The Genocide Continues

The Genocide Continues

Population Control & the Sterilization of Indigenous Women

Karen Stote

Fernwood Publishing
Halifax & Winnipeg

Copyright 2025 © Karen Stote

All rights reserved. No part of this book may be reproduced or transmitted in any form by any means without permission in writing from the publisher, except by a reviewer, who may quote brief passages in a review. The publisher expressly prohibits the use of this work in connection with the development of any software program, including, without limitation, training a machine learning or generative artificial intelligence (AI) system.

Development editor: Tanya Andrusieczko
Copyediting: Lisa Frenette
Text design: Brenda Conroy
Cover design: Evan Marnoch
Printed and bound in the UK

Published by Fernwood Publishing
Halifax and Winnipeg
2970 Oxford Street, Halifax, Nova Scotia, B3L 2W4
www.fernwoodpublishing.ca

Fernwood Publishing Company Limited gratefully acknowledges the financial support of the Government of Canada through the Canada Book Fund and the Canada Council for the Arts. We acknowledge the Province of Manitoba for support through the Manitoba Publishers Marketing Assistance Program and the Book Publishing Tax Credit. We acknowledge the Nova Scotia Department of Communities, Culture and Heritage for support through the Publishers Assistance Fund.

This book has been published with the help of a grant from the Federation for the Humanities and Social Sciences, through the Awards to Scholarly Publications Program, using funds provided by the Social Sciences and Humanities Research Council of Canada.

Library and Archives Canada Cataloguing in Publication
Title: The genocide continues : population control & the sterilization of Indigenous women / Karen Stote.
Names: Stote, Karen, author
Description: Includes bibliographical references and index.
Identifiers: Canadiana 20250254255 | ISBN 9781773637693 (softcover)
Subjects: LCSH: Involuntary sterilization—Canada. | LCSH: Reproductive rights—Canada. | LCSH: Indigenous women—Violence against—Canada.
Classification: LCC HV4989 .S76 2025 | DDC 363.9/7—dc23

Contents

Acknowledgements ix

Preface x

Introduction 1
    Corporate Philanthropy and the Formalization of Public Health 4
    The Expansion of Public Health in Canada 9
    The Politics of Reproduction in Modern Times 11
    A Note on Reproductive Agency and Choice 17

1   Corporate Philanthropy and Federal-Provincial
    Intersections in Public Health 22
    Tommy Douglas and the Expansion of Public Health in Saskatchewan .. 27
    Federal-Provincial Intersections in Public Health 39
    Giving and Taking — Jurisdictional Disputes and Indigenous Health 46

2   Emptying the Reserves —
    Indian Policy and the Welfare State 54
    Planning for the Expansion of the Welfare State 57
    Too Tough and Stubborn to Die — An Indian New Deal in Canada? 62
    The Hawthorn Report, 1966–67 70
    Integration, or Continued Segregation 74

3   From Eugenics to Family Planning —
    Canada's War on Indigenous Births 82
    The Special Planning Secretariat and the War on Poverty, 1965 85
    The Culture of Poverty among the Poor 86
    Overpopulation and Underdevelopment 89
    Legislating a War on Indigenous Births 92
    Post-legislative Reform — A Family Planning Program for Canada 99
    The Royal Commission on the Status of Women, 1967–70 105
    A Note on Abortion 109

**4   Family Planning in Post-1970 Saskatchewan —
    A Thirty-Year Review** 112

Proposals for a Family Planning Policy in Saskatchewan 113
The Advisory Committee on Family Planning, 1973 116
The Family Planning Association of Saskatchewan —
Planned Parenthood 120
A "Modern" Family Planning Program in Saskatchewan, 1977 126
Female Single Parents and the Saskatchewan Assistance Plan 129
A Proposal in Love, Saskatchewan 132
The Advisory Committee on Family Planning, 1993 134
Fetal Alcohol Syndrome and the Policing of Indigenous Mothers 137

**5   The Coerced Sterilization of
    Indigenous Women in Modern Times** 146

The Saskatoon Health Region Response 148
The Restart of the External Review, 2017 149
The Birth Alert Practice 151
R for Racial Profiling? 156
Sterilization by Numbers — Comparing Sterilization
Rates in Saskatchewan 158
Violence against Indigenous Lands and Bodies 171

**6   After the (Media) Storm —
    Responding to Genocide** 178

The Saskatoon Health Region Apologizes 181
Class Action Litigation and the Settling of Colonialism 183
Cultural Competency and Cultural Safety 187
Bill S-250 and Calls for Criminalization 198
Indigenous Rights, Responsibilities, and Resurgence 203

Conclusion 210

Endnotes 215

References 254

Index 281

To merely resist is not enough for me any more. I am interested in having a place that feels right and fits right ... resistance only gains mere survival. I cannot, and I suppose will not believe that the Creator gave us the walk, gave us life, to have nothing more ...

Sometimes we do not resist when we should. Sadly, some of us never learn how to resist or reject beyond resisting or rejecting ourselves ... Other times we resist each other because it is safer ...

[While] I must sometimes rely on acts of resistance ... I must always remember resistance ... means the only choice I have is to respond ... I do not have free choice about what it is I am going to do ...

I grow weary of talking about the pain, the statistics, the crisis. I understand that hope will not be built with these words. A step forward for me ... is to begin to imagine humanity, freedom and independence.

—Patricia Monture-Angus (1999a, 68, 72, 80, 87)

Acknowledgements

I want to thank the countless thinkers, speakers, writers, and dreamers who have informed my thinking. My analysis is not new. It is credited to those who have taught me. I am grateful for the lessons I have learned about what it means to remain committed in struggle. I am responsible for my shortcomings. To my colleagues and the institution that employs me, thank you for providing a home base to carry out this work, and some financial support as well. This work was partly supported by Wilfrid Laurier University and the Social Sciences and Humanities Research Council of Canada. To the archivists, librarians, and other point people who put in extra effort to help me locate the information I was looking for along the way. To the many research assistants who helped with parts of this project since its inception. To the reviewers who commented on my article "From Eugenics to Family Planning: The Coerced Sterilization of Indigenous Women in Post 1970 Saskatchewan," published in *Native American and Indigenous Studies Journal*, 9, 1 (2022) — portions of which appear mostly in Chapter 3 — your constructive criticism informed the overall direction of this larger work. To Fernwood Publishing for giving my writing a home, to Tanya Andrusieczko for your support in getting this project to completion, and to the reviewers whose comments strengthened this manuscript. I am grateful to Erin for tending to me when I could barely tend to myself. To Emily for always lending your ear. To Cheryl for reminding me to listen to that voice. To Melanie for creating space for me like it was your job. To my family and friends who put up with me disappearing for long periods even if they are unsure what requires so much of my attention. Finally, to the women who have come forward with their experiences or not; and to those who continue to teach me the most important lessons in life, about life and land, and how central one is the continuance of the other.

Preface

Bringing this book to completion was one of the hardest things I have ever done. This work began shortly after the sudden death of my partner; the grief of which I avoided for another six years. In that time, I was increasingly exposed to the personal and collective grief carried by Indigenous women who were coercively sterilized. In 2016, I was contacted by a woman in Saskatoon, and after by a lawyer acting on her behalf and that of others who were coercively sterilized. I began some of the research informing this book in 2017 to assist with a proposed class action lawsuit. I also came to know another Indigenous survivor who approached me about contributing to an edited collection on coerced sterilization. The first edition of *Sacred Bundles Unborn* was published in 2022, and a second edition in 2024. I refer to the finalization of the first edition of that project as "my undoing" because when faced with the outpouring of grief in those pages it became obvious I could no longer continue without facing my own. Thank you to Morningstar for creating that space, sharing your story, and bringing together a chorus of voices speaking out against coerced sterilization so that none of us feel as alone as we did before. And thank you for all the laughter and learning in times of grief.

The weight of this unfinished manuscript hung over me in the time I left my job to face uncomfortable aspects of my own life experiences. I often wondered if I had the wherewithal to return and finish what I had started. But life went on and struggles continued. I remember Wet'suwet'en resistance to pipeline expansion in their territory and the RCMP being called in to "sterilize the site" by arresting land defenders. Then, there was a COVID-19 pandemic. The "discovery" of unmarked graves of children who attended residential schools followed. Mass demonstrations took place in response to police violence against Black bodies, including the death of George Floyd, one of many Black people killed at the hands of the state. More Indigenous women who were coercively sterilized came forward to share their experiences before the Senate Standing Committee on Human Rights. The United States Supreme Court overturned *Roe v. Wade* to end or severely restrict abortion access. Queer and trans people have faced the renewal of a longstanding attack against them led by the religious and political right and some governments. There is a war in Ukraine, another in Sudan, longstanding violence in Gaza; and the list goes on.

I have done a lot of thinking about grief. The interconnections between these struggles and my own are more obvious to me today than ever before. I have come to the conclusion that we are all grieving even if our experiences are different, and even if some of us are making out better than others. My inability to tend to my grief, connected to my own experiences as a queer person in this world, was exhausting. It made me fearful and closed off to the possibility of doing differently. Denial and avoidance are strong impulses. Sometimes we tell ourselves this avoidance is a form of resistance. I know from experience when we avoid facing hard things, they rankle and fester and grow to such an extent it becomes difficult to think we could ever deviate from the path to which we have committed. Grief cracks a person open and there is pain in that. It is no wonder we try to avoid. But the cracks have formed and there are lessons in prying them open. In those cracks exist possibilities to do differently. It is only by facing what is uncomfortable, by opening space and shedding light, that things change.

Writing this book has confirmed to me that there are cracks in much of what Canadians hold dear. The institutions we rely on, the jobs we hold, our way of living, and many things we do for pleasure or comfort are embedded in violence and dehumanization. The functioning of this world as it exists depends on our continued denial of this reality, and this denial makes it difficult for us to imagine how things could be different. It is my hope this work is part of the cracking open of Canadian consciousness that is necessary for us to face what is uncomfortable; to acknowledge our own grief and that of others; to think about what is and how we got here; and to see each other in our humanity. It is only when we are taught to deny our own humanity that we become capable of denying it to others. The capitalist social relations under which we live, that link us to people and places beyond ourselves, exist at the expense of all our humanity. We are being tricked if we think otherwise.

If there is one useful thing I learned through countless hours of therapy is that our ways of coping serve a purpose; they allow us to survive. However, at some point we need to decide if these ways are working. They were not working for me, they are not working for you, and they certainly are not working for Indigenous Peoples. They never were. It is past time we pry open the cracks and re-imagine something new. We cannot continue to cover up the light. There are many trying to do differently despite the personal and collective grief they carry. We cannot let avoidance and fear paralyze us. It is only in doing that we find each other, forge relationships, and learn to do differently. Imagine all we could do if more of us worked together.

The territories we call Saskatchewan are home to Cree, Dakota, Dene, Nakota, Saulteaux, Métis, and an increasing number of Inuit. I want to acknowledge you. I realize I am speaking of you in these pages without you knowing me. It is not my intent to speak for you. I hope this work is useful in some way. I recognize the terms Registered Indian, Status and non-Status Indian, First Nation, Native, Aboriginal, or Indigenous do not reflect who you are. I also know the place names referred to are not your own names for these spaces. Neither does this work engage in the history of responsibilities set out in Treaties 2, 4, 5, 6, 7, 8 and 10, which cover Saskatchewan, how they are eschewed, or their consequences for you.[1] I refer to Indigenous women who have come forward with their experiences of coerced sterilization by their initials even though many names are easily findable in news articles. I do this to leave the decision up to women to identify publicly. This decision can change from day to day, and some have changed their mind after coming forward, partly because of the backlash they received. I want to acknowledge all of you and others who remain unknown to us. I know you are out there.

This work relies on research conducted at Library and Archives Canada, the Provincial Archives of Saskatchewan, and information accessed from the Saskatchewan Ministry of Health and Indigenous Services Canada. It also revisits sources other historians have relied on to tell histories of public health. While writing this book would have been much more difficult without the work of others, I was often taken aback by the lack of mention of Indigenous Peoples in these histories despite their appearance in many primary documents. I still wonder why they were left out. Linda Tuhiwai Smith wrote that if we think history is about justice, we are wrong. History has been about power; the story of the powerful and how they became so. If this is true, Smith asks, why write history at all? To which she responds, because there is unfinished business. Indigenous Peoples are still being colonized (and know it) and are still searching for justice (1999, 34). It is my hope this contribution is useful in that search. The history in these pages is one missing piece in broader histories of public health and it is unapologetic in seeking justice for Indigenous Peoples. It is also unapologetic in my own desire to live in a better world.

Scholars increasingly refer to the social, political and economic formation of colonialism in Canada as "settler colonialism" to highlight the structure social relations take when settlers assert sovereignty over and make home on lands they are exploiting, how Indigenous Peoples must be "disappeared" as a result, and the profound resulting violence perpetrated by the state and coordinated through its institutions that results in genocide.[2] I acknowledge this important scholarship but refer to "colonialism" throughout to better reflect the language of Indigenous struggles outside academia. Other times I refer to capitalism in a way that assumes colonialism because for Indigenous Peoples in Canada, colonialism cannot be separated from capitalism. It is what brought settlers here and it is the reason colonialism continues.

I highlight the intersections between capitalism and colonialism to stress the ties each has to the other. It has been my experience when many of us hear talk of colonialism, we assume this only involves Indigenous Peoples. We often fail to understand how violence committed against Indigenous Peoples involves other Canadians; that this violence arises from a way of life that impacts us too. We actively impose this violence on Indigenous Peoples through our assertions of ownership over these lands, the institutions we turn to for assistance and depend on for our livelihoods, the ways we think about the world, and how we live our lives. In our failure to locate ourselves within this reality we become complicit in genocide. A central argument in this work is that capitalism and the material requirement for access to Indigenous lands for profit is intimately connected to colonial violence against Indigenous bodies; one leads to the other and each involves us. Until we understand these connections, which form the basis of our collective relationship with Indigenous Peoples, we will not be able to end violence against Indigenous bodies *or* lands. We will not be able to engage effectively in our own struggles either.

I often refer to institutions of health and welfare as public health because each is concerned with the health of society however defined, and with social welfare issues, and both were drawn into an increasingly complex web of relationship through government policy in managing the effects of colonialism in Indigenous lives. Many problematic terms appear in this history referring to the "feebleminded," "mentally deficient," "retarded," and others. These terms say something about the arrogant disdain many in power held toward those suffering exploitation and marginalization. In terms of citational practices, the reader will find in text citations for published works; archival and other primary sources, and explanatory materials, are in endnotes.

The story in the following pages highlights some of the corporate-federal-provincial intersections that gave rise to coerced sterilization as a cost-effective public health measure. Each exerted influence over ideologies and knowledge produced and legitimated in universities and other public institutions, enacted through laws and policies, carried out in the careers some of us perform, and reinforced in the stories we tell about who we and Indigenous Peoples are. The Rockefeller Foundation features centrally here. Named after the richest man in history at the time, the Rockefeller Foundation is also symbolic of all capitalist interests that shape how society functions and why decisions are made to the detriment of many.

Following the publication of my first book, *An Act of Genocide: Colonialism and the Sterilization of Aboriginal Women* (Fernwood Publishing, 2015), I was accused by some of engaging in conspiracy theories. There is no need for conspiracy when attempting to understand the influence corporate interests have exerted on governments, lands, and people(s), or how these interests shape policies meant to control populations in the interest of the political economy. The connections are documented. Only some of them are highlighted here. The attempt to curb Indigenous reproduction has never been the result of "dark conspiracies"; it is simply the recognition and articulation of class interests (Brown 1982, 139) that some of us reinforce even if we do not like to admit it. To become aware of this reality holds the possibility for us to link struggles and engage in the collective action necessary to build a more just world.

Introduction

It is through institution building and the institutionalization of their personal fortunes that ... elites perpetuate their influence and give a stabilizing "class effect" to an elite organization — not class in relation to the market, but class as a ... legacy of ideas and institutions. (Marcus 1983, 43)

Indigenous women in Canada have been subject to coerced sterilization since the 1930s. In Alberta and British Columbia, sterilization legislation informed by eugenic theories of population control provided a mechanism to justify a practice that continued over four decades (Grekul, Krahn and Odynak 2004; van Heeswijk 1994; Dyck 2013). By the early 1970s, over three thousand people had been sterilized under eugenic legislation, which disproportionately impacted young Indigenous women. More than one thousand Indigenous women, and some men, were also coercively sterilized in federally operated Indian hospitals and the North, from the late 1960s into the early 1970s (Stote 2015). This history reveals a lack of informed consent, language barriers, inadequate use of interpreters, and racism and paternalism on the part of health and welfare professionals and policy makers that, when coupled with long-standing relations of colonialism, informed the coercive context of these sterilizations. Canadians have only begun to grapple with this history, let alone how it continues.

Since 2015, more than one hundred Indigenous women have come forward with their experiences of coerced sterilization — from the 1970s and as recently as 2019. In that year, an Inuk woman filed an individual claim against a doctor who sterilized her without consent at Stanton Territorial Hospital (formerly Stanton Yellowknife Hospital) in the Northwest Territories (Zingel 2022). The doctor who removed her ovaries and fallopian tubes has since apologized for his "unprofessional conduct" (Kotaska 2023). A Rae Edzo woman sterilized at this hospital in 1986, at the age of fifteen, filed a similar claim in 1997.[1]

In another, a woman was sterilized without consent after giving birth at the Whitehorse General Hospital in 2002.[2] Proposed class action lawsuits are now pending in Saskatchewan, Alberta, British Columbia, and Manitoba, and a civil suit is proceeding in Quebec, each naming different levels of government, health authorities, and physicians as responsible for coerced sterilization.[3] In these cases, women describe their own unique yet similar experiences of coercion, misinformation, and discrimination in health and welfare leading to their sterilization without informed consent.[4]

The coerced sterilization of Indigenous women intersects with other forms of reproductive coercion including abusive or forced abortions, the indiscriminate prescription of long-acting contraceptives — intrauterine devices (IUDs) and Depo-Provera — and obstetrical violence more broadly. In the 1980s, more than one hundred women said they were subject to abusive abortions at the Stanton Yellowknife Hospital (Lowell 1995).[5] In 1994, the British Columbia Task Force on Access to Contraception and Abortion found Indigenous women were sometimes pressured to agree to abortions, long-acting contraceptives, or sterilization.[6] More recently, in 2022, researchers spoke to thirty-five Indigenous women who experienced coerced sterilization, forced abortions, and obstetrical violence, with some experiencing all the above, in Quebec hospitals.[7] In one instance, Atikamekw mother Joyce Echaquan, who was previously sterilized against her will (Hachey 2021), died in the Centre hospitalier de Lanaudière, in Joliette, Quebec, moments after live-streaming footage of healthcare staff hurling racist remarks at her. A coroner's inquiry concluded racism and prejudice contributed to her likely preventable death as medical staff assumed she was suffering from drug withdrawal (Nerestant 2021). Still other women in Winnipeg, Regina, and Saskatoon have spoken of coercive experiences crossing multiple contexts including community-based organizations, group homes, and foster homes, in addition to health care (McKenzie, Varcoe, Nason et al. 2022). They too describe being subject to paternalism, racism, and stereotypes from health and social service providers; pressure to submit to sterilization, abortion, or an IUD; and being prescribed Depo-Provera without access to the necessary information to make an informed decision.

The trend on the part of health and welfare professionals to promote Depo-Provera, often to young women, is not new. In the 1990s, the drug was prescribed to Inuit women and girls as young as thirteen years old as a form of chemical sterilization to curtail the birth rate (Canadian Women's Committee on Reproduction, Population and Development 1995; Scoffield 1993). In the Eastern Arctic, doctors prescribed it as a first-choice option and in at least one instance, to a pregnant woman (Sarkadi 1995). All this, despite it not being approved as contraception until 1997 (Shea 2007). This trend continued into the 2000s (Tait 2008). Métis researcher Caroline Tait stated, "In a hurry, and in an effort to address family planning and high fertility rates ... dominant society turns to something like Depo-Provera ... there's a feeling of, 'Well, jeez, we've got to stop these people from having all these babies'" (cited in Hawaleshka 2005, 46).

These instances are more than a dark chapter in our history. The coerced sterilization of Indigenous women never stopped; it continued in different form — long after eugenics fell into disrepute. This work provides a context in which to understand this reality through a focus on Saskatchewan — the province from which many Indigenous women have come forward. Saskatchewan did not enact sterilization legislation, but a draft bill was proposed in 1930 (Dyck and Deighton 2017) and a history of eugenics, systemic racism, and colonialism shaped women's experiences.[8] This work demonstrates that population control — a concern with who occupied land and how resources were distributed — not race, was the central thread guiding public health interventions from eugenics to family planning. It traces the historical evolution of an idea, legitimized through a professional class of experts and the institutions in which they worked, that sought to control populations in the interest of the political economy and resulted in the coerced sterilization of Indigenous women.

By the 1930s, corporate interests played a central role in shaping institutions of health and welfare as they supported the training of those necessary to carry out reform work in ways that were beneficial to them. These interests guided the approach taken by the Canadian state and its provinces to public health issues resulting from social relations of exploitation, including those imposed on Indigenous Peoples — the original occupants of the lands and gatekeepers of resources on which the Canadian political economy depends. This historical material context fuels violence against Indigenous bodies in the interest of securing access to Indigenous lands, and makes the coerced sterilization of Indigenous women an act of genocide.

Corporate Philanthropy and the Formalization of Public Health

Eugenics, as one ideology of population control, featured prominently in health and welfare activities in Canada in the 1930s. During this time and to varying degrees across the country, social reformers, policy makers, and health and welfare workers promoted segregation, marriage regulation and sterilization as cost-effective interventions in the lives of those considered a burden to the newly industrialized capitalist state (McLaren 1990). The mental hygiene movement, a self-appointed body of experts — medical professionals, psychologists and psychiatrists — linked mental deficiency, or the arrested or incomplete development of the mind, to poverty, crime, illegitimacy, illness, hereditary defect, and high infant mortality rates (Dowbiggin 1997; McLaren 1990). Those involved in social hygiene — the network of religiously based reformers, charity organizations and social workers — viewed mental deficiency as contributing to sexual promiscuity, illegitimacy, alcoholism, tuberculosis, and venereal disease. Sexual health and racial purity were interlinked indicators of a healthy nation, and reform work reinforced a White Anglo-Saxon Protestant version of morality (McLaren 1990). The activities of each were practically and symbolically linked through public health (Valverde 1991).

While eugenics "meant different things to different people in different settings" (Dowbiggin 1997, 238), all were united in the goal of "efficient social management" (McLaren 1990, 112). Mariana Valverde writes the "synthesis of medicine, morality, and social reform was a powerful one, and the various wings of the movement all had a stake in preventing its fragmentation" (1991, 51). Corporate interests gave the above movements their roots and wings. The rise of organized corporate philanthropy emerged under industrial capitalism, which was impoverishing the working class as wealth was consolidated in the hands of the powerful few (Arnove 1982). This wealth, amassed through the exploitation of people's labour, bodies, and lives — and the expropriation of Indigenous lands — was partly reinvested through philanthropic foundations to shape the direction of public health in Canada and abroad.

No foundation had as much influence on the ideological approach informing public health expansion as the Rockefeller Foundation (RF).[9] John D. Rockefeller Sr., one of the richest people in history, became the first billionaire primarily through investment in oil and gas. When he died in 1937, he had given away about $550 million of his wealth to various causes — an amount more than any American before him had ever possessed (Folsom 2010). Through the RF, established in 1913 to "promote the wellbeing of mankind throughout the world" (Weindling 1988, 119), he and his successors helped build institutions, promote ideas, and train a class of experts to carry out reform work to keep the world safe for capitalism (Berman 1983; Brown 1979). Science and technology had recently rationalized industry through a focus on efficiency and productivity, and these were relied on to address social problems created by social relations of exploitation. Public health interventions based on medical and social sciences sought to mitigate the negative consequences of a capitalist mode of production on people and populations (Brown 1979) while keeping exploitative relations intact. Richard Brown (1979) explains:

> philanthropic capitalists who supported medical science [for one] believed it would do more than demonstrate their good works. First, reductionist scientific medicine bore a striking, and not incidental, similarity to the capitalist worldview. Second, scientific medicine would help integrate all members of society, whatever their occupations or social standing, into an industrial technical culture, unifying the fragmented and often fragile industrial-capitalist social order. Third, scientific medicine would help replace the widespread class theories of misery with the perspective that inequalities and unhappiness are technical problems susceptible to engineering solutions, thus depoliticizing medicine and legitimizing capitalism. Finally, scientific medicine would help elevate the medical profession, encouraging a stronger identification of its members with the highest class in society and the capitalist order itself. (133)

The goal of corporate philanthropy, by investing in public health, was to develop and strengthen institutions that would "extend the reach ... of capitalism throughout society" (Brown 1979, 9).

The RF funded eugenic activities like the Eugenics Records Office in Cold Spring Harbor, the epicentre of American studies on purported racial characteristics among groups (Black 2003), and a German program that included Nazi doctors and research with "distinct eugenic undertones"

(Weindling 1988, 130–1) which, whether fully anticipated, culminated in a Holocaust and the death of millions along ethnic, political, religious, ableist, and heterosexist lines, including Jews, Romani, Slavic, Polish, and Ukrainian people, queer people, people with disabilities, and leftists. It enabled studies seeking to locate the genetic and neurological basis of criminality; surveys on inherited diseases and the link between heredity and alcoholism; investigations into mental diseases through study of body fluids, brain cells, and "racial" variations based on blood group; twin studies of "illegitimate" children; and projects to eliminate feeble-mindedness, the "social evil" linked to prostitution, venereal disease, and sexual promiscuity (Weindling 1988, 122; Kühl 1994).

In correspondence with Charles Davenport, director of the Eugenic Records Office, John D. Rockefeller Jr. wrote that to incarcerate "feebleminded" women would keep them from "perpetuating [their] kind … until after the period of child bearing had passed" (cited in Black 2003, 93). Segregation may represent "an immense economy to the city and the state" (Rockefeller Jr. cited in Gunn 1999, 108), but it could not be relied on to manage entire populations. Birth control could address fertility differentials between groups and "fit" nicely (Gunn 1999, 111) under the RF mandates of public health and medical education. Population control was the "de facto organizing principle" and "unspoken mandate" (Gunn 1999, 97–8, 101) of the RF, and its support for eugenics and broader birth control activities were means of promoting its own self-interests by managing the impact of dispossession and exploitation on populations and as it sought to ensure unimpeded access to lands for profit.

In the first half of the twentieth century, the RF helped mobilize popular opinion on birth control by enticing public health officials, sociologists, social workers, demographers, professors, government functionaries, and other philanthropic foundations to support "voluntary family planning" along "eugenically desirable lines" (Gunn 1999, 110). From 1921–35, it offered grants toward the study of populations in the fields of behavioural and physiological sex research, child development, mental hygiene, and birth control (Gunn 1999). It also funded activities carried out by Margaret Sanger through her Clinical Research Bureau, the first birth control clinic in the United States, and the American Birth Control League (ABCL), founded in 1921, until the early 1940s (Gunn 1999; Zunz 2012).[10]

In *The Pivot of Civilization*, Sanger (1922) wrote on the "emergency problem" of feeblemindedness needing to be faced. The ABCL could help educate the public on the dangers of "uncontrolled procreation" and the "necessity of a world program of birth control," enable collaboration between scientists, statisticians, investigators, and social agencies on the relationship between "reckless breeding" and "delinquency, defect and dependence," and assist in studying how these affected maternal and infant mortality. It could also promote the education of medical professionals while encouraging the sterilization of the "insane," "feebleminded," and those afflicted with "inherited or transmissible diseases." Finally, it could enable the cooperation of legal advisers, statesmen, and legislators in the removal of statutes that discouraged "dysgenic breeding" and contributed to the "population problem" and "national and racial conflicts" (281–3). The ABCL joined Sanger's Clinical Research Bureau to form the Birth Control Federation of America and in 1942, it became the Planned Parenthood Federation of America.

In 1943, Raymond Fosdick, president of the RF, who had served as counsel to the ABCL, endorsed a proposal that population work should become a top priority (Gunn 1999). He wrote:

> the problem of population constitutes one of the great perils of the future, and if something is not done along the lines that these people are suggesting, we shall hand down to our children a world in which the scramble for food and the means of subsistence will be far more bitter than anything we have at present. Scientists are pointing hopefully to such methods as Mrs. Sanger and her associates are advocating. (Cited in Zunz 2012, 94–5)

The program he and Sanger elucidated was pursued through public health expansion in Canada and abroad, and in this, the RF and various iterations of Planned Parenthood played central roles (Bashford 2014; Mass 1974; Stote 2022; Takeuchi-Demirci 2018).

By the time the horrors of Nazi Germany came to light, eugenic claims that sterilization would "solve the problem of hereditary defect, close up the asylums for the feebleminded and the insane, [and] do away with prisons" were mostly considered unrealistic — sterilization on its own was unlikely to have much of an effect in the next generation (Dowbiggin 2008, 29). Post–World War II, the motivations of eugenicists in preventing the reproduction of the unfit merged with neo-Malthusian ideas focused on the need to reduce the fertility of some through birth control (Chase 1977; Connelly 2008; Hartmann 1995). They were joined by environmentalists who argued fertility regulation was necessary to ensure the capacity of the earth to support itself; and demographers, who studied fertility trends between populations — all of which were "so significantly enabled" (Bashford 2014, 289) by Rockefeller funding that by the 1960s their arguments were "more or less indistinguishable" (329). These arguments infiltrated the thinking of government officials and policy makers in Canada, as did the studies they produced.

In other words, population control was not a mid-century creation; it drove eugenics from the beginning (Bashford 2014). Alison Bashford highlights how the desire to control the quality *and* quantity of the population were questions of political economy — of land, resources, and the prevention of war — and these concerns were shared by traditional eugenicists, other population theorists, capitalist interests, and Western nation-states (2014, 328–9). A shared concern with who was doing the reproducing, based on notions of race, class, and gender, drew them together. Birth control, as population control, delivered under the banner of family planning, was compatible with the system of public health envisioned by corporate interests. Corporate backing gave scientific and medical legitimacy to these ideas, and by making contraceptive decisions dependent on the advice of physicians, medical professionals were positioned as the ultimate "arbiters" of population policy (Gunn 1999, 113).

The RF, through its International Health Division, shaped the global public health agenda by expanding the network of experts and agencies "fully co-ordinated through conferences, institutional cooperation and political programmes" (Barona 2021, 51). This included the League of Nations and its two arms, the League of Nations Health Organization and International Labour Organization, since their inception in 1919, and after 1945, the World Health Organization and the United Nations (Bashford 2014; Berridge 2016; Tournès 2014).[11] It funded public health campaigns against contagious diseases; promoted efforts against tuberculosis, influenza, and malnutrition; and institutionalized public health "country by country" by supporting local health units and national ministries, helping establish twenty-five schools and institutes of public health, and sponsoring 2,500 nurses, doctors, and engineers to study in public health (Birn 2014, 130).

The principle guiding its work was that public health was a function of government, but the RF would assist by providing expert advice, financial resources, and facilities to train health professionals (Iacobelli 2022). Support would be withdrawn when governments controlled their own operations (Birn 2014). The "scientific medicine" guiding public health became a powerful "ideological weapon" exonerating "capitalism's vast inequities" and "reckless practices" that shortened the lives of workers (Brown 1979, 10). The expansion of public health was also a form of imperialism (Arnove 1982; Navarro 1981) enabling Western medicine, its functionaries, and ideological approach to social problems to infiltrate an area and remain in the absence of military intervention, or after soldiers had left.[12] It was imposed on Indigenous Peoples in Canada as a tool of colonialism.

The Expansion of Public Health in Canada

Corporate philanthropy was instrumental in shaping the aims, purpose, and direction of public health in Canada. In 1911, Alice Chow, Secretary of the Kingston Charity Organization Society, which relied on corporate philanthropy to help people living in poverty, stated: "our charity, although intended for the victims of the present industrial system, sometimes indirectly benefits the employers ... let me say, what the poor want is not charity, but justice" (cited in Valverde 1991, 158). Neither did those living in poverty only want birth control; they wanted to be able to support the children they already had (Richardson and Fisher 1999).

In 1919, John D. Rockefeller Sr. offered a $5 million gift to the RF with the suggestion it use these funds to support medical education in Canada (Fedunkiw 2005). The RF promoted cooperation between different levels of government and universities in mental hygiene and the social sciences. This included the University of Toronto and its School of Hygiene and Public Health (Brison 2005), a central institution training experts in public health; McGill University, including a Social Science Research Project through which scholars, some of whom directly informed the expansion of the welfare state, conducted studies on health, welfare, and the political economy (Brice 1984); and the universities of Montreal, Manitoba, Saskatchewan, Alberta, and British Columbia.[13]

Between 1913 and 1950, RF funds helped establish the Social Sciences Research Council, the National Research Council, provincial departments of health, and field offices across Canada (Brison 2005; Fisher

1991; Mullally 2009; Twohig 2002). Donald Fisher explains, institutions like the Social Sciences Research Council served as "intermediaries" or a "buffer state" between social scientists and philanthropy, the state, and ruling class interests (1999, 75). RF funding shaped the work of the intellectual elite while creating a network of "like-minded" experts who could reform society in ways congruent with corporate interests (Brison 2005, 54). It also invested in the Canadian National Committee for Mental Hygiene (CNCMH), another intermediary, to encourage surveys on mental health and the training of students.[14] The RF supported the CNCMH until 1939, after which time it sought direct relationships with the universities and research institutions it helped expand (Pols 1999).

This work considers how corporate interests influenced federal-provincial intersections in public health expansion and its impact on Indigenous Peoples, with Saskatchewan as a case study. The period from 1944–61, under the premiership of Tommy Douglas, was an important one in the expansion of public health and the professionalization of experts who could intervene in social problems. In one sense, Saskatchewan, as home to the first state-funded health insurance scheme, was a "pilot project" (MacDougall 2009, 307) for the expansion of public health across the country. In 1933, Douglas had written his master's thesis on the problem of the "subnormal" family, which he defined as one exhibiting some combination of "mental defectiveness," questionable moral standards, delinquency, and "social disease," who may be reliant on state support (1933, 1). While he is said to have given up on his eugenic tendencies once taking office, as Premier and Minister of Public Health, Douglas supported restrictive marriage legislation and other policies that increased the segregation and pathologization of those labelled "mentally defective." Eugenics was not always openly promoted in Saskatchewan, but this work shows how the system of public health built under Douglas's tenure achieved similar goals by enabling the continued policing of people along race, class, gender, and ableist lines in the interest of the economy. The ideas guiding Douglas were informed and supported by corporate interests, and the federal government was influenced by these same interests as well.

In the post–World War II period, health services were positioned as one arm of the welfare state and the RF took a step back as governments invested more directly in public health expansion. The welfare state sought to place "a floor on the standard of living" for some as it managed an "upsurge of radicalism" (Finkel 1995, 222), but without reducing the power of capitalist interests. It also became one solution to the "Indian problem" in Canada — a means to undermine Indigenous connections to the land and reduce federal obligations. The system of public health in Saskatchewan initially excluded most Indigenous people, who were often segregated on reserves and in residential schools and Indian hospitals. This changed following revision of the Indian Act, in 1951, which increased the application of provincial laws to Indians and established a more complex administrative structure to manage Indigenous lives, one involving federal-provincial collaboration. The federal government sought to minimize treaty responsibilities as it supported the expansion of a provincial system of public health that further entrenched colonialism and systemic racism. The longstanding jurisdictional dispute on which level of government was financially responsible for the delivery of services informed Indigenous experiences, and as the federal government delegated responsibility to the province, each viewed Indigenous people as a fiscal burden.

The system of public health in Saskatchewan intersected in Indigenous lives to blame them for problems created by colonialism and federal neglect. Indigenous Peoples were forced into the choice between willingly participating in their own assimilation or facing continued segregation, now through a newly expanded provincial child welfare system, or in psychiatric institutions and jails. However, as both Rockefeller Jr. and Sanger pointed out, segregation only went so far in controlling a population. Birth control was more effective in the long term and by the early 1960s, as part of its War on Poverty — the policy approach underpinning the expansion of the welfare state — Canada began taking steps toward decriminalizing contraception.

The Politics of Reproduction in Modern Times

Reproductive politics were transformed by the 1960s as social conservatives, eugenicists, demographers, economists, and politicians spoke more openly of the need to decriminalize birth control to limit the reproduction of some (Appleby 1999; Dyck and Lux 2020; McLaren and McLaren 1986). The eugenic discourse of "race betterment" by preventing the reproduction of the "unfit" was replaced with the view that "unregulated population growth" caused poverty, resource scarcity, and social tensions that threatened political economic stability and corporate access to raw materials and cheap pools of labour (Mass 1974, 651, 656). This, despite a crude birth rate in Western nations that had been decreasing since the 1950s.[15]

Eugenicist C.P. Blacker described family planning as an attempt "to fulfill the aims of eugenics without disclosing what you are really aiming at and without mentioning the word" (cited in Kühl 2013, 148). However, any effort to manage the fertility of populations would be more effective if "grafted onto freedom, not force" (Bashford 2014, 331). Francis Galton, who coined the term eugenics, emphasized as much when he said, "eugenic reform must chiefly be effected ... [by] Popular Opinion" (cited in Gunn 1999, 102). Birth control was increasingly couched in human rights discourse (Bashford 2014), setting the stage for decriminalization.

Women have always desired the means to control their reproduction. Erika Dyck tells us that married women, whom she defines as "healthy" and "middle class," were seeking out birth control and sterilization as a means of fertility control by the 1950s, as others continued to be sterilized under eugenic legislation (2013, 92). Prior to legislative change, birth control was often available to those of "average means" if their private family physician was willing to offer it, but for low-income, single, or otherwise marginalized women, it was only available from health and welfare departments willing to break the law (Appleby 1999, 20). Brenda Appleby (1999, 14–16) points to slowing economic growth, rising unemployment, an increase in the federal deficit, and overburdened health and welfare departments as factors informing a reconsideration of the legal status of contraception. Family planning could reduce government budgets and long-term reliance on social welfare.

Family planning came to encompass a range of birth control methods, including sterilization, fertility and genetic counselling, marriage and family counselling, adoption, and associated assessments, diagnostics, referrals, and follow-up functions.[16] The concepts "family planning" and "planned parenthood" sought to highlight what voluntary organizations, namely Planned Parenthood, could do to encourage the spacing of children in the interest of ecological and economic stability while distancing the issue from the horrors of Nazi Germany (Bishop 1983, 105). "Free choice" was assumed, but family planning continued to intersect with issues of race, class, ability, and gender, including eugenics and fears of a "world population explosion" (Bain 1964; Dyck and Lux 2020; Stern 2005; Shapiro 1985), poverty and high infant mortality rates

(Palko, Lennox, and McQuarrie 1971), and societal views on promiscuity, illegitimacy, and adolescent births (Gurr 2015; Thomas 1998).

Population control policies, organized and funded by world elites, were the ideological and material catalyst for family planning activities in Canada and abroad (Connelly 2008; Gordon 2002; Hartmann 1995). The Population Council, founded by John D. Rockefeller III in 1952, was the "preeminent institute" for the study of contraception and family planning, and a hub for other players in the field (Connelly 2008, 159). The RF introduced birth control into the United Nations agenda with the assistance of aligned supporters who, as diplomats and other influential persons, sometimes continued to espouse eugenic ideologies as they took up central positions on the international stage (Mass 1976; Weindling 2012).

Family planning was declared a human right at the United Nations International Conference on Human Rights in Tehran in 1968. For the first time, a global agreement outlined that parents had a human right to determine "freely and responsibly" the number and spacing of their children.[17] Despite a very real want on the part of women to control their fertility, Alison Bashford tells us it is a mistake to say the expansion of family planning came at the behest of women. This "Rockefeller-led overture" (2014, 346) resulted from men involved in eugenics and population control who were invested in maintaining the status quo (347–50). The pretense of concern with the health of a mother, child, or family was an attempt to avoid "potential problems" from being overt about their goals (324–5). Population control was increasingly enjoined with feminist ideas of fertility control as a reproductive choice under a "modern project" — the responsible citizen central to the "economic planning of nations" (351).

The liberatory or coercive potential of reproductive technologies always depends on who has the power to control them, under what conditions, and for what ends, and through decriminalization the federal government increased the "bureaucratization, professionalization, medicalization and commercialization" of fertility control (McLaren and McLaren 1986, 141–2) as it intensified the possibility for coercion. Post-legislative change, family planning became an explicit feature of public health involving federal and provincial departments of health and welfare. The federal government engaged in family planning activities in jurisdictions under its control as it helped coordinate the uptake of activities on a provincial level. The notion of "responsible parenthood" focused on married couples and their social duty to limit their families to the number of children they could support, as non-married women continued to be deprived of the requisite conditions for exercising their responsibilities in a voluntary manner (Appleby 1999, 7–8, 56, 222–38). In this, class structures based on heteronormative, ableist, and racist assumptions of family life tied to a heterosexual nuclear family unit continued to be reinforced (Appleby 1999; Gurr 2015). These "ruling relations of reproductive health care" — which further marginalized those who were living in poverty, differently abled, transgender, and queer, along with women of colour — were imposed on Indigenous Peoples as a form of "imperialist medicine" (Gurr 2015, 157).

In the 1970s, the Indigenous birth rate was characterized as the "most important demographic trend in Saskatchewan for the next 25 years."[18] The provincial approach to family planning consistently framed Indigenous women as irresponsible parents due to poverty, sexual immorality, and a higher incidence of "illegitimate" births, often to young women (Gurr 2015, 99–134) — but also due to the political nature of their reproduction and the systemic racism resulting from material exploitation. As the original occupants of the lands upon which the political economy depends, Indigenous Peoples hold relationships, responsibilities, and forms of life linking them to these lands; Indigenous reproduction is one means of reproducing these linkages (Tuck and Yang 2012, 5–6). The province, in wanting to ensure continued access to Indigenous lands for development, and as it too sought to reduce government expenditures, focused on reducing the Indigenous birth rate. This resulted in the increased surveillance, criminalization, and sometimes, coerced sterilization of Indigenous women.

These themes are taken up, beginning in Chapter 1, which explores corporate-federal-provincial intersections, tensions, and congruities in public health expansion from the 1940s to 1960s through a focus on Saskatchewan. It shows how a series of interlinked health and welfare laws, policies, and practices worked to identify some as problematic while seeking to ensure economic efficiency. Premier Douglas relied extensively on the financial support and guidance of the RF and its trained advisors and mental hygiene experts — who were sometimes committed eugenicists but more centrally concerned with population control — to build a system which obfuscated the root causes of social problems by blaming individuals for their circumstances. The federal government shared connections with, and was influenced by, these same interests as it formulated a federal agenda to guide public health expansion in collaboration with the province. Here, the reader is challenged to reflect on the role of Western medicine as a tool of colonialism, but also how the system of public health worked to mitigate damages caused by exploitative social relations embedded in capitalism that, in the end, are detrimental to all of us.

Chapter 2 shows the influence of the RF coming to fruition in Canada through the expansion of the welfare state, shaped by experts it helped trained and the ideological approach it promoted, which informed the research studies and policy recommendations that guided federal and provincial Indian policy in the post–World War II period. The welfare state established a more organized means of intervening in poverty while reducing dependency on government supports and ensuring conditions conducive to capitalism. For Indigenous Peoples, it was a tool of colonialism. In a period of transition towards the integration of Indigenous people into Canadian society, the province worked in concert with federal Indian policy goals. It adopted a series of measures to "empty the reserves" by encouraging migration to urban centres where Indigenous people might be more easily induced to integrate, but where many faced continuing poverty as they increasingly relied on provincial services. Under the pretense of a humanitarian concern, and through extension of citizenship rights (Leslie 1999), newly trained experts in health and welfare were given a more direct role in managing these "dependent peoples" by attempting to enact development "with surgical precision" (Jahanbani 2023, 54, 46). Indigenous people who could not be induced to help themselves out of poverty often faced continued segregation.

Chapter 3 examines how the War on Poverty became a war against Indigenous births partly enabled through family planning. It revisits federal parliamentary debates culminating in the decriminalization of contraception in 1969, and a first federal family planning program in 1970, to show the extent to which legislative and policy change was influenced by broader concerns with population control — of who occupied land and how resources were distributed. In concert with international trends, the rhetoric employed by government officials and advisors centred on fears the Indigenous birth rate contributed to overpopulation and this, coupled with a culture of poverty and dependency among them, replaced eugenics as the central ideological tool justifying the need to curb Indigenous births through family planning — the most cost-effective public health measure. To decriminalize birth control and make it available to all would help avoid allegations of genocide.

Planned Parenthood features prominently in this history, guiding the federal approach until the provinces could take up their own activities. The Royal Commission on the Status of Women, established in 1967 to make recommendations on how to improve women's lives, also features. Its support for the expansion of family planning, assisted by Planned Parenthood, and its influence over second wave feminism more broadly, is as an example of how some women were incorporated into the work of creating the responsible citizen central to economic planning (Bashford 2014). The focus on reproductive rights and responsible choice erased Indigenous concerns as it reinforced a coercive context in which women were expected to make choices.

Chapter 4 shows how all this carried over in Saskatchewan, since the 1970s, to inform family planning policy and practice. A thirty-year review of family planning activities reveals how health and welfare professionals, by focusing on those considered "at risk" of poverty and dependency, consistently approached Indigenous reproduction as something needing to be curbed. Family planning became a cost-effective solution to public health problems created by colonialism; jurisdictional disputes on who was financially responsible for health and welfare services for Indigenous people; fears of a rising birth rate as Indigenous people migrated to urban centres and strained provincial services; and a desire for continued access to Indigenous lands.

In Chapter 5, demographic trends in Saskatchewan are considered together with health utilization data that reveals the number of deliveries, abortions, and sterilizations for Registered Indian women and Other Residents from 1972–2018. This comparative analysis shows Registered Indians, who are identified through a declaration of Indian Status on provincial health cards, were disproportionately represented among those sterilized and accessing abortions from the late 1970s onward. This data is considered squarely within the broader context of colonialism and systemic racism, a history of all levels of government approaching Indigenous reproduction as something to be curbed, and the ways family planning policy has sought to do this. This inherently coercive context — which informs, and is informed by, longstanding violence against Indigenous lands and bodies — leads to the coerced sterilization of Indigenous women.

Chapter 6 considers federal-provincial responses to the coerced sterilization of Indigenous women, and what is being done to address the practice. This includes an apology by the Saskatoon Health Region to women who were sterilized in its hospitals; a wave of class action lawsuits filed across Canada, including Saskatchewan; a focus on cultural competency and safety in health care; efforts to criminalize the practice through proposed legislation; and a push for government to respect Indigenous rights. This chapter critically engages each in turn to consider their effectiveness in achieving justice for Indigenous women and their peoples when each remains embedded in ongoing relations of dispossession and exploitation.

A Note on Reproductive Agency and Choice

It is important to ground instances of coerced sterilization and other forms of reproductive violence against Indigenous women within the broader context of colonialism, the oppression of women, and the denial of Indigenous sovereignty (Stote 2022; 2015). In one of the few works that engages the history of family planning in Indigenous lives in Canada, Erika Dyck and Maureen Lux (2016) consider the extent to which Indigenous agency intersected with "neo eugenics" to shape reproductive policy in the Global North (481). They write, while Indigenous reproduction was a "proving ground" for "competing interpretations" of population control (484), by the mid-1970s, reproductive politics were complicated by those who may have willingly sought out sterilization. They cite a 1976 letter to federal officials signed by five Indigenous women to support the view that access to family planning was desired by some and the wave of sterilizations engulfing Indigenous communities was not solely motivated by political and economic concerns:

> There are people like us here in ... [Nunavut] who have had such operations done ... we know the doctors do not perform operations on people without making sure that the person understands what they are being operated for. In this case the doctors do not decide whether to sterilize a person or not. There are those who especially ask for it ... Those people who are talking now on the radios regarding sterilization are saying that the doctors perform sterilizations on people

> without telling them ... We think that those statements are false, because the doctors can operate only after consulting with the patient. (Cited in Dyck and Lux 2016, 487)

This letter was subsequently cited by Brianna Theobald (2019, 154) as evidence of proactivity in seeking sterilization by Indigenous women. Reproductive justice scholars, in centring racialized, marginalized, and Indigenous women's experiences of reproductive violence and abuse, tell us reproductive options have different meanings for those facing systemic oppression, and while women exercise agency, they do not do so under conditions of their own choosing (Ross, Derkas, Peoples et al. 2017). This letter, then, and interpretations of history that engage Indigenous agency as choice must be approached critically.

In their work on the forced relocation of Inuit, which sometimes led to starvation and death, Frank Tester and Peter Kulchyski (1994) discuss other letters written to federal officials by Inuit who spoke favorably about their relocation and asked for their relatives to join them. Tester and Kulchyski argue there are good reasons to doubt the interpretation, based on these letters, that they viewed relocation favorably, whether because deference to authority was a "central trait" of Inuit or simply because they were aware if they wanted something from officials, it was important to tell them what they wanted to hear in a way that gave them the respect they were supposed to deserve (401, note 40). The fact that some women may have wanted sterilization does not mean others did not experience coercion, which the 1976 letter implies, or that the proliferation of family planning did not have larger intentions or implications.

Bashford (2014) cautions against wanting to clearly differentiate between population control and birth control as a reproductive right — this differentiation is "aspirational" more than "historical" (350) — one which separates family planning from its broader political and economic history which, for Indigenous Peoples, is embedded in colonialism. The material need on the part of the state to ensure access to Indigenous lands and resources in the interest of the political economy should never be underestimated. Neither should we underestimate the role this plays in shaping the choices presented to women — especially when Indigenous Peoples are considered "formidable and effective barriers" (Levitan and Cameron 2015, 270) to the development of industrial resource extraction. The material requirement for land and resources on the part of capitalist states has always required Indigenous Peoples to be "destroyed, removed, and made into ghosts" (Arvin, Tuck, and Morrill 2013, 12) and Indigenous women, in their ability to reproduce future generations, have long been targeted to these ends (Boyer 2014b; Stote 2015).

Despite children being valued in Indigenous communities, women have always had their own ways of regulating fertility, inducing abortions, and causing sterility (Anderson 2011, 40–2). Kim Anderson (2003) points to the role of the church in introducing large families, of Western medicine in suppressing Indigenous knowledge, and colonialism's undermining of the ability of women to raise children in their communities as factors upsetting Indigenous family planning. Mohawk midwife Katsi Cook highlights how a government attempt to create an "absolute dependence" (cited in Theobald 2019, 8) on Western medicine has left Indigenous women vulnerable to abuse. She views coerced sterilization as a symptom of "a more fundamental problem," how colonialism diminishes women's personal and social power and destabilizes "understandings of the meaning of Native womanhood" (Theobald 2019, 166–7).

Indigenous women do make use of Western forms of fertility control. However, to speak of reproductive agency as choice is to overlook a swath of feminist literature that critiques the tendency under capitalism, and within a liberal feminist discourse, to view the individual as paramount as it disregards the context in which women make choices, the options from which they must choose, and the role of private interests in crafting and constraining these. It also obfuscates any systematic abuse directed toward certain populations, or how tools considered central to reproductive freedom are the same tools that result in reproductive oppression (Hartmann 1995; Ross, Derkas, Peoples et al. 2017; Smith 2005; Solinger 2001; Stote 2017).

This work is not concerned with those who may have willingly sought out sterilization or any other Western form of reproductive control based on the options presented to them — but their choices too, are constrained. This work illuminates the historical, political, economic, and policy context in which agency is enacted, that informs choice *and* coercion for all Indigenous women. To quote the Committee to End Sterilization Abuse, formed the 1970s in response to the coerced sterilization of Indigenous and racialized women in the United States:

> Forced infertility is in no way a substitute for a good job, enough to eat, decent education, daycare, medical services, maternal infant care, housing, clothing, or cultural integrity … when society does not provide the basic necessities of life for everyone, there can be no such freedom of choice. (Quoted in Shapiro 1985, 144)

The attempt on the part of government to create an "absolute dependence" on Western medicine under ongoing social relations of colonialism, as Cook describes, fundamentally limits freedom of choice for Indigenous women as it contributes to the coercive potential of what is offered.

Dyck and Lux (2016) acknowledge how Indigenous women in their area of study have consistently struggled for the return of reproductive and political control to their communities. Theobald highlights how control over one's reproduction is an "essential element" of Indigenous sovereignty (2019, 147). Despite some Indigenous women making use of Western family planning options, many continue to view them with suspicion due to past violations and ongoing attempts to "wipe out" their populations (Theobald 2019, 149). Others may "choose" more permanent methods due to a lack of other options (153; also Gurr 2015, 125–6). Indigenous women have always wanted to control their fertility but have insisted this be on their own terms, based on their own cultural and value systems, and embedded in Indigenous sovereignty.

A reproductive justice approach asks us to consider how reproductive abuses like coerced sterilization are not only individual harms but are the tools of systems of oppression relied on to regulate entire populations (Silliman 2004, 1). Theobald writes, "colonial politics have been — and remain — reproductive politics" (2019, 4). In the United States, where Indigenous women were subject to coerced sterilization, scholars link the proliferation of family planning in the 1970s to funding priorities of governments, a lack of concern for the welfare of communities, and the theft of lands and resources — as part of a genocide against Indigenous Peoples (Ralstin-Lewis 2005; Smith 2005; Torpy 2000). The Canadian context is not so different. To discuss reproductive agency without centring how this context shapes women's choices amounts to "agency without choice" (Mann and Grzanka 2018, 334) — a misnomer to say the least.

We also need to consider that, for Indigenous and other marginalized women, the struggle is often for the choice to have children and raise them in safe and healthy communities (Ross, Derkas, Peoples et al. 2017), a reality so often erased in liberal feminist approaches to reproductive agency and choice. In Saskatchewan, women describe scare tactics by health and welfare professionals and being told sterilization was in their best interest, while others did not know they had a right to bodily autonomy.[19] Still others faced threats, and the reality, of having their babies apprehended at birth.[20] Yvonne Boyer and Judith Bartlett point to systemic racism in Western health care as central to understanding coerced sterilization — a systemic racism that needs to be grounded within the historical and material context of colonialism.[21] Violence against Indigenous bodies is connected to violence against Indigenous lands.[22] To focus on this reality, rather than agency and choice, is not to identify Indigenous women only as "victims" (Dyck and Lux 2016, 485), but to stress fundamental change is urgently needed for Indigenous bodies *and* lands to be respected.

Federal-provincial intersections in family planning policy and practice in Saskatchewan indicate that for Indigenous women, coerced sterilization remains a symptom of a broader context, one where the desire to undermine Indigenous connections to land and reduce obligations to Indigenous Peoples remains central. The lands of Cree, Dakota, Dene, Nakota, Saulteaux, and Métis, and the home to an increasing number of Inuit, continue to be contested in the interest of capital. In the process, Indigenous sovereignty — including reproductive sovereignty — is undermined. We must centre this historical and material context in our attempts to understand why the coerced sterilization of Indigenous women continues and what is required to stop the practice. This context must be *transformed* if we are to speak in any meaningful way about reproductive agency and choice for Indigenous women. Transformation requires the dismantling of colonialism and the political economy that supports it to ensure respect for Indigenous sovereignty — over lands, resources, forms of life, *and* bodies. Short of this, a genocide against Indigenous Peoples continues.

1

Corporate Philanthropy and Federal-Provincial Intersections in Public Health

> *The subnormal family presents the most appalling of all family problems ... the question of limiting the family of the subnormal is of paramount importance, since large families are undoubtedly one of the causes of their extreme poverty. This might be done by a discreet dissemination of contraceptive knowledge ... With fewer children there is little doubt that they could give their families greater opportunities for advancement.* (Douglas 1933, 1, 27)

Saskatchewan did not enact sterilization legislation, but eugenics featured in its history and segregation, marriage regulation, *and* sterilization were all considered as means to control the reproduction of those considered a social burden. In 1928, Rockefeller Foundation (RF) monies helped establish county-based health projects in the districts of Gravelbourg and Assiniboia, and field training for health officers, public health nurses, and sanitary inspectors under condition the province take over responsibility for costs.[1] The following year, the newly elected Co-operative government, an alliance of Conservatives and Progressives, proposed a public health platform that included "free consultative medical clinics," "a State Health Insurance scheme," and "the sterilization of mental defectives" (Russell 1970, 134). In a time of economic and social crisis, guided by principles of "strict economy" and "efficiency" (Kyba 1964, Appendix B, 5–6), the province enacted intersecting health and welfare legislation to assist in stabilizing the political economy while reinforcing the heteropatriarchal family as an economic unit. In doing so, it marked the reproduction of some as problematic.

The Child Welfare Act of 1927 consolidated legislation relating to the "protection" of children, mothers' pensions, adoption, and juvenile courts. Under this legislation, a mentally defective child was defined as "an idiot ... so defective of mind ... as to be unable to guard itself against common dangers," "incapable of managing its affairs or being taught," who required supervision and control "for its own protection and for the protection of others."[2] To enhance its ability to police unwed single mothers and putative fathers who might produce mentally defective children, the province sought to recoup costs for children born out of wedlock through Part VII of the Act, entitled "Children of Unmarried Parents," making it mandatory for the registrar of vital statistics or any public health institution to notify the Commissioner of Child Protection of unmarried pregnant women needing care.[3] In 1930, this section was amended to include those who were widowed, living apart from their husbands, or had borne children from adultery, and it applied to those under twenty-one years of age (Boyd and Flood 2015, 20–4). The goal of this type of legislation was twofold: to alleviate financial pressure on public support mechanisms by privatizing costs for children born out of wedlock, and to regulate the behaviour of parents by reinforcing notions of a good mother as someone who was white and legally married (Boyd and Flood 2015). This increased state surveillance reinforced discourses about "rampant immorality, family breakdown, and race suicide" (Chunn 1992, 28), and impacted Indigenous women in specific ways (Little 1998; Sangster 1999; Stevenson 2020; Maki 2021).

The province subsequently commissioned a study on mental health services by Drs. Clarence Hincks, head of the Canadian National Committee for Mental Hygiene (CNCMH), Samuel Laycock, a psychologist whose studies on behavioural problems in school children received CNCMH funding, and physician Oswald Rothwell. The authors explained, from sixteen years of age, mental defectives were the "greatest social problem" because of their tendency to live in unsanitary conditions and reproduce their own kind, which contributed to delinquency, immorality, and illegitimacy.[4] They highlighted the case of a twenty-four-year-old woman who left home at sixteen and who, over the course of eight years, "made four different alliances resulting in the birth of five illegitimate children. This woman [was] still at large."[5] If mental deficiency was not controlled, a problem associated with young and single mothers, the province would face "a great economic burden" from institutionalizing large numbers of individuals while providing social relief.[6] It should invest in training based on principles of sound child guidance; research and training in psychiatry and mental hygiene; mental hygiene outpatient clinics; psychiatric facilities for diagnosis and treatment; and the supervision of mental defectives by social workers.[7] Those unsuitable for training should be prevented from reproducing.[8] Here, the province should consider restrictive marriage legislation and sexual sterilization.[9]

That same year Progressive Member of the Legislative Assembly (MLA) S.A. Horner, part of the "left wing" of government (Russell 1970, 89), passed a motion proposing that, in the interest of eugenics, parenthood should be denied to mental defectives through marriage regulation, institutionalization, or sterilization (Dyck and Deighton 2017). Liberal MLA John Uhrich questioned the scientific basis of eugenic sterilization and whether it was possible to test for mental deficiency, arguing that segregation was as effective in preventing the propagation of "undesirables" (Deighton 2018, 73–4). Horner's motion was defeated and the province did not pass sterilization legislation, but it did enact legislation to segregate the "diseased" and "defective," and to regulate marriage.

The Mental Diseases Act, enacted in 1922, was indicative of the "growing power of the medical profession" in psychiatric care, and their increased reliance on "more nuanced diagnostic categories" to institutionalize "lunatics," the "insane," and the "mentally diseased" in newly established hospitals (Dyck and Deighton 2017, 14). The Mental Defectives Act of 1930, coupled with amendments to the Mental Diseases Act, enabled the committal of "idiots," "imbeciles," "morons," and "feebleminded persons" to training schools.[10] By 1936, both pieces of legislation were merged into An Act Respecting Mentally Defective and Mentally Ill Persons, or the Mental Hygiene Act.[11] Indigenous people would not be admitted to provincial institutions unless costs were guaranteed by Indian Affairs.[12]

Jennifer Creighton (2011) shows only ten female and twelve male "Indians" were identified on patient ledgers from the Saskatchewan Hospital, North Battleford, between 1929 and 1939. Erika Dyck and Alex Deighton report the highest number of Indigenous admissions to provincial institutions — thirteen patients — in 1936 and 1946, with none noted in the files reviewed, between 1948 and 1965. They argue "the economics of confinement resulted in few Indigenous patients" (2017, 11–12). While perhaps true in the first part of the century when Indigenous people were segregated on reserves, and in residential schools and Indian hospitals, as the federal government re-framed Indian policy and sought to devolve responsibility to the province for the delivery of health and welfare services, Indigenous admissions rose.

This was partially reflected in amendments to the Mental Hygiene Act in 1950, which specified the province would bear the cost of care and treatment for those considered mentally ill or defective but would enter into agreements with the federal government for those to whom the latter was responsible.[13] Legislation was broadened to include a section on "alcoholics," "drug addicts," and epileptics, and admissions became "almost entirely" (Mills 2007, 181) controlled by the medical profession.[14] The federal government enabled the increased application of provincial legislation by revising the Indian Act in 1951 to include a first definition of a "mentally incompetent Indian" as whatever a province deemed them to be.[15] Mental defectives capable of being trained were sent to provincial institutions under the auspices of Indian Affairs; Indian Health Services was responsible for those considered mentally ill.[16] Later, Indigenous admissions to psychiatric institutions increased twofold, with "significantly higher" diagnosis for epilepsy and schizophrenia (Roy, Choudhuri, and Irvine 1970, 385).

The province also enacted restrictive marriage legislation. In 1933, it altered the Marriage Act to exclude anyone from marrying who was considered an "idiot" or "imbecile," or suffered from a "chronic mental" or "communicable" disease.[17] By this time, feeblemindedness, prostitution, illegitimacy, and venereal disease — syphilis in particular — had become so "closely related ... they [could not] be discussed intelligently apart" (Pols 1999, 122). The RF explained the logic behind restrictive marriage legislation — considering "mental defects" were "variable and elusive," factors in the blood promised more direct genetic interpretation than was possible from "symptoms" or other instruments.[18] The rise of medical genetics, coupled with notions of eugenics and mental hygiene, informed amendments to the Marriage Act establishing mandatory premarital blood testing for syphilis, rubella, and later, maternal phenylketonuria.[19] The federal government implemented a form of marriage regulation under the Indian Act, including a definition of "Indian-ness" based on blood quantum, and other clauses that reinforced heteropatriarchal and heteronormative notions of marriage, family, and property relations that targeted women and their "illegitimate" children (Jamieson 1978; Palmater 2011). It also supported the provincial approach.

In 1938, Thos. Robertson, Inspector of Indian Agencies, Saskatchewan, inquired as to whether Indian Affairs would pay for the medical examination of "Indians" before marriage. In the File Hills agency, examinations were conducted free of charge by a doctor working on behalf of Indian Affairs. The Indian Agent from the Qu'Appelle Agency, where a two-dollar fee was charged, believed it was not the fee, but the medial examination itself to which Indigenous people objected. In Leask, the Indian Agent claimed the only thing that would stop Indigenous people from living together outside of marriage was an amendment to the Indian Act.[20] Robertson thought the matter of considerable importance to the department so it should bear the expense. E.L. Stone, Secretary, Indian Affairs, replied that this problem could not "be separated from the general problem of medical attendance. Under the law the Indian must be examined and if he has not got the money, I think the Department will have to pay in one way or another."[21] Indigenous resistance to the imposition of Western medicine was longstanding, which led the federal government to amend the Indian Act in 1914 and 1951 with the purpose of making hospitalization and treatment compulsory.[22] It also required Registered Indian marriages to submit to provincial legislation.[23] A follow-up letter to Indian Superintendents stated, if an "Indian" did not comply with provincial law pursuant to directives from a medical officer or doctor, this person was liable to prosecution.[24]

In 1977, when the province considered repealing the clause prohibiting the "mentally retarded" and "mentally ill" from marrying, Cabinet initially rejected the idea because of "unnecessary controversy" that may arise from those who agreed with the clause.[25] The Saskatchewan Mental Health Association argued, in a contradictory fashion considering its predecessor recommended its passage, that to retain this provision was discriminatory and if not repealed, it would make public debate of the matter.[26] Government feared its opposition might exploit the issue for political gain.[27] Minister of Health Ed Tchorzewski explained the power to pass legislation restricting marriage rested at the federal level and since judgment on who was "mentally retarded" or "mentally ill" under the Marriage Act was up to a physican, not a psychiatrist, it was a difficult to make this assessment given the brief contact had with the intending marital couple.[28] In 1978, the province repealed this clause.[29]

Tommy Douglas and the Expansion of Public Health in Saskatchewan

Saskatchewan's entanglement with eugenic approaches to social problems continued under the leadership of Tommy Douglas. As the first Co-operative Commonwealth Federation (CCF)–elected Premier from 1944 to 1961, Douglas served concurrently as Minister of Health from 1944 to 1949 and became the "ultimate architect" (Mills 2007, 180) of a system of public health granting increasing power to psychologists and psychiatrists, the medical profession more generally, and later, social workers, to manage the lives of those suffering the most negative effects of an exploitative political economy. Douglas had completed his graduate work under the supervision of Dr. A.L. McCrimmon, who trained in sociology and economics at the University of Chicago, an institution founded by John D. Rockefeller Sr. where "eugenic concerns" were "widely reflected" in curriculum and faculty activities (Clarke 2022, 112).

In his study on eugenics and the "problems of the subnormal family," Douglas (1933) echoed prominent ideological positions from the time. He described the "indigent" women in his study as "immoral," "non-moral" (2), "common prostitutes," and "mental defectives" (4), of lesser intelligence and poorer health, and who, through marriage, tended to "infect" (4) others. Not only were "these people" inferior, but they were also a problem due to their "rapid growth":

> Twelve women producing [ninety-five] children means a birth rate of 7.9, and for total descendants, an average of 16.6 children per each one of the original twelve women. When we remember that the average birth-rate is in the neighborhood of 3.1, we see just how alarming the situation is. If this group should continue to be as prolific as in the past quarter of a century, we would have well over one thousand descendants from these twelve women in another twenty-five years ... two-thirds of whom are mentally defective, and one-fifth morally delinquent, [and this] would create a problem of horrible magnitude. Surely the continued policy of allowing the subnormal family to bring into the world large numbers of individuals to fill our jails and mental institutions, and to live upon charity, is one of consummate folly. (5–6)

The "problem of the subnormal family" was for government to solve. Douglas recommended modification of marriage laws to require medical certification prior to issuing marriage licenses, segregation of the "subnormal" on state-run colonies, and the sterilization of those considered mentally defective to deprive them of "nothing but the privilege of bringing into the world children who would only be a ... charge to society" (25). To allow state-sanctioned sterilization meant there was possibility of abuse, but the ethics of medical professionals were of such "high order" (27) this would protect against injustice. He also suggested legislation allowing the "discreet dissemination of contraceptive knowledge" (27) to those having children they could not feed or clothe, and schools for those impressionable enough to develop new attitudes.

Douglas is said to have given up on his "eugenic tendencies" (McLaren 1990, 166; also Dyck and Deighton 2017; Mills 2007; Shevell 2012) once becoming Premier, but this narrative needs to be complicated (Shaheen-Hussain 2020). Prior to Douglas taking office, the province had initiated population control measures relating to marriage regulation and segregation. Douglas strengthened their scope and applicability and by the time he left, much of what he outlined in 1933, except for a clearly stated policy on sterilization and contraceptives, had been implemented — though he too considered sterilization. Months after being elected, he and members of his government inquired with officials in Alberta and British Columbia on the "operation and effectiveness" of their sterilization laws.[30] He then commissioned two surveys on mental health, both recommending the expansion of public health in a manner envisioned by his predecessors, which included sterilization.

The first was conducted in 1944 by Dr. Henry Sigerist, socialist medical historian and sometimes eugenicist, and long-time advocate for public health care subsidized by the state (Fee 1996; Jones 2019). Throughout his career, many of Sigerist's activities were funded by the RF, and Dr. Alan Gregg, director of the Medical Sciences and International Health divisions, was a close friend with a shared interest in cost-effective public health interventions (Brown and Fee 2003; Haraway 2003). Sigerist visited Canada – before being retained by the province at the invitation of the scholarly and medical community – to share his views on socialized medicine, a project that became a primary focus for Douglas. Sigerist viewed medicine as "social science" and "socialized medicine" as a means of ensuring "advances" were distributed to all (Duffin and Falk 1996, 660), especially those who could not pay.

In his report, Sigerist offered recommendations on how to administer a system of public health to address "pressing disease issues" like tuberculosis, mental health, and venereal disease (Jones 2019, 179). This included, among other things, the delineation of health districts and the establishment of rural health centres, district hospitals, a university-based hospital, and a medical school (Duffin and Falk 1996). The province should build a training school for the mentally deficient, provide outpatient services in urban centres, and travelling clinics in rural areas free of charge (Mills 2007) with the goal of "devolv[ing] most mental care to regular physicians" (Dyck and Deighton 2017, 98). Finally, it should consider sterilization.

The year previous, in *Civilization and Disease,* Sigerist explained it would be "a great mistake to identify eugenic sterilization solely with the Nazi ideology and to dismiss the problem simply because we dislike the present German regime and its methods ... The problem is serious and acute, and we shall be forced to pay attention to it sooner or later" (1943, 106–7). To the province, he recommended a focus on sterilizations carried out "humanely," "cautiously," and "with good results."[31] The humanitarian argument, common among eugenicists and other population controllers, was based on the idea that sterilization was for a person's own good, enabling them to participate in society while being protected from the burden of pregnancy and parenthood (Kurbegovic 2020). This argument was often coupled with an economic one — sterilization would protect state resources and society (Stern 2005; Dowbiggin 2006).

Sigerist's "vision" of public health reflected a "racialized and colonialist view" of the world (Jones 2019, 181). On Indigenous Peoples, Sigerist wrote:

> The Indians, about 13,700 scattered throughout the Province, constitute a reservoir of disease ... Ill health of Indians is a menace to the health of the white population since the two races mix freely. The Indians would, in all probability, receive more medical attention if they could be included into the provincial system of rural health services. An agreement might be reached with the Dominion Government, under

which the Province would assume responsibility for the health services of the Indians, and would be compensated for it by the Dominion Government.³²

Under the British North America Act, Indians were a federal responsibility, but the province had jurisdiction over education, health, and welfare more broadly. The federal government limited the provision of services mostly to reserves, in a coercive, partial, and underfunded way (Lux 2016; Shewell 2004). The province viewed the federal approach as an impediment to assimilation (Abel and Leslie 2000). To secure federal monies would allow it to expand its own system of public health as it engaged with the "menace" posed by Indigenous people while encouraging assimilation. However, to move in these directions it would need to wait until the federal government was prepared to subsidize this expansion (Jones 2019).

Douglas commissioned a second mental hygiene survey by Hincks.³³ Hincks recommended a reduction of the patient population in mental hospitals through a stronger community-based mental hygiene program "beyond the asylum," and reiterated the need to separate the "mentally deficient" from the "mentally ill" by establishing training schools.³⁴ Those who could not be trained should be sterilized.³⁵ On this, he wrote: "the Mental Hygiene Commissioner ... should study the Alberta Program and also the program in California, where sterilization has been conducted on an extensive scale. The observations and conclusions ... would be helpful to the Minister of Health in deciding upon the best course of action."³⁶

Following the release of Hincks's report, Douglas was hit with a deluge of protest stemming from a letter writing campaign organized by the Catholic Church.³⁷ The Prince Albert Catholic Women's League wrote that sterilization could not be justified on moral, ethical, or scientific grounds; the Nazis had resorted to maiming the bodies of those they viewed as belonging to inferior races and the world was shocked by this.³⁸ Members of the Sodality of the Christian Mothers wrote that considering Douglas was a Christian minister, it should not be necessary to point out how unchristian and unethical it was to propose to sterilize individuals.³⁹

In his standard response, Douglas stated that Hincks had not recommended sterilization "per se," only that the Commissioner of Mental

Services examine what was being done in Alberta and report to the Minister of Health, but "no policy of sterilization of mental defectives had been accepted or even contemplated at present time."[40] This correspondence appears to be the same evidence relied on by scholars who argue Douglas's views underwent a "massive change" (Marchildon 2011, 310) from "coercive" to "sympathetic" (Mills 2007, 181, 196, n. 4), leading him to give up his eugenic tendencies. If so, there is reason to doubt this interpretation. Douglas queried two governments on their sterilization laws, expanded the scope of legislation to regulate marriage based on eugenic principles, and continued to rely on Hincks, a well-known proponent of eugenics whose recommendations should not have been surprising — he had made them numerous times previous.

One of the few pieces of correspondence to Douglas in support of sterilization came from A.R. Kaufman — businessman, eugenicist, and "father of birth control" in Canada — who enabled the sterilization of over one thousand individuals living in poverty in Ontario from the 1930s to 1960s (Revie 2006, 128–9). Kaufman highlighted "[50 percent] of mental defects come from poor human stock, and by means of sterilization it was possible to prevent the transmission of defects to offspring."[41] Extra social services were a form of "national suicide," which aggravated social problems by encouraging breeding in dependent classes.[42] C.G. Sheps, Acting Chairman of the newly formed Saskatchewan Health Services Planning Commission, established to implement Sigerist's recommendations, advised Douglas that Kaufman's letter was an example of "lop-sided thinking."[43] Yet Douglas responded he was "very interested in the contents [of Kaufman's letter] as were some of the officials in the Department of Public Health." It was his hope that Hincks's recommendations would be "gradually and steadily implemented."[44]

These do not reflect the words of someone whose thinking has undergone a massive change, and while Douglas did not enact sterilization legislation, he did not condemn the practice. We also need to remember the point made by Alison Bashford (2014), that in the first instance, eugenic concerns were questions of political economy — of land, resources, and the prevention of war — embedded in population control, not notions of race. Further, by this time, the RF was being "extremely careful" to project an impartial and objective image by avoiding openly engaging in anything that might lead the public to "infer they were attempting to control any aspect of social life" (Fisher 1983, 209).

Douglas proceeded to expand a system of public health in ways that resulted in the increased control of populations in the interest of the political economy, and he relied on Rockefeller support to do so.

Douglas wrote to numerous American philanthropic organizations with racist, colonial, and capitalist roots in hopes of securing financial support to expand his system of public health, including the RF and its sister organization, the Commonwealth Fund, and the Carnegie Foundation and Julius Rosenwald Fund.[45] He engaged the W.K. Kellogg Foundation, the Millbank Memorial Fund, the Menninger Foundation, and the Russell Sage Foundation, though it is unclear whether he sustained any meaningful contact with these organizations.[46] Most of his requests for financial assistance were turned down. In a time of economic contraction, his attempt to engage the Carnegie Foundation was thwarted by its previous funding commitments that had stretched resources to their limit (Brison 2005). However, Douglas maintained extensive contact with the RF to expand a system of public health in keeping with the Foundation's approach — to avoid explicit reference to eugenics or more controversial proposals like sterilization, but while increasing the scope and expanse of interventions in people's lives.

On May 23, 1946, C.F.W. Hames, Deputy Minister of Public Health, outlined that the RF was interested in Saskatchewan's public health activities and would provide assistance on a cost-shared basis in three ways, in keeping with its investment principles: by providing long-term and short-term fellowships to enable professionals to be trained at Rockefeller-funded schools of public health; helping the Department of Public Health to expand health services, for example, by creating separate divisions for local health administration and assisting local health regions to become adjunct to medical schools; and financing research work.[47] Funding was temporary and would be withdrawn when government could control its own operations — governments were always expected to eventually "foot the bill" (Birn 2014, 130).

Douglas introduced a policy to fund "free" psychiatric care, with costs recouped when possible, from the estate of an individual after their death (Marchildon 2011, 308). The province rewrote the Mental Hygiene Act to specify any costs associated with this legislation after January 1, 1946, would be borne by government, and appointed Dr. D.G. McKerracher as Commissioner of Mental Health.[48] McKerracher later headed the Psychiatric Services Branch, positioning Saskatchewan as a "world leader" (Mills 2007, 185) in psychiatric research with a program partially supported by the RF.[49] Douglas also relied on Dr. Alan Gregg, who, together with the Canadian RF representative Dr. W.A. McIntosh, advised on how to expand public health services in Saskatchewan.[50]

In his various roles with the RF, McIntosh advised on the expansion of public health internationally and in other provinces in ways that overlapped with what was transpiring in Saskatchewan (i.e., Campbell 1945). He also influenced Dr. Harry Cassidy, one of Canada's "foremost experts on public health administration" (Mullally 2009, 103), who played a key advisory role to the federal government on the expansion of the welfare state. Gregg, a close friend of Sigerist, was "deeply embedded" (Sachse 2009, 105) in the eugenics movement, influenced by English geneticists who believed intelligence was hereditary (Haraway 2003). In one instance he corresponded with C.C. Little, former president of the American Eugenics Society and founding director of the ABCL, who "loudly and repeatedly advocated birth control, euthanasia, and eugenics" (Crow 2002, 1357). Gregg suggested to Little, who conducted cancer research on dogs and mice, that they begin a project to breed dogs based on intelligence to demonstrate the limitation of training programs for the mentally deficient (Paul 1998). The RF awarded over $600,000 to this project.

As head of the Medical Services Division, Gregg supported research in behavioural genetics, mental hygiene, psychobiology, and psychiatry (Paul 1998; Weindling 1988). Founded by Francis Galton, behavioural genetics sought to explain mental ability and social behaviour through reference to genetics. Under Gregg's leadership, developments in the field, often under the banner of medical genetics, maintained a "continuity of beliefs" and a commitment to demonstrating "the falsity of environmentalist assumptions" (Paul 1998, 56). Ian Dowbiggin (2003) demonstrates the central role of psychiatry in promoting sterilization as a mental hygiene measure, but claims Gregg had little sympathy for the discipline. However, he invested Rockefeller funds into surrounding fields including neurology, neuroanatomy, neurophysiology, endocrinology, genetics, psychology, and psychobiology, and more deeply integrated psychiatry as a legitimate part of the general hospital system (Summergrad and Hackett 1987).

Gregg and McIntosh met with Douglas and members of his government, presidents of universities, and deans of schools of medicine to discuss the expansion of a system of public health through provincial investment in a Department of Hygiene and Social Medicine, a university hospital, and medical research.[51] In anticipation of the launch of a hospital insurance plan, in 1947 the province developed hospital and professional standards; divided territory into health regions; began establishing local health units; and would expand public health services as rapidly as personnel became available.[52]

It also hired Dr. Samuel W. Hamilton as consultant to the Mental Hygiene Program.[53] Hamilton was a prominent psychiatrist who advised on mental hospitals and training schools, first for the American National Committee on Mental Hygiene, and later, for the United States Public Health Service, through RF support — he is said to have evaluated nearly every public and private mental institution in North America (Thorne 1952; Barton 1977). In a survey of Minnesota's mental health program, he concluded, while the "sterilization of defectives" was based on the "crudely unscientific" idea that inferior hereditary strains could be eliminated through sterilization, the practice was supported because it was cost-effective, allowing for de-institutionalization while avoiding additional costs should "feeble-minded" persons reproduce (Ladd-Taylor 2017, 168–9). In a report on the Vermont State School for the Feebleminded, which provides hints that queerness informed the label of mental deficiency, Hamilton posited a connection between low IQ, sexual deviance, and homosexuality (Allen and Fuller 2016).

Leonard G. Rosenfeld, Vice-Chairman, Saskatchewan Health Services Planning Commission, also engaged Dr. Hugh H. Smith, Assistant Director, International Health Division.[54] Rosenfeld held a Rockefeller Fellowship and studied with Sigerist at Johns Hopkins University (Jones 2019). Smith, and his colleague, Edward Flahiff, worked on a Rockefeller-funded Tuberculosis Commission in Jamaica, from 1927 to 1942, and a vaccine trial on patients from mental hospitals and children from an industrial school and orphanages, to determine whether race or "gradients of skin color" impacted disease susceptibility (Altink 2017, 1078). Some went unvaccinated, a fact that was not conveyed to participants. Despite showing socioeconomic status, not race, impacted vaccine effectiveness, the Commission "struggled to shake off the belief that there was a natural difference between whites and blacks" (Altink 2017, 1083).[55]

These are some of the individuals who guided the expansion of public health in Saskatchewan. In his first ten years as Premier, through the consultative and financial support of the RF and its trained associates, Douglas established a medical school at the University of Saskatchewan; set out a more comprehensive program focused on mental health and the training of mental defectives; engaged fellowship funding for medical officers to undertake post-graduate work at the School of Hygiene, University of Toronto; developed a manual for public health nurses; and organized public health care by regional centres and health authorities. By 1955, the Royal University Hospital opened, as well as a College of Medicine, and a training school in Moose Jaw, for which there was quickly over five thousand children waitlisted.[56] The Psychiatric Services Branch was established, and in addition to North Battleford and Weyburn Hospitals, there was a Munroe Wing in Regina, the McNeil Clinic in Saskatoon, the University Hospital psychiatric ward and clinic, a mental health clinic in Moose Jaw, and travelling clinics for other areas of the province.[57] By 1960, a mental hospital at Yorkton was "squeezed into the budget."[58] The expansion of a system of public health, and the making of "experts" to diagnosis and treat individuals, created demand and confirmed the need to continue investing in those who could operate institutions, conduct research, and deliver services. This had always been a goal of Rockefeller philanthropy (Richardson and Fisher 1999).

With respect to the training component of public health work involving children, support from the RF for Hincks and Laycock, and the CNCMH, shaped the psychological approaches to mental deficiency that dominated the post–World War II period, even after financial support ended (Richardson 1989; Turner 1999). Brian Low (2004) explains, RF support for proponents of "mental hygiene" provided an institutional base for them to "legitimate their ideals of child rearing" while "marginalizing alternate ideals and alternate research." As a result, in the post–World War II period, the "almost universal expert support for 'modern' child-rearing methods" in truth, reflected "almost universal authority over child-rearing expertise by Rockefeller philanthropy" (34). Guidance clinics and training schools were sites where young people were made into a "productive and democracy-loving citizenry," and deviancy was "diagnosed and defined" (Gleason 1999, 119). This was reflected, for one, in the professionalization of social workers, which Hincks referred to as society's "shock troops" (Irving 1992, 19), as they played a larger role as part of the welfare state in identifying and apprehending children from "maladjusted" families; something especially relevant to Indigenous people as they were increasingly subject to provincial child welfare policies and interventions, and Indigenous mothers faced the risk of having their children apprehended at birth.

RF support is significant because, through the institutions it helped build and experts it helped train, it — not government — drove a public health agenda meant to prepare "backward regions" and the people living in them for integration into the "capitalist world of production, trade and consumption" (Birn 2014, 130). The "narrow, biological approach" to disease underpinning Rockefeller philanthropy, harnessed through public health expansion, imparted "scientific knowhow" while "garnering population support for social amelioration," "upping labour productivity and investment prospects," and avoiding "social and political uprisings" (Birn 2014, 130).

More broadly, Douglas sought to ensure a "rational" and "efficient" administration (Lam 2011, 133) and relied on George Cadbury to do this. Cadbury, who became a central figure in the expansion of family planning in Canada, was British heir of the confectionary company of the same name, and a eugenicist and socialist. He met with Douglas in 1945 on the recommendation of David Lewis, fellow socialist, CCF member, and later head the national New Democratic Party (Kühl 2013; McLaren 1995). As Chairman of the Economic Advisory and Planning Board and Chief Industrial Executive, Cadbury was the "top CCF planner" (Quiring 2004, 102). He worked closely with Douglas under a "broad mandate" to apply his business approach to government through "restraint in social spending" to increase "the productivity of the economy" (Lam 2011, 134), including by purportedly nationalizing resource industries, monopolizing natural gas distribution, and establishing a state-owned power grid (McLaren 1995).

The CCF had run on an "aggressive" policy of socialization but, in concert with recommendations from the Economic Advisory and Planning Board in 1947, and again in 1948, it changed course by opening up Crown lands for private development to such an extent that, by the early 1950s, it had "formally abandoned the nationalization option" (Emery and Kneebone 2008, 425). In this period, thirty-six million acres of land were under lease for oil exploration (Western Oil 1949) and Imperial Oil, for one — a Rockefeller-owned Standard Oil subsidiary — became more active in the province (Taylor 2019). Cadbury also attempted to persuade the British government to support uranium mining as an alternative to Eldorado Nuclear, a Crown Corporation under federal control.[59] The focus on rationality and fiscal restraint also did not apply to the "golden child" — the Psychiatric Services Branch — which saw its budget increase "exponentially" from 1950 to 1964 (Marchildon 2011, 312).

There is much written on the purported socialist tendencies of the CCF, and of Douglas's "charismatic leadership" (Kowalewski and Mayne 2012, 62) in spearheading what became a national publicly funded healthcare system, for which he was "crowned" the "greatest Canadian of all time" (CBC Arts 2004). Yet both the party and man shared "ideological affinities" (Russell 1970, 127) and relationships with the most conservative and exploitative elements of society. Gad Horowitz writes, "The tory and socialist minds have some crucial assumptions, orientations and values in common, so that from certain angles they may appear not as enemies, but as two different expressions of the same basic ideological outlook" (1966, 158). Similarly, Herbert Emery and Robert Kneebone state, "the [CCF] party's official stand on the role of social ownership versus private enterprise moved from a prohibition of capitalism in 1933 to the aiding and encouraging of private business ... in 1948. The distinction between the CCF and the 'old parties' diminished further through the 1950s" (2008, 437, n. 23). Douglas's socialism was embedded in capitalism (Duffin and Falk 1996; Jones 2019), and his support for the expansion of public health can be understood as one means of ensuring the productivity of the economy while managing its negative effects on people and populations (Swartz 1993).

One also needs to consider the lands upon which Saskatchewan depends for its existence, out of which resources and profits are drawn — these are Indigenous lands. In this respect, Douglas's government was embedded in colonialism, sharing a similar desire as corporate interests in wanting to control resources, markets, and populations (Brown 1976). His view on the future for Indigenous Peoples, to "gradually blend them into larger society," would ensure control over lands and resouces for development (Quiring 2004, 47). The expansion of public health became one means of doing this, as social problems on reserves were framed as individual ones that could be solved through integration, and by subjecting Indigenous people to the increasingly organized gaze of health and welfare professionals. This does not make Douglas a hero, but an apologist for a system based on exploitation and theft.

In the post–World War II period, "gone were most references to mass eugenic sterilization laws as the catch all solution to cleaning up the nation's gene pool and eradicating poverty, crime, disease, and welfare dependence. In their place were statements that sterilization had to be based on the most up-to-date diagnostic precision and most thorough consideration of each patient" (Dowbiggin 2008, 30). It was not sterilization that was unacceptable, only the "wild talk of the most ignorant eugenicists" (31). As Sigerist stated, "It is never sound to continue to use terminology with which the minds of millions of people have been poisoned even when the old terms are given new meaning" (1951, 101).

While sparse, there are references to sterilizations being considered and sometimes performed on Indigenous women in this period. In one case, from 1933, both sterilization and segregation were considered for an Indigenous girl discharged from the Onion Lake Residential School who engaged in prostitution as a means of survival and had recently given birth.[60] The Medical Officer, Battleford Indian Office, wrote to the Secretary of Indian Affairs asking what should be done. Once she returned to the reserve, she would likely resume her "former ways," and this would result in additional births. Punishment would be mistaken for persecution and lead to resentment, but "Segregation, where? Sterilization? Sterilize a Catholic, Holy Horrors."[61]

In a later instance, J.P. Harvey, Regional Superintendent, Saskatchewan, wrote the Director of Indian Health Services with two appended applications for surgery, requesting approval from the Department.[62] The first was for a twenty-five-year-old Indigenous woman, "a waitress" from the Poorman's Band, Touchwood Agency, Punnichy, recommended for a "Hysterectomy, salpingectomy, etc." on the advice of Dr. McEwen, from Regina.[63] P.E. Moore, Director, Indian and Northern Health Services, later found it necessary to clarify sterilizations should not be performed for eugenic or economic reasons after an account came to his attention involving a woman from the Thunderchild Reserve, Battleford Agency, sterilized by Dr. John M. Richards, Turtleford, Saskatchewan.[64] Correspondence from T.J. Orford, Regional Superintendent, Saskatchewan Region, to Dr. A.C. Taylor & Associates, Regina, also spoke to an unauthorized sterilization performed on a woman from the White Bear Band.[65]

In one instance directly involving Douglas, a father whose daughter was institutionalized at the Saskatchewan Hospital, Weyburn, wrote to request her release.[66] Douglas inquired with Superintendent Dr. A.R. Coutler, who responded "[the] home situation is very poor. They are on relief, living in a very small, dirty, poorly kept home. The patient's father is at present living with a squaw [sic] from a nearby reserve. Social workers have been sent into the home which have confirmed our impression."[67] Because the girl had previously become pregnant and would likely again after her release, he was opposed to her discharge. Douglas agreed, and replied to the father that it would be unwise to release his daughter.[68] There is no indication sterilization was performed in this case, but segregation was justified on similar grounds, and the father living with an Indigenous woman was a factor preventing her release.

Federal-Provincial Intersections in Public Health

Significant efforts toward the expansion of a system of public health were advanced by William Lyon Mackenzie King, Canada's longest serving prime minister, who held office for three non-consecutive terms between 1921 and 1948. Mackenzie King viewed the principle that the federal government should refrain from becoming involved in health matters for constitutional reasons as a "vicious" one.[69] His efforts, together with those of Deputy Minister of Health, Dr. J.J. Heagerty, were central in motivating government to assist with public health expansion (MacDougall 2009; Taylor 2009). This support goes back to 1919 when, as leader of the Liberal Party, Mackenzie King updated the party policy platform to include health insurance measures (Swartz 1993). It also leads back to the Rockefellers through a personal request he made to his "closest friend" (Spaulding 1993, 74), Rockefeller Jr., which resulted in the first substantial investment by the RF in medical education in Canada, enabling the expansion of institutions, forms of knowledge, research, and the training of experts essential to the capitalist state — the network of "like minded" (Brison 2005, 45) individuals amenable to collaborating over the long term in shaping social policy. Mackenzie King was such an individual, having served as a labour advisor to the Rockefellers before becoming federal leader, during which time he made a "convert" of Rockefeller Jr. on the role of the state in managing relations between labour and industry (Kaufman 2004, 88). Once elected, he furthered a "statist" approach to social policy by supporting the expansion of the welfare state — which included health — in ways that gave "the appearance of reform" while "maintaining the essential capitalist configuration" of the political economy (Irving 1981, 24).

This thinking was shared by all political stripes, including H.E. Spencer, United Farmers of Alberta Member of Parliament (MP), Battle River, and founding member of the CCF, who proposed in 1930 that federal grants be made available for one-third of the cost of establishing provincial public health units.[70] An arrangement had been made with the RF by which it would cover a third of operating costs for each provincial unit for three years, after which time federal support was needed. British Columbia and Quebec had taken advantage of this arrangement, and Alberta, Saskatchewan, and Manitoba were organizing in these directions. Spencer explained, people are "the greatest national asset," but those who fail to retain their health "very soon become liabilities."[71]

It also influenced Conservative leader Richard Bennett, prime minister from 1930 to 1935. One of Canada's "leading capitalists" (Finkel 1995, 224) and a "most prosperous and influential" (Taylor 2019, 139) businessman, Bennett was "chief lawyer" (Finkel 1995, 224) for Rockefeller-owned Imperial Oil from 1924 to 1929, and president of Royalite, a Rockefeller subsidiary, from 1926 to 1930. On the eve of an election, in 1935, Bennett passed legislation promising a host of reforms, including employment and universal health insurance, pensions, a minimum wage, and the limitation on work hours (Scott 1937). Many aspects of his "New Deal," including health insurance, were invalidated upon Mackenzie King's re-election in 1936 for being outside the scope of federal jurisdiction (MacDougall 2009). It was not the proposals per se that were invalid, the tension rested on who would pay for them, and so planning continued.

In 1937, the federal government struck a Royal Commission on Dominion-Provincial Relations (RCDPR) to examine the financial relationship between it and the provinces in light of the strain caused by a depression that had placed Saskatchewan, for one, in "such financial straits" (Smiley 1963, 1–2) it had become impossible for it to meet its financial obligations while providing public services. The RCDPR retained Albert Grauer, political economist, businessman, and former director of the Department of Social Sciences, University of Toronto, to prepare a report on public health.[72] The function of a federal department was to "coordinate" policy; promote uniform standards of practice; "give leadership" through research, education, and publicity; and address health problems beyond the control of any one province.[73] With respect to mental health, Grauer suggested public education, the training of social service personnel, and community services for the mentally ill, which would lead to savings and a decrease in crime.[74] A "comprehensive" program would add to the national income by increasing the productivity of workers, and he cited studies funded by the Millbank Memorial Fund to support his conclusion.[75]

The infant mortality rate in Canada was higher than sixteen other "developed nations," highest in rural areas, as was the maternal mortality rate, and mental health services were inadequate (Kozyrskyj 1996). Indigenous health statistics showed a "very serious state of affairs," but the federal government did not provide the same facilities as the provinces, for the broader population.[76] This was reflected, for one, in a tuberculosis death rate twelve times higher than among whites, a situation that should concern government because infection was spreading from reserves.[77] The least costly route would be for the provinces to deliver tuberculosis programs with federal funding made permanent.[78] Similar arrangements could then be made in other areas until there was a nationwide system for which the federal government provided grants-in-aid to support provincial services.[79]

The RCDPR believed medical and hospital services should remain a provincial responsibility considering constitutional constraints and the difficulty in controlling costs (MacDougall 2009). However, it relied on Grauer's data, based on research conducted by Hincks, which implied an "open relationship" (Lampard 2012, 205) between the CNCMH and the RCDPR. This relationship was confirmed by CNCMH members, including Hincks, who sat on the Dominion Council on Health, together with representatives from the Canadian Medical Association, the Canadian Hospital Association, the Advisory Committee on Child Welfare, the Canadian Tuberculosis Association, the Royal College of Physicians and Surgeons, Indian Affairs, and medical faculties from McGill, University of Montreal, and Laval (MacDougall 2009). It was further cemented through the Mental Health Division, Department of National Health and Welfare (DNHW), established in 1944 to conduct surveys, disseminate information, and coordinate efforts in the field.[80] Hincks became advisor to the DNHW (Richardson 1989).

Throughout this period, the advocacy of Dr. J.J. Heagerty was central. Heagerty had long been involved in federal health matters. Following the formation of the Department of Health in 1919, he headed the Venereal Disease Control Division until 1928, during which time he toured the country with Dr. Gordon Bates, director of the Canadian National Council for the Control of Venereal Disease (CNCCVD), later known as the Canadian Social Hygiene Council, together with British feminist-eugenicist Emmeline Pankhurst, who was employed by the CNCCVD for a time and influenced the ideas of Emily Murphy and Nellie McClung, two of the "Famous Five" who supported eugenic sterilization legislation in Alberta and British Columbia (Carter 2017).

The CNCCVD and Bates, who was member of the CNCMH and the Dominion Council of Health, were preoccupied with eugenics (McLaren 1990). Sarah Carter describes the work of the CNCCVD as being about "more than venereal disease," this served as a "metaphor for other ills of society" linked to "racial and national health" and "the vitality and strength of the Empire" (2017, 140). Venereal disease was "inextricably intertwined" with feeblemindedness (McLaren 1990, 40). This was true for Heagerty, who advocated restrictive marriage regulation to delay marriage between those suffering communicable diseases, but also to prevent marriage among the "unfit" (Blacker 1935, 34). Heagerty promoted health insurance in his various roles "with the same vigor that he proselytized against sexually transmitted diseases" (MacDougall 2009, 285). However, as a "first generation" public health activist, he was being overshadowed by thinkers who advocated for the expansion of public health as part of a broader state-supported welfare scheme — those who had moved away from the "wild talk" of eugenics (Dowbiggin 2008, 31).

When, as director of Public Health Services, Ministry of Pensions and Public Health, Heagerty prepared draft legislation and a report on health insurance in 1943, his work was considered alongside Leonard Marsh's *Report on Social Security for Canada*, the "most important single document in the history of the development of the welfare state in Canada" (Moscovitch 2017, xxxvii). In this report, which reflected developments in the field of welfare economics and an increased role for social workers in public health, Marsh made a series of proposals for the expansion of welfare programs, including health insurance, unemployment insurance, and measures to promote "purchasing power and economic stability" (Moscovitch 2017, xxiv; Horn 1976). Heagerty focused on health insurance "closely linked up with public health and form[ing] an integral part of it" (MacDougall 2009, 291), with medical professionals at the centre of change. He explained:

The mere treatment of illness is of secondary importance to the building up of a healthy race. Good housing, good nutrition, adequate income, higher standard of living — all these factors are what concern us now and, if we do not take cognizance of the need and seize the opportunity that presents itself … I fear that the medical profession may miss the opportunity that presents itself by not giving leadership to the movement. (Cited in MacDougall 2009, 298)

To implement any plan, constitutional issues needed to be resolved. Government proceeded with family allowances (Christie 2000), something under federal jurisdiction which had long been advocated by eugenicists (McDougall 1934; Sear 2021), as it considered how to move forward with a broader welfare scheme. Dominique Marshall writes, family allowances were a means to "quell the discontented worker" while keeping wages low and stimulating the economy, and possibly, increase the lower birth rate among "Canadian women" by re-making children as a "source of joy" rather than an economic "burden" (2006, 20, 25). Mackenzie King committed to a consultative approach on a nationwide health plan with Saskatchewan as a "pilot project" (MacDougall 2009, 307).

The DNHW, established in 1944, indicated health and welfare were "intimately connected" (MacDougall 2009, 304). The DNHW was headed by Brooke Claxton, with Dr. Brock Chisholm as Deputy Minister of Health, and Dr. George Davidson as Deputy Minister of Welfare. Chisholm was "good friends" with Hincks (Dowbiggin 2006, 179). He too was grounded in the eugenics movement and while not always explicitly espousing the ideology, throughout his career he emphasized the importance of fertility control as a means of population control (Dowbiggin 2006; Farley 2008). Chisholm resigned as Deputy Minister and served as director general of the World Health Organization from 1948 to 1953 (Farley 2008) where he attempted to persuade the United Nations to incorporate contraception into its work (Bashford 2014). He also declined the opportunity to head the Rockefeller-funded Population Council (Weindling 2003), but later became an active member of the Association for Voluntary Sterilization, as did Cadbury and Kaufman, which promoted sterilization in "underdeveloped" countries (Dowbiggin 2014, 186).

Claxton, a McGill-trained lawyer active with the Civil Liberties Association, did not share Chisholm's eugenic tendencies, but was committed to capitalism, private enterprise, and the role of government in "satisfying consumer needs," believing if Canadians had "a house, food, a job" they would have "a chance" (Caccia 2010, 180). He too thought the political and ideological debates between conservative, liberal, and socialist governments would become "more and more irrelevant" as differences in their goals were "enormously reduced" (Caccia 2010, 180). The shared goal of economic prosperity sought by politicians all political stripes was based on wealth exploited from Indigenous lands.

Chisholm represented a problem for Claxton for many reasons, including speeches he gave which Claxton feared might cost government votes, and his advocacy of birth control, sterilization, and euthanasia (Farley 2008). Claxton too should have known about Chisholm's commitment to problematic ideologies — he had made it clear in 1936, as expert witness in the trial of Dorothea Palmer, a nurse employed by Kaufman who was arrested for illegally distributing birth control in a working-class community. Chisholm argued federal legislative change on birth control was necessary for eugenic reasons, and to free people from "emotional troubles" due to "frustrated sexuality" (Dowbiggin 2006, 181). Claxton left his post after overseeing the launch of family allowances. He was replaced by Paul Martin Sr. who, together with Heagerty, championed the expansion of a national health insurance plan (Ostry 2009).

In 1946, the DNHW organized the Federal-Provincial Conference of Mental Health Directors, chaired by Dr. C.G. Stogdill, Chief, Mental Health Division, DNHW, and attended by Dr. G.D.W. Cameron, newly appointed Deputy Minister of Health, Dr. A.L. Crease, Superintendent of Mental Hospitals, Essondale, B.C., Dr. R.R. McLean, Superintended of Mental Institutions, Ponoka, Alberta, Dr. R.O. Davidson, Commissioner of Mental Health Services, Regina, Saskatchewan, Dr. Clarence Hincks and Dr. J.D.M. Griffin, General Director and Medical Director of the CNCMH, and Dr. D.G McKerracher, Director of Psychiatric Services, Weyburn, Saskatchewan. This was the first in a series of conferences sponsored by the DNHW to assist the provinces in coordinating efforts to solve "common problems."[81] Mental health was the "most important" and "neglected" problem in public health.[82]

Those in attendance, representing the "best in the field of medical science," many of whom were embedded in eugenics, stressed mental issues accounted for nearly one-third of illnesses and one-half of hospital beds in the country; every province was spending more on this issue than any other.[83] Hincks emphasized public health problems needed to be tackled on a "national basis," something the CNCMH had been trying to do without consistent funding for twenty-six years.[84] Dr. Stogdill, DNHW, encouraged the provinces to consult with Hincks as a leader on this issue.[85] Rockefeller funding may have supported Hincks and other so-called experts who advocated coercive measures in the name of public health, but the federal government reinforced their legitimacy. In clarifying why the provinces should consult with Hincks, Dr. A.H. Mackay, member of the Nova Scotia Society for Mental Hygiene, who was also in attendance, indicated there were problems for which it would be "embarrassing" for the DNHW to implement any action — these were best be handled by a voluntary agency.[86]

In 1948, the National Health Grants Program made ten grants available to the provinces to develop and strengthen public health services (Taylor 2009). These grants were described by Mackenzie King as "the first stage in the development of a comprehensive health insurance plan for all of Canada."[87] Nine were continuing grants for hospital construction, professional training, public health research, mental health, tuberculosis, cancer, venereal disease control, and support for "crippled" children.[88] J.H. Horowiczs, Senior Research Assistant, DNHW, explained that mental hygiene was "the most important subject to be faced," affecting all branches of public health including maternal and child welfare, and any control in the field would require a 50 percent contribution from the federal government.[89]

The centrality of the National Health Grants Program to the expansion of public health activities supported, if not initiated, by the RF was noted in its annual report that year.[90] It referenced Cameron, Deputy Minister of Health, speaking at the annual meeting of the American Public Health Association, who described National Health Grants as a continuation of social security measures meant to assist the provinces in surveying their own problems. The "cooperative planning" between federal and provincial departments, and voluntary agencies, was "encouraging."[91] The RF took credit for this. Its investments were not only a "valuable foundation" for a national program, the plan articulated by the federal deputy minister was dependent on — and shaped by — Rockefeller support.[92]

The DNHW sought direct advice from representatives of the International Health Division, RF, and took advantage of travel grants provided for government officials to visit Rockefeller-funded medical schools in the United States.[93] This included Dr. G.E. Wride, who obtained a degree in Public Health from the University of Toronto, and joined the Saskatchewan Health Services Planning Commission in 1946 with the task of drawing up a "master plan" for provincial health services.[94] In 1951, Wride became Principal Medical Officer for Health Insurance Studies, DNHW, and with Cameron, promoted federal investment in provincial services.[95] Cameron, a former bacteriologist trained at the School of Hygiene, University of Toronto, worked on a Rockefeller-supported study on diphtheria and scarlet fever in the 1930s, and was later appointed to the Joint United Nations International Children's Emergency Fund and World Health Organization Committee on Health Policy (Cameron 1959). These are only some of the federal-provincial-corporate intersections in building a system of public health that benefitted private interests while obfuscating the social causes of poverty and poor health.

Giving and Taking — Jurisdictional Disputes and Indigenous Health

In response to the availability of federal funding through the National Health Grants Program, F.D. Mott, Chairman, Health Services Planning Commission, Saskatchewan, was so excited he wrote Dr. W.A. McIntosh, International Health Division, "This program has all of us busy as we try to plan extension of the public health program and … take advantage of the funds available this first fiscal year."[96] The Saskatchewan Hospital Services Plan had come into effect the year previous, on January 1, 1947, and provided publicly funded hospital care to most residents except for those entitled to services from other agencies.[97] It was the federal view that as "payer of last resort" it would cover costs for Indigenous people who were indigent and living on-reserve, not because of any treaty obligations, but for humanitarian reasons. Claxton stated, it was necessary "to stamp out disease at its source where it may be within the confines of the country" to protect the health of the rest of the population (cited in Lux 2016, 47).

The refusal of the federal government to uphold its responsibilities with respect to health led to a longstanding tension on who should pay for those referred to as Registered Indians under the Indian Act post-1951. Federal-provincial negotiations took place in a way that further abrogated treaty responsibilities while each attempted to avoid the "prospect of ever-increasing costs" as the Indigenous birth rate rose (Abel and Leslie 2000, 7). Hugh Shewell (2004) writes, each time the federal government conferred with the provinces it "was attempting to move … toward the termination of [its] constitutional relationship" with Indigenous peoples (320).

On May 1, 1957, under the leadership of Prime Minister Louis St. Laurent, the federal government passed the Hospital Insurance and Diagnostic Services Act, based largely on Saskatchewan's plan to assist in funding hospital services on a national basis.[98] This commitment came after what has been described as the third and final stage of RF funding (Fedunkiw 2005). As St. Laurent stated, "the time has come for us to depend in future somewhat more upon ourselves."[99] The Saskatchewan Hospital Services Plan was brought under a cost-sharing agreement on July 1, 1958, and Indian Health Services was expected to pay premiums for eligible Registered Indians.[100] To track this, Registered Indians would have an "R" placed on their health cards.[101] This system, devised by the Saskatchewan Hospital Services Plan in cooperation with the federal government, enabled each level of government to account for Registered Indian users of provincial services with a view towards cost efficiency, in an attempt to force the other to take financial responsibility.[102]

The province, motivated by a desire to access increased federal funding, offered support to the Federation of Saskatchewan Indians — now the Federation of Saskatchewan Indian Nations, previously the Union of Saskatchewan Indians, created with Douglas's assistance (Quiring 2004) — affirming its position that health services were a treaty promise for which the federal government was responsible. O.J. Rath, Regional Superintendent, Indian and Northern Health Services, explained that the provincial approach was interfering with the federal strategy of having all Indigenous people assume responsibility for their own health care. He referenced a newspaper article in which Douglas was quoted as saying that a central part of "Indian life" was based in treaty, and treaties should be interpreted in modern terms; for instance, "medicine chest" should refer to health services.[103] This support for health as a treaty promise should not be misconstrued as respect for Indigenous sovereignty (Pitsula 1994); his intent was in line with federal policy — to promote assimilation (Weaver 1981). Douglas hoped, by offering support, the federal government would meet its obligations by delegating responsibility, coupled with more funding (Marchildon 2011).

In 1959, Douglas announced details on the Saskatchewan Medical Care Insurance Plan to cover the cost of insured health services for all residents (Taylor 1990). Anticipating passage of this legislation, J.W. Monteith, Minister of National Health and Welfare, wrote to J. Walter Erb, Minister of Public Health, Saskatchewan, that inclusion of all Registered Indians was the next step to encourage them to assume a position of "responsibility" and "equal status" with other Canadians.[104] However, the year previous, P.E. Moore, Director, Indian Health Services, stated it would be wise to "farm out" responsibility for the provision of health services as quickly as possible to ensure assimilation.[105] The province did not want piecemeal transfer. If delegated, this should cover all services for Registered Indians "as regular citizens ... or not ... at all."[106]

Douglas resigned as Premier to take up federal leadership of the NDP before passage of the Saskatchewan Medical Care Insurance Act, 1961, which went into effect the following year.[107] The Federation of Saskatchewan Indians had secured promise of inclusion prior to his resignation. Meanwhile, it was assured by the federal government that it would purchase medical cards for Registered Indians once the province was ready to include them. The province wanted the federal government to pay a greater amount due to the cost of servicing remote areas with a "backlog" of health problems.[108] Moore then tried to "strong-arm" the province into accepting responsibility:

> I am instructed by my Minister, the Hon. J. Waldo Monteith to request that Indians resident in Saskatchewan be immediately included in your Medical Care plan. I note that you state that everyone who has been a resident of Sask. for three months is registered ... I am sending a copy of this letter to our Regional Superintendent, Dr. T.J. Orford who will take immediate steps to register the Indians ... the Indian population pays the same sales tax and other provincial taxes as any other resident of the Province. We are anxious that they receive the same benefits.[109]

Special cards with the distinctive "R" marker were produced for Registered Indians under the Saskatchewan Hospital Services Plan, but only for hospital plan benefits. The cards supplied to municipal offices for other residents were different in make-up and covered benefits under both plans. These "white" population cards were not available for Registered Indians on reserves.[110] Orford commented, it was "a shade difficult to understand how the provincial government is able to split an Indian down the middle and accept him into the hospital plan but exclude him from the medicare plan," this must be to "try and force Federal financial assistance."[111] The federal expectation, too, was for the province to include Registered Indians as other residents, but each level of government appeared more concerned with avoiding additional costs than meeting the health needs of Indigenous people.[112]

In 1964, the newly elected provincial government led by Ross Thatcher, a former CCF MP who defected to the Liberals before entering provincial politics, continued the struggle to secure the "maximum financial contribution possible" from the federal government (Marchildon 2011, 321). Concurrently, details were being finalized for a national medical insurance plan which, combined with health insurance, became known as Medicare. In 1965, Prime Minister Lester Pearson stated he would meet with the provinces "at an early date" to discuss how they could provide health services to Canadians on a "comprehensive basis."[113] Again, at a Federal-Provincial Conference, he stated, in contradiction to the position taken with respect to services for Registered Indians, that it was the "responsibility of the federal government to cooperate" in making Medicare available for all Canadians, and "government accepts that responsibility."[114] Despite claiming to be working toward health services for all, each level of government was actively attempting to limit responsibility for Registered Indians.

The Medical Care Act passed on December 21, 1966, and came into force in 1968, at which time a 50/50 cost-sharing plan went into effect.[115] To qualify for federal contributions, provinces needed to make coverage available to all eligible residents. Registered Indians were expected to have access to benefits under the Saskatchewan Medical Care Insurance Plan.[116] In anticipation, the federal government released its "Health Plan for Indians," indicating it would no longer directly subsidize care for Registered Indians; they would be expected to access services "as any other citizen" (Lavoie 2018, 285). The exception was when an individual was indigent and denied provincial assistance, in which case Indian Health Services would step in. Maureen Lux (2016, 154) describes this as a "mean-spirited and draconian measure" — one going back to the Poor Laws in England and resistance to a "free rider" mentality (Breman et al. 2019, 4) — that placed the onus on individuals to prove they were impoverished to receive services. Providers were to prioritize diagnostic and preventative care; control admissions to hospitals to prevent overutilization; avoid active case finding for mental illness; and limit all accounts (Lux 2016), putting them in a conflict of interest in needing to weigh the best interest of a patient against what services and amounts were covered.

Fees paid by Indian Health Services to physicians were less than those paid for services provided to the rest of the population. E.H. Baergen, Saskatchewan Medical Association, wrote to Jean Chrétien, Minister of Indian Affairs, that it was paying for services at 85 percent of a fee schedule, but only up to a certain amount each month. As a result:

> some of the designated physicians, reach their maximum on about the 20th day of each month. The last 10 days' service therefore constitute conscripted voluntary service. If one breaks this down to a percentage payment, it comes to (2/3 x 85) approximately 56%. When one considers that services to all other beneficiaries in Saskatchewan are paid at 85%, this policy for … Indians should surely be tolerated no longer.[117]

Physicians were considering either refusing services to Registered Indians except in emergencies, or leaving. Baergen accused the federal government of discriminatory funding practices. Considering it was within its power to develop a plan for all Canadians to access health services, it was within its power to extend these to all Registered Indians, who were such a small proportion of the population. John Munro, Minister of National Health and Welfare, conceded and agreed to pay fees for one year at levels equivalent to the province.[118]

On January 1, 1969, Registered Indians became beneficiaries under the Saskatchewan Medical Care Insurance Act after which time it was "only logical" all public health services be provided by the province.[119] However, tension over who would pay for services continued into the 1970s when the province, in an attempt to use the federal position against itself, claimed the federal government was responsible for all "needy" Registered Indians, including those on social assistance and living off-reserve who, up to this point, had been issued a supplementary provincial health card featuring a "Y" rather than an "R," entitling them to medical services not covered by the provincial plan.[120] The province would issue "R" cards to all Registered Indians regardless of place residence or social assistance status, passing responsibility back to the federal government.[121] Indigenous leaders responded that both parties continued to ignore that health care was a Treaty Right, and "the thing to remember" was each "feel that this is a privilege they can withdraw at any time" (Federation of Saskatchewan Indian Nations 1973).

The Canada Health Act, passed in 1984, combined hospital and medical insurance into one piece of legislation and outlined responsibilities in service delivery.[122] It made no mention of Indigenous people, for whom services are delivered

> through a complex array of federal, provincial and Aboriginal-run programs and services. Who delivers what to whom depends on a number of factors such as status under the Indian Act, place of residence (on or off-reserve), the location of one's community (non-isolated or remote) and whether Health Canada has signed an agreement to transfer the delivery of certain health services to an Aboriginal community or organization ... Status Indians who reside on reserves are entitled to the general health services provided by the provinces and territories that fall under the Canada Health Act such as hospitals, physician services, and other insured services covered by provincial and territorial health plans. Health Canada, however, provides direct primary care and emergency services on reserves in remote and isolated areas where no provincial services are available.[123]

Métis, off-reserve Registered Indians, non-Status Indians, and Inuit are the responsibility of territorial and provincial governments (Lavoie 2013, 2).

Federal devolution with respect to health services allowed government to begin closing Indian hospitals and divert funds toward public hospital expansion. In doing so, it attempted to dissolve "the links between the economic and political roots of ill health on reserve and the state's responsibility for health care" (Lux 2016, 14) and disappear Indigenous peoples *as peoples*. However, it made Indigenous individuals more visible within the provincial system. This longstanding jurisdictional dispute, only some of which is recounted here, reinforced the view that Indigenous people were a burden to society and directly informed a context leading to systemic racism in health care.

The personal objectives of a prime minister are often the "most crucial factor[s]" in the decision to initiate a government proposal (Taylor 2009, 9). Mackenzie King's views, and his relationship with the Rockefellers, were a "powerful force" (9–10) pushing public health forward while reforming social justice struggles in ways more conducive to capitalism (Swartz 1993). Mackenzie King said as much when he wrote "social insurance, which in reality is health insurance in one form or another, is a means employed in most industrial countries to bring about a wider measure of social justice, without ... disturbing the institution of private property, and its advantages to the community" (1973, 222). This sentiment was echoed by Heagerty when he commented that implementing health insurance in Britain had countered socialist tendencies in the working class while doing little to advance their actual health (cited in Swartz 1993). That Saskatchewan was a pilot project is significant considering Rockefeller philanthropy often sought to co-opt socialist ideals in ways profitable to capitalist interests (Arnove 1982).

The expansion of public health may have been influenced by working-class struggle and community mobilizations, and while this came at some cost to capitalist interests and governments, the public was meant to receive the message that "limited reformist pressures" (Swartz 1993, 222) would bring about clear returns. As Donald Swartz puts it, the "fruits of struggle," in the absence of continued struggle, were "lost to working people ... even turned against them" (222). The expansion of state-subsidized public health "effected no change in the nature of the health care system ... Its control remained firmly in private hands ... What [it] amounted to ... was a virtually unlimited subsidy ... in the form of a guarantee by the state of payment for any services and goods physicians mandated" (222, 231). Despite a long and protracted battle between the government of Saskatchewan and physicians on how to operate under this legislation, which led to a withdrawal of services in protest for twenty-three days (Taylor 2009), medical professionals benefitted greatly (Naylor 1986) as they acquired "full control over the definition of disease, as well as how, when, and where to treat it" (Swartz 1993, 229). They were positioned as the ultimate arbiters of population policy (Gunn 1999).

To secure state subsidies for a system of public health offered in a way that reinforced capitalist relations — which for Indigenous Peoples, cannot be separated from colonialism — was a strategy envisioned by corporate interests; to have the public pay for interventions to help mitigate negative impacts of the political economy, but without this motivation being apparent, even to the professionals involved, who may not be aware they were promoting imperialism in their work (Berman 1983; Brown 1982). Intended as a "gateway" to access to raw materials by ensuring admission to a territory under the pretense of concern with health, once the initial "seeding" period ended, the institutions and ideological approaches to social problems supported by corporate philanthropy were to become "so entrenched as to be self-perpetuating" (Arnove 1982, 9, 13). When considered in this light, corporate interests are the largest beneficiaries of all.

Throughout, Indigenous Peoples were used as pawns by both levels of government while exploitative historical material relations informing their health status continued unabated. In considering the expansion of a system of public health in Indigenous lives, one would do well to reflect on the words of RF President George Vincent, who wrote in 1918 that for the purpose of "peacefully penetrating" colonies and "placating primitive and suspicious peoples," Western medicine had some "advantages over machine guns" (31–2; also Brown 1976). The following year, Vincent offered the first RF investment in medical education in Canada. In the post–World War II period, public health interventions — which included policies in health and welfare — replaced religion as "the intimate arm of the social order" (Brown 1979, 124). For Indigenous Peoples, they remained a tool of colonialism. The next chapter examines how the expansion of the welfare state informed Indian policy post–World War II by enabling increased coordination between each level of government in managing Indigenous lives to ensure continued access to lands and resources.

2

Emptying the Reserves — Indian Policy and the Welfare State

The Indian birth rate is so high and the exodus from the reserves is so low that there is a large net annual increase in the number of unintegrated Indians on reserves. The on-reserve population is expected to continue to expand ... resources of reserves cannot support the present population even at subsistence levels. The only practical alternative ... is for Indians to become full participants in Canadian economic and social life through permanent wage employment off-reserve and a transition to urban living ... services to Indians must be oriented to encourage off-reserve movement ... An intensive survey of the present conditions and prospects for improvement for Saskatchewan Indian life must be made as the basis for planning an "empty the reserves" program for integration of Saskatchewan Indians.[1]

In the late nineteenth and early twentieth century, federal Indian policy focused on separating Indigenous Peoples from their lands to secure colonial settlement and control. Segregation, or containment on reserves, enabled the federal government to subject Indigenous Peoples to a "coercive and restrictive" (Shewell 2004, 14) legislative authority through the Indian Act, to destabilize Indigenous forms of life and promote eventual assimilation. The Indian Act targeted Indigenous women through the definition of an "Indian" that was paternalistic, racialized, and heteronormative, to undermine the ability to pass on connections to the land to future generations. The federal pass system, implemented in 1885 and carried out in Saskatchewan until the late 1940s, reinforced segregation by restricting the movement of Indigenous people (Smith 2009). When off-reserve without a pass or means of support, Indigenous people could be arrested and ordered back to their community. For

Indigenous women who refused to leave town, the North-West Mounted Police might take them to the barracks and cut off their hair, a practice a local newspaper reported had "a wonderful effect in hastening their movements" (cited in Carter 1993, 156). Leona Blondeau, George Gordon First Nation, who was subject to the pass system into her teenage years, stated, "We never went anywhere. We stayed on reserve. We were very segregated ..." (Smith 2016).

Off-reserve, Indigenous women were blamed for prostitution, venereal disease, and alcohol problems, and were said to represent a threat to the public. The National Aboriginal Health Organization writes, governments at all levels "implemented various legal and non-legal regulatory techniques to manage prostitution. Indian Agents, missionaries, and local officials openly condemned both intra- and inter-racial prostitution, many also emphasized the need for more 'stringently applied laws.'"[2] This approach, connected to the hyper-sexualized view of Indigenous women as "drunken, dirty and easy squaws" (Anderson 2000, 99–115), fuelled the "unfit mother" stereotype as it contributed to their incarceration.[3]

Residential schools, the first of which opened in the 1830s, were also sites of segregation and assimilation. After the federal government began legislating mandatory attendance, in 1884, the numbers of schools and enrolments grew.[4] More than 150,000 children were sent to government-funded and church-run institutions to be forcibly Christianised, instructed on gender roles within a heterosexual nuclear family, and trained to become a subservient class of workers within the Canadian political economy.[5] Separating Indigenous children from their lands, histories, and kinship relations worked to undermine the central role of women, as mothers of children and nations (Cull 2006). Residential schools began to be phased out in the 1950s, but the last in Saskatchewan did not close until 1998 (Niessen 2017).

Western medicine had long been imposed to reinforce segregation and assimilation (Lux 2016; Shaheen-Hussain 2020) while undermining Indigenous practices of health and wellness grounded in forms of life (Lawford and Giles 2012) based on reciprocal relationships with the land — the most useful form of preventative medicine. Segregation and assimilation occurred in federal and provincial institutions. In the 1930s, the province operated three public health sanitoria to treat tuberculosis among the non-Indigenous population, with segregated space for Indigenous people in the Prince Albert Sanatorium. The sanitoria at Saskatoon and Fort Qu'Appelle were for "taxpayers," but a forty bed "Indian Wing" was reserved at Fort Qu'Appelle to repay debts to the federal government, where "deserving patients" were admitted on the authority of Indian Affairs (Lux 2016, 11). Social, not necessarily medical, criteria determined who received care — often residential school students who demonstrated "progress" (Lux 2016, 11) on the path to assimilation. Federal Indian hospitals, established to control the spread of tuberculosis and protect the health of the settler population, were also sites of experimentation and abuse (Lux 2016). In Saskatchewan, the Fort Qu'Appelle Indian Hospital opened in 1936, and the North Battleford Indian Hospital in 1947. Indian hospitals operated into the 1960s as the federal government increased funding to expand health services for non-Indigenous Canadians, demonstrating its commitment to "Aboriginal isolation and exclusion in pursuit of white national health and welfare" (Lux 2010, 410).

In the post–World War II period, health services were positioned as one arm of an increasingly organized and expanding welfare state. While some form of state-subsidized social supports beyond charity date back at least to the early 1900s (Finkel 1995; Struthers 1983), it was not until the mid-1960s that these came to represent the "modern welfare state" (Moscovitch 2017, xxix–xxx). The federal government invested in health insurance and more broadly, in unemployment insurance, pension programs for the elderly, support for the sick, and family allowances (Finkel 2006). However, just as the expansion of a publicly funded health system worked to manage the most negative effects of the capitalist system, these broader supports undermined working-class movements while buttressing the political economy.

Alvin Finkel writes, the welfare state was meant to place "a floor on the standard of living" for some without reducing the power of capitalist interests:

> It was devised by governments that wished to preserve the power of the ruling class but saw that power threatened by working class militancy directed against an economic system that seemed unable to provide jobs or security. The upsurge of radicalism in the working class first in the Great Depression and then during the war forced an important section of the bourgeoisie to rethink its strategies with regard to the role of

the state. The Canadian state had financed much of the infrastructure for Canadian industry and had intervened, when necessary, to defeat working class attempts to improve wages and living standards through the formation of unions and the waging of strikes. Now, however, the provision of police and railroads alone could not create sufficient economic stability to fend off working class attack. The result was a rethinking among many businessmen of the proper relations between state, industry, and the people. (1995, 222)

This change in thinking, which became "common stock" (Moscovitch 2017, lvii) among policy makers in the 1940s, was based on the logic that industrialization and urbanization, coupled with a rising standard of living and state-subsidized social supports, would ensure greater productivity of the workforce and prevent social disorganization.

Planning for the Expansion of the Welfare State

In his 1943 *Report on Social Security for Canada*, or the *Marsh Report* — a key document in the history of the welfare state — Leonard Marsh described social insurance as means of "attacking poverty" by providing a "social minimum" to raise the standard of living (2017, 48). While an attempt to outline the "primary causes" of poverty would take the discussion "too far afield … into the nature of the economic system," the "secondary causes" and "methods of attacking them" were more easily defined (48). These were found in low wages, unemployment, and a system of poor relief that supported dependency. He wrote, "one direct cause" not ranked as clearly as it should was those who had "too large a family in relation to the income available" (48). Marsh's proposals, too, were based on a heteropatriarchal version of the family as an economic unit with a "representative" family headed by a male breadwinner and two to three children (Marsh 2017, 50; also Christie 2000).

There was a population control element underpinning proposals to expand the welfare state. A state-subsidized social welfare scheme might induce people to have more or fewer children depending on what approach one took. For Marsh, irrespective of whether the "right parents have the most children" (2017, 162), children should not be condemned to suffer. Social benefits like family allowances could make society a "more desirable place for children to live" (129) and, in a positive sense, might halt the falling birth rate among socially desirable classes by encouraging them to reproduce. For others, who sometimes still adhered to eugenic thinking, a certain level of social supports might induce dependent classes to have fewer children to preserve their standard of living, however marginal (Hodgson 1983). Social services should work together to ensure a stable and efficient economy. Marsh wrote: "It is finally necessary to recognize the essential unities of social security — to fit together, in other words, all the branches of social insurance and social provisions in such a way that they support each other, and work together as a coherent administration" (2017, 27, 69).

Marsh's ideas were stimulated by RF funding and RF-supported thinkers. Prior to coming to Canada, Marsh studied at the London School of Economics (LSE), where he was a "protégé" (Frost 1984, 152) of William Beveridge, British economist, social reformer, eugenicist, and director of the LSE (Moscovitch 2017; Sear 2021). Beveridge had a relationship with the British Eugenics Society, including secretary C.P. Blacker, who sought to establish links between the work of eugenicists and other social welfare movements (Ittmann 2003). As director of the LSE, Beveridge secured so much Rockefeller funding to "upgrade the social sciences" that the institution was informally called "Rockefeller's baby" (Kaufman 2004, 202). This included launching demography as a formal discipline; a project partly pushed for by Blacker to provide purported objective data to eugenicists in their arguments (Ittmann 2003). The field became centrally important to the production of studies in support of theories of overpopulation in the second half of the twentieth century (Bashford 2014; Hodgson 1983).

In 1942, Beveridge authored *Social Insurance and Allied Services*, or the *Beveridge Report*, which had such influence on post–World War II social planning that he is referred to as the "father of the welfare state" (Benassi 2010, 1). Mackenzie King expressed admiration for Beveridge (Taylor 2009). Douglas too, relied on the logic of the *Beveridge Report* in his plea for increased federal funding for public health (Marchildon 2016). His report sought to address the "five giants" plaguing post–World War II nations — idleness, ignorance, disease, squalor, and want — through a state-supported social insurance scheme.[6] It made no mention of eugenics, but on the day the report was debated in the House of Commons, Beveridge delivered the Galton Lecture to the British Eugenics Society, explaining that his proposals would influence the quantity and quality of the population (Beveridge 1943); they were "eugenic in intent and would prove so in effect" (Sewell 2009, 73).

Marsh came to Canada at Beveridge's recommendation, in 1930, as director of the McGill Social Science Research Project, a project funded by a RF grant applied for at Hincks's suggestion (Frost 1984). The interdisciplinary team, put together by McGill's Principal Arthur Currie and a committee of "faculty, local industrialists, and some Canadians with connections to the [RF]" (Moscovitch 2017, xii), planned thirty-two studies meant to promote research as an "instrument of policy" through a "scientific approach to social problems" (Irving 1981, 20). In *Health and Unemployment*, Marsh and colleagues recommended a state-supported health insurance scheme to counteract the breeding of a "new generation" of citizens plagued by poor health and employment handicaps common among marginalized families (1938, xxiii).

In 1941, as advisor to the Federal Committee on Post-War Reconstruction, Marsh authored the *Marsh Report*.[7] His recommendations, heavily influenced by Beveridge, were also informed by experts from the International Labour Organization (ILO). The ILO, an arm of the League of Nations, was formed in 1919, and together with the League of Nations Health Organization sought to "stabilize" international relations following the First World War (Barona 2021, 33–4). Much of its work was embedded in the field of industrial relations, which expanded in the first part of the twentieth century due to a "growing crescendo of labour violence and strikes" and concern among progressives that "capital-labour relations were spiraling out of control" (Kaufman 2004, 85). The field sought to manage the employee-employer relationship through a "problem solving" (209) approach focused on collective bargaining, welfare capitalism, labour law, and social insurance. Bruce Kaufman writes, "More than any other person, it was John D. Rockefeller Jr. — the son of the world's richest capitalist — who in this early period did the most to institutionalize industrial relations ... he should also be considered a founder" (2004, 85). The Rockefellers had faced their own labour turmoil, most notably in the Ludlow Massacre, the mass killing of striking coal miners and family members, which Rockefeller Jr. was blamed for orchestrating (Zinn 1990), and after which he sought out Mackenzie King as labour advisor.

The ILO helped put population questions "on the agenda" internationally (Bashford 2014, 20). However, the closest eugenics came to be incorporated in the work of the League of Nations was with respect to infant health and protection; it viewed eugenic concerns as a matter for national policy (Bashford 2014), an approach that was not shared by its successor, the United Nations, which did engage eugenic considerations of population questions post-1945 (Mass 1974). Despite avoiding eugenics, population questions were central to the ILO — who occupied land, how resources were allocated, and how populations could be redistributed to avoid threats to peace (Bashford 2014). Albert Thomas, ILO director, stated "there was an imperative as never before to redistribute population to 'empty' parts of the globe" (cited in Bashford 2014, 9).

This imperative guided Indian policy in Saskatchewan where, by the 1950s, policy makers undertook, under the pretense of a humanitarian concern, to "empty the reserves" to free up lands for development and integrate Indigenous Peoples. The expansion of the welfare state was one means of doing this. Marsh consulted ILO members who had taken residence at McGill University at the invitation of Mackenzie King (Kaufman 2014). In this spirit, the *Marsh Report* proposed strengthening unemployment insurance and implementing family allowances, disability-old-age-survivor benefits, maternity benefits for working women, and health insurance — the "most important basic measure" with "rapid beneficial effects" (Marsh 2017, 213).

A second influential report published in 1943 was authored by Dr. Harry Cassidy, an economist who worked in the Department of Social Science and later headed the School of Social Work, University of Toronto. Cassidy had previously served as Director of Welfare in British Columbia, where he worked on a failed provincial health insurance bill (Irving 1988). He became technical advisor on social security at the DNHW in 1947, and after was director of training for the United Nations Relief and Rehabilitation Administration — a "crucial agent" in the transition from the League of Nations to the United Nations, supported by RF funding and expertise (Tournès 2014, 324). He, too, admired Beveridge and was involved in studies on unemployment, the "supreme social evil" which, left unchecked, might cause "radicalism" to grow and threaten "capitalist institutions" (Irving 1981, 17, 16).

In *Social Security and Reconstruction in Canada,* Cassidy echoed many aspects of the *Marsh Report.*[8] He advocated for "scientific social welfare research" (Irving 1992, 10) and the extension of social services as a "new type of social engineering" with "expert guidance" by social workers (Irving 1981, 19). In a follow-up report, he recommended separate federal departments of health and welfare, with activities coordinated between each and with provincial and local health and welfare agencies.[9] This view was shared by Marsh, who saw federal leadership as crucial to overcoming inequalities at other levels of administration (Irving 1981). Neither Marsh nor Cassidy made mention of Indigenous people. However, Marsh stressed, "regions or districts where welfare services have been most greatly lacking or unorganized in the past" (2017, 26) were obstacles to progress, especially if a piecemeal approach was adopted. Reserves and remote regions were such areas, and policy makers came to view the conditions of life experienced by Indigenous Peoples as an impediment to assimilation and a threat to peace.

A notable study in the 1940s did focus on Indigenous Peoples. John Collier, American sociologist and "progressive reformer," is credited with developing "a comprehensive approach to the problem of poverty in the industrialized world and its colonial domains" (Jahanbani 2023, 31). Collier criticized the American government for its treatment of Indigenous Peoples. He described Indian policy as a "brutal act of theft" and "program of systemic annihilation," and viewed the "ever-deepening poverty" caused by colonialism as a "weapon of genocide" (Jahanbani 2023, 38–9). In 1933, as Commissioner of Indian Affairs, he sought to ensure Indigenous Peoples were included in relief programs as part of "New Deal" measures implemented to "save capitalism" during the Great Depression (Smith 2014, 31).

For Collier, Indigenous poverty resulted from centuries of material dispossession and paternalistic management. He executed reforms to address poverty through economic development — what he referred to as the "Indian New Deal" (Jahanbani 2023, 42), by replacing boarding schools with local day schools and implementing curriculum focused on vocational training while celebrating aspects of Indigenous culture. He promised economic assistance to Indigenous communities who organized as self-governing communities; advocated return of land taken through federal allotment; and proposed extending civil rights to Indigenous people (43–5). "Research and then more research" was the "master tool" to ensure "development" was guided by science (cited in Jahanbani 2023, 44). While legislators did not engage land reform or eliminate federal guardianship, and only authorized half the funds towards economic development, Collier set out to study the impact of his work (52).

Collier was supported by "unlikely benefactor" Nelson Rockefeller, director of the Office for Coordination of Commercial and Cultural Affairs, established in 1940 to reinforce trade relations between the United States and Latin America (Jahanbani 2023, 48). He helped form an Inter-American Indian Institute to promote collaboration between governments in studying "the social, education, health, economic, etc., problems of the thirty millions of Indians in the Americas," through which anthropologists would play a central role by producing reports to inform solutions to the problems of "dependent peoples" (49). With his wife, anthropologist Laura Thompson, he began the "Indian Personality Project" to assess whether the "Indian New Deal" was helping individuals "adapt to new modes of living" (53).

The study, which took place between 1941 and 1947, concluded that colonialism had left Indigenous Peoples "humiliated," "defeated," and "impoverished," and "produced personalities that resisted change," which was undermining assimilation efforts.[10] Policy changes and comprehensive reform to administrative bodies responsible for "improving Indian welfare" (Jahanbani 2023, 62) was required. For Collier, poverty indicated an absence of development, and community development was the means to achieve integration by enticing people to help themselves out of their circumstances.

Some argue Collier's goal, especially his opposition to the federal division of communally held lands, centred on preserving Indigenous cultures (Rusco 1991). However, Sheyda Jahanbani writes, Collier had not suggested ending the colonial administration of Indigenous Peoples; he proposed making this administration more complex through "a new" relationship, one of "indirect administration" (2023, 54, 46). These ideas, which in his view, could "settle the vast and vexing ethnic … problems in Asia, in Africa, in Eastern Europe, in Oceania," and even the "Negro problem" in the United States (cited in Jahanbani 2023, 58), influenced federal-provincial approaches to Indian policy in post–World War II Canada.

Too Tough and Stubborn to Die — An Indian New Deal in Canada?

Post–World War II, the federal government re-envisioned its approach to Indigenous Peoples as "new observers" (Shewell 2004, 135) — academics, professionals, and private organizations — pointed to Indian policy as responsible for the "slumlike conditions, ill health, despair, and suspicion" (167) in Indigenous communities. It was evident the health status of Indigenous Peoples was "inseparable" from their economic well-being and general welfare (Shewell 2004, 186). This period, characterized as one of "Indian citizenship" (Shewell 1995, 15), saw both levels of government engage in an increasingly cooperative and complex administrative relationship to ensure Indigenous integration into Canadian society. Integration was not unlike assimilation but while allowing for the continuance of "vestigial ethnic traditions" (Pitsula 1994, 22). Its purpose remained one of facilitating "economic dispossession and social displacement," as Hugh Shewell explained, "this was the darker meaning of Indian policy. The cultural banners of humanitarianism and the applied reason of social science were mere masks obscuring the real task … capitalist expansion" (2004, 263).

The "new" direction of Indian policy was not a "radical departure" (Abel and Leslie 2000, 5) from the past, but several changes took place. The Special Joint Committee of the Senate and House of Commons to Examine the Indian Act, established in 1946 to investigate and report on "amendments to the Indian Act, treaty rights and obligations, voting rights, education," and other matters relating to "the social and economic status of Indians and their advancement" (Abel and Leslie 2000, 4), recommended the reorganization of the Department of Indian Affairs, revision of the Indian Act, and the establishment of a land claims commission (Leslie 2004). With respect to health, welfare, and education, the Joint Committee thought "it should be possible to arrive at such financial arrangements as might bring Indians within … provincial legislation," to allow "mutual and coordinated assistance" in making Indigenous people citizens "proud of Canada" and "the provinces in which they reside."[11] Indian Affairs was transferred to the Department of Citizenship and Immigration (1949), the Indian Act (1951) redefined what constituted an Indian while increasing the application of provincial laws on reserves, and later, Indians were declared citizens (1956) and given voting rights (1960).

The federal government relied on the Canadian Welfare Council (CWC) as a "guiding light" in setting policy directions (Shewell 2004, 333). The CWC, founded in 1920, was the "first national voluntary [child welfare] organization" subsidized through federal funds (Hodson 1990, 1). It was headed by social worker and eugenicist Charlotte Whitton

(McLaren 1990) until her retirement in 1942, after which time Dr. George Davidson took over.[12] Davidson served as Deputy Minister of Welfare from 1944 to 1960, and after, as Deputy Minister of Citizenship and Immigration. In 1972, he became Under-Secretary-General of the United Nations and then, Special Advisor to the Population Fund (Leslie 1999; Splane 2003). Earlier, as Superintendent of Welfare in British Columbia, he trained under Cassidy and Laura Holland, a social worker and member of the provincial Board of Eugenics (McLaren 1990). Davidson helped write the *Marsh Report*, for which the CWC was a strong advocate, and while the report made no mention of Indigenous Peoples, the CWC had much to say.

In its appearance before the Joint Committee, together with the Canadian Association of Social Workers, the CWC stated that, in its judgement, the "only defensible goal" was "the full assimilation of Indians into Canadian life" by admitting them as citizens with the right to participate freely in community affairs.[13] The CWC referenced substandard housing, low educational levels, malnutrition, and high infant mortality and tuberculosis rates on reserves. Of particular concern, it noted "wide open prostitution" and "Indian girls becoming diseased and pregnant," "juvenile delinquents" who were apprehended and returned to reserve "without any attempt being made for their treatment or reform," and the adoption of "Indian children" without "careful consideration" or the protections afforded to white children.[14] Residential schools were "outdated" and ineffective in caring for "neglected" and "delinquent" children (Stevenson 2020, 114). Government should rely on provincial child welfare legislation and services expanded on reserves, with social workers at the centre of this work. It recommended a "long range plan" by which government should undertake "an imaginative and aggressive program," best achieved "through coordinated efforts."[15] It cautioned against setting aside large tracts of land for reserves as this would only impede access to resources and their development, but warned, if nothing was done, social conditions on reserves could "infect surrounding communities over a wide area."[16]

This "influential brief" was a "first signal" (Shewell 2016, 183) the federal government would devolve responsibility for the provision of welfare services to the provinces. In exchange for "equal access" to citizenship rights, including services offered through the welfare state, it was expected Indigenous people would adopt "Western standards of individual and family life" (Shewell 2004, 191) and participate in the political economy. John Leslie writes, by attributing "traditional Indian 'shiftlessness, indolence, improvidence, and inertia' not to hereditary traits, but malnutrition and poor health," the "Indian Problem" could be solved "by extending benefits of the welfare state to ... Indians" (1999, 181, no. 154).

The brief was important because what it proposed agreed with federal Indian policy. It provided "the state with legitimation of its political intent ... [and] mapped out a way for the state to achieve its goals" (Shewell 2004, 193). The federal government hoped the extension of services, coupled with a rise in the standard of living, would entice Indigenous people to "leave their old ways behind" (190). Social workers took on responsibilities previously held by Indian Agents in managing Indigenous lives, including in the delivery of child and family welfare. Their direct involvement in "extracting" Indigenous children from their communities linked them intimately and explicitly to the "extraction of natural resources" from Indigenous lands (Fortier and Wong 2019, 442).

Douglas, too, had "a strong personal interest" in Indigenous welfare and referred to the treatment of Indigenous Peoples as "one of the blackest pages" in Canadian history (Pitsula 1994, 21, 24). His government discussed the "inadequate housing, inferior furnishings, lack of electricity, telephones, modern amenities, inferior schooling, absence of job opportunities, low incomes and high death rates" (Pitsula 1994, 25) on reserves, and blamed Indian Affairs for these conditions. In 1946, D.M. Lozorko, MLA for Redberry, likened reserves to concentration camps where "the Indian sits quietly and stoically watches the extinction of his race" (cited in Pitsula 1994, 26). W.H. Wahl, representative from Qu'Appelle, compared the situation of Indian people to Soviet farm and slave labour camps during the Cold War (Pitsula 1994, 27).

A Conference on the Métis of Saskatchewan highlighted the destitute living conditions shared by Métis.[17] M.W. Knudsen, Saskatchewan Métis Society, stated Métis people faced the struggles of the white man and those of Indians, which made it hard to eke out a life, and a lack of housing and formal education, and the failure of government to respect Métis land scrips and hunting and fishing rights made it difficult to meet their own subsistence needs.[18] The Society petitioned the province to improve conditions of life; set aside suitable blocks of land for Métis communities; make available loans to enable the upstart of farming operations; and provide better medical care and housing.[19] O.W. Valleau,

Minister of Social Welfare, responded he could not do a great deal for Métis people, but Métis could do a great deal for themselves by developing a deeper sense of pride in themselves.[20] To provide land for Métis settlement would only prolong the "ultimate solution," he stated, "I don't think there is any doubt about that. There will come a time when there will be no distinction between Métis and white men. You will be absorbed through intermarriage."[21]

Douglas initially pursued a form of segregation with respect to Métis, building the first non-denominational children's institution in Saskatchewan in 1947 — the Green Lake Children's Shelter for Métis children.[22] The shelter closed in 1951 after the Department of Social Welfare and Rehabilitation deemed it unsuitable to integration and began placing children in white foster homes (Stevenson 2020). He also undertook a "rehabilitation experiment" of Métis families from the Punnichy area who were living on roadside allowances, to Green Lake (Barron 1997), where they were given forty acres of bush land to cultivate.[23] Métis people sometimes "disappeared" from these settlements due to difficult living conditions (Stevenson 2015, 120). Those who lived through this relocation viewed it as an attempt by government to avoid embarrassment by hiding Métis people further north (Stevenson 2020). Perhaps, but there was a political economic motivation as well, as it began leasing increasing swaths of these lands for resource extraction.

Victor Valentine, an anthropologist hired by the Department of Mines and Natural Resources, criticized the relocation policy, writing that prior to 1944, "each man provided for himself and his family in an isolated camp with the aid of simple tools." After, they were "almost totally dependent on family allowance and relief" (1954, 90). Settlements became a "hodge-podge of overcrowded homesteads" with many public health issues (94). D.F. Symington, also involved in the "rehabilitation project," described things differently when he stated that, prior to government intervention, Métis people were "untrained and unwilling to work," and "despised by" and "despising of the white man" (1953, 130). On Métis women, "most of them remain[ed] amoral, and illegitimacy occasion[ed] no stigma" (139).[24]

In northern areas, where by 1944 some Indigenous people had still not settled on reserves, Douglas pursued a policy of "nucleation into settlements" (Quiring 2004, 47). David Quiring explains the motivations of such a policy:

> First ... nucleation ... would make it easier to assimilate Aboriginals into white society. Village life would allow CCF to efficiently apply education, health, housing, social, and other services to the formerly mobile population, which would gradually blend them into larger society. Second ... the CCF believed that supplying these services would result in the improved health and welfare of northern Aboriginals. A third motivation came from the CCF desire to bring all aspects of the north under state control. (2004, 47)

This policy, assisted by the expansion of health services in towns and a family allowance system that tied benefit eligibility to children attending school, impeded the ability of Indigenous people to engage in subsistence activities and had a "devastating impact," making them "poverty stricken" (67). It also led to population growth. One government official claimed Indigenous people were "breeding like mink," while another viewed the population, "mounting in leaps and bounds," as a "serious threat to peace" (cited in Quiring 2004, 67).

The problems of "Indians and Métis" were "inextricably bound together" and could not be settled apart, as John Sturdy, MLA, Saskatoon, wrote in 1952 to federal Minister of Health and Welfare, Paul Martin Sr.: "Wherever there is an Indian reserve there is a contiguous Métis settlement each aggravating the problems of the other."[25] Arnold Feusi, MLA, Pelly, declared, "It is very necessary ... that we assimilate our Indians at an early date."[26] In 1956, William Berezowsky, MLA, Cumberland, introduced the motion "Equal Rights for Treaty Indians," proposing to remove restrictions denying Indigenous people the "rights, privileges, and responsibilities" enjoyed by others, and the creation of a federal-provincial entity to engage in planning in health, welfare, and education on a basis of "equality."[27]

For Douglas, the province had no choice but to deal with the results of increased migration of Indigenous people to urban centres, which meant more were relying on provincial services and taking up space in hospitals, jails, and asylums (Barron 1997). Full transfer of jurisdiction — and federal funding — was necessary:

> The Federal Government and the Provincial Government ought to get together to plan the health, welfare and education of the Indian people with a view to gradually assimilating them

> ... I don't mean by that that the Saskatchewan Government is now asking for the privilege of taking over the responsibility for the Indian — that is a federal responsibility which the Federal Government undertook when it signed the Treaty; but I do think that a good deal of the administrative work could be done by a provincial government. I think if we are going to bring these people into the provincial economy that gradually the separate administration of the Department of Indian Affairs ought to disappear, wither away, and these people be assimilated into the municipalities and the towns and the villages and come under the same jurisdiction as do the other people of the province. When I say that I am thinking of a long-term programme of ten or twenty years; and in my opinion it would take that long to do it; but if we never start in to plan a programme, then nothing is ever done ... Surely we would hope that in a quarter of a century or more, they will have become full-fledged citizens, carrying their share of the burdens, having their voice in the government of the country and of the province and of the municipalities, just as every other person does.[28]

The time to act was now because the Indigenous population was growing. A survey of reserve communities in the Pelly Agency revealed a near doubling of the population since 1940, which was projected to triple by 1965. Sturdy pointed out, overpopulation was an "immediate problem that must be faced up to and solved."[29] Expanding on the provincial approach, he stated, "minority groups in time die out or are forced to conform to the standards and behaviour of the majority population." While "the Indian [was] too tough and too stubborn to die," with "wise leadership" and "careful planning," at least some Indigenous people could be "persuaded" to integrate.[30] Under the pretext that Indigenous people were being denied rights and privileges enjoyed by non-Indigenous people, provincial services would be extended to them. Yet, as Allyson Stevenson (2020) writes, as services expanded, so did Indigenous poverty.

The province established an Interdepartmental Committee to liaise with the federal government and welfare, voluntary, and religious groups, to discuss social services for "minority groups" including "Indians and Métis" (Barron 1997, 83). The Committee, chaired by Douglas and headed by Sturdy, consisted of representatives from provincial departments and "special members" (Barron 1997, 83). This included Indigenous representative William Wuttunee from Red Pheasant First Nation, the first Indigenous lawyer in Saskatchewan and a "strong proponent" of integration (Cuthand 2015), and later, of the federal White Paper (Weaver 1981); and Dr. Morris Shumiatcher, a lawyer who worked as senior legal counsel and Douglas's personal assistant, who drafted the Saskatchewan Bill of Rights in 1947, the first of its kind in North America, preceding the Universal Declaration on Human Rights and Canadian Bill of Rights, in 1948 and 1960, with the goal of protecting "civil liberties and human rights" (Patrias 2006, 265).

To the Second Joint Committee on Indian Affairs, which sat from 1959 to 1961, the Committee on Minorities explained that the population on reserves was continuing to grow, by 9 percent from 1941 to 1946, 18 percent from 1951 to 1956, and 21 percent from 1956 to 1959. Three factors were central to this increase — the large proportion of the population under the age of twenty-one, a rising birth rate, and a falling death rate — and because the exodus from reserve was so low, the results were unsustainable.[31] Since imposed cultural change was "irreversible," new arrangements in program and service delivery were needed to smoothen this transition.[32] The distinctions between "reserve Indians, off-reserve Indians still 'in treaty,' out of Treaty Indians and integrated Indian-Canadian citizens" needed to be blurred, and all should be integrated through an "empty the reserves program" to encourage wage employment and a transition to urban living.[33] To empty the reserves would also, by default, secure increased control over lands, opening them up for exploitation.

The province, in moving toward integration, extended the "touchstones of full citizenship" (Barron 1997, 102) — the right to vote and to consume alcohol, demands which did not originate from Indigenous people but "white humanitarians" (98). Cree leader John Tootoosis stated the vote was "shoved down Indians throats" (cited in Pitsula 1994, 38). More broadly, there was "remarkable congruity" (21) between Saskatchewan Indian policy and that of the federal government; both had "virtually identical" views of the "Indian dilemma" and prescribed "remedies" based on "equality," "individual rights," and "non-discrimination" (23). The Second Joint Committee recommended Indian Affairs "speed up" the process of integration (Weaver 1981, 20) despite Indigenous leaders stressing the importance of collective rights, the special relationship between Canada and Indigenous Peoples as enshrined in treaties, and the need to settle land claims (Leslie 2004).

A solution came from Shumiatcher, who suggested the concept of "citizens plus," or that Indigenous people "receive the same social benefits and economic opportunities as other Canadians" but while retaining "rights-based benefits" (Leslie 2004, 22) unique to them. He wrote to Prime Minister John Diefenbaker:

> I base this argument [for Indians as citizens plus] on the principle that many groups in our society receive special aid, among them, veterans, mothers, in receipt of mothers' allowances, the blind, the aged, certain farm groups, etc. Since the Indian requires something more by way of assistance than other citizens of Canada why not, I ask, accord him the rights of citizenship, together with these additional benefits (treaty rights, tax exemption, etc.) he now enjoys. (Cited in Leslie 2004, 27)

Shumiatcher recommended treaty promises be taken up, not as agreements governing relations between sovereign nations, but as a social benefit offered through the welfare state.

The concept of "citizens plus" was echoed at the federal level, including in the *Hawthorn Report*, the culmination of a study proposed in 1963 to the outgoing Diefenbaker government by the Imperial Order of Daughters of Empire (Weaver 1981), a women's organization with racist and imperialist motivations that had supported sterilization legislation (McLaren 1990). Interestingly, its national president, Pauline McGibbon, was married to Don McGibbon, who had a long career with Rockefeller-owned Imperial Oil, including as vice-president and treasurer, and whose mother funded sections of the organization (Pickles 2002). The following year, in concert with the approach set out by Collier on how "to enact development with surgical precision" (Jahanbani 2023, 46), the newly elected Liberal government of Lester Pearson established the Hawthorn Commission to study social, economic, and political issues affecting "Indians" and recommend a way forward.

The Hawthorn Report, 1966–67

Harry Hawthorn, an anthropologist who had undertaken studies on the Doukhobors and coastal Indigenous Peoples in British Columbia, together with anthropologist Marc-Adélard Tremblay and a team of researchers, began surveying the conditions of life of "Canada's Indians" (Shewell 2002, 61). The *Hawthorn Report* put forward a series of proposals drawn from its own "Indian Research Project," meant to encourage Indigenous people to participate "fully and effectively" in Canadian society, with economic participation in "White society" as "the only feasible path."[34] Reflecting the post–World War II change in thinking among policy makers, the study explained, investments in social welfare to "put some sort of floor" under the feet of the "weak and the poor" would help prevent social disorganization while managing the costliest social problems; any expenditures were necessary to promote economic development and industrialization.[35] The "types of programs and their timing in relation to one another" was crucial.[36]

The *Hawthorn Report* clarified, to implement medical and health programs — which the federal government had begun supporting in Saskatchewan and was preparing to do nationally — but without "prior preparation for their end result," may have contributed to a level of population growth that had "outrun" economic development and was impacting human welfare.[37] This might suggest a "special birth control campaign" was "the most important" cornerstone for future development, but Indigenous people comprised a "minute fraction" of the population; it would be "unwise and discriminatory" to single them out.[38] Besides, Canada was underpopulated, and Indigenous people did not constitute "any conceivable threat of over-population."[39] This was only a problem where a community had outrun the capacity of resources and opportunities to support itself, which reflected shortcomings in government policies. Community development should be the first step toward economic development.

Ernest Grigg, Chief, Community Development Division, United Nations, described community development as a process by which "efforts of the people themselves are united with those of government to improve the economic, social and cultural conditions of communities, to integrate these communities in the life of the nation, and to enable them to contribute fully to national progress" (cited in McEwen 1968, 7–8). The proliferation of community development initiatives grew out of United Nations involvement in "poverty-ridden" societies post–World War II (McEwen 1968, 7). They were formalized in the late 1950s in Canada, shaping its approach to poverty in Indigenous communities at home and abroad, including through external aid to "developing countries" (Langford 2017, 40). However, their roots go back to Collier (Jahanbani 2023), who served as advisor at the first meeting of the United Nations Trusteeship Committee, established in 1945 to supervise the administration of "trust territories as they transitioned from colonies to sovereign nations."[40] By the 1960s, as a form of "applied social science" embedded in liberal individualism (Langford 2017, 19), community development became a means to counter the "widespread apathy, resignation and lack of motivation" among those in poverty by "imbuing residents" with the impetus to improve their own situation, "to help people help themselves" while ensuring economic relations conducive to capitalism.[41]

The Saskatchewan government viewed community development as a "proactive" and more "palatable" (Shewell 2002, 66) means of solving "problems of underdevelopment" (Quiring 2004, 158). As early as 1945, in hopes that Indigenous people could be induced to "internalize and apply" CCF ideals to their lives and become "productive" members of society, Douglas implemented various initiatives, in northern areas especially, to promote self-sufficiency and integration into white settlements (158). For the federal government, community development was meant to be part of a "package" (Weaver 1981, 27) that, when coupled with the devolution of responsibility for delivery of health, welfare, and educational services to the provinces, would accelerate transfer of responsibility to Indigenous communities for managing their own affairs while reducing welfare dependency (Shewell 2002).

The Community Health Representatives (CHR) program implemented by Medical Services, DNHW, in 1963, focused on training Indigenous people as liaisons between health workers and community members, to assist them in "coping with modernity" and "smoothen the jump" into the twentieth century by inducing them to accept Western medicine (McCallum 2014, 122). The CHR program involved "minimal financial contribution" and "no consultation" with Indigenous Peoples (123). Mary Jane Logan McCallum writes, the program was based on a view of Indigenous Peoples as "dependent, suspicious, stubborn, and disobedient" and "slow and uneducated," and part of a long history of government seeking to "evade treaty responsibilities, conserve federal funds, and erode services" (2014, 65).

The Department of Indian Affairs began implementing community development initiatives in 1964, which sometimes amounted to "sensitivity training" for workers on-reserve as part of existing programs (Weaver 1981, 28). Despite a recommendation by the *Hawthorn Report* that initiatives expand in collaboration with the provinces, by the late 1960s many were shelved at least partly due to a federal fear that Indigenous people were using them to foster more emphasis on the "Plus" than the "Citizen" aspect of integration (Shewell 2002, 70). Indigenous leader and former community development officer George Manuel explained, "community development [could] never take place without economic development. But economic development without full local control [was] only another form of imperial conquest" (Manuel and Posluns 2019, 151).

With respect to education, the proportion of Indigenous children attending provincial schools had risen, but over a twelve-year period, 94 percent did not complete high school.[42] The *Hawthorn Report* referenced cultural discontinuity and marginalization in schools as factors influencing retention, but found when Indigenous cultures were relatively stable and Indigenous cultural pursuits were highly valued, success was defined "in Indian terms" and schooling was devalued.[43] Yet, experts attributed high drop out rates to cultural "differences" (Bear Nicholas 2001, 15) and "deficient" home environments (Bowd 1977, 333). The rise of psychological research focused on the "cognitive and perceptual development" (335) of Indigenous people recast them a "scientifically proven liability," which legitimated moving ahead with assimilation through integration (Bear Nicholas 2001, 15).

In this, social workers were assigned the role of ensuring proper social development (Shewell 2001) of school-age children. Andrea Bear Nicholas comments that, "ironically," it was not physical, sexual, and emotional abuse in residential schools that led to their phasing out, but their segregated nature that failed to assimilate Indigenous children (2001, 13). The *Hawthorn Report* explained, to raise educational levels would help "adjust people" to a complex society by instilling necessary "work habits and motivations."[44] This, coupled with Indigenous people living closer to urban centres, would encourage "consumer tastes" that required "long-term saving" and "debt commitments," which was an inducement to holding steady jobs.[45] However, if Indigenous people could not be induced to help themselves, they faced continued segregation.

Integration, or Continued Segregation

The *Hawthorn Report* recommended the extension of provincial welfare services "as rapidly as possible," and "all possible efforts should be made to induce Indians to demand and accept them."[46] Direct welfare supports and interventions, a "palliative" and "less popular" option among government officials (Shewell 2002, 63), expanded after passage of the Canada Assistance Plan (CAP) in 1966, the "cornerstone statute" (Shewell 2016, 184) of the welfare state. Through the CAP, the federal government provided 50 percent of shared-cost welfare programs and benefits, with 30 percent paid by the province, and 20 percent by municipalities. Direct welfare assistance was based on economic need (Weinberg 2019). Paul Weinberg writes, "age-old prejudices and judgmental attitudes about the deserving and underserving poor" going back to the Industrial Revolution governed how welfare supports were administered (2019, 11). This form of "poverty alleviation," grounded in a history of capital accumulation, dispossession, and the commodification of land and labour was shaped by the "impelling need" to drive the poor away from rural habitats and into urban centres (Breman et al., 2019, 3, 4).

The CAP accelerated greater involvement of child protection workers in Indigenous lives, including through the "60s scoop" (Shewell 2016, 184–5), the adopting out of large numbers of Registered Indian, non-Status, and Métis children by the provincial welfare department and assisted by social workers. In response to overcrowding in institutions, the province had begun seeking foster care placement as an alternative to ensure children received supervision while accessing community services.[47] For Indigenous children already institutionalized, deinstitutionalization through placement in white families represented savings for government as it hastened assimilation. More broadly, the expansion of provincial child welfare services brought more children into the system.

In 1967, the province piloted the Adopt Indian and Métis project to convince white families to adopt Indigenous children (Stevenson 2020). Enabled through a federal grant from the DNHW, Alice Dales undertook a survey to identify Indigenous children for adoption (Stevenson 2020). An advertisement campaign appeared in local media asking white families to "consider a part Indian child if you are thinking of enlarging your family. The problems are very small and rewards are very great" (cited in Stevenson 2020, 135). Project architect Frank Dornstauder, a social worker trained at McGill University, commented that if successful, this would represent "a major saving in maintenance costs for children" (cited in Stevenson 2020, 161). Allyson Stevenson, who studied this history in depth, writes that "Aboriginal transracial adoption rose to prominence as a key solution to ... the 'Indian problem,' as social workers asserted their expertise in not only adjusting the personal deficiencies of Indian and Métis clients, but also enacting ... integration, one child at a time" (2020, 42). The involvement of child welfare in Indigenous lives was justified as a cost-effective means of intervening in substance abuse, poor housing, violence, and neglect, and it took place against the backdrop of an increasingly organized movement for Indigenous sovereignty (Jacobs 2014).

The first systematic study on child welfare trends across Canada conducted by Philip Hepworth, a social worker trained at the LSE, former Program Director of the CWC, and policy advisor to the DNHW, revealed that despite the high proportion of "illegitimate" Indigenous children, unlike white "illegitimate babies," few were relinquished for adoption (1980, 115). For Indigenous children, contact with child welfare was mainly due to poor housing, something under federal jurisdiction on reserves, which made it less likely for them to be able to return home. By 1977, more than 50 percent of Saskatchewan children in care were Indigenous despite making up 20 percent of the population, which rose to 67 percent in 1979 (Hepworth 1980). Hepworth offered his findings without any analysis, but an earlier speech to the Planned Parenthood Federation of Canada (Planned Parenthood) helps us better understand his views.

In 1977, Hepworth acknowledged the importance of children having access to adequate housing, health, and nutritional supports. He then stressed the role of the state, and of Planned Parenthood, in ensuring all children were "wanted" (1977, 3). The overrepresentation of Indigenous children in care, and even barriers to abortion experienced by young and vulnerable women, indicated social policy was not working. Instead of calling for transformational change to historical material relations that created conditions of poverty and poor housing, and served as pretext for funnelling large numbers of Indigenous children into care, he called on government to make contraceptives freely available (Hepworth 1977).

The segregation of Indigenous children continued. Patrick Johnston (1983), policy analyst for the CWC who coined the term "60s scoop," found that from 1976 to 1981 about 63 percent of children in care were

Indigenous, and Saskatchewan had the largest proportion of any province. Jurisdictional disputes contributed to this overrepresentation, a trend which is still playing out nearly fifty years later. Cindy Blackstock, Nico Trocmé, and Marlyn Bennett found the number of on-reserve Registered Indian children in the child welfare system increased by 71.5 percent between 1995 and 2001 — up to three times more than during the height of residential schooling — and apprehensions often took place for reasons of "poverty, neglect, and substance misuse" (2004, 905). In 2007, the First Nations Child and Family Caring Society of Canada and the Assembly of First Nations filed a human rights complaint against Canada for discriminatory funding practices on-reserve as the federal government provided 22 percent less funding per child, including for "least disruptive measures" intended to keep children at home.[48]

Many argue the child welfare system has continued the policy objective of residential schools under different guise and is part of a genocide against Indigenous Peoples (Blackstock 2007; Mercredi and Chartier 1981; Monture-Angus 1995; Stevenson 2020). More generally, Leslie concluded, "despite attempts at camouflage," the basic tenets of post–World War II Indian policy "maintained an eerie continuity" with earlier policy; the fundamental objectives remained "essentially the same" (1999, 406). Integration was purported to remove barriers preventing Indigenous people from enjoying the same rights and services as other citizens, but these were offered under the condition they assimilate or face continued segregation — in the child welfare system, or in psychiatric institutions and jails (Stevenson 2020).

The number of Indigenous people in psychiatric institutions increased in this time. Chunilal Roy, Adjit Choudhuri, and Donald Irvine (1970) found twenty-five Registered Indian men and twenty-six Registered Indian women were institutionalized in North Battleford in 1961, a twofold increase from the highest number of admissions noted in the 1940s (Dyck and Deighton 2017). Registered Indians were more likely to be admitted at a younger age, with 61 percent of admissions among those under thirty years of age, compared to 23 percent in the non-Indigenous population. In a visit to nine Cree reserves and one Saulteaux reserve in the Pine Lake area, researchers found approximately 50 percent of the population was under fourteen years of age, and "the welfare cheque," "family allowance," and "treaty money" were the only sources of income for most (Roy, Choudhuri, Irvine 1970, 386).

The North Battleford Hospital Register indicated that eighty-three individuals from the area suffered some form of psychiatric illness (Roy, Choudhuri, Irvine 1970). During their visit, these researchers claimed to have identified another forty-six cases, twenty-six in "emotionally disturbed children" (388). The purportedly higher incidence of psychiatric disorders among Indigenous people — 80 percent higher than among non-Indigenous people — indicated the problem of mental illness could not be dismissed lightly, and unless efforts were made to identify children suffering from emotional disturbances as early as possible there would be an increase in "maladjusted, problem youth." In a final comment, they indicated the higher prevalence of mental deficiency was not surprising, and questioned whether "inbreeding" was to blame (391).

In another study conducted by Wayne Fritz (1976), Psychiatric Services Branch, Saskatchewan, it was revealed 140 Registered Indians, and 149 Métis were hospitalized in provincial psychiatric treatment centres in 1973, with a mean age of twenty-nine and thirty years, as compared to forty-three years for non-Indigenous people. Indigenous patients were less formally educated and less frequently married, but more likely to be hospitalized involuntarily. On involuntary admissions to institutions operating under the Psychiatric Services Branch, Aldred Neufeldt, Director of Operations Research, wrote there had been "a rather large increase" between 1965 and 1972.[49] The majority of these were at the mental hospitals in Weyburn and North Battleford, which represented 54 and 38 percent of admissions, but by 1972, the rate of involuntary admissions at psychiatric units at Munroe, University Hospital, Moose Jaw, and Yorkton had also risen, from 3 percent in 1965 to 17 percent in 1972. This led Neufeldt to wonder whether "concerns for civil liberties [were] slacking off somewhat."[50]

Fritz (1976) found Registered Indian and Métis inpatients were 76 percent and 135 percent more likely to be identified as suffering from personality and behaviour disorders, and had a higher incidence of hospitalization in every ten-year age category, especially in the thirty- to thirty-nine-year age range, when Indigenous women were hospitalized 118 percent more frequently than their non-Indigenous counterparts. In subsequent research, Fritz (1978) revealed, even as the province moved away from institutionalization and toward community psychiatry, which involved a shift from inpatient to outpatient services for non-Indigenous people, the trend was reversed for Registered Indians — more

Registered Indians were institutionalized. This trend was projected to increase into the 1980s as the Registered Indian population grew more rapidly than other residents (Fritz and D'Arcy 1982). To institutionalize large numbers of Indigenous people during their childbearing years is a means of preventing reproduction — it was considered as such by many in the population control movement. This is especially relevant when they were also being incarcerated in prison.

In 1957, shortly after a new provincial jail for women opened in Prince Albert, roughly 85 percent of those incarcerated were Indigenous.[51] Twenty-two years later, John Hylton indicated Registered Indian men were 2.3 times more likely, and Métis and non-Status Indians 7.5 times more likely, to be admitted to provincial correctional institutions.[52] In 1979, Registered Indian women were 88.2 times more likely, and Métis and non-Status Indian women 19.2 times more likely to be institutionalized.[53] Hylton, too, projected Indigenous incarceration rates would continue to increase as non-Indigenous admissions declined.[54] His projections were also correct. Indigenous incarceration rates increased every year since 1960 (Chartrand 2023). In 2023, Indigenous women were were 28.5 times more likely to be incarcerated in provincial facilities than non-Indigenous women, the highest overrepresentation of any province.[55] Saskatchewan's Ministry of Corrections, Policing, and Public Safety indicated that, between 2018 and 2023, on average, 85 percent of female provincial inmates identified as Indigenous (James 2023). Correctional Investigator Dr. Ivan Zinger, who examined Indigenous incarceration rates at federal and provincial correctional institutions, concluded "it is astonishing that the rate of Indigenous over-representation has increased unabated."[56]

In the early 1970s, George Manuel wrote, "the height of Canadian racism" was manifested through the incarceration of Indigenous people:

> Native people are not greater criminals than whites ... We are jailed for minor offences that stem from the frustrations of living in a racist and colonial society ... In one far northern community, the judge sentenced so many natives in one day that it took three days to transport them all to jail. (Manuel and Posluns 2019, 185–7)

The incarceration of Indigenous people has led some to refer to prisons as "the new residential schools" (MacDonald 2016), too, and a continuing strategy of genocide (Monture-Angus 1995). Vicky Chartrand states, "I don't think it's a coincidence that in the 1950s and 1960s, as we started to see Indian assimilation policies begin to recede, we also started to see the prison and the child welfare systems silently take their place ...."[57] She views Indigenous incarceration as a form of "containment, segregation, and reformation" (Chartrand 2019, 78) that facilitates "colonial interventions, racialized dispossession, and exploitation of land" (Chartrand 2023, 261).

Indian policy in the post–World War II period transitioned towards the integration of Indigenous people into Canadian society, assisted through the extension of citizenship rights and the expansion of the welfare state. Under the pretense of a humanitarian concern, so-called experts in health and welfare were given a greater role in carrying out a more organized and complex form of administrative control over Indigenous lives. For Indigenous Peoples, the choice remained to willingly participate in their own assimilation or face continued segregation. Most Indigenous people are not confused about what is at stake. Through their longstanding resistance to assimilation, by consistently raising the need to respect treaties and Indigenous sovereignty, and in their unwillingness to forget their own responsibilities to the lands upon which we depend, Indigenous people are not only still here but continue to challenge and confront the problematic functioning of the Canadian political economy.

For those concerned with questions of population control, sterilization was always intended to accompany segregation efforts. In the early 1920s, Margaret Sanger called for every "feeble-minded" girl to be segregated during her reproductive years and cautioned the "male defective" was "no less dangerous" (1922, 101). In her view, segregation could be carried out for one or two generations, but this would only partially control the population problem. Only a policy of sterilization would address population problems once and for all (101–2).

On June 25, 1968, Pierre Elliott Trudeau was elected Prime Minister of Canada. Having run on the slogan of a "Just Society," he explained this was one in which all people have the "means and the motivation to participate," where personal and political freedom are paramount, and in which "Indian and Inuit" enjoy "full rights of citizenship" and "meaningful equality of opportunity," to ensure "the most humane and compassionate society possible" (cited in Graham 1999, 16–20). However, once taking office, he stated, in reference to the welfare state, "We have had enough of this free stuff," and the "days of Santa Claus" are over (cited in Jones 1968, 10).

Trudeau viewed the expansion of the welfare state as "a disincentive" to society, which held the risk of promoting "revolutionary tendencies among the masses" should they come to expect supports (Aivalis 2018, 74). This potential for violence might stem from the poor, but particularly from Indigenous people (Weinberg 2019). It was also costly. During his tenure, he focused on "empowering capitalists" to ensure a "thriving capitalist economy," and distanced himself from previous planners by bringing an end to the "handout machine" (Aivalis 2020, 70, 74, 125) through austerity measures (Langford 2017; Weinberg 2019).

It was becoming increasingly clear the expansion of the welfare state was failing to induce Indigenous people to fully integrate. This situation became especially problematic as Indigenous activism grew more organized in its demands that government respect Indigenous land and sovereignty (Palmer 2009). This resistance was galvanized in 1969 when Trudeau introduced the White Paper, proposing, under the guise that Indigenous people were being discriminated against, a plan to eliminate Indian Status, fully incorporate Registered Indians as a provincial responsibility, and do away with treaties.[58] The White Paper was viewed by many as a "thinly disguised programme of extermination" (Cardinal 1969, 1) in its dismissal of Indigenous struggles and the proposed termination of Indigenous Peoples *as peoples*. In response to this vocal resistance, which led to the withdrawal of the White Paper, Trudeau is said to have responded, "We'll keep them in the ghetto as long as they want" (Lagace and Sinclair 2015).

More broadly, population transfers as a means to ensure control over lands and resources were proving "too hard" (Bashford 2014, 18) and, in keeping with trends in other parts of the world, the Canadian government turned its efforts toward controlling Indigenous fertility. Since the early 1960s, as part of the War on Poverty underpinning the expansion of the welfare state, it had been considering proposals to decriminalize contraception. Shortly after being elected, Trudeau amended the Criminal Code to allow for the open promotion and use of birth control, and a first federal family planning program followed.[59] If Indigenous people could not be induced to help themselves out of poverty, government would assist by reducing their birth rate. The following chapter demonstrates how a concern with overpopulation in "under-developed" areas around the globe, coupled with a culture of poverty among those most marginalized, replaced eugenics as the central ideological tool relied on by government officials, policy advisors, and those working in health and welfare to justify birth control as population control, under the banner of family planning. In this context, sterilization became the ultimate austerity measure in the fight against poverty and welfare dependency, and a final solution to the Indian problem in Canada.

3

From Eugenics to Family Planning — Canada's War on Indigenous Births

> *What will be the result of this clash of low and high birth rate nations in the future world? In the last analysis, numbers will count ... The low birth-rate nations ought to form a league ... even though the low birth-rate nations control the raw materials without which industrial and military strength is impossible, they cannot retain this control if their populations dwindle.* (Spengler, cited in Mass, 1974, 655)

Connections exist between eugenic sterilization and coerced sterilization under the banner of family planning. In 1963, A.R. Kaufman, eugenicist and a "prime mover" (Bain 1964, 336) of family planning in Canada, lobbied federal officials to offer more permanent forms of birth control to Indigenous people whom he described as living in "tragic conditions" made worse by overcrowding and high birth rates, because welfare work without family limitation would not solve intergenerational poverty.[1] The following year, S. Mallick, Zone Superintendent, Sioux Lookout, stated that while the department provided family planning on request, this was not working because of the costs involved and women either not taking birth control regularly or being "too lazy" to ask for more once their supply was depleted.[2] He suggested the plastic coil method, which field workers could insert while saving the department money and enabling "scientific" research on many people.[3]

The intrauterine device (IUD) — the plastic coil method in particular — has its roots in the population control movement (Takeuchi-Demirci 2018) and a history of being imposed on women in other colonial contexts, some of which is only now coming to light (Greve-Møller 2024). Alan Guttmacher, Director and Vice-President of the American Eugenics Society in the 1950s, Chairman of the Medical Committee of the

International Planned Parenthood Federation in the 1960s, and former President of the Planned Parenthood Federation of America, reported conventional measures were "not working" to curb the birth rate (Reed 1978, 306). He advised the Population Council, founded by John D. Rockefeller III in 1952, that it should address "world overpopulation" (306) by investing in the IUD. The Population Council touted the IUD as "particularly appropriate" in "developing countries" due to its "high effectiveness" and "single application for long term effect, obviating any need for sustained motivation, repeated action, and continued provision of supplies" (Takeuchi-Demirci 2018, 202). Mallick's views were informed by this context, and in 1965, Medical Services contacted Kaufman about the procurement of IUDs.[4] The desire to curb Indigenous reproduction through more permanent methods, whether IUDs or sterilization — Indigenous people were being sterilized under eugenic legislation — was shared by other medical professionals who employed similar language to Kaufman, no longer couched in eugenic terms, but framed around concerns with overpopulation as the main cause of poverty.

The personal reflections of a medical officer employed from 1965 to 1971 at the Fisher River Indian Hospital — in the middle of the Peguis reserve, north of Winnipeg, which also served the Fisher River and Jackhead reserves — provide insight into the approach some doctors took toward family planning in Indigenous lives. Dr. Ah-Yin Eng wrote, when he arrived at the hospital, the institution was beyond repair. A decision to replace the "shack" was made in 1959, but any available funds were being diverted to finish the Charles Camsell Hospital in Edmonton. Eng was "shocked" to see the poor state of health in the community, which he described as "poverty stricken," "closed," and with "early sexual experiences" (1999, 26). He began performing Pap smears on all adult females and without the "slightest doubt," the biggest problem facing these reserves was their high birth rate:

> It is pure nonsense to tell me the Indian women wanted more children and therefore we should help them have large families. Nothing could be further from the truth. Once the communication barrier was broken, we found the great majority … have similar aspirations and desires to any non-Indian. To be misled or intimidated by the shrill cries of a few Indian fanatics like Kahn Tineta-Horn, who at the time advocated against birth control of any kind for the Indian women, is

> to prolong the suffering and agony of thousands of women. Tineta-Horn, a former fashion model, naturally did not have to raise her own children in a log cabin without heat, electricity or water. (Eng 1999, 26)

Kahn Tineta-Horn, a long-time advocate of Mohawk sovereignty from Kahnawake, had written to Indian Affairs expressing concern that birth control was being used to reduce the birth rate in her community.[5] In dismissing her concerns, Eng implicitly acknowledged how chronically underfunded housing and social services on reserves, or conditions of poverty created through colonialism and federal neglect, informed Indigenous reproductive choices. He continued:

> We were told that oral contraceptives were never issued (although the hospital had a stock of 15000 Enovid) because ... Indian Affairs discouraged birth control to conform with what was then the law of Canada. I had no idea to advocate birth control was a criminal offence ... We limited our efforts in family planning to individual counselling behind closed doors — by requesting permission to do tubal ligations for women who had had too many children and for those who had serious obstetrical complications ... Every year, we sent four or five women to Winnipeg for tubal ligations. At the time we had 50 or so women on the Pill and another 30 using the [Lippes] Loop. By 1968 the birth rate showed a 35 [percent] drop. (Eng 1999, 27)

Eng's reflection is imbued with Eurocentric assumptions and paternalism when it comes to the ideal number of children and the spacing of births. However, in this, he indicates it was medical professionals who were requesting permission to perform sterilizations and over the course of three years, these requests effected a substantial drop in Indigenous births.

It is possible Indigenous women wanted to prevent conception through sterilization, but it is not clear how communication barriers were broken down, and sometimes, how voluntary these operations were. Erika Dyck and Maureen Lux (2020, 86) recount the experiences of a doctor working at the Fisher River Indian Hospital, and while they do not identify the individual by name, the evidence cited supports the view that this is Dr. Eng. They write, in one instance:

the physician ... "obtained consent" from a woman (and her husband) for tubal ligation after her current pregnancy. Upon return from her confinement in Winnipeg the woman stopped at the Indian hospital to register her shock at the attempt to perform surgery. "They wanted to cut me open, so I came home," she said. Disgusted with medical care she refused to spend another minute in the Indian hospital and stepped out into the November night with her five-day-old infant to walk to her home reserve miles away.

Dyck and Lux conclude that clearly this woman's consent to surgery was not informed but she had the "wherewithal" (86) to refuse it. One must wonder what happened in cases where a woman did not have this wherewithal. Dr. Eng's reflection involves him as a federally employed medical officer in arranging at least one sterilization that cannot be described as consensual.

Shortly after the formation of the Special Planning Secretariat of the Privy Council (Secretariat) in 1965, which was responsible for coordinating a War on Poverty in Canada, government considered whether it was feasible to limit Indigenous births through birth control. It was in a precarious legal situation since its use and prescription were prohibited under law. Over the next four years, numerous bills were proposed to effect legislative change that culminated, in 1969, with decriminalization. This was followed, in 1970, by Canada's first federal family planning program. Throughout, the rhetoric employed by officials centred on a fear the Indigenous birth rate contributed to overpopulation and this, coupled with a purported culture of poverty and dependency among them, reproduced from one generation to the next, replaced eugenics as the central ideological tool to blame individuals for their circumstances as it divorced the causes of poverty from their roots in social relations of exploitation.

The Special Planning Secretariat and the War on Poverty, 1965

The Secretariat was established under the government of Prime Minster Lester Pearson with a mandate to "coordinate and promote initiatives against poverty" across Canada (Tough 2014, 177). Headed by Policy Chief and Director Tom Kent, who viewed "full employment policies" and "social security" as key to ensuring "equality of opportunity for all" (Langford 2017, 1, 2), the Secretariat oversaw the introduction of several initiatives central to the modern welfare state, including Medicare and the CAP (Moscovitch 2017). The work of the Secretariat, referred to as a War on Poverty by journalists and then by government, sought to encourage federal-provincial collaboration with health and welfare departments and social welfare organizations engaged in poverty issues so that, as staffer W.A. Dyson described, action flowed "from many sources ... with greater and greater precision" (cited in Tough 2014, 186).

The Secretariat's place in the Privy Council Office, and its direct link to Pearson through Kent, signalled its importance to the formation of social policy. The War on Poverty was directed at those "pockets of poverty" that still existed in "ghettos," "rural areas," and others "isolated from contact with, or sight of, anybody else" (Tough 2014, 180–1). The Secretariat's view of poverty isolated from the social relations producing it set the stage for rhetorical attacks on the poor and allowed officials to intervene in ways that sought to improve the performance of the economy while reducing welfare dependency (Tough 2014).

The concern among Western states regarding the effectiveness of state-sponsored programs in alleviating poverty, and a reluctance to rely on public funds to do this, had been a preoccupation since at least the 1930s. In the 1960s, governments undertook concerted efforts to rethink the "heavy, rusting bureaucratic machine," which resulted in an "unprecedented production of rhetoric" about a "culture of dependency" among those living in poverty (Tough 2014, 186, 206, 181, 200). Gareth Davies writes, a worry among officials about "rapidly rising welfare rolls," the "strong distaste" welfare administrators had toward their clients, and concerns among experts with family instability, including the "moral panic" that welfare families were reproducing from one generation to the next, informed the War on Poverty in Canada (1997, 439–40).

The Culture of Poverty among the Poor

The notion of a War on Poverty against Indigenous Peoples goes back to the work of John Collier and research carried out through the Inter-American Indian Institute, which became part of the "modus operandi" of the "global war on poverty" in the 1960s (Jahanbani 2023, 31). In this, Collier was assisted by Oscar Lewis, an anthropologist who previously served as director of the Strategic Index for Latin America, an offshoot of the Rockefeller-funded Institute on Human Relations at Yale University (Jahanbani 2023) on the recommendation of Ralph Linton.

Linton, anthropologist and author of a terribly racist piece on the "disappearance of the Negros" (1947, 139), influenced Western approaches to "acculturation" at the Rockefeller-funded Social Science Research Council (Patterson 2018). In 1943, Lewis began research that made him an "expert" in the "transnational Indian problem" and "acculturation" — read, assimilation through integration — in "less developed counties" (Jahanbani 2023, 73).

In a study of the peasant population in Tepoztlán, Mexico, a "community in transition" that faced widespread poverty despite "modernization," Lewis located the cause of poverty in villagers who, in his view, preferred to live with problems rather than solve them (Jahanbani 2023, 79; Lewis 1951). Historical inequities had been internalized in Tepoztecan culture and the mentality of people, and "only a small percentage" of youth were "willing or able to strike out on new paths" (Lewis 1951, 448). In a follow-up study examining the impact of urbanization among people in the "slums" of Mexico City, Lewis found they too shared similar characteristics with villagers in Tepoztlán, those in "lower class" neighbourhoods in London and Puerto Rico, and the "Negroes in the United States" (Jahanbani 2023, 84; Lewis 1960, 965).

Poverty was a dynamic factor affecting the ability of those living in it to participate in national culture — it created a "sub-culture" (Lewis 1960, 965). Its "basic values" were a feeling of "fatalism, helplessness, dependence and inferiority" (Lewis 1966a, 23); it was a way of coping that flourished under specific conditions including "a cash economy, wage labor, and production for profit," a "high rate of unemployment," "low wages," "a bilateral kinship system," and "a set of values in the dominant class" stressing "the accumulation of wealth," and "upward mobility and thrift" (Lewis 1966b, xliii–xliv). Capitalism and its associated ideologies centred on private property, individualism, and meritocracy played a role in creating poverty, but it was the failure of those living under these circumstances to uphold a heteropatriarchal version of family life that was responsible for re-creating the poverty cycle. Once it came into existence, it was perpetuated "from generation to generation" (Lewis 1966b, xlv).

The culture of poverty discourse was taken up by Western governments to "blame the victims" of exploitative social relations (Ryan 1971) while silencing calls for social change. In the United States, in 1965, Assistant Secretary of Labour Daniel Patrick Moynihan, in considering the problems faced by Black people in America, argued civil rights alone would not address racial inequality.⁶ The "Moynihan Report," heavily influenced by Lewis's work, argued the circumstances of Black Americans may have been shaped by slavery and government failure to ensure freedom *and* equality for Blacks, but this population was now overrepresented among the unemployed and in "every index of family pathology" including divorce, separation and desertion, female-headed families, and "illegitimacy."⁷ Current problems could be traced to a "tangle of pathology" perpetuated by unemployed and unmarried Black mothers on welfare who threatened the health of the political economy.⁸ A cycle was at work — parents having "too many children too early" made it difficult to complete their education, produced lower income levels, deprived children of opportunities, and "the cycle repeats itself."⁹ To address this:

> a national effort ... must be directed towards the question of family structure. The object should be to strengthen the Negro family so as to enable it to raise and support its members as do other families ... To this end, the programs of the Federal government bearing on this objective shall be designed to have the effect, directly or indirectly, of enhancing the stability and resources of the Negro American family.¹⁰

The reproductive behaviour of women living in poverty was an obstacle preventing them from escaping their circumstances. This view informed the passage of the Family Planning Services and Population Research Act in 1970, as it justified the sterilization of Black and Indigenous mothers in the United States into the 1990s (Ralstin-Lewis 2005; Roberts 2016).

The culture of poverty discourse gained "wide political purchase" in all levels of government in Canada (Langford 2017, 16). Paul Weinberg (2019) demonstrates how the Canadian Welfare Council (CWC), by espousing the culture of poverty ideology, avoided focus on social and economic relations. The CWC, the "guiding light" in shaping federal Indian policy, helped fuel the "eternal fear" of Indigenous dependency (Shewell 2004, 185). For government, self-reliance was key to integration, but Indigenous people were "lazy, idle, and intemperate" (Shewell 2004, 236, 328). These purported cultural traits, not broader relations of colonialism and federal neglect, explained Indigenous poverty while justifying assimilation. The culture of poverty discourse appears in debates on decriminalization, offering policy makers one ideological justification for the control of Indigenous reproduction.

Overpopulation and Underdevelopment

The shift from eugenics to family planning was also connected to global conversation among Western nations on how to best apply "contraceptive technology" (Takeuchi-Demirci 2018, 13) to solve public health problems stemming from imperialism, exploitation, and threats to capitalism (esp. 181–210). Bonnie Mass (1974) documents the evolution of population control activities under the banner of family planning at the United Nations from its inception in 1945, until the early 1970s. Corporate philanthropies, including the RF, worked in tandem with the Population Council to influence international institutions like the United Nations and World Bank, and imperial nation-states, to ensure continued access to lands, resources, and cheap pools of labour (Mass 1974). The head of the Carnegie Corporation noted, "American industry could ill-afford the loss of cheap sources of raw materials which could only be secured in the nations of Africa, Asia, and Latin America"; Paul Hoffman of the Ford Foundation acknowledged, "our own dynamic economy has made us dependent on the outside world for many critical raw materials"; and Philip E. Mosley, RF staff member stated, "the resources which the United States needs are not located in Europe, but are in the underdeveloped areas of the world" (cited in Marshall 2015, 784). Policy makers and corporate interests agreed, changes taking place in "underdeveloped" areas, many of which had recently freed themselves from the chains of colonialism, should be "evolutionary rather than revolutionary" (Marshall 2015, 784).

Political instability and threats to the political economy abroad were also arising at home. William Langford (2017, 30–1) writes:

> Most vividly, anti-imperial activism in Canada drew inspiration from the Third World struggles ... More than simply a collection of coexistent leftisms, antiwar, student, labour, Indigenous, women's, gay and lesbian, anti-racist, urban, environmental, and nationalist mobilizations shared in the global movement to make a better world. The Sixties marked a significant historical period during which demands for greater democracy and social justice in Canada were powerfully sustained from below.

Birth control, as population control, under the banner of family planning became a solution to political instability and threats to peace (Bashford

2014). It was not until 1965, at the second United Nations Population Conference, that a "special section on family planning" was established to study the benefits of conception control to curb "overpopulation" and address its purported effects, whether poverty, high infant mortality rates, or environmental destruction (Appleby 2001, 46). The "population establishment" had expanded to include eugenicists and neo-Malthusian theorists concerned with the "control" aspect of population control; environmentalists focused on the need to conserve "resources" to ensure the capacity of the earth to support itself; and demographers who studied fertility trends among and between populations — all of which were "so significantly enabled" by Rockefeller funding that by the 1960s, their arguments became enmeshed (Bashford 2014, 288–9) in the call to reduce the birth rate among those most marginalized.

This call infiltrated the thinking of government officials and policy makers in Canada, as did the studies they produced. Of note was the 1958 study by Ansley Coale and Edgar Hoover, produced at the request of the Population Council, funded by the World Bank, RF, and Millbank Memorial Fund, and carried out through the Office of Population Research (Merchant 2022). Coale, a Princeton demographer, spent his career at the Office of Population Research, while Hoover, a Harvard economist, trained employees from "underdeveloped" countries in demography as part of a Ford Foundation research program. Their study, focused on population growth and economic development in India, was meant to inform government approaches to "underdevelopment" in any country. Focused on the economic benefits that would arise if the birth rate was "cut drastically" in one generation, the authors concluded a country's per capita national income would be 40 percent higher in the next thirty years if the birth rate was reduced to half (Coale and Hoover 1958, v). The conclusion, that high fertility was "an impediment if not a total barrier" to economic development, provided "definitive proof" (Merchant 2022, 546) for governments to justify population control through family planning to slow population growth, spur economic development, protect the environment, and prevent widespread famine. However, all this was "a victory for demography and the Population Council, which largely controlled the terms of the solution to the perceived population problem" (Merchant 2022, 546–7).

As a "global industrial power" in the post-war period, Canada sought to "bestow the blessings of 'technical assistance' on 'under-developed' populations" (Meren 2017, 345). This was a priority of the Pearson government when elected (Brushett 2015). By the mid-1960s, Canada funded "Third World" aid requests through grants to the International Planned Parenthood Federation and United Nations Fund for Population Activities (Marsh 1999, 252) as it increasingly supported resource extraction activities in Latin America and Africa (Gordon and Webber 2016; Engler 2015). This continued through the Canadian International Development Agency and the International Development Research Centre, two federally funded institutions created, in 1968 and 1970, to address "problems of the developing world."[11]

Pearson, a former history professor from the University of Toronto, held an "esteemed role" in nearly every international forum since the 1930s (Brushett 2015, 87). Prior to becoming prime minister, he advised on the Charter that guided development of the United Nations, was President of the General Assembly, and shared in planning that led to the creation of the United Nations Relief and Rehabilitation Administration. He was a former Cabinet minister and Secretary of State for External Affairs in the governments of Mackenzie King and St. Laurent, and he was offered the opportunity to become president of the Rockefeller Foundation (Ward 1973). He is said to have come to power following a Rockefeller-supported coup under the Kennedy administration, fuelled by its opposition to Diefenbaker's desire to protect Canadian political economic interests (Boyko 2016). Despite receiving the Nobel Peace Prize in 1957 for his role in creating the first United Nations peacekeeping force, Pearson is accused of being a war criminal for his role assisting with the conflict in Vietnam (Engler 2012).

Pearson took up the rhetoric of overpopulation as the cause of poverty, and upon his retirement, he became further entrenched in promoting family planning as population control. In 1968, he was recruited by Robert McNamara, President of the World Bank, to undertake a "comprehensive review of plans" for the United Nations Second Development Decade (Mass 1974, 665). The Pearson Commission on International Development, composed primarily of bankers and economists (Brushett 2015), was provided data and perspectives on population from a body of experts assembled by the United Nations Association of the United States — under the leadership of John D. Rockefeller III and consisting of "veterans" of the population establishment, notably, Frank Notestein from the Population Council, and Ansley Coale from the Office of

Population Research (Mass 1974, 665).

The *Pearson Report*, released in 1969, recommended the expansion of world trade and foreign investment in "developing countries" to assist them in reaching a path of sustained growth and an increase in gross national product; Western aid needed to be closely linked to these economic objectives. The need to control the birth rate should be stressed by donors and recipient countries, and family planning should be made available through the work of United Nations agencies with assistance of the World Bank, and in consultation with the World Health Organization.[12] In a subsequent speech delivered before the World Bank and the International Monetary Fund, Pearson (1970, 13) stated:

> it is increasingly clear that nothing we do in the development field ... will be of lasting significance unless and until there is a substantial slowing of the rate of population growth which now threatens in many countries to overwhelm all other progress ... no aid-providing agency can ignore performance in this area any more ... we are aware that economic and social progress is in the long run the best way of stabilizing population growth. But we haven't a long run any longer. There is an immediate population explosion and immediate action is needed. We would hope that ... family planning will gain even more momentum in the years ahead.

David Meren highlights the "entangled history" of Canadian foreign aid and Indian policy, and "how race and the logic of white supremacy" were embedded in government's approach to development across borders (2017, 369). Similarly, Tina Loo writes, "not only did the Canadian government's views and policies regarding Indigenous Peoples influence its understanding of foreign aid, but Canada's experiences in the global South came to inform its relationship with Indigenous peoples" at home (2019, 16). The line of thinking Pearson espoused guided the War on Poverty in Canada, which was, partially at least, a war against Indigenous births. It too is reflected in parliamentary debates on the decriminalization of contraception.

Legislating a War on Indigenous Births

Following formation of the Secretariat, Commander J.R.B. Coulter contacted H.A. Proctor, Director of Medical Services, requesting he inquire with each Zone Superintendent and other senior officers on his staff on whether it was feasible to reduce the size of Indigenous families through birth control to reduce the "size of the homes" the federal government would need to provide (Stote 2015, 60). On August 27, 1965, Proctor wrote:

> In connection with [the Secretariat's] war on poverty among the Indians ... Medical services has been asked to express an opinion as to whether birth control techniques would actually affect the size of Indian families in general and hence the size of the home requested. Naturally, the question is somewhat hypothetical so long as the Criminal Code remains unchanged. However, it is an aspect of the problem which the Special Planning Secretariat must examine and it is our obligation to co-operate in this study in any way possible.[13]

The responses Proctor received make clear that prior to legislative change, officials were already considering how to limit Indigenous births (Stote 2015, 60–7).

M.L. Webb, Zone Superintendent, North Battleford, Saskatchewan, wrote to advocate birth control techniques amongst "the Indian population" would reduce the size of the average family, though this may take several years. However, "some Indians will not want to practice birth control, and others are not capable of following any regime," and in these cases, the IUD might be the answer.[14] J.H. Wiebe, Regional Superintendent, Eastern Region, noted the contradictory nature of this inquiry: "It is anomalous that inadequate housing in many instances produces circumstances under which crowding prevents the successful practice of birth control measures ... larger homes would ... aid to control family size."[15] He recommended material improvement to living conditions on reserves so Indigenous people could limit family size — a suggestion that continues to be resisted by government as many communities face overcrowding and destitute living conditions.[16]

In his summary, Proctor wrote that despite Indigenous beliefs about premarital sex or the ideal number of children wanted by families, the main difficulty in relying on birth control to reduce the birth rate was a lack of motivation on the part of Indigenous people.[17] They were very tolerant of premarital sexual relations, which resulted in a much higher percentage of children born "out of wedlock" to young mothers. If a birth control program was implemented, it needed to be extended to "unmarried schoolgirls of child-bearing age." However, their "casual attitude" towards timed instruction might make the IUD more effective. There was a "very heavy reliance on financial assistance" in Indigenous communities determined based on family size, which seemed to encourage having as many children as possible. He concluded:

> There are many factors militating against any early or marked reduction in the size of the average Indian family by birth control techniques but birth control techniques are being used by Indians and increasingly so and are having some modest effect … A more intensive program to encourage birth control by an official government agency, in defiance of present legal restrictions, can hardly be advocated. An intensive educational program, directed towards older school children and young adults and continued over an extended period of years, would probably be effective, particularly if the present financial incentive to having large families could be removed. Modern methods of controlling conception are comparatively cheap, simple and effective but they cannot be imposed on people. In the absence of personal motivation of individual parents, any program to control procreation by these techniques is bound to fail.[18]

While government could hardly advocate a more intensive program considering legal restrictions, a year later, T.J. Orford, Regional Director, Saskatchewan, wrote the prescription of birth control in Indigenous communities was proving almost "impossible to control."[19]

Canada first began considering legislative change in 1963, when Robert Prittie, NDP Member of Parliament (MP), Burnaby-Richmond, put forward Bill C-41 to amend the Criminal Code and decriminalize birth control. Under section 150 (2)(c), it was an offense to advertise or have for sale or disposal "any means, instructions, medicine, drug or article intended or represented as a method of preventing conception or causing abortion or miscarriage."[20] Prittie, member of the national executive of the Family Planning Federation of Canada (Planned Parenthood), proposed deleting "preventing conception or" from this section.[21] This proposal did not make it pass first reading, but was reintroduced the following year. During debate on Bill C-48, Prittie stated

Canadian law was archaic because it was illegal for competent professionals to advise on family planning.[22] Most couples of higher education and average income disregarded current law and accessed family planning from family physicians, but those who relied on public health services through hospitals and social welfare departments could not.[23] To amend the Criminal Code would allow these agencies to promote family planning to those of lesser means.

In opposition to Prittie's motion, Joseph O'Keefe, Liberal MP, St. John's East, suggested rather than threaten the family and corrupt the morals of young unmarried women, which might further contribute to promiscuity and out-of-wedlock births, government should concern itself with the material betterment of the people. O'Keefe argued "the answer to the problem of poverty ... is obvious. We must increase the supply of food and jobs, and certainly not decrease the population."[24] For Charles Willoughby, Conservative MP, Kamloops, overpopulation was the concern, and legislative reform could address it. He explained:

> the world population today is almost three billion ... four out of every five deaths in the world today are directly or indirectly the result of lack of proper nourishment ... in 40 years the population of this continent will have doubled, and ... in 65 years, at the present rate of growth, the world population will be in the neighborhood of 50 billion ... I suggest there are only two ways out of the problem created by world population explosions. One is to create more arable land and grow more agricultural products ... or assist in curtailing the increase in the world population.[25]

This concern, that the birth rate would outstrip the availability of arable land on which people could subsist, had been vocalized by the Saskatchewan government with respect to Indigenous people. To the Joint Committee on Indian Affairs, Douglas had outlined the reserve population was increasing at "an accelerating rate" as the limits of cultivatable acreage were quickly being reached.[26] This unsustainable increase — not colonial policies of land expropriation and government neglect — resulted in high levels of poverty, unemployment, and poor health.[27]

The Standing Committee on Health and Welfare, struck in 1965, considered four bills proposing legislative changes to increase the ability of individuals to access, and of practitioners to promote, birth control as family planning. During deliberations on Bill C-64 in 1966, Ron Basford, Liberal MP, Vancouver-Burrard, urged government to understand the connections between family size and poverty.[28] Family planning should be a personal matter between couples, but government should be concerned with overpopulation and to decriminalize birth control could help shape foreign policy. While not a specialist in world population, Basford cited "disturbing" statistics showing population increases in parts of Latin America and Africa, and read from a speech by the President of the World Bank on the state of housing in India:

> Calculations have been made about the cost of providing houses in India during the next generation, if the population continues to grow at its present rate ... if you disregard the cost of rural housing ... you still have to pay for the homes of nearly 200 million extra people ... living in India's cities in the next 25 years ... I would hope the domestic laws of Canada would be such that we could take a larger part in this area in foreign affairs ... we cannot remain neutral against poverty.[29]

The concern Basford was highlighting in an international context in relation to housing, which Coale and Hoover viewed as one of the "largest categories of social welfare investments" (1958, 249), had been raised that year by the Secretariat, in relation to its War on Poverty and Indigenous people at home. The intersections between these discussions are difficult to ignore.

The Standing Committee continued to receive opinions, including from Planned Parenthood. The Canadian branch of Planned Parenthood, founded by George Cadbury, was an alliance of birth control societies, family and population planning groups, and representatives of five protestant churches.[30] Cadbury, member of the British Eugenics Society (Kühl 2013, 154), came to Canada through Saskatchewan in 1945, where he served as Chief Economic Advisor to Douglas in opening up Indigenous lands for development. In 1951, he left to work as United Nations advisor to "less developed" countries (Webster 2011). In 1959, as director of the International Planned Parenthood Federation, with its close ties to the population control movement, he served as liaison to the United Nations (Kühl 2013). In 1961, he and his wife Barbara formed the first Planned Parenthood Association in Toronto to push for legislative reform (Bishop 1983).

He founded the national organization in 1963.[31] Cadbury participated in the second United Nations Population Conference, in 1965, as representative of the international organization, and was member of the Association for Voluntary Sterilization, which promoted sterilization in "underdeveloped" countries (Dowbiggin 2014, 186).

In its brief to the Standing Committee, Planned Parenthood proposed government make family planning an integral part of domestic health and welfare programs, and external aid to requesting countries.[32] The decision to use birth control should be voluntary, but because family planning was not readily available or widely used, society was bearing the cost for "maladjusted children" who were often wards of the state. It cited a study showing an inverse relationship between family income and size, and the prevalence of children from low-income families who ended up in child welfare.[33] President Dr. Frank Fidler stated that Planned Parenthood was particularly interested in those who depended on public health services.[34] This sentiment was echoed by Dr. Phillip Rynard, Conservative MP, North Simcoe, who specified, "the people we are aiming at are the people with a low standard of living … who have not been able to increase the gross national product along with the increase in their birth rate."[35] Cadbury claimed they were not "attempting to be dictators" or advocate state control of family size, only to provide information to help people to make up their own minds.[36] However, members of Planned Parenthood were arguing for population control at home — against Indigenous Peoples.

In a report submitted to the Secretariat in 1966, Erick Schmidt, University of Alberta, recommended family planning to attack poverty and "illegitimacy" in Indigenous communities.[37] He cited Dr. C.A.D. Ringrose, President, Planned Parenthood, Edmonton, whose words reflect post–World War II ideologies on "dependency" and "underdevelopment":

> there is a global problem which none of us can ignore, but we in our own community and province have a similar problem … The Indian and Métis of Alberta have a [4 percent] annual increase in population (higher than South East Asia and Central America) at a time when their productivity is not increasing at anywhere near this rate. They have an illegitimacy rate much higher than the [7 percent] average for Alberta's population.[38]

In another instance, he cited Dr. Mary Jackson, who served the Keg River District, in her address to Planned Parenthood, Edmonton:

> How could one hope for a rising standard for living in the Métis and Indian unless they could reduce the size of their families? The PILL has a dramatic impact ... A school superintendant remarked that it would really be cheaper for the school divisions in the north to give pills free, than to build the classrooms required for the hundreds of unwanted children pouring into the schools each year.[39]

Indigenous people on reserves continue to struggle for adequate funding for schools in their communities, a discriminatory situation that often leaves children with the difficult "choice" of dropping out or moving away to complete their education.[40] Schmidt concluded that poverty, disease, and neglect were linked to a lack of family planning, and birth control would reduce illegitimacy rates and government budgets.[41]

In his appearance before the Standing Committee to request the DNHW approve an increase in funds for health services to Registered Indians, Proctor reiterated, "the Indian population will not stand still, sir. It has the highest increase, perhaps, on average, of any population in the world."[42] Dr. R.A. Armstrong, Adviser, Medical Services, clarified that Indigenous individuals cost less per capita than non-Indigenous people but more *per family* because families were bigger.[43] That same year, Ross Thatcher, Premier of Saskatchewan, acknowledged the living standards of Indigenous people were "the poorest in the world." He then expressed concern they were "breeding faster than rabbits," and considering a large proportion were on social aid, government would not be able to create enough jobs to "keep up."[44] While family planning was not explicitly named in either instance, both levels of government were concerned with the Indigenous birth rate.

The CWC thought family planning could address the "multi-problem family," those who showed a recurring pattern of dependency, inadequacy, and poverty from one generation to the next.[45] Legislative reform would allow child welfare agencies to bring family planning to the "poor and uneducated."[46] The Unitarian Council echoed this when Rev. Pohl highlighted that legislating against birth control when it was accessible to those with higher income levels made this discriminatory class legislation.[47] To put another way, the act of *decriminalizing* birth control was motivated by class considerations. John McNab, United Council of Churches, concluded, "As far as the whole war on poverty is concerned, family planning is an integral part of it."[48] The War on Poverty guiding legislative change was a war against Indigenous Peoples. One need only to ask — who are the poorest of the poor in Canada?

The Standing Committee recommended amendment to Section 150 (2)(c) of the Criminal Code to allow dissemination of knowledge and literature on family planning and birth control, and amendment to the Food and Drug Act to ensure oversight on how means of contraception could be advertised (Appleby 1999). Another two bills, Bill S-22 and Bill S-15, were debated between 1967 and 1969 prior to legislative change. Bill S-15, An Act to Amend the Food and Drug Act and the Narcotic Control Act and to make a consequential amendment to the Criminal Code passed on May 14, 1969 and received Royal Assent on June 27, 1969.[49]

Post-legislative Reform — A Family Planning Program for Canada

Bill S-15 was sponsored by John Munro, Minister of National Health and Welfare (Appleby 1999). Mary Bishop notes that Munro was "in frequent touch" with Cadbury, the "prime mover" of Planned Parenthood, and Planned Parenthood was a catalyst for government action on legislative reform (1983, 109). On February 8, 1969, Munro and seven staff met with Planned Parenthood, when Cadbury instructed "once the door to family planning was opened" (110) government should proceed with a program. Munro recommended a Family Planning Division within his department, and that Cabinet approve as national policy a concept of family planning that respected individual choice while enabling government to provide financial, research, and training support to outside agencies (Collins 1982).

Cabinet approved, but resisted the idea of a national policy. The federal approach was guided by the principle that abortion was not an acceptable method of birth control; use of contraception was based on "free choice" within the context of "family life"; no fertility research or population policy would be undertaken; and the division would not initiate programs, only respond to requests for information (Collins 1982, 6). Family planning could reduce social welfare costs, and while those with higher incomes could already access family planning, to make it available to the entire Canadian population would quell Indigenous fears of population control (Collins 1982). Less than a year later, Munro announced a family planning program that would distribute educational materials on family planning and sex education; provide consultative services to the private sector, local governments, and other federal departments, including Indian Affairs and Northern Development; and financially support voluntary associations, local government agencies, and university-based research (Collins 1982).[50]

In a news release, Munro declared, in adopting this program, government was recognizing and supporting the right of Canadians to exercise free choice in the practice of family planning — there would be no suggestion of coercion toward anyone.[51] He then wrote to Cadbury that he was able to give some indication on the federal position, "Freedom of choice implies the absence of all kinds of restrictions, either material or psychological ... There is opposition to the plan for fear that contraceptives and information would lead to abuse and license. Health and welfare is a provincial responsibility, but the Government has opened the door" (cited in Bishop 1983, 111–12).[52] Planned Parenthood received "the largest single grant given by the department to any national organization," enabling it to establish national headquarters and local offices (Collins 1982, 10). From 1972 to 1976, it received 37 percent of the Family Planning Division grant budget. The federal government also contributed to provincial planning programs under the Medical Care Act and the Hospital and Diagnostic Services Act, and shared-cost agreements for those meeting provincial "needs tests."[53]

J.H. Wiebe, Assistant Deputy Minister, Medical Services, stated this new program was "unquestionably applicable" to Indigenous clientele.[54] However, to impose measures to prevent births within a group when done to undermine its ability to exist is an act of genocide (Stote 2015). Indigenous people were already alleging genocide in response to their treatment by government, most especially its attempt to impose the White Paper, which effectively proposed to terminate Indigenous Peoples as peoples (Cardinal 1969). Wiebe was "acutely aware" of these allegations, but if government was going to break the "cycle of poverty," it needed a more positive, but subdued, approach.[55] He subsequently outlined a family planning policy aimed at reducing the birth rate to address child "neglect" and a host of other social issues, which would remain "low key" except where "local or native support" was given.[56]

In the early 1970s, allegations of coerced sterilization began to arise, and Indigenous political leaders increasingly viewed family planning as a means of carrying out genocide.[57] Both the White Paper and a family planning policy aimed at reducing the Indigenous birth rate shared a similar end result — of undermining Indigenous connections to the land and reducing obligations to Indigenous Peoples. To reduce the Indigenous birth rate can be seen as one means of weakening Indigenous resistance to these goals — a resistance that was increasingly organized by this time — by reducing the number of Indigenous people who can resist.

Despite the claim by Cabinet that government did not wish to enact a population policy or become directly involved in family planning, Munro tabled a report on his achievements in May 1971, indicating health and welfare officials had launched "a Canada-wide family planning program" in cooperation with the provinces, and professional and voluntary organizations.[58] The minutes of the Ad Hoc Meeting on Family Planning from 1971 indicate that in Northern Canada:

> The eskimo [sic] birth rate is the highest in the world. There are, at the same time, a large number of infant deaths, especially in large families or where children were not wanted ... [but] doctors carry on the ethical practice of medicine in the north. They do not push birth control, but give information when it is requested. Sterilization and abortion are carried out if the medical evidence indicates that such actions are warranted ... Medical Services Branch ... will be involved in the Department's family planning program, as will the Food and Drug Directorate, the Health Services Branch, and other parts of the Department.[59]

As early as June 11, 1968, G.C. Butler, Chief Medical Officer N.W.T. had called on the Northwest Territories Council to pass a motion to "immediately undertake ... a formal universal and intensive scheme for the dissemination of information about birth control and family planning ... through which various birth control devices can be made freely available to anyone wishing them."[60] Jim Lotz (1968, 292), Canadian Research Centre for Anthropology, Ottawa, commented:

> Despite the demand by the government for people to go North and develop the area, the same government manages

to give the impression that there are too many Eskimos [sic] and Indians. At their Spring 1968 Session, the Council of the Northwest Territories noted high infant mortality in the North, squalid living conditions, reduced health services, and came up with the inevitable statement that birth control services were needed. If Eskimo [sic] women keep losing children — a source of wealth and comfort to them — then no amount of propaganda about birth control will convince them of the need to keep the population down. The Northwest Territories showed a curious paradox in 1968 — all the official talk was of boom and economic expansion and the need for labour in the North, whereas the Territorial Council endeavored to keep the native people from reproducing.

This initiative, in an area under federal jurisdiction, was in keeping with activities taking place in other "Third World" countries where Western governments identified overpopulation as a central concern. This, despite acknowledgement by some population planners that, considering a high infant mortality rate often accompanied a high birth rate, a rise in their standard of living was the most effective form of family planning (e.g., Mass 1976).

Government officials and medical professionals sometimes appeared committed to family planning rather than improving the material conditions of Indigenous lives no matter what the cost to Indigenous women or their children. Discussing the potential dangers posed to breastfeeding mothers if they were given the contraceptive pill, Dr. Jeffrey Bishop, Drug Advisory Bureau, indicated the general consensus amongst the American Academy of Pediatrics' Committee on Drugs, for which he was a liaison member for the Canadian Food and Drug Directorate, was that the pill was contraindicated for breastfeeding mothers on the principle that "even small quantities of steroids should not be allowed to reach the nursing infant." Studies in rats had also shown sterility could result in female offspring when mothers received oral contraceptives during lactation.[61]

It became evident there was a lack of agreement on these findings since little was known about the long-term effects of progesterone and estrogen on women or nursing infants. The National Advisory Committee on Birth Control Medication thought it was best to be cautious, and recommended mothers avoid the pill when breastfeeding.[62] However, the Obstetrical and Gynaecological Committee at the Charles Camsell Hospital, led by Dr. Parlee — who proposed a research study on the issue with Indigenous women as test subjects — suggested there was no danger in prescribing the pill to lactating mothers.[63] Bishop concluded, based on available information, it would be "premature to interdict the use of oral contraceptives in the nursing Eskimo [sic] mother, in light of the attempt to interrupt a population explosion there."[64] He agreed this was an "ideal situation" for a controlled study, if women in one isolated village were given oral contraceptives while those in another were not, this would allow for "careful prospective evaluation of the offspring."[65] In response, Wiebe acknowledged the conflicting advice from the medical community, but without making any explicit recommendation on a course of action, concluded, "It will take 20 years to find out whether the children who were nursed by mothers taking the pill are sterile."[66]

In 1972, the DNHW organized the First National Conference on Family Planning to promote provincial participation in a "Canada-wide family planning program."[67] Family planning was to be voluntary, but planners should place high priority on "isolated" communities and groups, including "people in remote rural and northern areas, native peoples living in self-contained settlements, and adolescents living away from home."[68] While these categories were not mutually exclusive, Indigenous people were a segment of the population for which it was essential to understand their values, attitudes, and motivations for having children. A study by the Canadian Institute on International Affairs found Indigenous Peoples had "a tradition of close ties within a larger family," assigned parenthood a "high community value," and sometimes considered family planning a "white strategy" to limit their population while relieving pressure for social change.[69] Since most communities lived in poverty, for family planning to be successful, systemic change was needed.[70] However, because it was "not feasible nor likely" social and economic conditions would improve, family planning was a priority.[71]

Family planning had been declared a human right at the United Nations International Conference on Human Rights in Tehran, in 1968. The Proclamation of Tehran outlined that parents had a right to "determine freely and responsibly the number and the spacing of their children."[72] The following year, the United Nations General Assembly encouraged member states to take steps toward developing and coordinating "policies and measures designed to strengthen the essential functions of the family as a basic unit of society," while establishing population programs "within the framework of national demographic policies and as part of the welfare medical services."[73] The United Nations World Population Conference, planned for 1974, featured a "World Population Plan of Action" as a major agenda item (Finkle and Crane 1975, 87). Debate on what approach governments should take was a "polarizing" one, between Western nations who viewed population growth as an impediment to "development," and "Third World" countries who viewed population problems as a consequence of "underdevelopment" (102). Canada faced increasing pressure to adopt an explicit population policy in concert with this "major step" toward a global policy. It also had its own "Third World" at home — in Indigenous communities.

Planned Parenthood continued to press Canada to recognize fertility rates as an obvious component of population growth, and family planning programs as a critical part of any population policy — at home or abroad.[74] In the lead up to the World Population Conference, in collaboration with the Conservation Council of Canada, Planned Parenthood co-hosted a two-day seminar, "A Population Policy for Canada?" with Cadbury as opening presenter.[75] In his address, Cadbury outlined, while people were the basic unit of any nation, in Canada, planners and policy makers had largely neglected "their numbers" and "qualities" (1973, 2). Indigenous people had become "conscious of their relatively small proportion" of the population and this, coupled with a high birth rate and "immensely improved health facilities," made them "the fastest growing sector of the population" (2). Canada was still "basically a European country with a heritage of European customs and habits," but the problem of "over-large families" was only beginning to be met by the Ministry of Health and Welfare (2). All levels of government had a responsibility to address the consequences of population growth and age distribution on the economy. Cadbury referred to "explosive pressure" in Latin America and parts of Asia that might bring an influx of people to Canada at a rate "far greater" than space could accommodate, and this alone should push government to develop a domestic population policy (1973, 4). Decriminalization allowed government to assist with the "world population crisis," but an explicit domestic policy was needed to better support this work home.[76] This policy, which did not come to fruition until 1977, was influenced by Cadbury and Planned Parenthood.

The Royal Commission on the Status of Women, 1967–70

The Royal Commission on the Status of Women (RCSW), appointed by the Privy Council on February 16, 1967, was tasked with inquiring on the status of women in Canada and making recommendations on how to ensure "equal opportunities" in all aspects of society.[77] The RCSW supported federal activities as informed by Planned Parenthood. The RCSW was chaired by broadcaster, journalist, and later, Liberal Senator, Florence Bird; accompanied by Lola Lange, a rural feminist from Alberta; Jeanne Lapointe, a Quebec academic; Elsie MacGill, Canada's first aeronautic engineer and president of the Canadian Federation of Business and Professional Women's Clubs; and Doris Ogilvie, a judge in the juvenile court system. The two men on the Commission were John Humphreys, drafter of the Universal Declaration on Human Rights, and Jacques Henripin, a demographer specializing in "population projections" and "family policy."[78]

The RCSW received 468 briefs and nearly one thousand letters of opinion, conducted public hearings across ten provinces and northern cities, undertook forty special studies, interviewed 890 witnesses, and made 167 recommendations. The report, tabled in December 1970, recommended a series of actions to support pay equity, universal child care, and maternity leave, and to increase representation of women in public life. It also made recommendations on how to ensure better access to birth control, abortion, and family planning.[79] The work of the RCSW, considered significant to second wave feminism in Canada, was imbued with a "liberal hegemonic feminist ideology," or racist, classist, ableist, heterosexist, and nationalist assumptions (Bunjun 2018, 1). Most submissions to the RCSW were by "white middle-class women," and "no Indigenous person sat as a Commissioner nor staffed any of the studies on Indigenous Peoples" (Bunjun 2018, 8–9).

The general absence of Indigenous involvement was described by at least one journalist as "disappointing" and "puzzling" (Freeman 2001, 202). However, Indigenous women did speak in various capacities to the RCSW. Media reported on a delegation of Mohawk women from Kahnawake, including Mary Two Axe Early, who highlighted how the Indian Act had revoked the status of some women and their children, leaving them with no "voting, property or burial rights" on-reserve, and under constant threat of eviction (Freeman 2001, 196–7). The Alberta Native Women's Conference attempted to shift the focus from "equality" to "healthcare, education, poverty, residential schools, and housing ... [and] self-determination and agency" (194). Alice Steinhauer, June Stifle, and Christine Daniels, two Cree women and one Métis, expressed how they were "tired of federal interference in their lives" and "had enough of seeing their families torn apart" as their children were sent to residential schools and stripped of their language and culture (194).

The RCSW heard testimony on violence against Indigenous women, including sexual violence committed by "transient men" (Freeman 2001, 201) working on construction or survey crews in northern communities. Chair Florence Bird explained why this issue was left out:

> We did not ... hear as much about violence as people do today because it was not a subject that was discussed as openly as it is now. I myself, at a private, confidential meeting, heard a shocking story about violence against Inuit women perpetrated by men working on the Dew Line. After I told the commissioners about this, they decided that they had some doubts whether our terms of reference would justify our undertaking the study of such a complicated legal and moral issue. (1997, 194)

Commissioner Henripin stated, while the RCSW acknowledged the "privations" faced by Indigenous Peoples in terms of health, education, and standard of living, and "every means should be taken" to address them, these subjects were outside its "terms of reference" (cited in Turpel-Lafond 1996, 74). The RCSW stated it was not qualified to deal with the "complex problems which arise when attempting to introduce social and economic changes in cultures which are so very different from ours," "goodwill in these matters is often, and sometimes quite rightly, interpreted as a form of paternalism" and "a more or less conscious attempt to destroy these cultures," and some recommendations "may have been drawn up a little too hastily" (74).

Despite Indigenous women raising urgent issues of concern for their peoples, Barbara Freeman documents how media focused on "common-law marriages, high 'illegitimacy' rates and ... addictions, sexual exploitation and imprisonment," presenting these issues as "the lot of 'tragic' and 'destitute' [A]boriginal women on urban 'skid rows'" (2001, 190), which further entrenched stereotypes of Indigenous women as sexually promiscuous. Benita Bunjun writes, it is clear the

RCSW, "as a colonial project," reproduced ideologies supporting the regulation of Indigenous women — a regulation which continues to this day (2018, 11–12). The RCSW report had "very little in it about Native women and the few relevant recommendations made were integrated into other chapters which primarily concerned White women" (Freeman 1998, 103).

The act of leaving out Indigenous concerns reflected the inability, or intentional refusal, of the RCSW to grasp how violence against Indigenous lands is connected to violence against Indigenous bodies, and in doing so, it reinforced colonial relations. In her study on the entrenchment of the RCSW agenda in the women's movement, Bunjun interviewed "Sydney," who explained how RCSW recommendations constructed "legitimate" (2018, 16) women's issues while erasing those of importance to queer, racialized, immigrant, and Indigenous women. Reflecting on her attendance at a Vancouver Status of Women meeting when an Indigenous woman raised the centrality of land claims to Indigenous struggles, "Sydney" stated, "The land claims [issue] was a surprise because we had violence against women, we had issues we thought would touch on women from every culture, but we never thought land claims, which I still don't think is specifically a women's issue" (cited in Bunjun 2018, 13).

The RCSW discussed family planning and birth control as a means of "responsible parenthood."[80] It recognized families with higher education and income had access to birth control, while the "poor and less well educated" did not, but fertility rates had been decreasing overall.[81] It supported the "excellent work" initiated by Planned Parenthood and endorsed its request for a "much wider" family planning program.[82] Social workers informed the RCSW that some "young unmarried girls" neglected to use contraception out of "sheer ignorance," often becoming mothers as a result, and consequently, they should be advised on birth control.[83] It supported "imaginative" programs, including having hospitals give maternity patients information on family planning and birth control, and recommended increased collaboration between all levels of government and health and welfare departments to ensure family planning was accessible, including to those in remote areas.[84]

In its discussion of sterilization, while referring to eugenic legislation in Alberta and British Columbia as "prohibiting" compulsory sterilization, it commented that no law in Canada expressly prohibited a physician from sterilizing an individual on request.[85] Despite this, the possibility existed for a physician to be found criminally responsible if a court ruled sterilization caused bodily harm; or civilly, if carried out without consent of a patient and their spouse. It recommended legislation to ensure sterilization was available for non-medical reasons, when performed by a qualified medical practitioner at the request of his [sic] patient, without requiring spousal consent.[86] This recommendation, centred on protecting physicians from potential liability rather than shielding women from coercion, should cause us to reflect on whether *criminalizing* coerced sterilization holds potential to stop the practice.

Policy changes recommended by the RCSW have improved the lives of *some* women. However, as with any liberal, reformist change, they benefitted some more than others, and have failed to address the systemic aspects of women's oppression, including that of racialized, marginalized, and Indigenous women (Abner and Mossman 1990; Gimenez 2005; Tuck and Yang 2018). The support of liberal feminists for family planning as a reproductive right and responsible choice provided a veneer of legitimacy to an agenda that joined family planning to the economic planning of nations (Bashford 2014; Ordover 2003). Alison Bashford writes, through the efforts of "states, international agencies, health organizations, philanthropic funds, and family-planning organizations to persuade, to enjoin citizens — of nations, of regions, of the world — to reproduce responsibly and to practice family planning ... individuals were not just freeing themselves from the prospect of pregnancy, they were becoming subjects of freedom" (2014, 350). By supporting the expansion of family planning without centring the multiplicity of issues that directly inform the context in which Indigenous women are presented reproductive options and must make choices, and in failing to call for a fundamental transformation of the exploitative social relations that inform *all women's experiences*, the RCSW, and second wave feminism more generally, *became* the master's tool (Ahmed 2023, 63). Not unlike how first wave feminists reinforced social relations of oppression by seeking rights from within a system based on exploitation and theft, as they supported eugenic sterilization legislation (Stote 2015), this "ideological complicity" (Ordover 2003, 132) contributed to the coerced sterilization of Indigenous women in modern times.

A Note on Abortion

Many involved in the population control movement were "generally ambivalent" toward the abortion issue, and while abortion was considered a personal choice, population planners viewed the need for abortion as "proof of program failure" with respect to family planning (Critchlow 1999, 177). Bonnie Mass writes that the avoidance of the abortion issue in the late 1960s and early 1970s was a "minor concession" (1974, 667) granted to the Catholic Church in exchange for its non-opposition to the expansion of birth control activities globally. This changed when Rockefeller III became involved in the struggle against legislative restrictions on abortion. Some intepret this involvement as a political strategy, based on his understanding of the importance of women to ensuring economic development through family planning (Critchlow 1999) — a way to bring more women into the fold of population work by giving primacy to abortion as a reproductive right. However, abortion remains a polarizing issue that continues to cause deep divisions between those concerned with the reproductive rights of women, the religious and political right (including anti-abortionists focused on the rights of the fetus), and marginalized and racialized women who struggle for an end to systemic oppression as a necessary step toward ensuring reproductive justice and choice (Ross 2017).

Federal discussions that culminated in the decriminalization of birth control and allowed for the open promotion of family planning took place concurrently with, but separate from, those on abortion. Omnibus Bill C-150, The *Criminal Law Amendment Act*, passed on the same day as Bill S-15, exempted from prosecution those who performed abortions in accredited hospitals if a Therapeutic Abortion Committee determined a pregnancy would endanger the "health" of a woman.[87] The RCSW also addressed abortion, calling on the federal government to implement legislative change to allow abortion at the request of a women if the continuation of a pregnancy would endanger her physical or mental health, or there was a substantial risk that, once born, a child would be "handicapped," either mentally or physically — a recommendation with definite eugenic undertones.[88]

Many scholars have studied the significance and shortcomings of Canada's abortion law in its formation and aftermath (Brodie, Gavigan, and Jensen 1992; Ackerman and Stettner 2019; Haussman 2000). Jane Jensen (1992) states a primary motivation for legislative change was to clarify the legal liability of doctors performing abortions while increasing the ability of the medical establishment to decide what should be done to women's bodies. Legislative change allowed for the continued regulation of women in line with the objectives of the federal family planning program. Therapeutic Abortion Committees emphasized economic factors when determining whether a pregnancy would endanger a woman's health. Jensen writes, "Most simply, if doctors saw any pregnancy as 'unhealthy' they could legally abort it" (1992, 19).

Some continued to experience barriers to abortion post-1969, namely white middle-class and rural women, as others were pressured to consent to sterilization as a prerequisite to obtaining the service.[89] Indigenous women experienced abusive abortions into the 1990s (Stote 2015). More recent research demonstrates the continuation of this trend.[90] The inequitable operation of Canada's abortion law mobilized the reproductive rights movement under second wave feminism, one which was led by white middle-class women. In its hyper-focus on securing abortion on demand as a fundamental requirement of reproductive agency and choice, some voices were given primacy as Indigenous experiences of reproductive oppression were erased.

While this work does not engage abortion directly, legislative change on abortion intersected with and informed family planning policy and practice in an important, though perhaps, non-obvious way in keeping with the position taken by population planners. In 1973, Dr. R.W. Tooley, Director, Family Planning Division, explained, in line with the federal objective, that "every child should be a wanted child," both the incidence of "illegitimate births" *and* the number of abortions could provide clues as to how many pregnancies were "planned" and hence, how many were "wanted."[91] To rely on "illegitimacy" rates alone was misleading considering the act of living together without the "formal blessing of the church and state" was more acceptable, or perhaps was never the norm for some; but it was reasonable to suppose the number of abortions was indicative of "unplanned conception."[92] If there were unplanned pregnancies, the need for family planning services was not being met.[93] Post-legislative change, newly available abortion utilization data reinforced the need for more concerted family planning efforts. When filtered through a racist and paternalistic lens focused on cost efficiency, it helped justify the increased surveillance of young, single Indigenous women, and the promotion of more permanent means of fertility control to them. Abortion was a politically sensitive issue. Sterilization was "much cheaper in the long run" than even the long-term use of contraception.[94]

In the post-legislative change era, sterilization was left to medical discretion when performed at the request of a patient.[95] Rather than defer to a given law, eugenic or otherwise, in deciding the feasibility of sterilization, medical practitioners were the "ultimate arbiters" of population policy (Gunn 1999, 113). The federal government established the parameters in which medical practitioners could act, and as it liberalized this context, it was aware coercion was possible and sometimes taking place. In failing to address the conditions allowing for coercion — the context in which choices are made — it holds a responsibility for how family planning was experienced by Indigenous women. The expansion of family planning was a cooperative federal-provincial venture involving both health and welfare, based on a "reciprocal relationship" between each level of government — federal policy influenced provincial action and was modified in light of provincial experience.[96] Throughout, it was given shape by corporate and other private interests. The next chapter examines how this unfolded in Saskatchewan to inform family planning activites that consistently approached Indigenous reproduction as problematic, and culminated in the coerced sterilization of Indigenous women.

4

Family Planning in Post-1970 Saskatchewan — A Thirty-Year Review

The most important demographic trend in Saskatchewan for the next 25 years is the growth in the Indian ancestry population both in absolute terms and also as a proportion of the total population ... Given the present attitudes and policy orientations of non-Indians and judging from past experiences in Indian/non-Indian relationships, the next 25 years could be years of racial turmoil in Saskatchewan. If racial turmoil does occur in Canada, it is likely to begin in Saskatchewan and spread to other areas ... [setting] the stage for events in all of Canada in the area of Indian/non-Indian relationships.[1]

In an address to the Saskatchewan division of the Canadian Public Health Association in 1967, Dr. Waldron, Indian Health Service, Zone Superintendent, Prince Albert, indicated Indigenous people were the fastest growing population in Canada. The Indigenous birth rate was more than twice that of the rest of Canada, their fertility rate was "exceptionally high," and "illegitimacy" represented 45 percent of provincial births.[2] The infant mortality rate was three times the national average and northern areas, heavily populated by Indigenous people, were largely responsible for these rates. Infant mortality was a "very high priority" for Medical Services and mortality was higher among illegitimate births.[3] M.L. Webb, Medical Services, stated it was unlikely there were "ever so many Indigenous peoples living in the whole of Canada at any other time," and high birth and infant mortality rates were a "special health problem" facing them.[4] Poverty was common on reserves, which were noted for their "alcohol problems, violence, neglect of homes and children," and additional issues were the "retention of ancient customs and habits" and "refusal to accept medical care and advice."[5]

Earlier, at an in-service training session for public health nurses, T.J. Orford, Indian and Northern Health Services, stated the degree of nutrition in most Indigenous homes was not equivalent to Canadian standards, and low-income levels and lack of ability to ensure a balanced diet influenced Indigenous circumstances, but poor management of income and "reliance on handouts" were ultimately to blame.[6] Indigenous people who left reserves to seek out opportunities may encounter discrimination, but "this [was] played up much more than [it] actually exist[ed]."[7] While deliberate and conscious neglect of children was rare, many lived in "filthy condition with serious malnutrition and inevitable illness" due to "ignorance on the part of the parent." Higher illegitimacy rates would continue "as long as slum conditions exist" and young women "move into urban centres without sufficient educational and moral background. Their environment is not conducive to strong moral fibre."[8] Reflecting on how far Indigenous communities were from "the ideal public health," Dr. F. Porth, Indian and Northern Health Services, stated it was important to remember the "Indian" had "only recently progressed" from the "Stone Age" and "we cannot push him, he must lead."[9]

Post-legislative change, the Canadian Public Health Association — a non-governmental body with links to the international health community whose members regularly advise decision makers on public health reform — passed a resolution endorsing the need for family planning programs.[10] Health departments should educate the public on family planning, encourage physicians to make it an integral part of their medical practice, and provide services to single women with children, especially "known promiscuous women," while offering "special adoption services" based on genetic counselling.[11] Indigenous women had already been singled out as the cause of public health problems — the "tangle of pathology" plaguing Indigenous communities; they were the "known promiscuous women" the Canadian Public Health Association referenced. The racism and paternalism imbuing the federal approach to Indigenous public health was also embedded in the provincial approach to family planning.

Proposals for a Family Planning Policy in Saskatchewan

Saskatchewan was one of the first provinces to take organized steps toward a family planning policy.[12] In May 1970, the Department of Public Health requested government approval to allow physicians to advise women on fertility control, and for public health nurses to provide services in remote areas, including northern health districts, at no charge.[13] By October, its policy manual outlined family planning should be promoted to everyone "in need" through the free supply of devices to medically indigent patients.[14] Public health nurses should discuss family planning during prenatal and post-natal visits on request, or when warranted by "family circumstances."[15] A.W. Sihvon, Deputy Minister of Welfare, issued a policy statement permitting staff to advise individuals on how to plan the size of their families, with the cost of oral contraceptives, IUDs, and diaphragms covered for welfare recipients.[16] Social workers, who up to this point had taken a passive role in family planning (Argue and Schlesinger 1974), now had a responsibility to provide information to their clients, often single mothers facing the possibility of their children being taken from them, to enhance their "quality of life."[17]

In November 1971, the Department of Public Health formed the Thrust Group to undertake two separate probes: one on abortion, another on family planning.[18] The "Probe Committee" conducted a comparative analysis on the number of abortions across the province, reviewed the adequacy of abortion facilities and referral procedures, and considered the legal implications of expanding abortion services under federal law.[19] With respect to family planning, it examined the adequacy of services and recommended areas for expansion.[20]

In a brief report on abortion, the Committee found the number of abortions rose 850 percent in the first year post-legislative change, from 20 to 171, but this rate was about half the national average.[21] Regina and Saskatoon accounted for 85 percent of all abortions.[22] It recommended more Therapeutic Abortion Committees and a reduction in time spent in hospital when accessing the procedure.[23] The age of consent for medical treatment was nineteen, but the Department of Welfare considered anyone sixteen or older to be an adult. Provincial legislation should allow consent from individuals "capable of understanding" that to which they were consenting.[24] Medical professionals should place more emphasis on male sterilization, as a simpler procedure, and hospitals should accommodate demands for tubal ligation as a gynecological matter. Many female sterilizations were performed as hysterectomies; these could be performed on an outpatient basis if a laparoscopy device was used.[25] The "tragic problem of the unwanted child" among "disadvantaged groups" might be influencing abortion rates, though it was impossible to know for sure.[26] The Committee passed a resolution that Cabinet approve a family planning program to reduce the number of abortions, and the Department of Public Health should prepare a "considerably expanded" program the following year.[27]

The report on family planning was more extensive. The Committee was concerned the Department of Public Health was operating a family planning program without authority of official government policy. This situation should not be allowed to continue.[28] The program, implemented in 1970, placed staff in an awkward situation.[29] For example, a nurse in a northern community facing "multiple health and socio-economic" problems discussed family planning "unofficially," but experienced "unpleasant opposition" from a Catholic priest.[30] The provincial population was declining, but women of childbearing age had a higher fertility rate than the national average and a rising percentage of "illegitimate" births.[31] This was especially true for young Registered Indian women, who had an illegitimacy rate more than five times the provincial average, and an infant mortality rate nearly three times higher.[32] This indicated there was "a need for information on family planning for our native population."[33]

The Committee recommended government adopt a "positive family planning policy" to minimize "unwanted pregnancies," directed at the population of reproductive age, with emphasis on "young women, native and white, single and married." The Regional Health Services Branch should assume responsibility for coordination and implemention, and health workers, social workers, and teachers should be given training on methods of dissemination. In the interim, the Family Planning Association of Saskatchewan (Planned Parenthood Saskatchewan) should be encouraged to expand its program, with financial support from government and participation from women's groups. The newly created Department of the North should disseminate birth control information to Indigenous people, and the Department of Social Services, to "indigent persons."[34] Finally, the age of medical consent should be lowered to sixteen years of age.[35]

Overall, government was receptive. It produced a revised version of the report to account for changes in birth, illegitimacy, and abortion rates since the Probe Committee report, and notably, removed all language alluding to "target populations." This was released for comment as the "Proposals for a Family Planning Program for Saskatchewan."[36]

In a press release, Walter Smishek, Minister of Public Health, repeated that every child should result from the responsible decision-making of parents, but this required "coordinated efforts" to ensure individuals had access to birth control.[37] The number of "unwanted children" was rising at an "alarming rate," reflected in the number of illegitimate births and abortions. A positive family planning program was needed.[38] Despite removal of inflammatory language alluding to "target populations," on the day of the press release, S.L. Skoll, Deputy Minister of Public Health, restated "special attention will have to be paid to ... the socially disadvantaged and the Native people."[39] This led Associate Deputy Minister of Health M.B. Derrick to reiterate the long-term policy objective was *not* to be interpreted as an attack on welfare clients.[40] Yet this focus remained at the Advisory Committee on Family Planning.

The Advisory Committee on Family Planning, 1973

Cabinet approved in principle the "Proposals for a Family Planning Program for Saskatchewan" and agreed to develop an expanded program.[41] It struck an Advisory Committee to recommend the way forward.[42] The Advisory Committee on Family Planning, chaired by Alice Caplin, Assistant Professor of Nursing, University of Saskatchewan, included representatives from health and welfare, media, churches, and Planned Parenthood Saskatchewan.[43] It attempted to include Indigenous representation.[44] Smishek wrote to invite Isobel McNab, President of the Saskatchewan Indian Women's Association (SIWA), an organization formed in 1971 to represent "Treaty" or "Registered Indian" women on reserves, to participate.[45] He wrote again a few months later asking if his letter had "gone astray."[46] McNab agreed to serve, but never attended any meetings.[47] Vicki Wilson, representative from the Saskatchewan Native Women's Association (SNWA), also formed in 1971 to represent "Treaty/Status," non-Status, and Métis women on- and off-reserve, was involved, but resigned in 1975 and her spot remained vacant.[48]

The Advisory Committee was tasked with reviewing the Probe Committee report and current family planning initiatives.[49] At its first meeting, it inquired on whether giving unsolicited family planning advice to minors would influence the legal responsibilities of physicians and health workers.[50] In 1972, women under nineteen years of age accounted for 47 percent of births outside of marriage and 53 percent of abortions; to lower the age of consent would allow a focus on this group.⁵¹ This issue, at what age a person could consent to birth control, sterilization, or abortion, had been raised many times previous.

Much earlier, in 1948, Dr. G.G. Fergusson, Registrar of the College of Physicians and Surgeons, Saskatchewan, wrote to C.F.W. Hames, Deputy Minister of Health, to request his opinion on the legality of performing sterilizations.⁵² Hames forwarded a memorandum from Deputy Attorney General Alex Blackwood stating "any person performing a surgical operation for sterilization without just cause and for the benefit of the patient as cure or extirpation of disease would not be excused from criminal liability."⁵³ What disease would warrant sterilization as "cure" was not expanded on. Consent needed to be freely given, but with respect to children, practitioners had legal protection if consent of a parent or guardian was sought, and this rule applied to "insane" persons.⁵⁴

In 1958, F.S. Lawson, Director, Psychiatric Services Branch, inquired with Department Solicitor R.G. Ellis on consent for operations performed on mental patients. He then wrote to Dr. A.J. Beddie, Superintendent, Saskatchewan Training School, Moose Jaw, that "after 15 minutes of talk and his annoyance, I pinned him down to saying definitely that it was legal for a Superintendent to prescribe any kind of treatment for a mentally ill person in his institution."⁵⁵ By 1971, R. Baxter, Coordinator of Therapies, revealed the impetus for sterilization was emanating from professionals in the field who were "not in accord with the predominant values of Canadian society" to ensure "human rights are preserved."⁵⁶ The Northern Regional Director clarified this decision should be decided "on a case-by-case basis."⁵⁷

The Canadian Medical Association, concerned with the lack of uniformity in the age of medical consent across the country, drafted a motion recommending a uniform age lowered to sixteen.⁵⁸ However, the provincial Coming of Age Act, 1970 established the age of consent at nineteen, with medical treatment to minors subject to parental consent, except in emergencies.⁵⁹ A draft memorandum prepared for Deputy Minister Skoll, addressed to physicians and nurses employed in mental health, family planning, and venereal disease treatment clinics, proposed guidelines to preserve "secrecy" when treating minors for mental disorders or engaging the non-medical use of drugs.⁶⁰ Those providing services without consent could be found guilty of negligence, but if clinics required parental consent, minors may leave without obtaining services.[61] To avoid this, minors should receive services after being examined by a physician.[62]

This proposed policy was contrary to law and the position of the Canadian Medical Protective Association (CMPA). The CMPA intended to lobby the federal government to implement a uniform age of medical consent across the country, but in the meantime, doctors needed to obey the law. Secretary Treasurer T.L. Fisher wrote, "To repeat myself, this must be, not just should be … the starting point," otherwise medical professionals would "stand in some peril."[63] Despite clarification, Skoll indicated, in Quebec, the Hospital Plan issued instructions that consent need not be sought for patients who were sixteen years old. Saskatchewan had not issued such a directive, but "probably in practice, individual physicians and perhaps hospitals too, might … be following the policy enunciated in Quebec, particularly … if they judge the patient would refuse treatment if parents were notified."[64]

Later that year, C. Beek, Executive Director, South East Regional Hospital Council, said he had received questions from a hospital with "a large Indian patronage" on whether it was legal for persons under eighteen to consent to abortion, sterilization, or hysterectomy, and asked whether patients "should be made aware that a tubal ligation or complete hysterectomy is irreversible before consent is obtained."[65] It is difficult to believe permanent procedures like a tubal ligation or hysterectomy — performed as a form of sterilization — were being requested by those under the age of majority to such an extent as to warrant an inquiry. It is also concerning there was any confusion on whether the irreversibility of either needed to be conveyed.

Solicitor Ellis indicated the problem of informed consent was creating "fairly serious concern" at the Parkland Hospital and "a number of other general hospitals" in the province.[66] Consent for surgery could only be obtained if the procedure was medically indicated, not through a blanket form signed upon admission.[67] Ellis had indicated government would be jointly liable for any negligent employee.[68] This point was later reiterated by Skoll when he indicated that he had been instructed by the provincial treasurer to advise all physicians employed with the department that government "would assume full responsibility for all costs incurred by an employed physician in connection with a malpractice claim."[69] It is unclear how one should interpret this, or how it was interpreted by medical professionals who might be inclined to forgo seeking informed consent. Were they deterred or further enabled by such a statement?

When a child was apprehended under the Child Welfare Act, the Minister of Welfare became guardian and "by an internal arrangement ... the welfare worker acquainted with the case may authorize surgical procedures."[70] In much later correspondence, J.D. Fraser, Regional Director, Qu'Appelle Region, recounted being asked to provide consent for abortion for a young girl of Indigenous origins:

> I found the decision a heavy one as there were no consultants available or other staff to discuss the decision ... She is not yet 18 years of age but I was quite impressed by her maturity. She attends a business school during the day and works from 5-9 each night so that she pays most of her own costs. Her boyfriend is white and is gainfully employed. He is 19 and states that although they plan marriage in the future she felt they were too young to take on the responsibility of a child. I interviewed the girl alone and then saw them together and although I didn't have the time required to deal with the matter fully, they made the decision to proceed with abortion. I saw the Doctor and signed the consent ... but advised him that I felt the girl really didn't want to proceed and was doing so because she was fearful of losing her boyfriend ... As of this date the abortion has not been completed.[71]

Fraser wanted to discuss the lack of policy on abortion, but his response illustrates factors weighed when granting consent on behalf of wards of the state. One must wonder how these factors were weighed when a young person did not impress such maturity.

Despite all these "red flags," the Advisory Committee recommended lowering of the age of consent to sixteen.[72] It was purportedly concerned with the coercive nature of any program that implied family planning sought to "reduce the number of unwanted children."[73] The potentially coercive nature of a program was exemplified when it came to Indigenous people who "faced serious dislocations of family patterns [and] family life."[74] Family planning was not to be "a panacea for the ills of society," the decision to regulate reproduction should be arrived at without pressure, and programming should not be aimed at any group.[75] It then identified "unmarried" mothers as those who could most benefit from family planning, and cited statistics on births occurring outside of marriage, which were "steadily increasing" and "to a certain extent" reflected "the high proportion of Indian births ... to unmarried mothers aged 19 and under."[76] Among its sixty-one recommendations, it suggested "high risk" pregnancies by young and unmarried women be referred for follow-up services; social workers, doctors, and nurses take a "team approach" to ensure "unprejudiced" care; "preventative" services be provided under the Family Services Act; and the Department of Northern Saskatchewan rely on Indigenous health workers under the supervision of nurses and physicians to provide family planning information.[77] With respect to sterilization, patients should be informed of its consequences and written consent obtained.[78]

The Advisory Committee report was tabled on April 18, 1975.[79] Cabinet agreed with the recommendations but wondered if it should make a positive statement on family planning by directing staff in provincial departments to provide services whether or not these were requested.[80] It would expand postpartum family planning counselling but wanted detail on costs and whether this could be done by health and social workers.[81] The following year, Alice Caplin wrote W.A. Robbins, new Minister of Health and Chairman of the Committee of Ministers on Family Planning, requesting a meeting to discuss the "lack of action" on the Advisory Committee's report.[82] In minutes from this meeting, Robbins stated, while the proposed program was "interesting," it was "controversial" and "expensive" in a time of fiscal restraint.[83] H.H. Rolfes, Minister of Social Services, indicated many problems relating to family planning were social, promiscuity was "a way of life" for some, and information alone would not help alleviate the problem.[84] The Committee of Ministers decided government would avoid taking an explicit policy stand.[85] In October 1976, it disbanded the Advisory Committee.[86]

The Family Planning Association of Saskatchewan — Planned Parenthood

Planned Parenthood Saskatchewan formed in December 1971 with funds from its parent organization, the federal government, and the province.[87] Saskatoon was the first centre with a Planned Parenthood branch, followed by Regina, Prince Albert, North Battleford, Melfort, Yorkton, and Meadow Lake.[88] Planned Parenthood Saskatchewan saw its long-term role as one of "community activator," but was prepared to provide direct family planning services, at least temporarily.[89] The Probe Committee recommended a key role for Planned Parenthood Saskatchewan in expanding services, with the province funding activities until regional health staff could take over.[90] In response to a similar recommendation from the Advisory Committee, the Minister of Health provided a grant to Planned Parenthood Saskatchewan for the following year, but indicated this should not be interpreted as a long-term commitment on funding.[91]

The first family planning clinic opened in Regina in 1971, focused on "hard to get at" groups — including "Indian-Métis."[92] However, according to clinic director Dr. G.W. Piper, it failed to attract any significant clientele in its first two years of operation, so he looked to Planned Parenthood Saskatchewan for help.[93] It suggested Piper secure funding for an "Indigenous Worker Project" to train people from particular social groups, "say high school students or the Indian and Métis community," and geographic neighbourhoods, "say College Ave. to Victoria, or Winnipeg to Broad," in the theory and technique of contraception in order to offer counselling services in their communities.[94] The "door-to-door" campaign would involve workers chosen "from those receiving social assistance" who could offer information and refer people to a doctor or clinic.[95]

The Committee of Ministers met with Planned Parenthood Saskatchewan on the same day it struck the Advisory Committee. Sally Anne Williams, Executive Officer, Planned Parenthood Saskatchewan, explained the organization wanted to ensure everyone had access to family planning through information, education, and the use of medical facilities; a family planning program should be based on quality of life, not just contraception; government and private agencies should help disseminate information; and staff in education, social services, and public health and medicine should be versed in how to discuss these issues.[96] She emphasized Planned Parenthood Saskatchewan had no contact with the North due to a lack of funding but had given thought to problems in the area.

Family planning was needed for Indigenous people, but this was not a "high priority" amongst them, and "difficulties in communication, culture and religion" made an effective program challenging.[97] In a follow-up brief, Williams explained:

> The attitude of native people towards family planning has been strongly influenced by events which have occurred in this and other provinces. In a recent conversation with the [SNWA], it was apparent that the late Premier Thatcher's comments on "Indians breeding like rabbits" still rankles. In addition, the women were aware of cases of involuntary sterilization of native women in other provinces and naturally took exception to this. It is also apparent that, as with non-native women, information on the IUD and the contraceptive pill is very limited ... unless a broad educational campaign on contraception is initiated there will continue to be mistrust and suspicion amongst native people ... Our contact with politically aware native peoples' groups indicates that family planning is not one of their priorities. However, this does not necessarily mean that native women on reserve do not want family planning.[98]

More research on methods of conception control used prior to white settlement was needed, when "native people ... had to control the number of children they had for reasons of survival and were therefore highly motivated."[99]

Family planning information was geared "in attitude" toward the "white middle class city dweller" in its emphasis on the material advantages of not having children and the increased "freedom" resulting from the use of contraception.[100] Isobel McNab, SIWA, had told Williams a better approach would be to emphasize the "strong healthy children" resulting from controlled conception.[101] Williams then directed a comment to the Minister of Public Health regarding the provision of contraceptives free of charge in the North:

> This may have been construed as a policy of genocide on the part of the government since nowhere else in the province is this available. Since a precedent has been set ... we suggest the Public Health Department ... begin distributing free contraceptives to every person in this province needing and wanting [them] ... Any attempt to provide free birth control devices to so-called under-privileged peoples ... which usually refers to native and poor people, will always be construed as genocide."[102]

One could read Williams's words as a warning to government should it want to avoid charges of genocide in relation to its family planning work. They could also be read as directives on how to ensure the increased cooperation of Indigenous people in regulating their own reproduction. Or, by suggesting Public Health provide free birth control to all, she might have been seeking increased financial support for the work of Planned Parenthood Saskatchewan. Whatever the case, her words were in line with the federal position that, by making birth control available to all, policy could focus on Indigenous people without attracting charges of genocide.

Planned Parenthood Saskatchewan engaged family planning initiatives focused on and sometimes in relationship with Indigenous people. It partially funded the Tansch Women's Centre in Meadow Lake in cooperation with the SNWA, to provide family planning to Indigenous and low-income people.[103] Other branches were involved in similar activities.[104] It conducted education programs for the local Native women's association and helped incorporate family planning into counselling services.[105] In Prince Albert, the local coordinator conducted door-to-door visits on ten reserves together with Indian Health Services, and educational programs at the Pinegrove Institute for Women and the Native Women's Halfway House.[106]

In a report from the early 1970s, the SNWA highlighted priorities as the need to address the large number of Indigenous children adopted into white homes; unemployment, poverty, lack of housing, over-incarceration, and alcohol-related issues faced by Indigenous women; and hunting and fishing rights.[107] It was trying to establish daycare centres to help mothers, halfway houses for women transitioning out of prison, counselling services for incarcerated and young women moving from rural to urban centres, and only lastly did it mention birth control information for those who wanted it — but this service should be delivered by Indigenous instructors.[108] Allyson Stevenson writes, two themes figured largely on the SNWA agenda, namely "women's ability to birth and rear children" and "building up the Native family" (2020, 186). She states, "In one meeting, women raised concerns about involuntary sterilizations of Native women in Saskatchewan and suggested speaking to the College of Physicians and Surgeons about the issue. They recognized that they needed to combat what they saw as genocide through forced sterilization and birth control" (186–7). The SNWA highlighted the differences between Indigenous and Canadian society, and that Indigenous women needed to establish their own approaches to dealing with issues under their control and leadership.[109]

While there was a certain amount of collaboration between Planned Parenthood Saskatchewan and Indigenous organizations, it was not always clear who was setting priorities, or under whose "control and leadership" these activities rested. With respect to a "Local Initiatives Project" funding proposal entitled "Health is Wealth" submitted to the federal government, Nadia Greschuk, Executive Officer, Planned Parenthood Saskatchewan, wrote to Lizette Ahenakew, SIWA, with the idea of employing five Indigenous women, four living on the Littler Red River, Sioux Wahpoton, John Smith, and Cumberland House reserves, to conduct a health education program for women.[110] Greschuk wrote: "The following are a few thoughts … that could employ some of your field workers for six months this winter … The task I envision for the project is to … involve women in a health education program … by now you have also received the … application form. What do you think? Should we give it a try?"[111]

The prospect of six months of employment on-reserve, where unemployment rates are often exceptionally high, is not inconsequential. In additional correspondence on this proposal, but with the federal Job Creation Branch, Greschuk wrote that while she was familiar with the socio-economic profile of Indigenous people on reserves, including high unemployment rates, Indigenous "lifestyles" needed to "keep pace" with economic development and monies earmarked for housing would be better spent employing Indigenous women to influence their families to practice "preventative health" — read, family planning — and "utilize health delivery systems more effectively."[112]

In other correspondence a few months before she reached out to SIWA, Greschuk indicated that Planned Parenthood Saskatchewan wanted to initiate discussion on a population policy but was "holding back" because the province still had not formalized a family planning policy.[113] This goal — to establish an explicit population policy — was in step with its parent organization, which had continued lobbying the federal government to adopt a population policy to guide its activities, domestically and internationally.

In June 1976, the federal government announced a formal policy statement was "in the works."[114] In response, Planned Parenthood

Canada convened a workshop to discuss what this policy should look like.[115] It recommended a "Population Policy of Stabilization" working, possibly in five-year increments, to produce a population that would stabilize, then replace itself. This would involve careful monitoring and policies for "Native peoples" and "our bicultural heritage and constitution," and give Canada a role in shaping global population.[116] The policy should rely on "proper contraceptive knowledge," and when necessary, abortion facilities, coupled with "educational courses in population," to help stabilize population levels.[117] Indigenous reproduction was a hindrance to economic development because this development centred on the expropriation of Indigenous lands. Similarly, "underdevelopment" in Indigenous communities was linked to expropriation. To promote family planning would help enable the political economy to continue functioning in a cost-efficient way. Planned Parenthood Saskatchewan's efforts in "collaboration" with Indigenous women's organizations are linked to these broader goals regardless of any desire by Indigenous women to control their reproduction.

In March 1977, federal Minister of Health and Welfare Marc Lalonde announced a new family planning policy:

> I propose now to change the policy underlying these joint objectives of information, training, research and financial assistance from a basic "response to request" to a policy of active promotion and publicity of family planning information ... The availability of family planning services will also be considered in light of the proposed Social Services Legislation, wherein provisions have been made for the universality of availability of such services ... Officials of my Department will be advised to develop and prepare inserts for the Family Allowance cheques in which it will be pointed out that responsible parenthood involves consideration of the use of family planning methods. These steps will serve to reduce the incidence of unwanted children and thereby materially reduce the problems of child neglect, abandonment, desertion, dependency and abuse.[118]

The proposed insert for Family Allowance cheques was dropped following "negative caucus reaction."[119] Federal-provincial "joint promotion of birth planning" would focus on "at risk" groups, with possible targets including those "who now have abortions," "recent immigrants of neither French or English heritage," and "Indians and Inuit."[120] In contrast to a consistent focus on women, the list included "young males."[121]

A "Modern" Family Planning Program in Saskatchewan, 1977

On June 10, 1977, the Saskatchewan Department of Health followed suit with an updated family planning program to guide activities into the 1980s. The "Statement on Family Planning" outlined family planning was an intrinsic part of any "modern" health service, and the department would ensure everyone had access to educational and counselling services through public health staff and grants to agencies, including Planned Parenthood Saskatchewan.[122] Teenage pregnancy was a "critical family planning problem" and on this, it would sponsor studies to inform program development.[123] Its first comprehensive review of the health needs of Saskatchewan children and youth, in 1979, recommended "preventative programs" in the area of teenage pregnancy, including intensive interventions with "high risk" youth.[124] Poverty, age, and Indigenous status were all potential "risk" factors.

In 1982, a Symposium on the Prevention of Adolescent Pregnancy was held with a grant from the federal Family Planning Division allocated through the Saskatchewan Department of Health and the Saskatchewan Chapter of the College of Family Physicians, where presenters compared the behaviour and demographic profile of Indigenous and non-Indigenous adolescents. More than half of Registered Indians and slightly more than one-third of Métis and non-Status Indians were estimated to be under twenty years of age.[125] Chair of Proceedings Margaret Norum explained, people with "higher education" and "special training" pursued educational and occupational goals before having children.[126] While experts should avoid defining adolescent pregnancy as a "problem" in Indigenous cultures, and even if family planning was not compatible with some value systems, for most, poverty was "a way of life" and single parenthood "guarantee[d] they w[ould] remain poor."[127] Dr. Melvyn Lavallée, stated:

> It is safe to say that all Native adolescent females are at a higher risk for succumbing to the social ills in our society. The rapidly changing social and economic scene has shocked

> the Native community and has truly affected its physical and mental health. The Native community has not kept pace and remains highly dependent on bureaucratic services ... As we move along into the 1980s there is evidence to suggest that alcoholism (as well as other rampant social ills) has severely affected all women and especially Native adolescent girls. As a result, the sins of mothers are increasingly visited upon their hapless offspring in the form of child abuse and fetal alcohol syndrome ... the protection of their future offspring must become a public health goal of high priority.[128]

These words reflect the approach underpinning family planning activities in Saskatchewan, based on ideologies that portrayed Indigenous women, particularly young Indigenous mothers, as a threat to their children, communities, and society (Salmon 2004).

The Department of Social Services would contribute to a modern family planning program. Deputy Minister F.J. Bogdasavich agreed to make staff aware of provincial efforts in family planning, assist with research on teenage pregnancy, and provide training to social workers.[129] The legislative mandate to visit all women giving birth "out of wedlock" meant it had useful information at its disposal when dealing with illegitimacy and teenage pregnancy.[130] Under The Children to Unmarried Parents Act, the Director of Vital Statistics was required, on receiving notification of the birth of a child to a single woman, to alert Social Services within thirty days, after which time the director would conduct a "full investigation" in the interest of the child.[131] When a single woman presented for care during pregnancy, the person in charge was required to notify the director within two weeks of the birth of a child using "report of birth form SSS2090."[132] Failure to report could result in conviction for a summary offence and a fine.[133]

The Family Services Act outlined that every person who had information on a child "in need of protection" was required to report this to the appropriate person appointed to enforce the Act.[134] A child in need of protection was without "competent supervision," living in "unfit" circumstances, or whose life, health, or emotional welfare was endangered through caregiver "neglect," when a parent was "unfit, unable or unwilling" to provide care.[135] The department, upon receipt of a report, would investigate and provide services.[136] While a person defined as an "Indian" under the Indian Act was not subject to this legislation unless an agreement had been reached with the federal government, in 1978 this provision was repealed.[137]

The Saskatoon Region was having trouble obtaining information from rural hospitals on births to unmarried women and sent a reminder to comply with the duty to report.[138] The administrator of the Rosetown Hospital, about an hour southwest of Saskatoon, protested that being forced to report a birth by a single woman, even when she chose to forgo supports, was a violation of her rights.[139] Don Cameron, Chairman, Social Services Policy Coordinating Committee, acknowledged compulsory "after the fact" contact was not an efficient approach to the problem of illegitimacy, but "unmarried mothers' supervisors" wanted to retain this legislation and the department would do so, at least until an alternative was developed.[140] Revised legislation went into effect in 1979 and this clause was retained.[141]

The "Services to Single Parents" program operated under this legislation to support "family functioning" and prevent children from becoming "in need of protection."[142] The target group was single and pregnant women, self-referred or referred by another agency, whether public health, hospitals, the Social Aid Program, or Indians Affairs.[143] Referrals might originate from physicians, nursing staff, private social services personnel, government workers, teachers, or clergy.[144] Given it was impossible to conduct a "full investigation" of all single women who gave birth, when a woman had no previous contact with Social Services, or if she was over eighteen years of age and no other concerns were reported, a letter outlining services was mailed out.[145] When the single mother was under eighteen, or if the child was considered "at risk," a worker would visit the woman in hospital, open a file, and record information regardless of whether services were provided.[146] All cases were reviewed by a supervisor, and instances of suspected neglect were referred to a child protection worker.[147] The "Services to Unmarried Parents Committee" thought those living common law, who were pregnant for a second or third time, or who were living on-reserve would benefit from this program.[148]

W.G. Bayne, Social Services Supervisor, was concerned the province was laying itself "wide open for attack through the courts, the media, etc." in its failure to investigate all reports of "neglect, abuse, exploitation or cruel treatment" of children as required under legislation.[149] The policy of intervening in "life or death situations" and then, only at the request of Indian

Affairs, was in contravention of its own laws.[150] In 1980, Social Services released a new policy indicating field workers would remove children from reserves when their safety was in jeopardy if parents refused to voluntarily consent to their placement by Indian Affairs in another home.[151] Bayne again raised concerns. The new policy allowed field workers to decide, without the benefit of a judicial review, that neglect or abuse occurred, but the department could "forget" this if the parent "voluntarily" placed their child in another home.[152] This placed Indigenous parents "between a rock and a hard place" and was a "flagrant abuse" of their rights.[153] Services for families in crisis were inadequate, and Indigenous children were placed in foster homes as a result, without parental consent.[154] Forty years later, this situation has not changed greatly.

Female Single Parents and the Saskatchewan Assistance Plan

In 1978, the province identified the Indigenous birth rate as "the most important demographic trend in Saskatchewan for the next 25 years."[155] Increased urban migration and a birth rate nearly three times the provincial average meant Indigenous people were "grossly over represented in all factors associated with poverty," which was straining provincial services.[156] Indigenous people were not the only ones living in poverty, but they were the "poorest."[157] A "special computer program" extracted data on social assistance cases by region, costs, employment status, female-headed household, and reason for assistance, whether age, ill health, disability, "retardation," desertion of spouse, or "personality problems."[158] The number of Indigenous households facing poverty outnumbered non-Indigenous households five to one, and Registered Indians were five times more likely to be on the Saskatchewan Assistance Plan.[159] Nearly three-quarters of these cases were female-headed families, and 30 percent were women twenty-four years old or younger — an increase of nearly 50 percent from 1977 to 1980.[160] Births to Registered Indian mothers under the age of nineteen were also increasing.[161] In Regina, where approximately 42 percent of all Registered Indians lived, 44 percent of households on social assistance were single and female-headed families.[162] The Métis population "would show at least as badly" if their vital events could be extracted and analyzed.[163] The single parent in need of intervention was female and most likely young, Indigenous, and living in poverty.[164]

In 1982, a "Teen Parent Project" was initiated under the "Services to Single Parents" program to intervene in the lives of young single mothers and their children. Sharon Kelly, Coordinator of Preventative Services, wrote that adolescent pregnancy and childbearing was a significant health and social problem. Young mothers and their children were "a large identifiable group ... at risk ... as a result of social, environmental and biological circumstances." Children parented by teenagers had "significant physical and psychological handicaps," lower IQ scores, higher "retardation" rates, and higher levels of deviant behaviour.[165] The pilot project, begun in Regina and Saskatoon, hired four child development workers to provide in-home demonstrations to mothers on how to interact with their infants, provide employment and family relationship counselling, and initiate referrals.[166] Len Soiseth, Coordinator of Foster Care Services, indicated there was value in this program in "very high risk communities" including Métis settlements at La Loche and Pinehouse, where neglect and teenage pregnancy were high.[167]

The Regina Native Women's Association (RNWA) was approached by Kelly to support the initiative.[168] In a brief submitted to the Social Planning Secretariat, it said it realized "it is us, as Native women and as mothers, who are the most affected by existing problems. We are the largest target group of any future programming and planning." Indigenous women were "doubly disadvantaged" because of their sex and racial origin, and represented a large percentage of adults living in poverty.[169] The RNWA, well aware of the issues facing Indigenous women, had solutions. Indigenous women were no longer prepared to sit back and have "government and male dominated organizations" decide what was best — they wanted to be involved.[170] One of the most important aspects of Indigenous culture was the ability of the family unit to care for its members, but this ability was broken down over centuries.[171] Childcare laws needed to allow for more Indigenous foster parents, field workers should be paid better wages, and supports should be given to single mothers — including more housing options.[172] Funding was needed for Indigenous cultural values to be taught in schools, and incarcerated people needed to be protected from "forms of punishment."[173]

Despite these clearly articulated demands, provincial correspondence indicates Indian Affairs refused to grant any form of financial assistance to Indigenous people living off-reserve for more than a year and there had been a dramatic increase in the number of social assistance cases borne by the province — more than 40 percent between March 1980 and 1981 — and this "did not appear to be slowing down."[174] Chris Bailey, Research Officer, Planning and Evaluation Branch, feared costs could total over $10 million in 1981–82, nearly 30 percent more than the year previous.[175] The province previously acknowledged Indigenous urban poverty was "appalling" and the acceptance of Registered Indians living off-reserve as a provincial responsibility, the approach taken in Alberta, was an inappropriate "policy of legal and cultural genocide."[176] However, a "confidential report" from the Social Services Planning and Evaluations Branch reiterated female-headed, one-parent families received social assistance at a "disproportionate rate" and, referring to the family planning program laid out by the Department of Health, concluded there was an "obvious need" for family planning counselling which, if provided at an early age, could influence whether young women ended up on welfare.[177]

In 1983, the Public Health Division, Department of Health, held health assessment seminars in collaboration with the SNWA and local membership in Prince Albert and Yorkton.[178] The purpose was to obtain grassroots input on "preventative health issues" of importance to Indigenous women but the department identified family planning as a topic of discussion before proceedings began. Fifty-five Indigenous women from across the province attended. There was brief discussion on Indigenous methods of fertility control and how these were undermined through the imposition of "alien" institutions.[179] Indigenous women desired some form of fertility regulation but shyness and fear informed access. The relationship between Indigenous and non-Indigenous people was not "very good," and methods of birth control were not "adequately explained or interpreted to the user."[180]

An excerpt from a report prepared by the Saskatchewan Task Force on Women's Health (STFWH) appended to the "summary of proceedings" identified poverty, an ambivalence toward the imposition of Western culture, health care delivered by white people, and an identity tied to childbearing as primary issues for Indigenous women.[181] The STFWH made a series of recommendations related to Indigenous health that included involving Indigenous women in planning and implementing their own health services; training them as health workers in hospitals and the community; and employing translators and advocates to facilitate informed decision-making.[182] The summary of health assessment seminars facilitated by the SNWA concluded parents should be responsible for educating their children and the decision to practise birth control should rest with them.[183] The RNWA also stated Indigenous women, as "heads of households," should ensure delivery of health or family education programs, but adequate funding was needed.[184]

Indigenous women did not dismiss family planning entirely. The tension existed because Indigenous women had different visions of what this "planning" should look like and who should lead. If Western forms of family planning were incorporated into Indigenous ways, this needed to happen on terms set out by Indigenous people. However, provincial bureaucrats and health and welfare professionals, imbued with racist and paternalistic assumptions, and appearing more concerned with how to balance budgets while containing the "threat" posed by Indigenous reproduction, returned time and again to family planning as a cost-effective means of addressing public health problems that strained government resources, even if they were the ones causing these problems. This tunnel focus led to calls for the coerced sterilization of Indigenous people.

A Proposal in Love, Saskatchewan

On January 24, 1980, a town hall was held in Love, Saskatchewan. With fifty to sixty people in attendance, including McKenzie MP Stan Kordinski, a twelve-member Employment Support Council proposed "there should be a compulsory birth control program for people who can't or won't look after or support their children" with possible sterilization after two children, or less if the person applies for social assistance.[185] Committee Chairman Alvin Tatlow stated children of welfare recipients tended to go on welfare rather than seek work, which left the taxpayer facing a financial burden.[186] This resolution proposed legislation that would require welfare recipients who were not "looking after" their children to submit to sterilization or forfeit their right to assistance (*Leader Post* 1980, 3). It carried with 25 yeas, 4 nays, and 20–25 abstentions.[187]

In his report on this meeting, L.M. Flynn, Northern Supervisor, Employment Support Services, wrote that debate was "lively and open, with people frankly suggesting that Hitler's policies on genocide were good, that the native population would outbreed the white unless we did something about it, and that the people were sick and tired of supporting their neighbors."[188] Problems in this community were likely no different than in any other except perhaps there was greater ignorance of policy and more open racism and intolerance of the poor. Flynn explained, "the economic distance between the haves and have nots ... is very short and this undoubtedly explains some of the greater feelings of anger, hostility and fear of their neighbors and relatives on assistance because of the open knowledge that it is so easy to trade places."[189] Flynn was indirectly acknowledging a purpose of racism, classism, and other ideologies of discrimination — while individuals blame each other for systemic issues linked to exploitative social relations, these relations are allowed to continue unchecked, to the peril of all people.

Rod Durocher, Association of Métis & non-Status Indians of Saskatchewan, referred to the proposal as a "Hitler type" resolution and called Murray Koskie, Minister of Social Services, "gutless" in his response that he was "not particularly excited" about the resolution but needed to study its intention before deciding on its worth.[190] Premier Allan Blakeney stated this did not represent government policy, but the Committee had a right to express its opinions — diversity of opinion was a "hallmark of this province" and made Saskatchewan "one of the most exciting" places to live (*Leader Post* 1980, 3). Journalist Clare Powell reported on the irresponsibility of this statement:

> Blakeney makes being a bigot or a racist sound like a virtue! Do we want diversity of opinion that suggests that Indians or welfare recipients should be treated as sub-human? That those whose religious or political beliefs are different from the status quo should be thrown in jail or tortured? Or that witches should be burned at the stake? ... these and worse things have occurred in countries where people with "diverse" opinions went unchallenged and finally got the opportunity to put their opinions into practice. (1980, 7)

Durocher subsequently wrote to Koskie that to contemplate the sterilization of welfare recipients was "disgusting," and to blame Indigenous people for the failures of the economy was a "trick" used by racist governments.[191]

Despite receiving numerous letters of support, Koskie released a statement indicating "no needy person in Saskatchewan will ever have to surrender his or her ability to have children as the price for receiving social assistance. The idea is extreme and does not merit consideration by this government."[192] However, he continued:

> We need to do more than just reject one mistaken idea. The problems of child abuse and neglect are very real. Every day, government and the province must deal with such tragic situations. I am charged by the Family Services Act with legal responsibility for protecting children whose wellbeing is threatened. Further, The Children of Unmarried Parents Act provides legal recourse for obtaining financial assistance for children whose parents are not married. These Acts and their related programs provide the means for detecting and preventing child abuse, and shielding its victims. I call on all who are concerned to join in actively supporting this province's child protection program.[193]

Koskie was affirming the federal family planning policy announced in 1977, and reinforcing a link between the costly burden posed by those living in poverty and child abuse and neglect among young and single mothers — who were disproportionately established to be Indigenous. Shelagh Day, Saskatchewan Human Rights Commission, stated the Love proposal influenced how people felt (*Prince Albert Daily Herald* 1980, 2). Considering the large number of Indigenous women reporting coerced sterilization since the 1970s, it is safe to conclude this resolution and the context informing it also impacted how people were treated.

The Advisory Committee on Family Planning, 1993

In the 1990s, Saskatchewan initiated major health reform based on a "wellness approach" meant to encourage a "healthy life" by reducing disparities in "preventable deaths, disability and illness" within populations.[194] Family planning was central to this.[195] Louise Simard, Minister of Health, appointed a second Advisory Committee on Family Planning to advise on how to promote reproductive health, healthy pregnancies, and healthy births by improving access to family planning programs, particularly for adolescents; recommend implementation strategies and resources allocation; examine economic, psychosocial, and educational issues contributing to unintended pregnancy; and facilitate cooperation between stakeholders.[196] It received seventy-four submissions and held consultations with community groups.[197]

The Advisory Committee found considerable progress had been made on unintended pregnancies but by 1987, funding cuts to family planning programs meant Saskatchewan still had the second highest provincial teen pregnancy rate, fourth overall behind Manitoba, the Yukon, and the Northwest Territories.[198] In 1991, the number of births to married teenage mothers was 48 percent lower than in 1987, but over 90 percent of teen births were to single mothers, resulting from "desperate socio-economic conditions on many reserves," "urban poverty," "geographic isolation," and "substance abuse."[199] Its focus would be on health and social issues that had gained recent attention, including violence against women; gender inequities in health; the rising incidence of HIV/AIDS acquired through unprotected sex or drug use; and the role of substance abuse in perpetuating cycles of violence, abuse, and poverty.[200]

To better understand the needs of Indigenous people, a single-day consultation was held with "about fifty people" from "a variety of Aboriginal groups." Those in attendance agreed young women were having babies, often lacked parenting skills, and substance abuse played a role in unintended pregnancy.[201] They recommended family planning information in schools, but material should be culturally relevant and focused on methods grounded in Indigenous value systems. It was important to raise self-esteem among youth, and family planning should be taught on reserves and to Indigenous foster parents, but Elders should have a role in educating youth.[202] Aside from a mention that family planning programs should be "culturally sensitive," none of these recommendations appear in the Advisory Committee's proposed sexual and reproductive health strategy.[203] It implemented a "Family Planning Community Grants Program" to foster cooperation among community groups to reduce unintended teenage pregnancy through increased access to family planning, established a provincial toll-free "facts of life" referral line on a sexual and reproductive health issues, and recommended government continue promoting family planning as an essential component of healthcare reform, with district health boards providing services tracked via a geographic information system.[204]

In 1993, the Regina Health Board identified family planning services for youth as a community need and entered into a contract with Planned Parenthood Regina to initiate a youth-focused reproductive health clinic.[205] Despite this partnership, Barb Shonhoffer, Executive Director, Planned Parenthood Regina, requested a meeting with Health Minister Eric Cline to secure increased funding. He directed her to speak directly with the Regina Health District.[206] This request was followed by another from Bonnie Johnson, Executive Director, Planned Parenthood Canada, who stressed a continued need for government support.[207] Poverty was the greatest indicator of unintended teenage pregnancy, and in times of economic contraction and cuts to health care, government needed to recognize the "long term real dollar costs associated with short term savings." Planned Parenthood services were "cost-effective prevention."[208] However, the role of Planned Parenthood was one of "community activator," providing services until other agencies could take over.[209] By the mid-1990s, health districts began to do just this.

When the Advisory Committee released its second report in 1995, statistics showed the number of teen births had increased over 3 percent.[210] The proportion of children in the population was expected to decline, but that of Registered Indian children and youth was expected to increase.[211] There was a continuing need for "concerted, coordinated and integrated efforts" to address sexual and reproductive health among "high risk and marginalized" individuals and groups.[212] Comprehensive solutions were needed to address the complexities of teen pregnancy, sexually transmitted diseases, and HIV/AIDS — private issues, but with "so many public dimensions."[213] To these ends, it undertook a first initiative in collaboration with the Saskatchewan Institute for Prevention of Handicaps (SIPH), focused on alcohol abuse prevention among young, pregnant, and Indigenous women.

Ann Schulman, Chair of the Advisory Committee, was Executive Director of the SIPH, which had been involved in alcohol prevention activities since the 1980s. As a public health issue, alcohol abuse intersected with the concerns of the Advisory Committee in the notion that excessive drinking could lead to unintended pregnancies among "high risk" populations and consequent adverse health outcomes for women and children. Those experiencing "child neglect, family dysfunction, violence and abuse, substance abuse, disabilities, and multiple health problems" were at risk of unintended and problem pregnancies.[214] Those most "at risk" lived in poverty as young single parents and Indigenous people were overrepresented in this group.[215] This "preventative program" reinforced the labelling of Indigenous children as suffering birth defects purportedly caused by alcohol abuse on the part of their mothers during pregnancy, and resulted in the surveillance, criminalization, and sometimes sterilization, of Indigenous women.

Fetal Alcohol Syndrome and the Policing of Indigenous Mothers

Researchers Kenneth Jones and David Smith (1973) first described fetal alcohol syndrome (FAS) as a condition based on anomalies in infants born to women who ingest alcohol while pregnant. The diagnosis is marked by the presence of pre- and/or post-natal growth deficiency (e.g., low birth weight and height); central nervous system dysfunction; and characteristic cranio-facial malformations (e.g., short palpebral fissures [short eye slits], flat upper lip, flattened philtrum [the groove between the nose and upper lip], and a flat mid-face) (Tait 2003, 8). Fetal Alcohol Effects (FAE), often discussed in the same breath as FAS, refers to other potential "Alcohol-Related Birth Effects" including "behavioural" or "cognitive" problems in children exposed to alcohol in utero but not presenting with the diagnostic features of FAS. This term has been subject to criticism for a lack of precision (Tait 2003, 9).

The first case of FAS in Canada was diagnosed at the Royal University Hospital, Saskatoon, in the 1970s (SIPH 1997). Saskatchewan became a centre of research and treatment through the Alvin Buckwold Child Development Program (ABCDP) (Habbick, Nanson, Snyder et al. 1996, 204). The ABCDP, associated with the Kinsmen Children's Centre, is a major referral centre for children with mental and physical "handicaps" from Central and Northern Saskatchewan. It opened as the Alvin Buckwold "Mental Retardation Unit" in the 1960s, offering assessment, guidance, and treatment for individuals; training for medical students and paramedical personnel; and research into the "causes" of "mental retardation."[216] By the 1990s, the Kinsmen Children's Centre had an FAS/FAE clinic with a team including a pediatrician, psychologist, physiotherapist, speech therapist, and social worker, which travelled to remote areas to assist with diagnosis before satellite clinics were opened in North Battleford and La Ronge.[217]

In a study considering the incidence of FAS in Saskatchewan over a twenty-year period, Brian Habbick, Josephine Nanson, Richard Snyder et al. (1996) found that out of 207 identified cases of FAS, 178, or 86 percent, were among Indigenous children. Of these cases, only 25 percent were living with their biological parents, 72 percent had been in foster care, and most had an IQ of less than 70. The overall incidence rate of FAS had remained steady, averaging 0.585 per 1,000 live births, but was higher in Indigenous populations. In a study of children diagnosed with FAS at two Vancouver hospitals, researchers extrapolated the prevalence of FAS in Indigenous communities surpassed non-Indigenous people 10:1 (Sandor, Smith, MacLeod et al. 1981). Habbick, Nanson, Snyder, et al. concluded, considering public education and professional training programs had failed to lower the incidence of FAS, new strategies, potentially targeting "high risk" women, were needed (1996, 206-7).

The claim that FAS/FAE is more prevalent among Indigenous children is "questionable" (Tait 2003, esp. 93–120). To make a valid comparison of FAS/FAE rates between Indigenous and non-Indigenous people is difficult considering differences among and between populations (Bray and Anderson 1989). Standard diagnostic criteria, including IQ tests, do not always apply across cultures, and facial characteristics can differ between Indigenous and non-Indigenous people, making it problematic to rely on this as a criterion for diagnosis (Abel 1998). The idea that Indigenous people consume excessive amounts of alcohol on a regular basis or possess a genetic predisposition to alcohol consumption is false (Tait 2003). Indigenous mothers are no more likely to drink alcohol (Godel, Pabst, Hodges et al. 1992) and may be *more likely* to abstain than men and non-Indigenous women (Roberts and Nanson 2000).

A survey of physicians in Saskatchewan uncovered a "detection bias" may play a role in the high FAS prevalence rate among Indigenous people (Nanson, Bolaria, Snyder et al. 1995), a bias that also influences the decision to place children in state care (Trocmé, MacLaurin, Fallon et al. 2006). To say symptoms linked to FAS/FAE reflect a mother's alcohol consumption overlooks possible confounding factors that can lead to associated symptoms — whether poverty and food insecurities, vulnerability to violence, lack of prenatal care, or environmental pollution — all of which impact fetal development and are realities for many Indigenous mothers (Tait 2008; Wiebe and Konsmo 2014). A diagnosis of FAS/FAE locates the causes of these symptoms within Indigenous children and their mothers.

The 1990s saw a wave of funding to increase awareness on the "causes" and "effects" of alcohol consumption during pregnancy.[218] A Fetal Alcohol Syndrome Coordinating Committee, formed in 1993 and headed by the SIPH, enabled cross-collaboration between organizations, all levels of government, and the community.[219] In 1996, Minister Cline announced funding for the "FAS/FAE in Saskatchewan: Programming for Education and Prevention Initiative," led by the SIPH, to "prevent" and "intervene" in FAS/FAE.[220] In her extensive work on the subject, Caroline Tait states, out of twenty community development initiatives, "sixteen were located in reserve communities, and the other four urban and prison based initiatives were run by Aboriginal organizations or had a strong Aboriginal component" (2003, 316). Professionals often view pregnant Indigenous women as "high risk" due to a "culture of pathology" and inability to make "good lifestyle choices" (Tait 2008, 71). Reflecting the "tangle of pathology" and "culture of poverty" discourses, this "uncritical approach" taken by practitioners, policy makers, and governments reinforces the belief that Indigenous women and their children are not only at higher risk for FAS but may constitute the entire risk group (71).

As a result, Indigenous women have been "singled out as objects of blame for the extra lifetime costs they will incur to society" (Salmon 2004, 117) if they or their children are left untreated. Minister Cline estimated over five hundred children were treated in twenty years, and an additional ten cases were born each year. This represented "staggering costs" for health, education, social services, and justice sectors, estimated at $1 million for each child.[221] Lorne Calvert, Minister of Social Services, agreed FAS-diagnosed children required significant support and his department would collaborate on provincial initiatives.[222]

The federal government also promoted FAS/FAE initiatives. In 1999, it offered $11 million dollars for a national strategy focused on prevention, awareness, and surveillance.[223] In 2001, it provided another $25 million for initiatives that identified young Indigenous women on reserves as a primary target (Salmon 2004). Indigenous communities sometimes implement FAS/FAE initiatives and access grants from the provincial and federal government.[224] However, Tait cautions, Indigenous involvement is not simple; some communities "take ownership" by using this as an opportunity to secure increased support for much needed community programs, while others remain worried about the impact of engaging with a "government ploy" to undermine their communities (2003, 316–17).

In 1999, the Advisory Committee began supplementing SIPH "prevention and intervention efforts" for "at risk and chemically dependent women" in Métis and off-reserve Indigenous communities.[225] Judy Junor, Associate Minister of Health, indicated that through increased funding, Saskatchewan Health would continue its "tradition of silent partner" in community-based programming.[226] This included the Baby Safe program for pregnant women using alcohol in Prince Albert; FAS/FAE educational sessions for provincial judges; supports for women in treatment facilities; and training for workers at young offender facilities to assist in identifying FAS/FAE clientele.[227] Tait writes, training sessions were often "oversimplified," offering "only a basic understanding" of FAS/FAE, and leaving workers with the assumption they could identify a "typical" person with the condition without any medical assessment (2008, 73). Her review of support programs revealed "very few to none" of those identified with FAS were medically assessed or diagnosed (Tait 2003, 18, 148–9).

At an FAS/FAE "Train the Trainer" conference, Gitxsan speaker Audrey Lunquist highlighted that FAS was a "complex issue" linked to colonialism and jurisdictional disputes; it was one of many manifestations of the damage done to Indigenous Peoples.[228] To effectively address the issue, governments needed to negotiate land and political rights with Indigenous Peoples and help strengthen and rebuild Indigenous values, beliefs, and cultural and spiritual practices.[229] The provincial approach, while purporting to be "community focused, non-stigmatizing, and culturally sensitive," focused on the individual, leaving unaddressed the confluence of factors impacting the health and well-being of Indigenous women and children.[230] In one instance, Saskatchewan Health turned down a proposal to establish a clinical teratology program at the University of Saskatchewan to consider the effects of methyl mercury, lead, polychlorinated biphenyls, and other environmental contaminants on fetal development, in addition to alcohol or other drugs, because of the magnitude of its budget.[231] The failure to consider broader determinants of health is especially problematic considering only 5 percent of birth defects are estimated to be the result of prenatal exposure to teratogens.[232]

Psychologist Josephine Nanson (1997), associated with the ABCDP and Royal University Hospital, indicated many women she encountered at the FAS clinic drank as a way of coping with emotional pain. For Indigenous women, emotional pain stemming from violence and abuse needs to be understood within broader social relations of oppression. However, the portrayal of an FAS "epidemic" in Indigenous communities pushed programming beyond "preventing pregnant women from drinking alcohol," and toward "pregnancy prevention," including through long-acting contraception and sterilization (Tait 2008, 69).

The long-acting hormonal contraceptive Depo-Provera, which inhibits conception for up to three months, has a history of being imposed on young, Indigenous, and other racialized women as a form of chemical sterilization (Lewis 1995; Roberts 2016; Sarra 1982; Smith 2005; Stote 2012). Tait found that physicians and clinics serving high concentrations of Indigenous people regularly prescribed Depo-Provera, sometimes to young girls thought to be unable to "take a pill every day," to prevent pregnancy *and* FAS (2008, 73). In one case, a "high risk" Indigenous woman consented to tubal ligation following the birth of her son after nurses told her he was born with "debilitating health problems" due to her substance abuse (Tait 2013, 3). She writes, "elevated fertility rates among Indigenous populations imply to many Canadians that the 'Indian problem' will increase exponentially if solutions are not found. The added dimension of a serious illness such as FAS further fuels this sense of urgency" (2008, 75).

The FAS/FAE "epidemic" affecting Indigenous communities has fuelled and been fuelled by racist stereotypes that resulted in calls to regulate Indigenous reproduction in the name of public health. In one instance, in correspondence to the Minister of Health, a member of the public highlighted FAS/FAE was "particularly prevalent" among Indigenous people and offered to single-handedly put together a "prevention-awareness-education" program for use in schools and on reserves; all he needed was a government salary and vehicle.[233] The author attached an editorial by Jim Short appearing in the *Saskatoon Star Phoenix* that linked the prevalence of FAS to Indigenous women and their children, and blamed the death of a white woman on the province's failure to "take effective action." Short wrote the province should be less afraid of "hurting the feelings of the Indians" and not "shrink from shaming both the establishment and Indian people into action" (1999, A17).

The death referred to was the 1997 killing of a woman who operated a group home in North Battleford at the hands of two fifteen-year-old Indigenous girls in her care, both of whom were tried as adults and sentenced to life for the crime (Zakreski 1999). The press focused on the "troubled life" of one girl, placed in the home as part of a manslaughter sentence issued for a previous offence (Perraux 1999, A1). She had a childhood "fraught with violence, neglect and alcohol abuse," and was diagnosed with FAS during her first trial (Zakreski 1999, E1). When asked about the case, Sherrie Tutt, a former nurse who taught Indigenous Health at Saskatchewan Indian Federated College, stated "alcohol abuse is much higher amongst Native people, and this is strictly connected to alcohol use of the mother. Because [of this] ... fetal alcohol syndrome is higher. I think it's a pretty direct equation" (cited in Zakreski 1999, E1).

In another article published in the *Star Phoenix*, journalist Randy Burton described FAS as a "time bomb under the seat of Saskatchewan society," and those who suffered brain damage because of their mothers drinking were "permanently damaged" with "no conscience" or "hope of recovery" (1999, A2). He cited Nanson, the psychologist associated with the ABCDP, who believed at least half of young offenders were affected by FAS because their mothers drank during pregnancy. The price society was paying, which she estimated at more than $300 million, was becoming "increasingly apparent" through "a series of high-profile crimes across the country" resulting from the condition, including the armed standoff at Gustafson Lake, British Columbia (cited in Burton 1999, A2).

The 1995 "standoff" at Gustafson Lake involved Ts'Peten land defenders of the Secwepemc Nation asserting their right to practise the Sun Dance on Secwepemc lands, which were not ceded or surrendered but claimed as personal property by a cattle rancher (Shrubsole and Lackenbauer 2014). The RCMP attempted to remove land defenders in one of the largest paramilitary operations in provincial history. It is not clear why Nanson referred to this event as resulting from FAS or how she could have known about the health status of individuals involved, but to criminalize and pathologize Indigenous people has done much to enable land theft.

Raymond Denson, a psychiatrist who worked twenty-seven years with the Saskatchewan Psychiatric Services Branch but later transferred to Lakehead Psychiatric Hospital, Thunder Bay, suggested to Pat Atkinson, Minister of Health, cash "bonuses" for "any female alcoholic of reproductive age" who agreed to sterilization. Denson explained, a single case of "severe retardation" might cost the community over $1 million over an individual's lifetime; to offer bonuses to two hundred "alcoholic females" would be of significant financial benefit, and considering the "voluntariness" of the program, it would be free from "racist overtones" and avoid contravening human rights.[234] Judy Junor, Associate Minister of Health, responded that while she understood Denson would like to see this type of program, it would raise ethical and legal questions and was not something government would support.[235]

What Denson suggested was not new. By this time, at least thirteen America states had introduced legislative proposals to offer impoverished women cash incentives if they agreed to long-acting contraceptives (Hardon 1992). In some instances, additional benefits for children born to women receiving public assistance were denied as a means of reducing welfare costs (Roberts 1995). In others, women convicted of child or drug abuse were ordered to submit to long-acting contraceptives or face jail time (Ginzberg 1992; Scully 2000). All these examples had racial undertones, leading Dorothy Roberts to conclude that contraceptive welfare proposals "in the name of science, social policy, or fiscal restraint" disguise "racist and classist judgments about who deserves to bear children ... [and] a belief that impoverished people, especially Blacks [or Indigenous people], are less entitled to be parents" (1995, 944).

Canada had its own examples. In 1994, the government of Alberta covered the cost of Norplant, another long-acting contraceptive, for welfare recipients. Alice Hanson, Edmonton-Highlands-Beverley representative, claimed government approval of the drug was a veiled attempt to lower welfare costs (Verburg 1994). Nancy Miller, Calgary Project Coordinator, Alberta Status of Women, criticized the province for funding Norplant as it cut social assistance, and was concerned women felt pressured to consent to the drug for fear of having their benefits revoked (Lewis 1995). Larry Shipka, Director of Pharmacy Services, Alberta Health, replied that he was aware of controversy surrounding Norplant, but its adoption was based on a federal safety assessment; it remained an option, particularly for the "non-compliant patient who has trouble taking medication on a daily basis" (cited in Coutts 1994, A7).

In another instance, a Manitoba judge ordered the forcible detention of Ms. G, a young and pregnant Indigenous mother, to the Health Sciences Centre, Winnipeg, to undergo substance abuse treatment until childbirth on the basis that her glue-sniffing addiction placed her fetus at risk of developmental harm (Dawson 1998). This order was overruled but Child and Family Services appealed to the Supreme Court of Canada.[236] Interveners saw this as part of a broader trend of criminalizing Indigenous women under the pretense they are "bad mothers," and in this case, despite the woman giving birth to a healthy child. That this woman was young, Indigenous, indigent, had repeated pregnancies, and lacked resources to deal with these problems informed the request to have her held against her will (McCormack 1999, 79).

Indigenous people experience life-threatening effects from living under colonialism that sometimes result in personal, social, and public health problems. To acknowledge this does not negate their uncompromising strength, beauty, and health. However, to name these issues as individual defects ignores their broader causes and is to pathologize, criminalize, and deny the humanity of Indigenous women as it reinforces violent and unhealthy social relations. FAS/FAE is not a neutral diagnosis, it must be located in a broader context that acknowledges the "persistent colonial practices of the Canadian Nation-State, unequal and oppressive gender and race relations, inadequate access to resources and services on and off reserves, political under-representation at the local, provincial, and national levels of government, poverty, and on-going State intrusion into ... families and communities" (Salmon 2004, 121).

We must also remember Indigenous Peoples have histories of dealing with problems in their communities in their own ways and on their own term, histories that pre-date colonialism. In commenting on the trend of diagnosing Indigenous children as "special needs," including as suffering from FAE/FAS, Oneida scholar Roland Chrisjohn (1999) writes:

> In speaking with traditional people and elders in several different communities, they were unanimous in asserting that there was no such thing as a "special needs" child in former times. They didn't mean that there weren't occasions where some physical or even psychological problems arose, or that everyone was more-or-less moderately competent at everything. They meant that everyone was respected for the strengths and weaknesses they brought to the life of their community ... People weren't "fiscal burdens" on the "competitive economic well-being" of a society; they were people. The interdependence of all the members of any society wasn't hidden behind commodity production or specialization, and that interdependence was not seen as a weakness of some sort. Rather, it was taken as the fundamental meaning of "community." In diversity was strength, and the underlying tenet of First Nations societies was that greater ability justified greater

responsibility, not greater privilege. How distant this reality is from a system built to foster privilege, and blame inequities in the quality of life on largely internal and unchangeable defects of individual people ... The issues surrounding special needs and First Nations are not medical or psychological; they are historical, economic, and moral.

This review demonstrates a consistent concern on the part of decision makers with the "fiscal burden" Indigenous reproduction poses to the "economic well-being" (Chrisjohn 1999) of Canadian society. Rather than address longstanding historical material relations giving rise to public health issues, a family planning approach has further criminalized and pathologized Indigenous women, framing them as "an enemy of the state" (Cull 2006, 144).

The systemic racism and paternalistic arrogance reflected in the words of a long line of bureaucrats, coupled with more than fifty years of actions and inactions, laws and policies, and a failure of government officials, together with health and welfare workers, researchers, journalists, and community members, to acknowledge how colonialism shapes Indigenous lives, implicates all of us in the denial of their humanity. In our collective failure to end this violence and work in relationship with Indigenous Peoples to build alternative ways of relating to each other and the land, a genocide is being carried out; one that is feeding a system that ultimately, will not serve any of us. The next chapter considers the significance of the historical, political, economic, and policy context sketched out thus far as it intersects in the reproductive lives of Indigenous women to inform their reproductive choices, or lack thereof, through coerced sterilization — a most intimate form of violence that is directly connected to the ongoing violence committed against Indigenous lands.

5

The Coerced Sterilization of Indigenous Women in Modern Times

> [Was] sterilization abuse prompted by individual racism among doctors? Were their actions a dying gasp of government sanctioned eugenics ... or was it a reprisal for gains in Indigenous sovereignty? Violations against the reproductive rights of Indigenous women did not occur because of the efforts of any one individual or agency, nor can a single explanation or theory account for them. Rather, these violations resulted from sexism and racism, remnants of eugenics, population-control measures, and family-planning programs that drew large subsidies from the federal government. Complicating this situation are the unique political and social realities of Indigenous peoples, who were often dependent on ... government for health care while also demanding federal recognition of their ... land and sovereignty. (Ralstin-Lewis 2005, 72)

Indigenous women began publicly sharing their experiences of coerced sterilization in 2015. When interviewed by reporter Betty Ann Adam (Adam 2015a), B.P. described how healthcare workers forced the procedure on her after the birth of her child at the Royal University Hospital, Saskatoon, in 2010. As a recovering addict in a methadone program, she recounted being pressured by medical staff and social workers to consent to sterilization despite protests she "didn't want it done," and expressed this was because she was "Native," "a recovering addict," "low income," and had just delivered her seventh child: "Anything that they could use against me was used against me" (cited in Crozier 2017). B.P. was followed by T.B., who described how, in 2012, a nurse and members of a family support team repeatedly urged her to consent to sterilization after the birth of her ninth child (Adam 2015a). In T.B.'s case, her obstetrician intervened to stop the sterilization.

The act of these women sharing their experiences opened the flood gates for others, including R.L., a recovering addict and HIV-positive woman, who was told she needed to be sterilized or face being called a "negligent mother," in 2006 (*CBC News* 2015b). M.P., a single mother of two, was pressured to consent to sterilization while in full labour and preparing to undergo an emergency C-section, in 2008 (*CBC News* 2015a). S.L. described how she was sterilized in 2010 after the birth of her sixth child (Flett 2016). She recalled being "talked into" the procedure, which she did not want, and when she attempted to push her wheelchair away, was "turned around" by a doctor and sterilized without consent (*CBC News* 2015c). Over one hundred Indigenous women from across Canada have come forward with their own unique yet similar experiences, and proposed class action lawsuits are pending across the country.[1] A civil suit was also launched on behalf of an Inuk woman sterilized without consent in 2019 at the Stanton Yellowknife Hospital, Northwest Territories (Zingel 2022).

Alisa Lombard, lead counsel in the proposed class action in Saskatchewan, stated, of the women who have contacted her, at least sixty-four are from that province — all are Indigenous.[2] In summarizing their experiences, Lombard expanded:

> The women report going into hospital to have a baby, being pressured into signing a consent form while in the throes of labour and the immediate aftermath of delivery or not signing consent forms at all. In most cases, women report being told that the procedure was reversible ... They would be approached, harassed, coerced into signing these consent forms or simply told that they could not leave before their tubes were tied or cut or cauterized, depending on the procedure that was used, or that they could not see their baby until they agreed, or that [Children's Aid Society] would be called or that they had to do this for their own health, for their children's health because they may have children who won't be healthy. (Cited in *CBC Radio* 2018)

These women are significant as the first to share their experiences publicly. Their stories demonstrate how a history of family planning policy and practice has intersected with a systemic racism resulting from colonialism to inform coerced sterilizations since the 1970s.

The Saskatoon Health Region Response

The act of women coming forward triggered an amendment to the tubal ligation consent policy in Saskatoon Health Region (SHR) hospitals. The "Post Partum Tubal Ligation Policy Number PP 7-3.6" outlined that a nurse could identify a patient requesting tubal ligation within seventy-two hours of delivery and while informed consent was required, a patient was kept in "holding" until it was obtained — a situation that may have created pressure to obtain consent in an "efficient" manner to "move the patient along."[3] The revised "Post Partum Tubal Ligation Policy Number 1300," implemented in October 2016, specified any patient delivering vaginally needed to discuss tubal ligation with her physician before admission to hospital and this discussion must be documented on the prenatal record.[4] If this did not take place, a woman needed to wait to be seen as an outpatient at a later date.[5] Women requiring emergency C-sections would no longer be offered sterilization as part of this "sudden urgent surgery."[6] In non-emergent cases, a woman could be offered the choice to be sterilized at the time of consent for a C-section, prior to hospitalization.[7] Jackie Mann, Vice-President of Integrated Health Service, said this new policy would ensure women "had that conversation [about tubal ligation] with her physician prior to coming to the hospital."[8] However, it was immediately criticized by health professionals and Indigenous women for negatively impacting those who wanted to be sterilized after childbirth but were without a family doctor or obstetrician prenatally with whom they could discuss this option.[9] The revised policy made it more difficult for those coming from northern areas to give birth in urban centres to make this choice.[10] It also did not stop coerced sterilization.

In May 2019, Lombard described the experience of an Indigenous woman who was sterilized in December 2018 — two years after this policy went into effect.[11] D.D.S., a Nakota woman scheduled for delivery of her third child by C-section, was pressured by the attending doctor to such an extent she believed she had no choice but to sign a consent for sterilization, despite her desire for more children.[12] Lombard's review of this woman's medical records, created by many different medical professionals, revealed repeated references to her Indigeneity, employment and marital status, and the number of pregnancies and miscarriages characterized as abortions that she experienced.[13]

Internal Ministry of Health correspondence indicates that health regions are expected to provide "patient centred, safe and high quality care" to all, including by ensuring "free, prior and informed consent" for any medical procedure.[14] However, the newly implemented policy did not define what constituted "free, prior and informed consent."[15] The Ministry noted, all patients who came forward were from "visible minority groups" — they were Indigenous. It feared parallels drawn in the media between these instances and the "historical mistreatment and sterilization of First Nations, Métis and marginalized populations in Canada," and other forms of "mistreatment and cultural insensitivity in the medical system."[16] Yet rather than acknowledge how it was implicated in this history, it expressed concern with the "insinuation" these "unfortunate incidents" resulted from government directives.[17] Clinical decisions involved patients and their physician and care team; to suggest coercion because of government policy was "offensive, inflammatory, and flat-out wrong."[18] It failed to recognize how a history of family planning policy and practice approaching Indigenous reproduction as something needing to be curbed may have contributed to these circumstances.

Despite these deflections, in February 2016, the SHR retained retired Justice Merri-Ellen Wright to "work with" those who had come forward to build a "collaborative process" of change.[19] By June, it quietly terminated Wright's contract. The CEO of the SHR claimed attempts to contact the original two complainants were initially unsuccessful, and once contacted, these women did not respond to requests for interviews. Hence, it had no choice but to suspend the review (*Star Phoenix* 2016). Yet at least one woman, M.P., expressed "outrage" she was not asked to participate despite having spoken publicly (Charlton 2016, A8). Leanne Smith, Director of Maternal Services, said she was aware of media stories reporting on this woman's experience, but was unable to locate a phone number for her and besides, she was not sure she wanted to be contacted (*Star Phoenix* 2016). An editorial in the *Saskatoon Star Phoenix* suggested the province put less than "full effort" into making contact (2016, A8). M.P. spoke out again, stating that by terminating the review, the province was effectively denying systemic racism and genocide through sterilization (Charlton 2016).

The Restart of the External Review, 2017

Public pressure placed on the province by women like M.P. resulted in the SHR retaining the services of Yvonne Boyer and Judith Bartlett, in

January 2017, to "restart" the External Review.[20] The review, limited to those who experienced coercion "post-delivery," led to the exclusion of at least one woman coerced to consent to sterilization while pregnant.[21] It focused only on the SHR, one of thirteen health regions in the province. Boyer and Bartlett identified other limitations, including the anxiety women may experience in coming forward and their fear of potential breaches in privacy and confidentially; that a previous review was attempted but failed; its narrow timing and short duration; and the deep mistrust among Indigenous women stemming from their experiences of systemic racism within and outside health care.[22] The review sought input from those who had negative experiences to support them in telling their stories, to assess tubal ligation processes and the broader SHR environment to better understand how these contributed to women's experiences, and to provide recommendations going forward.[23]

Sixteen women contacted Boyer and Bartlett. The review documented the experiences of seven, who described receiving no explanation or a misrepresentation of the permanency of sterilization. In some cases, healthcare providers advised them the decision to have a tubal ligation was "in their best interest," but failed to fully explain the procedure in terms that were understandable.[24] One woman said, "It was just, like, we're going to do this," and after, "I wasn't told anything, no explanation that it was permanent."[25] They described being harassed by labour and delivery staff or social workers until they signed a consent form, which sometimes involved the use of scare tactics about potential health dangers they or their children would face if a tubal ligation was not done.[26] Some reported having their wishes ignored while being subject to physical and psychological pressure, which made them feel powerless to stop the procedure. Boyer and Bartlett concluded these were all signs of a power differential between Indigenous women in labour and healthcare providers. In one instance, a woman indicated she told the anesthesiologist directly "I don't want this" before the procedure was performed against her will.[27] All those interviewed were clear: they either were coerced, felt coerced, or felt an attempt to be coerced into sterilization by health professionals or social workers operating under the mandate of the Ministry of Social Services.[28]

Interviews conducted with care providers revealed covert and overt forms of racism in the hospital environment with some staff holding openly racist views towards Indigenous women. One provider stated, "I do think there may be coercion but I don't think it's in your face type of, 'have a tubal ligation or else.'" Another said, "staff — and it may well be that the physicians involved as well — sit around the desk and talk about women having five children, and four have been apprehended — 'it's time to stop.'"[29] Some expressed concerns about what may be happening to Indigenous women in their care to such an extent at least one submitted a formal complaint to a charge nurse about racial bias.[30] The reviewers emphasized the "grave concerns" raised by those they spoke with on how Child and Family Services (CFS) staff operating under a mandate from the Ministry of Social Services interacted with hospital staff and the "harsh consequences" experienced by Indigenous women who had previous involvement with CFS.[31]

The Birth Alert Practice

The interconnections between the department of health and social services in policing young, single, and Indigenous women have been well documented. By the 1990s, the Children of Unmarried Parents Act and the Family Services Act merged into the Child and Family Services Act and any reference to "single mothers" was dropped. However, section 12(1) continues to require every person who believes a child is "in need of protection" to report this information to a "designated official," whether a child protection worker in the Ministry of Social Services, a First Nation Child and Family Services Agency, or a peace (police) officer, who must investigate.[32] The Ministry of Social Services, through CFS, then issues an alert to the Saskatchewan Health Authority (SHA, which the SHR is now part of, since twelve regional health authorities transitioned to a single provincial health authority), and maternal units are tasked with monitoring these alerts. When a mother presents to access care, the unit social work team contacts CFS, at which point it becomes directly involved with the patient.[33] This "birth alert" practice, which can result in newborns of "at risk" mothers being apprehended at birth, has disproportionately impacted Indigenous women.

In her extensive research on the involvement of the child welfare system in Indigenous lives, Allyson Stevenson interviewed Nora Thibodeau, who described her experience as follows:

> When ... I had my four children and I was pregnant with my fifth ... They decided that because my first husband and

> I separated ... they tried to take my children. "We will give you the oldest boy, and we will take the younger boy and the babies." I said you will take nothing ... And I remember he had his feet up and I took his feet, and I said, "Send a social worker to my house, I will hammer her. You are not taking my babies." And they didn't take my babies. Cause I stood up for me. And I know how they did it ... I had a half-sister who moved away to Edmonton and they tried to take her baby. And these things happened in the city and they happened on the reserve and they happened in our community ... I was more fortunate because I had my mom, my grandmother, my aunties. I was more fortunate. Other Métis didn't have that support. And fell into that system, and lost their children. (Cited in 2020, 184)

Indeed, not all women were this fortunate. Another woman had her child removed after giving birth at the hospital in Wakaw, Saskatchewan. Her child was adopted and never heard from again (Stevenson 2020).

The Inquiry into Missing and Murdered Indigenous Women and Girls (MMIWG), being carried out at the same time as the External Review, heard testimony on the "birth alert" practice in other provinces.[34] Cora Morgan, a First Nations Family Advocate, Assembly of Manitoba Chiefs' First Nations Family Advocate Office, testified that simply being Indigenous put women "at risk" of being flagged for birth alerts.[35] She cited the example of a woman who had her first child at thirty-eight years of age, and despite having been out of the child welfare system for eighteen years, her file was "flagged."[36] In another, Morgan described the first "birth alert" to which she responded:

> this young woman had aged out of care and she was exploited as a youth and ... had addiction issues. And, now, she was 23, having her first baby, attended every parenting program, and it was all self-motivated. Her and her partner prepared for the baby, and her baby was at risk of apprehension. And so, when I arrived at the hospital an hour before the agency was there to pick up the baby, they had six bags of baby clothes, they had their car seat. They were all ready. The paternal grandmother was there. When I arrived, she was breastfeeding her baby, and you know, I couldn't believe what was going on ...

the worker came in with their agency car seat, and they took the baby. And I had found out later that they had issued that birth alert when the mom was three months pregnant, and they held onto it for her entire pregnancy. And then when the agency got a call from the hospital, they responded. And so, there was over six months of time that they could have went to that home and got to know that mom, and taken — you know, given her the opportunity.[37]

Métis physician Janet Smylie spoke of how apprehensions at birth disrupt the ability of mothers to establish the relationship of care necessary to parent their children and criticized the colonial and biomedical understanding of "risk" relied on by health and welfare professionals to justify apprehensions for negating the centrality of birth and birthing practices to cultural continuity.[38]

Some of those who have come forward with experiences of coerced sterilization experienced the "birth alert" practice. Boyer and Bartlett emphasized how women, many of whom had current or past involvement — sometimes many years past — with the provincial agency, felt "extremely impacted" and racially profiled by CFS.[39] One woman expressed "if one had contact with [CFS] at some point in life, it would follow them for the rest of their lives ... there's a birth alert [on her chart]."[40] Another indicated, "My records were flagged by the Ministry of Social Services."[41] A woman who was coercively sterilized in 2008 explained:

> Upon my release from the hospital on the following day after I brought my newborn baby home, due to the birth alert, my son's human rights were violated when, on his first day home, he was apprehended by Child and Family Services. While I had the resources to access justice to have my son returned to my care, many of the survivors who suffered the same fate did not and lost their children to the system ... Later, when I reviewed both mine and my son's Child and Family Services file, to my utter horror, it had read that, prior to the birth of my son, he was earmarked for permanent wardship.[42]

Still another said, "I just think they, with the birth alert, that they just basically targeted [me]."[43]

The External Review offers a picture of how healthcare providers and social workers in the employ of the hospital or CFS worked together to carry out the policing of Indigenous women. While the role of the hospital social worker goes beyond child protection concerns, requests for consults based on "risk" are often submitted to them by a nurse or physician, and they serve as the "middle person" between a mother, the medical team, and CFS.[44] Social workers operating under the CFS mandate may receive referrals from hospitals or "family, police, medical personnel, neighbors, schools ..."[45] One CFS social worker stated, "The hospital's pretty good about phoning us right after the baby is born."[46] If a hospital calls CFS and it does not conduct an investigation, the information remains on file for future reference.[47] One healthcare professional questioned how CFS gained access to patient information.[48] Another wondered how CFS social workers knew if a woman had been using drugs, asking, "Who's letting your tox[in] screen information go to CFS?"[49]

Health professionals acknowledged many Indigenous mothers fear child apprehension in hospital, a possibility that becomes more likely if she refuses to meet with CFS.[50] This fear can influence whether she comes to the hospital at all, which is a barrier to health care for her and her family.[51] Boyer and Bartlett wondered if every woman having a child is subject to her whereabouts being reported to an external agency.[52] A rhetorical question perhaps, as we know Indigenous women have been disproportionately policed and criminalized, including in their reproductive lives. One healthcare professional acknowledged "high risk" women are more easily coerced into sterilization.[53] The history of family planning policy and practice in the province shows how health and welfare workers consider young, single, and Indigenous mothers as being at the "highest risk" of all. The caregiver "neglect" informing "risk" often refers to "poverty, poor housing and substance misuse" (Trocmé, Knoke, and Blackstock 2004, 583) which, for Indigenous women, is connected to "colonialism, efforts to civilize and assimilate Indigenous Peoples, the Indian Residential School system, and other institutionalized systems of genocide" (Cattapan, Moore, and Lawford 2021, 3).

The Saskatchewan Ministry of Health acknowledged "bedside apprehension" results in trauma to the infant, mother, and family.[54] A provincial review revealed, between 2015 and 2019, out of 439 children aged thirty days or younger who were placed in state care, 341 — nearly

78 percent — were Indigenous (Vescera 2021). In response to calls from Indigenous women and the MMIWG Inquiry for governments to end the practice, Paul Merriman, Minister of Social Services, initially refused, stating the alert system only applied in "extreme circumstances" and besides, almost half of these alerts originated from health professionals and there was no alternative in place for mothers considered "high risk" (Taylor 2019a and 2019b). Merriman failed to acknowledge it was legislation his ministry oversaw that gave rise to the practice in the first place.

In October 2019, "birth alerts" were standard practice for "high risk" infants at all delivery sites, except Saskatoon.[55] Here, the SHA began an alternate care model for a subsection of the population captured within the birth alert system. The pilot program "Eat, Sleep, Console" (Moore and Cattapan 2020) was triggered in part by the "sterilization controversy" and seeks to reduce apprehensions resulting from drug use and other "high risk" behaviours on the part of the mother.[56] The goal is to enable an opioid-exposed mother to remain with her child and work through detox "naturally," after which both enter supportive care and receive "detailed follow up."[57] The SHA delivers this program in collaboration with Sanctum 1.5, a community-based organization that works with populations affected by HIV/AIDS, substance dependence, homelessness, mental health issues, and poverty (Moore and Cattapan 2020). Women in the program are accompanied by a Sanctum worker upon hospital entry, and the Ministry of Social Services agrees to not send a birth alert, or if already sent, will call the hospital to have it removed.[58] This, a better alternative to the apprehension of children at birth, applies only to a portion of the population in one area of the province, and is a partial solution that does nothing to address the realities of life contributing to the prevalence of HIV/AIDS, substance dependence, homelessness, mental health issues, or poverty in the lives of some. It is important to note, not all Indigenous women, including those who were coercively sterilized, experience these issues. The overarching commonality among those who have come forward is they are "visibly and audibly" Indigenous, which points to the practice being a manifestation of systemic racism toward Indigenous Peoples.[59]

On January 26, 2021, the province announced it would end the birth alert practice. Sanctum Care Group and others have called for government to expand support programs for vulnerable women across the province to ensure adequate prenatal care and post-delivery "wrap around" services (Cattapan, Moore, and Lawford 2021, 4). There is an immediate and urgent need to support individuals who experience HIV/AIDS, substance dependence, homelessness, mental health issues, and poverty to enable them to have healthy pregnancies, but there is also a need to address the conditions which contribute to these realities. Cindy Blackstock, Executive Director, First Nations Child and Family Caring Society, warns birth alerts "risk being kind of a red herring in the real issue of ensuring that children have an adequate opportunity to grow up with their families ... What we really need to get at is issues of systemic racism, poverty and domestic violence" (cited in Malone 2022). Jeannine Carriere, Métis professor of social work, echoes that, while ending birth alerts was a good decision, "poverty is the No. 1 factor for Indigenous kids coming into contact with the child welfare system" and its structural causes, linked to ongoing colonial relations, are what need to be addressed (cited in Malone 2022).

R for Racial Profiling?

Public attention paid to Indigenous women's experiences of coerced sterilization has brought to light the practice of identifying Registered Indians in Saskatchewan with an "R" identifier on their health cards.[60] In Saskatchewan, "Registered Indians" — those who are registered with the federal government under the Indian Act — are asked to disclose their status when applying for health coverage.[61] Shaylene Salazar, Vice-President of Strategy, Quality, and Risk at eHealth, the Crown Corporation responsible for maintaining electronic healthcare records, stated the "R" marker was a "historical practice" currently "under review" (Moore 2018). The practice, arguably a form of racial profiling, is alleged to have influenced jury selection, allowing jury lists drawn from eHealth data to be culled of "Registered Indians" to limit Indigenous representation, an issue that is particularly important in cases involving violence against Indigenous people (Moore 2018). Lombard argues the practice is a symptom of systemic racism embedded in Canadian society, which contributes to the differential treatment of Indigenous women and girls in health care.[62]

The plan to track Registered Indians through an "R" marker was co-devised by the federal government and the province in 1958, in response to the longstanding jurisdictional dispute on which level of government was fiscally responsible for health services for Registered

Indians.⁶³ In 1979, the Office of Registration and Benefits acknowledged the practice was contrary to human rights legislation.⁶⁴ However, N.D. Adams, Assistant Deputy Minister of Health, wrote the identification of Registered Indians was important for allocating costs in relation to cost-sharing agreements and charging these back to the federal government: "the "R" prefix gives us that capability ... I do recognize that identification on the basis of ethnicity does have human rights implications. However, in this special case the benefits outweigh the disadvantages."⁶⁵ Despite any human rights implications arising from the collection of "race-based data," Adams indicated the practice was in the interest of the Federation of Saskatchewan Indians (FSIN) in its struggle to ensure the federal government uphold treaty responsibilities with respect to health. Perhaps, but the practice was beneficial to the province in wanting to ensure increased federal funding for the operation of its health system.

Despite Adams claiming the FSIN would likely "object strenuously" to the "R" marker being deleted from the provincial system, no correspondence has been located to confirm whether it was consulted on this. The "R" prefix continued to appear on Registered Indian health cards, the reasoning for which is in line with a history of concern with the Indigenous birth rate:

> The Indian population is growing rapidly and has special health problems. When designing programs to meet these needs, it will be crucial to be able to identify where the client group is located as well as its age, sex, utilization and morbidity characteristics. The 'R' prefix gives us that flexibility now.⁶⁶

The "R" marker has allowed the province to produce studies informing family planning policy and practice, whether on the number of births and age at which they occur, teenage pregnancy rates, or social assistance cases headed by single females, with a primary purpose of calculating the costs involved, not improving the conditions under which Indigenous people live.⁶⁷

In one instance, Doug McArthur, Director of Socioeconomic Policy, Planning, and Research, stated, excluding any costs associated with the Department of Northern Saskatchewan, the province had spent over $60 million on programs and services for Registered Indians in one year and over half of this was never recovered from the federal government.⁶⁸

The longstanding jurisdictional dispute over which level of government is responsible for services provided to Registered Indians has contributed to a view of Indigenous people as a financial burden and a drain on provincial resources — a burden projected to increase with each Indigenous birth. To view Indigenous people in this way is dehumanizing and makes government efforts to reduce this financial burden by reducing the number of Indigenous births more likely.

Registered Indians can choose a regular six-digit health number like other residents. If they do, by consequence, they must give up one means of tracking health service usage in a way that may support the struggle to have the federal government uphold treaty responsibilities. On the other hand, this has made those who retain the "R" marker on their health card more likely to be subject to racial profiling and possibly, coerced sterilization. Lombard states, "at the very least," the practice "facilitates discriminatory treatment," and she called on Canada and Saskatchewan to issue new cards without this designation.[69] Of course, all this could be avoided entirely if the federal government simply upheld its treaty obligations to Indigenous Peoples.

Sterilization by Numbers — Comparing Sterilization Rates in Saskatchewan

Tracking Registered Indians through the "R" marker on provincial health cards allows for a comparative analysis of sterilization rates between Registered Indians and Other Residents in Saskatchewan. This section joins discussion of population and fertility trends together with a consideration of reproductive health services utilization data, including deliveries, abortions, and sterilizations, from 1972 to 2018.[70] This data, disaggregated by Registered Indian Status, does not reflect all Indigenous women, whether because they hold a regular six-digit health card or are otherwise considered non-Status, Métis, or Inuit — all of whom are hidden in data for Other Residents. It also does not tell the individual experiences of each woman represented by these numbers — and there are women behind these numbers, with personal histories and life stories that shape how they accessed and experienced reproductive health services. Despite this, the reader is urged to consider how this data fits within a broader context known to constrain the reproductive choices of all Indigenous women — the historical material context of colonialism, a consequent systemic racism, and a history of family planning policy and practice that has approached Indigenous reproduction as something to be curbed.

Demography as a purportedly scientific means of studying populations rose to prominence in the early twentieth century (Hodgson 1983). The size, density, and composition of populations have been central to the development of Western societies and questions relating to the quantity of population have intersected with concerns about its quality (Bashford 2014; Ittmann 2003). Post–World War II, through financial support from the Rockefeller Foundation and the work of the Population Council, demography became a central tool to study "overpopulation," or the threat posed by the reproduction of some to a capitalist political economy (Critchlow 1999, 26). Frank Notestein, who is often credited with formalizing the theory of demographic transition, viewed "overpopulated" regions as a threat to peace, "troublesome to administer," and "unsatisfactory to do business with" (cited in Connelly 2008, 122). The theory of demographic transition guided nation-states in setting population targets and identifying groups in need of intervention, as it justified state-sponsored family planning programs (Connelly 2008; Kirk 1996).

The "colonial explanation" for demographic transition contended that "modernization" brought about by colonial domination resulted in a reduction in deaths as famine and epidemics were brought under control through introduction of Western medicine, but fertility remained high, which led to population growth (Hodgson 1983, 8). The solution for governments was to "short-circuit" growth before it threatened international stability (Ittmann 2003, 436) by assisting with "development," having people move to cities, earn paycheques, and enrol their children in school (Connelly 2009, 122). The extent to which "westernization" (Kirk 1996, 371) was voluntarily undertaken by non-Western groups is not addressed, but the process of urbanization and industrialization central to the rise of capitalism was not voluntarily undertaken by Western populations (Federici 2004; Perelman 2000). With respect to Indigenous Peoples, all this sounds like assimilation through integration.

There are countless government-sponsored studies discussing Indigenous population characteristics and projections that hold as an underlying assumption that higher Indigenous fertility rates must meet overall trends of the general population even if the explicitness of this has softened over the years. Éric Guimond and Norbert Robitaille write, while it may be "easy to be judgemental" and interpret the "choice" of Registered

Indian girls to have children, "other lifestyle choices" like completing their studies, finding gainful employment, leaving the family home, and then starting a family are often "close to non-existent" for them; to debate early motherhood without taking into account the living conditions faced by many Indigenous people is "overly simplistic" and "ethnocentric." If societies were organized more "healthily," more children could be born to young mothers. However, even under "excellent conditions," "there is every reason to believe" fertility rates would be "much lower." They conclude, regardless of how early motherhood is "judged or justified," "the negative consequences" are "irrefutable" — it "strengthens and contributes to dependence from generation to generation" (2008, 51).

Beyond the economic burden posed by Indigenous reproduction, the assumption that, barring a drastic improvement in living conditions, reproduction must be contained, cannot be separated from broader concerns with land and who controls access to it. Capitalist nation-states, in managing populations in the interest of the political economy, have long focused on women's reproduction (Cooper Owens 2018; Ehrenreich and English 2005; Federici 2004; Washington 2006; Smith 2005). Alison Bashford demonstrates how, for Western nations, "a geopolitical problem about sovereignty over land ... morphed into a biopolitical solution, entailing sovereignty over one's person ... those troubled by population growth and distribution were concerned with the fertility of soil a[t] least as much as the fertility of women" (2014, 3). For a colonial nation like Canada, to "usurp the land and extract its value," Indigenous Peoples "must be destroyed, removed, and made into ghosts" (Arvin, Tuck, and Morrill 2013, 12). Family planning became one means of doing this and the study of demographic trends helped justify proposed policy interventions targeting Indigenous women.

The exact number of Indigenous people who occupied the lands we call Canada prior to colonialism is not known with certainty. Some estimate pre-contact Indigenous population levels ranged from the thousands to millions (e.g., Romaniuc 2000; Thoronton 1987). What is certain is any estimate is influenced by who is doing the counting and for what purpose. Olive Patricia Dickason writes, while the earliest European accounts of the "New World" spoke of the "great multitudes of people," once colonization gained momentum, large stretches of territories were said to be unoccupied and the notion of an "empty continent" gained currency (1992, 27). In other words, numbers tell a story, but only a partial one.

Any attempt to calculate the number of Indigenous people in Canada is complicated by a history of Indian policy seeking to bureaucratically define them out of existence to secure access to lands. It is further convoluted by how Canada has defined, classified, and accounted for some Indigenous people over time — whether as First Nations, Registered or Treaty Indians, Status or non-Status Indians — which does not always reflect how Indigenous people define themselves. In Saskatchewan, this largely includes Cree, Dakota, Dene, Nakota, Saulteaux, and Métis, and an increasing number of Inuit. Inconsistencies in data collection are magnified by the reality that it is not always in the interest of government to gather accurate data, which might provide fodder to those who seek to prove the health status of Indigenous people is tied to colonial policies and federal neglect. Indigenous people might resist the data collection process as well.

Despite this "fuzziness" (Guimond, Robitaille, and Senecal 2015, 231), studies engaging federal census data and vital statistics, sometimes coupled with estimates from the Indian Register — the official record of Registered Indians compiled and maintained by Indigenous Services Canada (Indian Affairs) — tend to come to similar conclusions.[71] The Indigenous population, particularly the Registered Indian population, is younger and reproducing at a higher rate than Canadian averages (Amorevieta-Gentil, Daignault, Robitaille et al. 2014; Loh and George 2003; Morency, Caron-Malenfant, and Daignault 2018; Ram 2004; Romaniuc 2000).

Prior to European contact, Indigenous population levels were relatively stable, subsequently experienced a three-century period of decline and then, a more recent period of growth (Maynard and Kerr 2007; Ram 2004; Romaniuc 2000; Trovato 1987). Indian Affairs estimates indicate the number of people of Aboriginal ancestry underwent "slow growth," from 127,900 to 160,900, between 1901 and 1941. The period from 1941 to 1971 saw "rapid growth," when the population nearly doubled to 312,800 individuals. The 1970s–2000s is characterised as a time of "population explosion," when the population grew to more than 1.8 million.[72] The original myth that Indigenous lands were largely uninhabited has been replaced with the view that an exploding Indigenous population represents as a threat to an overburdened health and welfare system, the political economy, and society.

Bali Ram and Anatole Romaniuc write, for "Status and non-Status Indians," the crude birth rate, or the number of live births per 1,000 people in a population in a given year, was "basically stable" to the mid-1940s, between 38 and 42 births per 1,000 people. It underwent a "rather significant increase" in the post–World War II period, to 47 births per 1,000 people. There was a "sharp turning point" in the 1960s, when the birth rate took a "nose dive," falling to 29 births per 1,000 by the late 1970s (1985, 1–2). The total fertility rate, or the average number of children born to a woman of childbearing age, declined between 1968 and 1981, from 2.5 to 1.7 for Canada as a whole, and from 6.1 to 3.2 for Registered Indians. In Saskatchewan, where the Registered Indian fertility rate was the highest in Canada in 1968, at 8.87 births, it too declined at a "very rapid pace," to 4.1 by 1981 (17). Downward trends were reflected in data inclusive of all Indigenous Peoples, including Métis and Inuit. While rates were still nearly twice the provincial average, "a major feature" of Indigenous fertility trends was their convergence towards overall Canadian levels and by 1985, Indigenous groups entered "the demographic transition" from a "traditionally high" to a "moderately low" fertility typical of "modern society" (1, 17).

Subsequent national projections revealed that, from 1986 to 2006, the population of Indigenous origins increased by 136 percent — six times the 22 percent increase in the non-Indigenous population (Guimond, Robitaille, and Senecal 2015). This increase was projected to continue, possibly reaching 2.633 million people by 2036, at which time Indigenous people might represent up to 6.1 percent of the total Canadian population, compared to 4.4 percent in 2011 (Morency, Caron-Malenfant, Coulombe et al. 2015). Generally, about half of Indigenous people in Canada are Registered Indians, and looking to 2036, the Registered Indian population, approximately half of which live on-reserve, is projected to grow at a higher rate than non-Status Indians or Métis (Morency, Caron-Malenfant, Coulombe et al. 2015) in all provinces, with Saskatchewan possibly experiencing the most rapid growth.

In Saskatchewan, Indigenous people were 15.6 percent of the population in 2011, higher than other parts of Canada except for Manitoba and the North, and this proportion is projected to increase to between 18.5 and 22.7 percent by 2036 (Morency, Caron-Malenfant, Coulombe et al. 2015). In 2011, Registered Indians were 9.7 percent of the population, compared to non-Status Indians, Métis, or Inuit, who made up the other 5.9 percent. All Indigenous groups are projected to see population growth, but Registered Indians are projected to be "greatly overrepresented" (Morency, Caron-Malenfant, Coulombe et al. 2015, 31), between

11.4 and 14.8 percent of the population in 2036, higher than any province and the Canadian average of 2.5 to 2.8 percent.

Researchers tell us that a population characterized by higher fertility tends to be younger, and children born to teenage mothers are more likely to have children as teenagers (Amorevieta-Gentil, Daignault, Robitaille et al. 2014). The increase in the Registered Indian population is projected to be most prominent among young people. Registered Indians aged 15–19 are about seven times more likely to have children than the Canadian average (Guimond and Robitaille 2008; Ram 2004). For teenage girls younger than fifteen, the rate is estimated to be as much as eighteen times higher than other Canadians; a rate comparable to "least developed countries" like Nepal, Ethiopia, and Somalia (Guimond and Robitaille 2008, 49). Saskatchewan has the second highest teenage pregnancy rate in Canada, and Registered Indians are projected to grow to between 23 and 35.5 percent of the population in that age group by 2036 (Morency, Caron-Malenfant, Coulombe et al. 2015). Éric Guimond and Norbert Robitaille conclude the fertility rate among young Registered Indian girls is nothing less than phenomenal (2009, 305). To say Indigenous Peoples are the "fastest growing" and "youngest population" requires acknowledging how young Registered Indian women contribute to this trend.[73]

Socioeconomic status and education level, the rise in "mixed unions" (i.e., between an Indigenous and non-Indigenous person), a "pronatalist subculture," "ethnic mobility" (changes to how one identifies), and "modernization" (i.e., assimilation) are factors influencing Indigenous fertility trends (Morency, Caron-Malenfant, and Daignault 2018, 36–8; also Ram and Romaniuc 1985). Population levels need to be considered in relation to a series of legislative amendments to the Indian Act, which, since 1985, have enabled some Indigenous women and children previously denied Indian Status (Palmater 2011) to apply for reinstatement. Indian policies meant to encourage off-reserve migration also reinforce living conditions that impact every aspect of life and death for Indigenous people reflected, for one, in infant mortality rates that, while still high, are lower than they were in the mid-twentieth century.[74] Infant mortality rates are the "single most comprehensive indicator" of the health of a population (Smylie, Fell, Ohlsson et al. 2010, 143) and a determinant of fertility decline (Bashford 2014).

The geographic remoteness of many communities can influence the birth rate, including by limiting timely access to health services (Morency, Caron-Malenfant, and Daignault 2018; Lawford and Giles 2012). It is not possible to assess the degree to which the proliferation of family planning has impacted population trends, but it needs to be considered, especially when the sharp "nose dive" described by Ram and Romaniuc (1985, 1) can be seen in parts of Latin America, for one, where governments implemented family planning programs in the same period (Kirk 1996; Mass 1976). Guimond and Robitaille refer to fertility decline among Indigenous women as an expression of the "desire to have fewer offspring," but they cite the increased availability of contraceptives for making this possible (2008, 51).

Table 1: Average Total Fertility Rate, Registered Indians in Canada, Compared to Canadian National and Provincial Averages

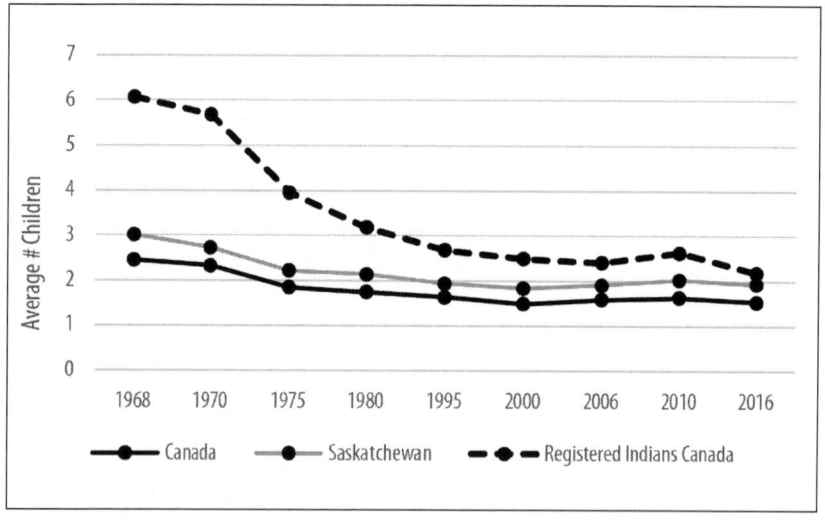

Table 1 provides a visual representation of the average Registered Indian total fertility rate in Canada compared to overall provincial and Canadian averages from 1968 to 2016.[75] In 1968, the Registered Indian total fertility rate was at 6.07 births, which fell to 2.18 in 2016. This compares to 3.01 and 2.45 births for Saskatchewan and Canada in 1968, falling to 1.93 and 1.54 births, respectively, in 2016. The Registered Indian total fertility rate in Canada is now only slightly higher than provincial and Canadian averages. This amounts to Registered Indian women giving birth, on average, to only one more child, with continued signs of convergence with provincial and national trends (Morency, Caron-Malenfant, and Daignault 2018).

Data from the Indian Register made available by the Statistics and Research Unit of Indigenous Services Canada (INSTAT) allows us to understand the proportion of the population made up of Registered Indians and Other Residents in Saskatchewan from 1972 to 2018.[76] In 1972, Registered Indians were approximately 4 percent of the provincial population, at 39,168 people. This proportion increased steadily to 13.5 percent in 2016, and 13.7 in 2018, or 159,386 people. The 2016 census, which provides demographic information on populations that self-identify as Aboriginal (First Nation, Métis, and Inuit), puts the Registered Indian population at 9.9 percent.

From 1972 to 2018, the Registered Indian population saw consistent positive growth, highest in 1986, at 6.6 percent, while Other Residents saw very low to no growth, and negative growth from 1986 to 2006.[77] The provincial population remained close to one million over the entire forty-six-year period. The steady provincial population, coupled with higher out-migration, particularly among youth, and low immigration to 2006, after which time economic conditions improved and trends reversed somewhat, has resulted in an aging provincial population (Moazzami 2015). Indigenous people have a much younger population overall (Ram 2004), but it too is aging. In 2001, the median age of the Indigenous population in Saskatchewan was 20.4 years, compared to 36.4 for the general population. In 2026, the median age for each is projected to be 27.8 and 42.8 years, respectively (Steffler 2008). In the meantime, if nothing is done, Indigenous people will constitute a larger *proportion* of the *overall* population.

The infant mortality rate in Saskatchewan, and for Registered Indians, has been consistently higher than national averages. In 1981, the provincial infant mortality rate, or the number of infants who die before age one expressed in a rate per 1,000 live births, was 11.8 for Saskatchewan overall, 26.1 for Registered Indians in Saskatchewan, and 9.6 for Canada as a whole.[78] Despite a lack of comparative data, general consensus is that the infant mortality rate among Indigenous populations remains more than twice that of non-Indigenous people, at 5.9 and 4.4 for Saskatchewan and Canada in 2021, and while it has decreased over the years, there remains a "striking and persistent disparity" (Smylie, Fell, and Ohlsson 2010, 147) among Registered Indians and in communities with a high proportion of Inuit.[79]

In 2017, twelve of thirteen health regions transitioned to a single Saskatchewan Health Authority, in addition to the Athabasca Health Authority. Data in the following section is broken down by former health region groupings which includes, in the north of the province: Mamawetan Churchill River, Keewatin Yatthé, and Athabasca (MCR KY AHA), Prairie North, Prince Albert Parkland (PA Parkland), and Kelsey Trail; and in the south: Sun Country, Five Hills, Cypress, and Heartland (SC FH C H), Sunrise, Saskatoon, and Regina Qu'Appelle.

Statistics Canada describes the SC FH C H, Kelsey Trail, and Sunrise regions as mainly rural, with an "average percentage" of Indigenous people and high employment rates. Regina Qu'Appelle and Saskatoon have an "urban-rural mix" and "average percentage" of Indigenous people. PA Parkland and Prairie North are "rural northern regions" with a "high proportion" of Indigenous people, while the MCR KY AHA regions, northern and remote, have a "very high proportion" of Indigenous people and "very low" employment. This last grouping comprises approximately 44 percent of the provincial land mass but only 3.3 percent of the total population, while 53.4 percent of the population resides in the Regina Qu'Appelle and Saskatoon regions, and 43.2 percent among the remaining regions.[80]

Information acquired through an Access to Information Request to the Saskatchewan Ministry of Health provides the number of "deliveries" for Registered Indians and Other Residents.[81] Table 2 shows the number of Registered Indian deliveries from 1972 to 2018, together with the percent of all deliveries and overall population represented by Registered Indians. In 1972, there were 1,368 Registered Indian deliveries, a high of 3,260 in 2009, and 2,991 in 2018. This represented 8.5 percent of all deliveries in 1972, and 20.4 percent in 2018. The highest proportion of Registered Indian deliveries in 1972 was in MCR KY AHA (23.2 percent), Prairie North (22 percent), and PA Parkland (18.3 percent). In 2018, MCR KY AHA continued to have the largest proportion of Registered Indian deliveries (19.6 percent), followed by Regina Qu'Appelle (19.1 percent), PA Parkland (18.7 percent), and Saskatoon (17.5 percent).

The number of live births to women of childbearing age (15–49 years) in each five-year age category, a measure relied on to calculate the total fertility rate, cannot be disaggregated for Registered Indians in Saskatchewan. While the number of "deliveries" does not correlate exactly to the number of "live births," this data was relied on to calculate

Table 2: Deliveries — Registered Indian Deliveries By Year and % of Population and Deliveries, Saskatchewan

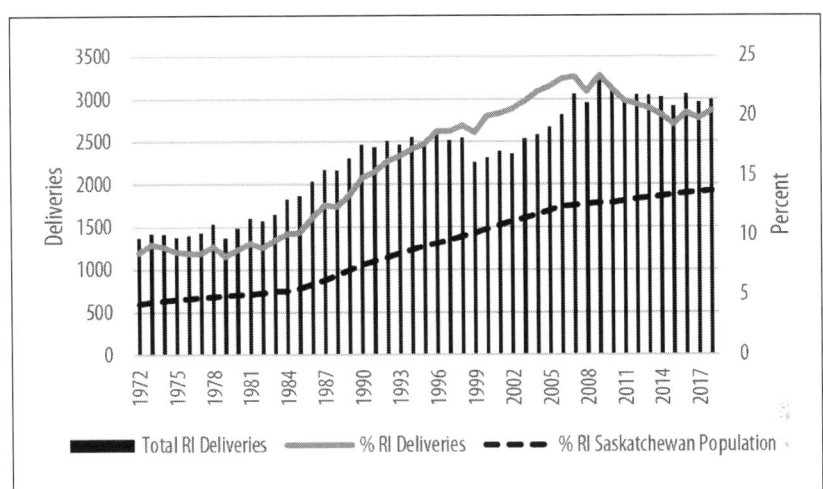

a rate per 1,000 for Registered Indians and Other Residents, similar to a "General Fertility Rate," or the number of births per 1,000 women of childbearing age, for comparison purposes.[82] In 1972, the delivery rate for Registered Indian women was 178.5 per 1,000, compared to 74.8 per 1,000 for Other Residents. By 2018, this rate dropped to less than half, or 68.0 per 1,000 Registered Indian women, much closer to the 54.2 per 1,000 for Other Residents. Overall, the number of deliveries per 1,000 Registered Indian women has been consistently above Other Residents, 2.4 times higher in 1972, and in 2018 it was 1.25 times higher, a pattern reflective of overall fertility trends in Table 1.

Infant mortality rates cannot be broken down by Indigenous status, but public health data indicates the seven year average, from 2001 to 2007, was higher, sometimes much higher, than the provincial average (6.2 per 1,000) in areas with a "very high" or "high" proportion of Indigenous people, namely Mamawetan Churchill River (10.9 per 1,000), Keewatin Yatthé (7.7 per 1,000), Athabasca (17.2 per 1,000), Prairie North (7.4 per 1,000), and Prince Albert Parkland (6.6 per 1,000).[83] Considering infant mortality rates are correlated with poverty, food insecurity, unemployment, lack of adequate housing and access to maternal care, among other factors (Smylie, Fell, and Ohlsson 2010; Smylie, Crengle, Freemantle et al. 2010), these higher rates reveal something about the conditions into which children are born.

Registered Indians are also more likely to have abortions. Table 3 shows the number of Registered Indian abortions performed each year from 1972 to 2018, together with the percent of all abortions and overall population represented by Registered Indians.[84] The number of Registered Indian abortions rose from 24 in 1972, to 416 in 2018, for a cumulative total of 10,445. The proportion of abortions performed on Registered Indian women rose mostly consistently, from 2.5 to 24.5 percent of all abortions in the province. The abortion rate per 1,000 Registered Indian women rose from 3.1 per 1,000 in 1972, to a high of 13.7 per 1,000 in 2009, after which it declined to 9.5 per 1,000 in 2018. In contrast, the rate for Other Residents was 4.6 in 1972, declining to a low of 0.5 in 1985, and rising to 5.9 per 1,000 in 2018. Prairie North represented 25 percent of Registered Indian abortions in 1972. All other regions represented 12.5 percent, with the exception of SC FH CH, where none were noted. In 2018, 39 percent of Registered Indian abortions were performed in Regina Qu'Appelle, and 24 percent in Saskatoon.

Table 4 shows the number of Registered Indian sterilizations performed each year between 1970 and 2018, together with the percent of all sterilizations and overall population represented by Registered Indians.[85] The number of Registered Indian sterilizations rose from 69 in 1970, to a high of 330 procedures in 2001, falling to 194 in 2018. The cumulative total of Registered Indian sterilizations in this period was 10,654. The total number of sterilizations performed on Other Residents was higher, at 91,355, as was their proportion of the population. Registered Indians

Table 3: Abortions – Registered Indian Abortions By Year and % of Population and Abortions, Saskatchewan

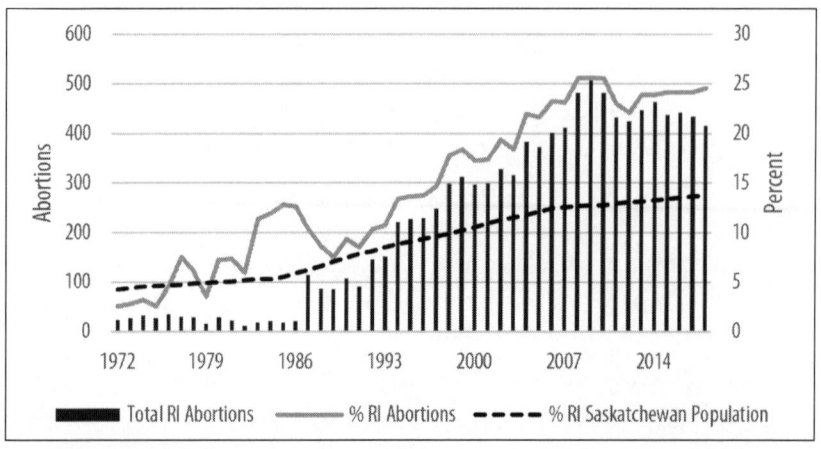

represented 4.2 percent of all those sterilized in 1972, and 17.5 in 2018. In 1972, the highest percentage of Registered Indian sterilizations were in Prairie North (28 percent), and MCR KY AHA and Regina Qu'Appelle (both 19 percent). In 2018, the highest percentage was in MCR KY AHA and Regina Qu'Appelle, both representing 20 percent.

When the proportion of sterilizations performed on Registered Indians is compared to their proportion of the population, it is clear Registered Indians began to be disproportionately sterilized in 1978, when they accounted for 4.9 percent of the population, but 5.7 percent of those sterilized. This overrepresentation nearly doubled by 1986, when Registered Indians were 5.9 percent of the population but 10.3 percent of those sterilized. It was at its highest in 2001, when Registered Indians were 10.9 percent of the population but 19.5 percent of those sterilized, or they were 1.8 times more likely to be sterilized. The number of sterilizations for Other Residents has fluctuated over the years, but their proportion of overall sterilizations matches, or most often falls below, their proportion of the population.

The sterilization rate per 1,000 Registered Indian women has been consistently higher than Other Residents, sometimes only slightly, every year between 1972 and 2018, except 1987, when the rate for Other Residents was 12.5 per 1,000 and 11.4 per 1,000 for Registered Indians. Overall, the sterilization rate for Registered Indians dropped from 17.7 to 4.4 per 1,000 between 1972 and 2018, while that for Other Residents

Table 4: Sterilizations – Registered Indian Sterilizations By Year and % of Population and Sterilizations, Saskatchewan

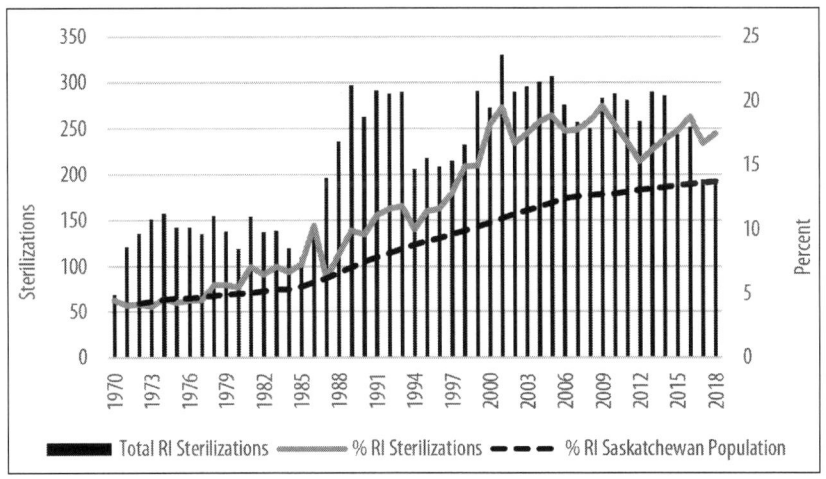

dropped from 15.9 to 4.2. Considering this data disappears non-Status, Métis, and Inuit within that for Other Residents, these comparative numbers underrepresent overall trends for Indigenous Peoples in Saskatchewan.

Scholars tell us because Indigenous populations are so small, to sterilize even a small proportion of the population has a much larger effect over time (Cohen and Baskett 1978; Smith 2005; Stote 2015). When considering sterilizations together with higher abortion and infant mortality rates, and the chronic poverty and other public health issues that impact all aspects of life and death for many Indigenous people, this point is magnified. It is also important to remember how higher birth, infant mortality, and abortion rates have served as indicators for policy makers of the need for more concerted family planning efforts, including more permanent methods like sterilization.

Based on available data, Registered Indians were disproportionately sterilized in Saskatchewan beginning in 1978. This is not to imply all sterilizations were performed against the will of Indigenous women — Indigenous women are as capable as any other of wanting sterilization as a legitimate reproductive option. However, these sterilizations need to be considered within the broader context of colonialism and its consequent systemic racism, a history of all levels of government approaching Indigenous reproduction as something needing to be curbed, and the ways family planning policy has sought to do just this. This inherently coercive context constrains Indigenous women's reproductive choices.

In the mid-twentieth century, population controllers were aware that to implement public health measures might compound population growth (Bashford 2014). For some, this confirmed that this form of "death control" (320) — the increase in public health measures aimed at reducing disease and death — needed to be coupled with birth control. For others, another form of birth control was useful — the active withholding of effective public health interventions to allow for "natural death control" (320). When considered in this light, the longstanding failure of government to effectively intervene in public health issues facing Indigenous communities becomes a form of population control, too.

In failing to do what is necessary to address the countless premature, avoidable, and tragic Indigenous deaths caused by violence and disease; chronic poverty; the large number of missing and murdered Indigenous women, girls, Two-Spirit people, and men; substance abuse and overdoses resulting from marginalization and unresolved trauma; or the disproportionate body burden carried by many due toxin exposure, which ties environmental justice to reproductive justice, Canada is effectively reducing the Indigenous population by consequence, if not by intention. To this we must add the incarceration of Indigenous people in psychiatric institutions, prisons, and the child welfare system. Segregation is not the most efficient means of managing reproduction, but it too keeps some from "perpetuating their kind" (Black 2003, 93).

Former Director General of the United Nations Economic and Social Council Julian Huxley once wrote, "Wherever there is no birth control there will be an outwards population pressure which clearly indicates the danger of war" (cited in Bashford 2014, 215). One wonders if the Indigenous birth rate is really what is at issue — we are talking about Indigenous women having, on average, only one more child than Canadian averages. Or is it the *proportion* of the population Indigenous people will grow to represent without intervention, and the threat this poses to assertions of Canadian sovereignty and the smooth functioning of the political economy? This question is heightened if one considers the ongoing resistance waged by Indigenous people to expropriation and exploitation. How tenable will claims to Indigenous lands be if the Indigenous population continues to grow? Perhaps coerced sterilization and the failure of government to effectively intervene in public health issues facing Indigenous people are two sides of the same coin. Intended or not, each enables the expropriation of Indigenous lands to the benefit of the political economy and corporations that depend on them for profit.

Violence against Indigenous Lands and Bodies

The political economy is dependent on wealth extracted from Indigenous lands. In 2021, this wealth was described by the government of Saskatchewan as "the envy of nations."[86] In the North — the area encompassed by the MCR KY AHA Health Regions, where Indigenous people make up the largest proportion of the population and where, together with Regina Qu'Appelle, the highest proportion of Registered Indian sterilizations took place in 2018 — much of this wealth comes from the world's largest high grade uranium deposits, copper-zinc, gold, graphite, iron, and nickel, and oil, gas, and bitumen deposits that make Saskatchewan the second largest oil producing province.[87] In the South — especially the area covered by the SC FH C H Health Regions — there is a large crop economy that has increased since the 1960s to become one of the most productive in the world, based largely on the growth and export of wheat, barley, oats, canola, peas, mustard, lentils, canary, and flax seed.[88] The Saskatchewan potash industry, the largest segment of the mining industry, experienced a "record breaking year for revenues" in 2022, positioning the province as the "world's largest producer with the largest reserves" (Schlesinger 2022). The potash industry, considered by some as a key to combating world hunger because of the use of potash in fertilizers, crosses the province from the southeast to the northwest, contributes billions in revenue to the political economy and corporate interests, and employs countless people.[89] Meanwhile many Indigenous people live in poverty and experience some the worst social determinants of health.

The province encourages Indigenous people to work for these industries under the guise of increasing self-sufficiency and in an effort to promote economic development. In 2013, Premier Brad Wall stated, "Do you know what the best program for First Nations and Métis people in Saskatchewan is? Not a program at all it's Cameco" (cited in Clarke 2013, A3). Cameco, together with Orano Canada Inc., are responsible for producing all of Canada's uranium.[90] Some communities enter into "collaborative agreements" to secure benefits from resource activities taking place on their lands, which often results in tensions between and among nations and the criminalization of those who defend these lands against potential "ecological scars" (Harding 2007, 21).[91]

When one community enters into an agreement with a resource extraction company, its impacts are often felt by others. Candyce Paul, from the English River First Nation, which signed agreements with uranium companies, states, "Cameco and [Orano] are busy sewing up approvals for all future projects. Both Pinehouse and English River collaboration agreements have these administrations locked into supporting everything ... this compromises the region's ability to ensure that our land, water, and health are protected over the long term" (cited in Hande 2013). Melanie St. Pierre, a resident of Wollaston, stated: "We mothers have a lot of young children. The greatest concern of the mothers today is what the children are going to live on if the water, land and animals are destroyed" (cited in Goldstick 1987, 139).

It is not the place of this author to comment on the decisions Indigenous Peoples must make when faced with centuries of colonial violence and the undermining of lands, sovereignty, and ability to subsist without outside interference. However, there is nothing close to consensus within Indigenous nations on whether collaboration with government and industry should take place — and there is often active resistance. In 2014, trappers from Birch Narrows Dene Nation erected a blockade on a piece of highway running from La Loche to the Cluff Lake Mine, a uranium mine operated by Areva Resources Canada Inc. that closed in 2002, to stop exploration by uranium and bitumen companies without community consent. The blockade was dismantled by the RCMP, but campers remained on the side of the highway for months (Toledano 2015).

In 2012, the leadership of the Métis community of Pinehouse, together with Kineepik Métis Local Inc., signed an agreement with Cameco and Areva (now Orano Canada Inc.), for approximately $200 million in "jobs, cash payments and other economic benefits over 11 years" (Larson 2014, C1). Some claim the uranium industry "bought" the village of Pinehouse (Hande 2013). Nine individuals from the community, with others from outside the region, filed a legal challenge against Cameco, Orano Canada Inc., Pinehouse leaders, Kineepik Métis Local Inc., and the federal and provincial government, arguing the agreement violated international law, Treaty Rights, and the duty to consult Indigenous Peoples about what happens on their lands. They also worry about the potential harm to waters used for drinking, washing, fishing, agriculture, and recreation.[92] The claim was dismissed in 2014 (Larson 2014).

Much earlier, there was more consensus on how to approach this "neocolonial" (Harding 2007, 26) situation. In 1977, at the Cluff Lake Board of Inquiry meant to assess the potential effects of expanding uranium mining in northern Saskatchewan and avoid grassroots pressure for a moratorium on development, all Indigenous organizations present — those who had not boycotted the inquiry altogether — expressed a clear and explicit "no" to uranium mining, at least until land claims were settled (Harding 2007, 26). The Chiefs iterated that uranium development was unacceptable unless Treaty Rights to hunting, fishing, trapping, and gathering were guaranteed, the Treaty Right to health, economic development, and resource management were assured, and Indigenous nations had the time and resources necessary to consider other questions related to the industry (Harding 2007, 29). The Association of Métis and Non-Status Indians argued uranium development was an attempt by government and industry to "commit robbery, theft and even genocide against our people" (cited in Harding 2007, 31).

In another instance, Chief Hector Kkailther of Hatchet Lake Denesuline Nation at Wollaston Lake, addressed a crowd erecting a blockade at the Rabbit Lake uranium mine:

> It seems like those people are only looking out for money … These governments and the people who are owning the mine … should have settled with the people and discussed things over … they never did that … But they make money out of our land. They damage the lake, the land, everything, animals, fish. We're left behind with nothing … it's not too late if we fight back. The land is still beautiful. Look around. So let's keep it that way … no matter what, let us all work together and stop that uranium mine. (Cited in Goldstick 1987, 195–6)

The leadership at Pinehouse was also against uranium mining and fully supported Hatchet Lake Denesuline Nation. In his letter to Chief Kkailther, Pinehouse Mayor George Smith wrote:

> Uranium mining is no good. Fishing is more important. Our planning study shows that for Pinehouse what we get in one year from commercial and domestic fishing is worth over 3 times what we get in town in wages from the Key Lake mine … uranium pollution might poison your fish for decades … Anybody who isn't against such a stupid and dangerous idea is either being paid by the uranium industry or just plain crazy. (Cited in Goldstick 1987, 159)

It took less than thirty years for Pinehouse leadership to change course.

In March 2021, Fission Uranium Corp. and Clearwater River Dene Nation reached an agreement allowing a proposed uranium project in the Patterson Lake area to progress to the next phase of development. Chief Teddy Clark stated his nation was "pleased" to sign this agreement, which "affirms the importance of respecting, understanding, and considering [Clearwater River Dene] rights, culture, and traditional land and resource uses when projects are proposed." The agreement would benefit the community by "building capacity," "supporting skills development," and "providing employment and contracting opportunities."[93]

Two months later, members of Clearwater River Dene Nation erected a security checkpoint because the province granted exploratory approvals to uranium companies without meaningful consultation and as families were on the land seeking protection from COVID-19 (*CBC News* 2021b). Band Manager Walter Hainault stated:

> governments allowed destructive uranium projects like the Gunnar Mine to go ahead that is now a toxic uranium legacy. They approved the Cluff Lake uranium mine to the north of us and our people have mostly left the area due to their fears over radioactive contamination and as our cultural connection to the area was broken. We now have two major uranium mines being proposed in one of our Nation's most culturally important and vital areas ... All this starts with the [Government of Saskatchewan] granting uranium mineral tenures, rights and exploration permits in the absence of meaningful consultation or sound analysis of its impacts on our rights, culture or People. Our People are kind, patient and have shown good will, but that patience is running out.[94]

The Clearwater River Dene Nation was not opposed to economic development, but government had an obligation to consult and accommodate their constitutionally protected rights. The province responded it was committed to "meaningful consultation," and while the lands of interest were used by Indigenous people, "mining contributes significantly to the economy in northern Saskatchewan, including partnerships with First Nations and Métis communities and employment opportunities for northern residents" (Bramadat-Willcock 2021).

The jury is out on what will result from these and other resource extraction projects, whether corporations will engage in an ethical way, or if it is even possible for development to take place without detrimental impacts to Indigenous lands, lives, and forms of life. If history is any indication of what is to come, risks will be disproportionately borne by Indigenous Peoples. Facing a "take it or leave it" (Harding 2007, 30) predicament, Indigenous Peoples try to make the best of the situation by capitalizing on the "trickle-down benefits" (26). However, this situation which was manufactured by those most in a position to profit — governments and corporations.

To keep Indigenous Peoples dispossessed of their wealth is a strategic move making them easier to control and possibly more amenable to working for, or entering into agreements with the very parties who are undermining their ability to live self-sufficiently on their own terms. It also lays the foundation for genocide, as the late Art Manuel wrote:

> Under the present Canadian system our dependence and our poverty are almost total. Suffering from this impoverishment is even more painful when we are forced to watch the settlers who live on our land enjoy almost 100 percent of our natural wealth and resources. Colonialism in Canada means we either live in poverty or we assimilate … The real cause of our distress is, of course, that we do not have power over any land or resources in our Aboriginal and treaty territory except for the 0.2 percent of our territories … to build a sustainable economy for our people … the ugliest part about the Settler-Indigenous relationship is that Canada secretly looks at our poverty as a final solution toward our ultimate extinction as a peoples … if we can be made to disappear as peoples, the land, finally, will be theirs alone. (2017, 80, 83)

This historical and material context is inherently coercive. The material requirement to exploit wealth from Indigenous lands gives rise to systemic racism against Indigenous peoples. It is also what informs longstanding concerns on the part of governments with the Indigenous birth rate.

When governments focus on the reproductive behaviour of Indigenous Peoples, they do not need to address broader structural aspects of poverty — what is being done with lands and how wealth acquired from these lands is distributed. The view that poverty in Indigenous communities is compounded by their reproductive behaviour is "untenable" considering the enormous importance resources drawn from Indigenous lands have for the enrichment of some. Vincente Navarro writes, it is not "scarcity of resources, nor the process of industrialization, nor even the much heralded population explosion" which is really at issue, but rather "a pattern of control over the resources … in which the majority of the population has no control" (1981, 5–6, 7). Wealth drawn from Indigenous lands enables the enrichment of the Canadian state, capitalist interests, and private citizens, and this enrichment results in poverty and public health issues in Indigenous communities. Through this process, violence against Indigenous lands is connected to violence against Indigenous bodies.

To date, over one hundred women have come forward with experiences of coerced sterilization. At least sixty-four are from Saskatchewan. But we know not all those subject to violence are willing to speak up.[95] Indigenous women have experienced negative personal, social, economic, and health effects as a consequence of being coercively sterilized including but not limited to physical side effects of the procedure, hormonal imbalances, early menopause, and sterility; mental anguish, anxiety, and depression; a decreased sense of value as a woman; and suicide or cycles of addiction.[96] When women come forward, they may experience online harassment; the re-triggering of past trauma; and negative mental or physical health outcomes, including the magnification of underlying health conditions; stress from being in the public gaze; even difficulties securing housing or health care because they are viewed as troublemakers. They also run the risk of not being believed. The decision to come forward is not an easy one. No one can know for certain how many of the 10,654 documented Registered Indian sterilizations from 1970 to 2018 were coerced, or how many other Indigenous women experienced this violence. That even one woman has been coercively sterilized should shock our collective conscience and spur us into action to ensure it never happens again.

Indigenous reproduction remains a threat to the political economy because it is tied to the continuance of Indigenous Peoples with rights, responsibilities, and relationships to lands which others depend on for profit. The direct connection between this and systemic racism against Indigenous people is the historical material context that makes Indigenous women vulnerable to coerced sterilization. Unless and until it is addressed by respecting treaties, rematriating land, and defending Indigenous sovereignty — over lands and bodies — a genocide against Indigenous Peoples is at risk of continuing. The next chapter explores how governments have responded to the coerced sterilization of Indigenous women and how these responses may serve as further attempts to avoid addressing these longstanding historical and material issues.

6

After the (Media) Storm — Responding to Genocide

Something sacred was taken away from me. I demand immediate action to resolve and fix this, fix what has happened to all the women in Saskatchewan. (Giesbrecht 2019)

In response to Indigenous women coming forward with their experiences of coerced sterilization, Saskatchewan NDP health critic Danielle Chartier referred to these instances as "disturbing," "disgusting," and a "heinous" attack on the reproductive rights of women (Adam 2015b) and called on Premier Brad Wall to make clear to all health regions that coercion under any circumstances is a violation of human rights.[1] Minister of Health Dustin Duncan indicated that while he took these "accusations" seriously and wanted to "find out what went wrong," he had "great concerns" with the insinuation that this resulted from government directives (Adam 2015b). Premier Wall referred to the National Inquiry into Missing and Murdered Indigenous Women and Girls (MMIWG Inquiry) which was underway, and stated Cabinet may have "something to offer going forward" to help young women after reviewing recommendations from the final report of the Truth and Reconciliation Commission (TRC) (Adam 2015b).

The federal government announced the MMIWG Inquiry in December 2015, as the TRC was concluding its work, to investigate the disproportionate violence faced by Indigenous women, girls, and 2SLGBTQQIA people.[2] The MMIWG Inquiry was empowered to report on the systemic causes of "all forms of violence" and make recommendations on how to address it.[3] It began its work in September 2016, but not without tension. In its first year, one commissioner and four staff resigned (Hamilton 2017). Some criticized the MMIWG Inquiry for being disorganized, "shrouded in secrecy" (Tasker 2017), and a "bloody farce" (Tunney 2017). Métis legal scholar and Commissioner Marilyn Poitras, who resigned in July 2017, expressed concern with the "status quo" colonial structure that, she claimed, made it unable to fulfill its terms of reference.[4] She explained:

> The traditional colonial style says: You go in, you have a hearing, people come and tell you their problems and you figure it out … You tell us your sad story and we'll figure out what to do with you. And we're headed down that same path. And if it worked, we would all be so fixed and healthy by now. It doesn't work … If your expectation is hearings and families telling stories, that's not failure, that's success. Justice systems and commissions and inquiries and inquests are set up to do certain things and if they do what they're set up to do then you can't be disappointed … But it's not going to get at the roots of systemic violence. I don't know how it's going to do that. (Cited in *CBC News* 2017)

More than 2,380 individuals, family members, and survivors of violence, experts, and Knowledge Keepers participated through written testimony, artistic expression, and public hearings. A 1,200-page report was released in June 2019. In speaking to a crowd gathered in Gatineau, Quebec, Chief Commissioner Marion Buller stated, an "absolute paradigm shift" was necessary from all levels of government and public institutions to "dismantle colonialism" (cited in Tasker 2019b).

The MMIWG Inquiry found "persistent and deliberate" human and Indigenous rights violations at the root of Canada's staggering rates of violence against Indigenous women, girls, and 2SLGBTQQIA people.[5] This violence included:

> [the] deaths of women in police custody; [Canada's] failure to protect Indigenous women, girls, and 2SLGBTQQIA people from exploitation and trafficking, as well as from known killers; the crisis of child welfare; physical, sexual, and mental abuse inflicted on Indigenous women and girls in state institutions; the denial of Status and membership for First Nations; the removal of children; forced relocation and its impacts; purposeful, chronic underfunding of essential human services; [and] coerced sterilizations.[6]

With respect to coerced sterilization, this form of "directed state violence" contributed to the dehumanization of Indigenous women, and the totality of Indigenous experiences was genocide.[7]

The MMIWG Inquiry made connections between violence against Indigenous lands and bodies, including resources extraction activities and the "man camps" that accompany industrial projects in northern and remote communities, and the violation of Indigenous rights — as individuals and collectives — through historical and ongoing practices embedded within Western institutions, including health care, child welfare, and the criminal justice system.[8] With respect to health, services provided to Indigenous people were "grossly lacking" and "often inappropriate," which informed the violence they experience. The fact that many Indigenous people needed to travel outside their communities to give birth was a factor making them vulnerable to abuse, and jurisdictional neglect and the failure of health systems to respect human rights were central concerns. A healthcare system largely designed and delivered by non-Indigenous people was problematic, and there was a need to remove systemic barriers preventing Indigenous people from pursuing health training to ensure culturally relevant services grounded in Indigenous worldviews, cultures, and languages.[9]

Following the release of the MMIWG Inquiry final report, newly elected Premier Scott Moe spoke against the conclusion of genocide:

> While the historic violence highlighted ... is extreme and unacceptable, when viewed through the lens of other examples of deliberate and systematic destruction of ethnic, racial, religious or national groups; such as the Armenian genocide, the Holodomor, the Holocaust, or the Rwandan Genocide; the Premier does not agree with the use of the term ... It is unfortunate that the use of this term has distracted from the recommended action highlighted ... recommendations our government is reviewing diligently. (Cited in Tasker 2019a)

This "diligent review" has resulted in funding to support "culturally responsive" service delivery in health, welfare, and justice, and the establishment of a Community Response Fund to support projects promoting safety for women, girls, and Two-Spirit people.[10] It would ensure "system-wide" cultural safety for First Nations and Métis people by working with local organizations to develop "health and wellness training, education and programs to address violence and abuse," and "other culturally safe and trauma-informed practices and services."[11]

There were no suggestions for addressing historical material relations which contribute to violence.

Proposed interventions to address the coerced sterilization of Indigenous women are in line with previous approaches, focused on the need to respect Indigenous and human rights; to criminalize the practice through federal legislation; to ensure cultural competency and safety in health care; to hold perpetrators accountable through class action litigation; and, on the day of the release of the report, the offering of an apology. Each of these is considered in turn, the last considered first, and each is complicated, not to dismiss the important work being done by those who want to stop the practice, but to explore their implications in addressing violence against bodies *and* lands — the context leading to coerced sterilization.

The Saskatoon Health Region Apologizes

On July 22, 2017, the day the final report of the External Review was released, the Saskatoon Health Region (SHR) offered an apology to those who were coercively sterilized. SHR Vice-President Jackie Mann thanked those who came forward and acknowledged racism exists within the healthcare system. She stated: "I want to apologize ... I am truly sorry ... you were not treated with the respect, the compassion and all of the support that you needed and deserved ... No woman should ever be treated the way you were treated." She referenced the "clear direction" provided by the External Review on how to "truly start" healing, let women know they had been heard and would be listened to, and committed herself to doing all she could "to bring about real change" (cited in The Canadian Press, 2017).

There is a history of government apologies in response to claims of coercion and abuse, including with respect to coerced sterilization (Stote 2015). British Columbia passed legislation related to the issuing of apologies for past wrongs in April 2006. The Apology Act outlined that the issuing of an apology would not constitute an admission of fault or liability, but it could be used in assessing damages in court.[12] This legislation followed on the heels of the province facing numerous class action lawsuits, including one dealing with coerced sterilization.[13] The province described the act of apologizing as having the potential to reduce the number of claimants in a case by almost 40 percent, thereby reducing the number of suits and court costs.[14]

Saskatchewan passed its own legislation in November 2006. During debates on the Evidence Amendment Act, Attorney General Frank Quennell stated similarly that in many cases, people or institutions may want to apologize but do not, based on legal advice that an apology may be used to establish liability or due to a fear insurance coverage could be voided.[15] If issued quickly, however, an apology could mitigate damages in medical malpractice situations:

> Our mediators who have experience with apologies in the context of mediation have told us that the biggest impact of this legislation will be felt shortly after the events giving rise to the injury if people feel free to say the right thing when it is most appropriate without fearing that it will haunt them later ... they have also told us that after hearing a long-overdue apology, participants in mediation often say that if they had heard it earlier, it would have saved them a lot of pain and they likely would not have pursued the matter.[16]

One needs to approach the apology issued by the SHR with a critical, if not a skeptical eye, regardless of any real or purported sincerity on the part of the individual issuing it, when the act of apologizing is considered a strategic tool to avoid liability and mitigate damages. This is especially relevant when, not two months later, the SHR was named as a defendant in a proposed class action for its role in the coerced sterilization of Indigenous women.

During her appearance on CBC's *The Current*, when asked about the apology and any policy changes implemented by the SHR to ensure Indigenous women were no longer subject to coerced sterilization, lawyer Alisa Lombard responded:

> I think apologies are good. I think actions are better ... I have not been told what measures are being taken to prevent, to investigate, to prosecute, to remedy, to make amends with these women and their families who have suffered so greatly and so, although that apology is a good first step, I think being accountable and taking responsibility involves changing one's behaviour. (Cited in *CBC News* 2018)

With respect to policy changes, the SHR revised its Tubal Ligation and Consent Policy in 2016. The External Review recommended it revisit this policy, which did not prevent the coerced sterilization of D.D.S., in 2018, by first consulting with those directly affected and then by ensuring all staff sign a document indicating they understood and would comply with it.[17]

It is important to remember healthcare providers have a legal, ethical, and moral obligation to ensure the informed consent of their patients — one that does not depend on this additional and potentially non-binding paperwork. As Dr. Jennifer Blake, Chief Executive Officer, Society of Obstetricians and Gynecologists of Canada, stated, "physicians are fully aware that obtaining free and fully informed consent is a fundamental component of the therapeutic alliance between the patient and the health care provider" and are required to recognize "their ethical responsibilities with respect to preserving the autonomy of the patient, particularly in cases of irreversible elective surgical procedures such as tubal ligation."[18] In addition to an apology, the External Review called on the SHR to provide reparations to those impacted. Boyer stressed the importance of involving those impacted and asking them what they want and need to heal, whether it is to have more children or for therapy and other supports (2020). The Survivors Circle for Reproductive Justice, formed in June 2023, consists of over two hundred survivors of coerced sterilization from Saskatchewan and beyond.[19] These women are still waiting for reparations for the harms done to them.

Class Action Litigation and the Settling of Colonialism

In October 2017, Lombard filed a statement of claim naming the Attorney General of Canada, Government of Saskatchewan, Regional Health Authorities (now Saskatchewan Health Authority and Athabasca Health Authority), and individual doctors as responsible for the coerced sterilization of Indigenous women.[20] The claim alleges battery of a sexual nature, trespass against the person, false imprisonment, and negligence and negligent misrepresentation; breach of fiduciary duty, or the obligation to act in the best interest of Indigenous women; and a violation of rights guaranteed under the Charter of Rights and Freedoms, including to freedom of conscience, belief, and religion; to life, liberty, and security of the person; to not be subject to cruel and unusual treatment; and to access health care free from discrimination. Each plaintiff is seeking $7 million in damages.[21]

Class action litigation is a tool that can bring attention to injustices as it places pressure on those responsible to do something to address the harm caused. However, even when successful, it has rarely, if ever, amounted to justice for Indigenous people. Take, for instance, the Sixties Scoop Class Action Settlement Agreement that sought to address the claims of Indigenous children who were removed from their homes between 1951 and 1991 and adopted out, often to non-Indigenous families, which was finalized in November 2017. This action, which began in Ontario, grew to include over thirty thousand claimants from across the country, represented by a conglomerate of some of the largest law firms in Canada including Klein Law, Merchant Law Group, and Wilson Christen LLP, Morris Cooper, and Koskie Minsky.[22] The undertaking grew so big it led to the retention of services from several corporations including Collectiva Services, to administer claims; Donna Cona Inc., to provide call centre support; and Argyle PR – Integrated Public Relations Agency, to coordinate communication with claimants.[23]

The Settlement Agreement offered $875 million in federal compensation, with $50 million for a Healing Foundation to support survivors, and $75 million for law firms.[24] In 2018, the conglomerate of law firms was "slammed" as "opportunistic" by Justice Edward Belobaba, Ontario Superior Court judge, who was "stunned" some were collecting $10 million each for not "having done not much at all" (The Canadian Press 2018). Meanwhile, some of the thirty-four thousand survivors who applied for compensation, of which over ten thousand had their claims denied, received a total of approximately $25,000 each despite being told by Minister of Crown-Indigenous Relations Carolyn Bennett they would receive up to $50,000 (Martens 2022; Hyslop 2021). This compensation, limited to Status Indians, left out non-Status and Métis individuals, despite individuals from these groups sharing similar experiences.[25] In a statement from the Office of Crown-Indigenous Relations, Bennett explained there was more work to be done with Métis and non-Status people, but those compensated had waited "far too long" for the harm done to them to be acknowledged.[26] In December 2018, Koskie Minsky began a proposed class action on behalf of Métis and non-Status Indian persons.[27] In April 2024, Crown lawyer Catherine Moore filed a statement of defence arguing this claim should be dismissed because Canada was not responsible for what happened and besides, it was filed outside of the statute of limitations.[28]

While this wheel is still in spin, it is wise to reflect on where it is headed and who benefits from proposed class action litigation. Marlene Orgeron, member of the Sixties Scoop Class Action Settlement Agreement from the Sapotaweyak Cree Nation, who was adopted by a family in New Orleans, asked about the meagre compensation offered to claimants: "Was this just to shut us up? There is no integrity in this process. Justice was not served" (cited in Warick 2018). Sixties Scoop Survivor Sandra Relling, from Alberta, stated: "I'm tired of the leaders of this country telling me what's in my best interest. I feel victimized again" (cited in Warick 2018). Survivor Colleen Cardinal (n.d.) described what it was like to receive the initial $21,000 payout:

> Nothing prepared me for the grief that manifested at a cellular level; my body remembering and reliving decades of physical and emotional pain. It was a reminder of what we, as Sixties Scoop survivors, collectively lost – large extended families, our communities, our languages, ceremonies and the knowledge that comes from ancestors who hunted, fished and thrived since time immemorial on their traditional lands ... I felt disconnected and weepy. (1–2)

She also described the consequences for others:

> The next few weeks left some Sixties Scoop survivors weepy, grieving and triggered. Without comprehensive support services in place, Sixties Scoop survivors sought support from one another. After the initial payments were distributed, we heard stories of survivors involved in front-line support work relapsing, overdosing, being taken advantage of, or dying from alcohol and drug related self-medicating to cope with the triggers and unresolved traumas connected to the loss of culture and identity. Even worse, many survivors who had just found out about the settlement discovered they had missed the deadline with no recourse at all. (Cardinal, 2–3)

Class action litigation is one of the only avenues victims of state violence can pursue to hold perpetrators to account and seek redress as criminal cases are often more onerous and require a higher standard of proof, and a willingness on the part of the RCMP to investigate (Cheng 2023). Monetary compensation cannot be dismissed as a necessary part of rectifying injustices, most especially for those living in poverty — which Indigenous people too often are. However, compensation cannot address what is destroyed through the Sixties Scoop, and pursuing this avenue comes at a great personal cost to survivors. It has also done nothing to address the many other forms of violence that result from living under conditions of colonialism.

Notably, Cardinal's piece is entitled "The Sixties Scoop Payoff: Canada's Strategy for Settling Colonialism." Indeed, the act of removing large numbers of Indigenous children from their families — a practice that continues to this day — undermines more than Indigenous culture and connections to community, though it does often do this; it works to undermine Indigenous connections to the lands upon which Indigenous forms of life depend, as it reduces federal obligations to Indigenous Peoples. To compensate survivors without addressing the purpose for which the practice was enacted, how it continues, or what is achieved through its implementation, works toward "settling" the land question for good. This example, one of many Indigenous experiences with class action litigation, pushes us to return to the question — who benefits from class action lawsuits? In many ways, it is everyone *but* Indigenous Peoples. These lessons should be heeded as law firms undertake steps down this well-travelled road, again.

Coerced sterilization is an intimate form of violence, but it too is only one form of violence resulting from colonialism. How does one ensure Indigenous women are compensated for the personal-individual *and* political-collective consequences of coerced sterilization? More than this, how does one ensure ongoing violence against Indigenous bodies *and* lands, which undermines Indigenous forms of life, embedded in Indigenous sovereignty, is stopped? What court deals with such issues? The late Mohawk scholar Patricia Monture-Angus tells us the Canadian legal system is incapable of addressing these issues; to do so would undermine its very legitimacy as an institution embedded within and serving as a tool of colonialism. Indigenous women, in "agreeing to the litigation process to resolve a claim," are implicitly agreeing to the terms upon which this system is based, often to their own detriment and that of their peoples (1999b, 52, 65). To take this critique seriously means we must ask what role class action litigation plays in reinforcing rather than challenging ongoing relations of colonialism. This is especially important as proposed class action lawsuits dealing with coerced sterilization are now pending across Canada. No doubt, in this process there will be continued attempts by those responsible to individualize systemic issues, limit liability, and divide those victimized into two groups — those deserving of reparations and those who are not.

Commenting on class action litigation, Lombard states the women she represents know "legal remedies can only go so far to restore what they have lost ... no judicial pronouncement, class action or otherwise, like so many in the past, can replace what they have lost, and most importantly, make future generations safe from the devastating violations of forced sterilization."[29] Litigation can take years, if not decades, and regardless of outcome, what is achieved will be partial and incomplete. The coerced sterilization of Indigenous women is an *individual-personal* harm and a *political-collective* harm. It is important to protect Indigenous women and girls from this form of violence before it happens. It is equally important to protect future generations of Indigenous Peoples *as peoples*. As one woman who was coercively sterilized stated: "where the violated have Indian status, such as myself, the repercussions reflect in an inability to pass that status on to future generations and decreases the numbers of our people. This practice is, in all manners, nothing short of genocide."[30]

Cultural Competency and Cultural Safety

In 2017, the Saskatchewan Ministry of Health restructured twelve health authorities into a single Saskatchewan Health Authority (SHA), with the Athabasca Health Authority remaining separate. This was a prime opportunity for the Ministry to undertake "extraordinary measures" to deliver "culturally grounded" health care created by and for Indigenous women and their families.[31] To push beyond tokenistic inclusion, or "indigenization," the External Review recommended it appoint an advisory council with authority, consisting of Elders, grandmothers, and community members, to work with representatives of those affected by its tubal ligation policies and advise on an Indigenous health engagement strategy that would enable Indigenous people to "reclaim their rightful place in society."[32] It recommended implementation of the report *Awaken the Power of Change: Representative Workforce Strategic Action Plan, 2010–2014, and 2014–2018* to increase Indigenous representation in the workforce while addressing false stereotypes held by some healthcare providers through "cultural competency training."[33] The TRC made similar recommendations when it called on all levels of government to close the gap in Indigenous health outcomes by increasing the number of Indigenous professionals in health care; ensuring the retention of Indigenous healthcare providers in Indigenous communities; implementing cultural competency training; and requiring all medical and nursing school students to take courses focused on Indigenous health issues, the legacy of residential schools, the United Nations Declaration on the Rights of Indigenous Peoples (UNDRIP), treaties and Aboriginal rights, and skills-based training in conflict resolution, human rights, and anti-racism.[34]

The SHR announced its "Commitment to Reconciliation" and promised to foster and maintain "respectful relations" with Indigenous Peoples by recognizing Indigenous "worldviews, knowledge and practices," including with respect to health, and ensure "culturally safe care" by increasing the number of Indigenous employees and training non-Indigenous professionals in "cultural competency."[35] Boyer and Bartlett point to the willingness of the SHR to undertake the *External Review* as "concrete evidence of a desire to make positive changes" and a "move toward reconciliation."[36] On the day the report of the *External Review* was released, the Ministers of Health, and Rural and Remote Health, issued a joint statement:

> We want to ensure that the perspectives of our [sic] Indigenous peoples are considered from day one in the governance and operations of the [SHA]. To that end, we have directed the newly appointed SHA Board of Directors and the SHA Transition Team to read this report and give its recommendations and calls to action full consideration in the planning and implementation of the [SHA] ... The Saskatchewan Advisory Panel on Health System Structure recommended engaging with [I]ndigenous peoples to help inform how best to address First Nations and Métis health needs in a culturally responsive and respectful manner. (Cited in Adam 2017)

The Saskatchewan Advisory Panel on Health System Structure formed an Indigenous Health Working Group (IHWG) with representatives from First Nations and Métis communities to advise. The IHWG met for the first time in February 2018 and released its report in June.[37]

It called on the SHA to implement a "Cultural Responsiveness Framework" — one respectful of Indigenous worldviews on health and well-being and attentive to the different care needs of Indigenous patients depending on, among other things, how one identifies, in what area of the province one lives, and whether one is fluent in English.[38] The "Cultural Responsiveness Framework" referred to by the IHWG was conceived in 2008, resulting from a Memorandum of Understanding signed by the Federation of Saskatchewan Indian Nations (FSIN), Health Canada, First Nations Inuit Health Branch, and Saskatchewan Ministry of Health, as part of a ten-year plan to eliminate health disparities and improve Indigenous health. At the time, the FSIN explained how, from these tri-partite discussions, "culturally appropriate and competent health services quickly emerged as one of the top priority areas that needed to be addressed."[39] Funding from the Saskatchewan Ministry of Health enabled the FSIN to develop the "Culturally Responsive Framework," with "cultural competency" and "cultural safety" as the foundation of a "culturally responsive health care system."[40]

The notion of "cultural competency" has become prominent in health, education, and social services since the 1980s (Polaschek 1998), but its origins are found in the activism of the civil rights movement in the United States (Gallegos, Tindall, and Gallegos 2008; Sivanandan 1985) — over which the Rockefeller Foundation exerted strategic influence — and corporate-led equal opportunity initiatives meant to increase the number of Black people in the workforce (Dobbin 2009; Marshall 2015).[41] In Canada, it is often associated with discourses on multiculturalism (Beagan 2018; Grenier 2020). To practise "cultural competency" in healthcare is to "deliver professional services in a way that is congruent with behaviours and expectations normative for a given community ... adapted to suit the specific needs of individuals and families from that community" (Green 1999, 87). It means one has the skills to understand the "values, attitudes and behaviours of patients" (Schouler-Ocak, Graef-Calliess, Tarricone et al. 2015, 423) and can assess patient needs through an attitude of empathy, openness, curiosity, and respect (Beagan 2018; McNaughton 2002). It is achieved when providers offer "culturally safe care" that is "empowering" of the cultural identity of the patient, and by acknowledging the power differential between a provider and patient by cultivating a relationship of trust.[42]

While cultural competency and cultural safety are often used interchangeably, they exist on a continuum, one is the precondition of the other.[43] Cultural safety is often credited to Māori nurse Irihapeti

Ramsden, whose work in the 1990s led to the implementation of "culturally safe" nursing and midwifery training in New Zealand (Ramsden 1990). The National Aboriginal Health Organization explains, cultural safety refers to "what is felt or experienced by a patient when a health care provider communicates with the patient in a respectful, inclusive way."[44] This requires healthcare providers to recognize the negative attitudes and stereotypes they may hold, and how the realities of colonialism impact overall health (Polaschek 1998; Papps and Ramsden 1996). It is rooted in education through "culturally safe" curriculum that reflects Indigenous experiences and histories and recognizes Indigenous forms of knowledge.[45]

If curriculum is "culturally safe" and delivered by "culturally competent" educators, so the logic goes, this will help ensure health professionals deliver quality care as it promotes the retention of more Indigenous health workers. The underlying premise is that, as healthcare workers challenge their own racial biases and more Indigenous care providers are embedded in the workforce, this will work toward addressing systemic racism and improve the overall health of patients. However, a longstanding and growing body of literature is critical of this approach for being, at best, unable to address systemic racism, and at worse, a continuation of systemic racism — a means of undermining the struggle against colonialism and genocide.

Some less convoluted critiques revolve around how to measure a person's level of cultural competency, or whether cultural competency does anything to improve health outcomes for marginalized populations (Azzopardi and McNeill 2016). For some, the ineffectiveness of this approach is demonstrated by the many continuing health inequities and instances of racism experienced by Indigenous and other racialized populations despite it being prominent in health care for over twenty years (Grenier 2020). Others point out how this approach conceptualizes culture as a set of unique characteristics based on one's racialized or Indigenous status without acknowledging how gender, class, sexual orientation, level of ability, or citizenship status intersect to inform a person's experiences (Beagan 2018; Kumaş-Tan, Beagan, Loppie et al. 2007). Still others wonder whether the uptake of this approach is motivated by a desire on the part of health administrators to minimize risk and ensure cost efficiency rather than promote systemic change (Paul, Hill, and Ewen 2012; Polaschek 1998).

There are other critiques as well. Cultural competency relies on essentialized and homogenous notions of culture (Carey 2015) and while Indigenous Peoples certainly share commonalities, including in how they are treated in health care, there is great diversity among nations. The tendency to group Indigenous Peoples together originated in racism and bureaucratic convenience (Wasacase 2003). This raises the question, in the quest to become culturally competent, which cultures are care providers supposed to learn about and what, specifically, should they focus on learning? Can one be culturally competent in delivering health care to Cree patients, but not to Nakota? Is another culture even knowable and how is it learned?

The assumption that a culture can be learned by those who do not practise it is based on a reification of culture — the idea that Indigenous culture exists *outside of Indigenous forms of life* (Wasacase 2003). In a recent report on systemic racism in health care in British Columbia, culture was defined as "a group's shared set of beliefs, norms and values ... the totality of what people develop to enable them to adapt to their world, which includes language, gestures, tools, customs and traditions that define their values and organize social interactions."[46] While these elements are important, culture is not confined to expressive activities — these expressive activities are tied to political and economic activities explicitly linked to Indigenous forms of life, on Indigenous lands, grounded in Indigenous sovereignty (Kulchyski 2013; Simpson 2017).

When cultural practices are not grounded within Indigenous forms of life — based on histories, relationships, and responsibilities to lands that give cultural practices, languages, and traditions meaning — they risk being reduced to something that can exist apart from, or despite their necessary preconditions. To put another way, when culture is disaggregated into its constituent parts (Sivanandan 1985), it becomes open to assimilation. Consequently, ongoing struggles against colonialism — historical and material relations which actively undermine Indigenous cultural practices *and* forms of life — are overlooked. Through this process, living and dynamic forms of life are turned into cultural aspects to be incorporated into Canadian society. Tanya Wasacase (2003) explains:

> This approach requires us to misunderstand the relation between what it means to be an Aboriginal person and how to engage and maintain our forms of life ... It ignores the

fundamental fact that who we are is based entirely on what we do, which is a matter of engaging in practices, and these are material, historical, and social ... this line of thinking enforces Canada's position of assimilating Aboriginal peoples into mainstream society while avoiding charges of committing the act of genocide. Since what it means to be an Aboriginal person (including culture and language) resides in the ... individual, Canada can acquit itself of the charge of genocide because they are not physically destroying the person ... [and] continue unimpeded the on-going assimilationist attack of systematically destroying the material, historical, and social forms of life of ... Cree [people], or anyone else that stands up for the right to engage the world in the way they see fit.

This point is articulated differently by Audra Simpson (2014), when she writes:

This fixation on cultural difference ... occludes Indigenous sovereignty. Looking for "culture" instead of sovereignty ... is a tricky move, as sovereignty has not in fact been eliminated. It resides in the consciousness of Indigenous peoples, in the treaties and agreements they entered into between themselves and others and is tied to practices that do not solely mean making baskets as your ancestors did a hundred years ago, or hunting with the precise instruments your great-grandfather did 150 years ago, in the exact spot he did ... This is a historical attitude that supplants the ravages of settler colonialism with definitions of "difference." Tolerance, recognition, and the specific technique that is multicultural policy are but an elaboration of an older sequence of attitudes toward "the problem" of Indigenous people, rendered now as populations, to be administered to by the state. This moves Indigenous peoples ... from nations, to people, to populations — categories that have shifted ... in relation to land and its dispossession. (20–1)

Through a focus on "cultural competency" and "cultural safety," Indigenous sovereignty struggles are narrowed to struggles against obvious manifestations of racism perpetuated, for one, by healthcare providers in their failure to be aware of or sensitive to Indigenous "culture." In doing so, Indigenous Peoples are rendered "ethnic groups suffering racial discrimination rather than ... nations [actively] undergoing colonization" (Smith 2012, 66).

To suggest cultural competency and safety as a solution to the coerced sterilization of Indigenous women, or systemic racism more broadly, undermines the possibility for a discussion of why these and other forms of violence are committed against Indigenous bodies *and* lands, and what kind of transformational change is required for this violence to end. Gordon Pon (2009, 66) writes, the cultural competency framework is a manifestation of Canada's desire to forget its "contentious relationship" with Indigenous Peoples as an active and ongoing genocide. It then becomes as a logical product of systemic racism, not a means of addressing it (Grenier 2020). The belief "if we just include more peoples [or aspects of their "culture"], then our practice will be less racist" (Smith 2012, 75) operates on the assumption that Western medicine is a means of ensuring health and wellness. This overlooks the viability of Indigenous ways of doing so, which are not only based on traditional medicines and cultural practices but forms of life embedded in relationships that seek to ensure healthy bodies *and* lands.

The tendency to view Western medicine as inherently good, or value neutral, obfuscates the central role it has played in violence against women (Ehrenreich and English 2010; Federici 2004), including racialized women (Cooper Owens 2018; Washington 2006), and how it functions as a tool of capitalism, colonialism, and imperialism (Lawford and Giles 2012; Lux 2016; Navarro 1981). We would do well to recall the role of capitalist interests, including the Rockefeller Foundation, in supporting the institutional structure, biomedical understanding, and ideological approach to health that is central to Western medicine in ways intended to benefit them and the political economy. The technologies and approaches embedded in Western medicine carry "ideologies and relations of power that are not only foreign but harmful," and the values transmitted are not capable of solving poverty or poor health, rather they contribute to the strengthening of relations that cause both (Navarro 1981, 6).

While it may seem radical to address racism by connecting it to institutions like health care, those institutions are rarely connected to the exploitative social relations they reinforce, or to demands for their transformation. The result is discrimination is severed from exploitation;

institutional racism is severed from state racism (Sivanandan 1985). In an illustrative example from March 2021, Prime Minister Justin Trudeau stated that government would always stand up against "systemic racism and intolerance in all its forms" (cited in *CBC News* 2021a). He continued, "There are many institutions that we have in this country, including ... Parliament, that has and is built around a system of colonialism, of discrimination, of systemic racism." However, rather than address colonialism — the exploitative social relations giving rise to systemic racism against Indigenous people — Trudeau stated:

> the answer ... is not to suddenly toss out all the institutions and start over; the answer is to look very carefully at those systems and listen to Canadians who face discrimination every single day and whenever they interact with those institutions, to understand the barriers, the inequities, and inequalities that exist within our institutions that need to be addressed, that many of us don't see because we don't live them. That's what fighting systemic discrimination is all about: listening, learning, and improving and transforming our institutions. (Cited in *CBC News* 2021a)

By invoking this "reconciliation lite" discourse (Midzain-Gobin and Smith 2021, 488–90), Trudeau divorces systemic racism from historical and material relations that give rise to its manifestations as he ignores how dehumanization and discrimination are linked to an active and ongoing expropriation of Indigenous lands, violation of treaties, and undermining of Indigenous sovereignty. Systemic racism becomes a problem of the individual, or many individuals, within institutions, that can only be addressed through individual interventions. On this, Ambalavaner Sivanandan (1985, 21) writes, "what better way could the state find to smooth out its social discordances while it carried on, untrammelled, with its capitalist works"?

Despite longstanding critiques, Indigenous-led and government-funded commissions, organizations, associations, and studies look to cultural competency and safety as a solution to systemic racism, and this approach is increasingly reflected in healthcare mission statements and medical training programs (Baba 2013; Campbell 2020).[47] Granted, some argue there is a need to turn away, partially at least, from cultural competency and toward cultural safety. The Indigenous Physicians

Association of Canada acknowledged the "real limitations and concerns" associated with cultural competency, but a "cultural safety approach" remains key to improving healthcare access.[48] The Indigenous Nurses Association reiterated that cultural safety addresses the limitations of cultural competency because it is predicated on understanding power differentials and redressing inequities through education, "it is action orientated."[49]

For others, "cultural humility" is needed to ensure healthcare practitioners provide respectful care to their patients (Beagan 2018; Hook 2014; Kirmayer 2013).[50] Joshua Hook explains, the focus on "humility" is intended to "allay pressures" for care professionals to "get it right" and "not make mistakes" as they begin questioning their hidden biases and "blindspots" by complicating the idea that one can ever become "sufficiently proficient" to the point of being "competent" (2014, 277–80). Again, it is important to note health professionals are required to be competent when it comes to ensuring informed consent before performing the many potentially life endangering and complex medical procedures their jobs entail.

Cultural competency and safety are rationalized as necessary to "prompt transformative shifts in healthcare practitioners and in the culture of health care" (Browne, Varcoe, Smye et al. 2009, 174). The learning this approach encourages may educate willing healthcare providers on how to be more respectful to their patients and this could, possibly, lead to political activism. However, on its own, it does nothing to address historical and material relations giving rise to systemic racism, nor does it address the institutional role played by Western medicine in reinforcing colonialism. It also fails to hold healthcare professionals and the systems within which they operate, criminally, morally, or ethically accountable for the violence they commit.

What has all this talk of cultural competency and safety amounted to in Saskatchewan? The *External Review* recommended the SHR partner with the Indigenous Nurses Association and the Indigenous Physicians Association to develop "cultural content" in health care.[51] In 2019, the SHA began streamlining recruitment of Indigenous staff to improve health outcomes and "reduce health care costs," and at the end of the year, it graduated a first cohort of Indigenous Birth Support Workers.[52] It also offered training to maternal nurses and physicians on informed consent and cultural competency. This training included providing healthcare professionals an opportunity to attend a "conversational" Cree language class.[53] Primary Health Care Manager Rhonda Teichreb explained, "people wanted more access to the Cree language so that they could engage in more meaningful conversations as a way to build trust with clients. We understand we are only learning a few words, but it is a good start."[54] It is not clear how these activities will put an end to coerced sterilization or push forward the broader systemic change necessary to end violence against Indigenous bodies and lands. It is difficult to understand how they might do so when these issues are not part of the conversation.

The federal government also remains committed to cultural competency and safety in its approach to combatting anti-Indigenous racism in health care. In January 2020, it supported a Forum on Culturally Informed Choice and Consent in Indigenous Women's Health, facilitated by the National Collaborating Centre for Indigenous Health.[55] It held a series of National Dialogues, in October 2020, and January and June 2021, to address anti-Indigenous racism in health care. Following the third National Dialogue, it announced an initial response, co-led by Indigenous Services Canada and Health Canada, that increased funding to improve access to "culturally safe services" through support for Indigenous midwives and doulas; ensure Indigenous women's voices are reflected in policy development; support Indigenous navigators and advocates to assist patients with the regulatory complaints process; gather data to better understand and address anti-Indigenous racism; and develop "distinction based health legislation" to build Indigenous capacity in the delivery of federally funded health services.[56]

The return of birth to Indigenous communities is a significant undertaking. In 2022, the Sturgeon Lake First Nation experienced the first baby born on-reserve in more than fifty years (Eneas 2022). Through the assistance of Elders, Knowledge Keepers, birth experts, and midwives, Sturgeon Lake is one of three communities in a pilot project to "bring cultural birthing back" to Indigenous people by allowing women who are considered "low risk" to remain in the community to give birth (Eneas 2022). In partnership with the National Aboriginal Council of Midwives and through an agreement with Health Canada, the community is the first in Saskatchewan to receive funding for a birthing centre (Adam 2022), for which a sod-turning ceremony took place in October 2023 (Vecchio 2023). In commenting on work being done, project director Shirley Bighead stated, "We are rebuilding our nation, is actually what we are doing, because when we have healthy babies, healthy children, then we will have a healthy community" (cited in Eneas 2022).

This type of initiative, for those who are willing and able to take part, is important to Indigenous reproductive sovereignty and choice. However, we must remember, even in the 1940s, the federal government was willing to support "home birthing" as a means of reducing expenditures, as hospital births were costlier (Lawford and Giles 2012, 333). In parts of Mexico and Peru where women experienced coerced sterilization, and where "cherry-picked" aspects of Indigenous birthing practices were incorporated into the biomedical system, separated from their broader cultural systems, power dynamics remain "unchanged and as problematic as ever" (Guerra-Reyes 2019, 7). Many Indigenous people will continue to access Western medicine and consequently, systemic change is needed to ensure they are not subject to systemic racism or coerced sterilization when they do. It is also necessary to ensure the healthy community referenced by Bighead, which requires healthy lands on which Indigenous Peoples can practise all aspects of Indigenous forms of life.

Adam Gaudry and Danielle Lorenz argue there is a fundamental difference when speaking of *decolonization*, which entails the "wholesale overhaul" of Western institutions and power relations between Indigenous Peoples and Canadians with the goal of creating something "dynamic and new" (2018, 219). They ask:

> Will mandatory courses be an end to themselves? Is their objective merely to ensure a disengaged multicultural appreciation of "the other" and their colonial containment ... or will complex and demanding issues such as settler colonialism, land rights, dispossession, state violence, heteropatriarchy, racism and sexism form the core of the curriculum? (163)

This point is repeated differently by others who, while not dismissing the need for us to undertake "a fundamental reconstitution of ourselves" (Smith 2013, 264) in ways that push us to problematize settler society and "reject domination and exploitation" (Tuck and Yang 2012, 19), stress the need for this to occur concurrently with a broader project to transform historical and material relations of colonialism. Otherwise, "the frontloading of critical consciousness building can waylay decolonization, even though the experience of teaching and learning to be critical of settler colonialism can be so powerful it can feel like it is ... making change. Until stolen land is relinquished" critical consciousness does nothing to disrupt colonialism (Tuck and Yang 2012, 19). To say cultural competency and cultural safety is a step toward systemic change is not borne by reality. One does not necessarily lead to the other. In fact, a focus on the former may be a strategy that can "rather effortlessly be co-opted" (Simpson 2017, 50) so the latter is avoided.

Bill S-250 and Calls for Criminalization

Indigenous women who have been coercively sterilized have consistently raised the need for those responsible for committing harms against them to be held accountable. This was echoed by Vice-Chief of the Federation of Saskatchewan Indians Heather Bear, who described coerced sterilization as a "total intrusion" upon the sovereignty of Indigenous women and demanded the federal government criminalize the practice (Fitzpatrick 2018). The Assembly of First Nations Chiefs passed a similar resolution.[57] Ontario Regional Chief RoseAnne Archibald stated:

> Women have a right and sovereignty over their own bodies and the forced and coerced sterilization of Indigenous women goes against the grain of our collective existence. Indigenous women, and all women, carry and share the greatest energy on the planet and that is love. It is love that grows our families, our communities and our nations, and the doctors involved have interfered in this sacred process of life. I ask all women of every race and creed to become our allies and join us as we fight this great tragedy.[58]

Chief Denise Stonefish, Women's Council Chair, described this attack as the robbing of future generations and "no less than a form of genocide."[59] Minister of Justice Jody Wilson-Raybould responded that government believed "everyone must receive culturally safe health services," and while coerced sterilization "is a serious violation of human rights," existing provisions under Canadian law already forbid "a range of criminal behaviour" relating to the practice. Instead, her office would take a "public-health approach" to the issue (Kirkup 2018a). What this means is unclear but should be considered troublesome since it was a "public-health approach" which contributed to the coerced sterilization of Indigenous women in the first place.

In 2018, Canada underwent a periodic review before the United Nations Committee Against Torture (UNCAT), a process whereby State parties to the United Nations Convention Against Torture and Other Cruel, Inhuman or Degrading Treatment or Punishment submit to a peer review process to assess the human rights situation in their national territory.[60] In Canada, this Convention's implementing framework rests primarily with Article 12 of Charter of Rights and Freedoms prohibiting cruel and inhuman treatment and punishment.[61] In its concluding observations, the UNCAT expressed concern regarding reports of "extensive" coerced sterilizations of Indigenous women and girls going back to 1970s.[62] It called on Canada to impartially investigate allegations, hold persons responsible accountable, provide redress to victims, and adopt legislation to criminalize the practice.[63]

In a follow-up report submitted to the UNCAT in February 2020, Canada responded that coerced sterilization "is a form of gender-based violence and evidence of a broader need to eliminate racism and discriminatory practices in health services and ensure cultural safety and humility ... [so] that Indigenous women receive all of the information necessary to be able to give their informed consent."[64] It sent a letter to provincial and territorial ministers, medical associations, and professional bodies "expressing concern" over recent reports, and it would work in collaboration to eliminate "discriminatory practices" and improve "cultural competency and cultural humility" by supporting training and professional development.[65] However, coerced sterilization was already a criminal offence under assault (section 265), assault causing bodily harm (section 267), and aggravated assault (section 268) in the Criminal Code.[66]

It was primarily through the efforts of Senator Yvonne Boyer that proposed legislation to criminalize coerced sterilization appeared before the Senate. In 2019, the Standing Senate Committee on Human Rights undertook a preliminary study on the "extent and scope" of coerced sterilization in Canada. The report, released in 2021, concluded based on evidence presented through witness testimony that coerced sterilization was "clearly continuing," its prevalence was "underreported" and "underestimated," and not only were Indigenous women affected, so were some women with disabilities, racialized women, intersex children, and institutionalized persons.[67] It recommended government respond to the report without delay and that a parliamentary committee conduct further study to identify solutions to stop the practice.[68]

The Senate Committee undertook further study, in March 2022, to hear from survivors and provide tangible recommendations to end the practice. During proceedings, many survivors spoke to the importance of explicitly criminalizing coerced sterilization. Witness A, Anishinaabeg from Fishing Lake First Nation, who was sterilized in 2008, stated: "It is my opinion that criminalizing this gross human rights violation is a critical step toward ending the disturbance of our people's survival as a distinct nation and toward ensuring justice and healing."[69] Witness S.T., Cree from Peepeekisis First Nation, who was sterilized in 2001, said:

> I am standing up to protect our future generations and our nations from this genocide. We can't be scared of that word. Imagine all the little spirits who would be here in our lives to teach us and learn from us and to form the backbone of strong Indigenous nations. What they did to me and my family, and so many others, was wrong, and they need to be held accountable, including criminally, for these horrendous, tortuous and genocidal acts.[70]

A third witness, Saulteaux from Zagime Anishinabek First Nation, sterilized in 2018, stated: "I do believe that some of the people involved should be held criminally responsible for what they have done. I feel bad about it, but I don't think that they really thought about me while I was in their care."[71] In her testimony, M.M., who experienced reproductive violence when she was fourteen years old, commented: "I can assure you of a few things ... cultural sensitivity? That won't cut it. Ultimately, the end game for me, personally — and I believe I share this sentiment with others — is that it needs to be criminalized in Canada."[72]

Nevertheless, some expressed skepticism about legal remedies. Virginia Lomax, Legal Counsel for the Native Women's Association of Canada, referenced murder being a crime, but this had not stopped large numbers of Indigenous women from going missing or being murdered: "It's clear to me that this is a much larger systemic issue. Criminalization will only be a small piece of the puzzle. Every moving part of the system that creates these injustices must be informed in a way that will prevent, not simply react."[73] Madeleine Redfern, President, Amautiit Nunavut

Inuit Women's Association, highlighted how difficult it was to bring about criminal charges for assault and was "not entirely sure" how changes to the Criminal Code would assist.[74]

To criminalize coerced sterilization is not without limitations — it is a carceral remedy vested in the colonial state that depends on the RCMP to investigate and prosecute, and it is an individualized, after-the-fact intervention that frames coerced sterilization as something arising only from within the doctor-patient relationship. It does not go far enough in preventing this violence before it occurs or addressing the broader context allowing for it. One need only consider sexual assault is a crime, but not all women who are victimized come forward, and when they do, very few perpetrators are convicted. The deterrent quality is questionable. Our collective willingness to hold perpetrators to account may more accurately reflect the value we place on women — or how the devaluation of women embedded in the criminal justice system reflects heteropatriarchal relations underpining capitalism, as these intersect with colonialism and white supremacy. There is much work to be done to ensure Indigenous bodies and lands, for one, are valued. This requires a transformation of social relations based on dehumanization, which informs increasing calls, led by racialized and Indigenous people, for the abolition of carceral solutions and creation of alternative means of justice, including reproductive justice, through systemic change (i.e., Davis, Gent, Meiners et al. 2022).

Bill S-250 was introduced by Senator Boyer on June 14, 2022.[75] It proposed to amend section 268 of the Criminal Code covering aggravated assault offences to include a new offence dealing with coerced sterilization. Section 268.1(7) would establish that "anyone who takes part in coercive measures to cause or attempt to cause someone to be sterilized is guilty of an indictable offence that holds a maximum of 14 years in prison."[76] Other amendments would have required medical practitioners to inform patients of all possible alternative contraceptive options to prevent conception; ensure patients understand consent could be withdrawn at any time leading up to, and immediately before, the procedure; and that consent be fully informed and provided in the absence of external pressure. Consent could not be obtained when the person was under eighteen years of age, or if the request for sterilization was not voluntarily initiated by the patient. There would be a final opportunity to withdraw consent before the procedure occurs.[77]

During debate at second reading, Senator David Wells acknowledged this proposed legislation would not address harms of the past, but it would prevent future violations and possibly provide comfort to survivors.[78] It was a crucial first step sending a clear message that government acknowledged coerced sterilization is a violation of human rights that would not be tolerated.[79] The failure of government to act would also constitute a "a de facto acquiescence to the practice."[80] Following study at the Standing Senate Committee on Legal and Constitutional Affairs, a drastically parred down version of this legislation, which only defined for greater certainty what constitutes a sterilization procedure under Section 268 (1) of the Criminal Code, passed third reading on October 8, 2024.[81] This legislation, which died when government prorogued in January 2025, was reintroduced as Bill S-288 on June 5, 2025.[82] It was again referred to the Standing Senate Committee on Legal and Constitutional Affairs after being read a second time on June 16, 2025, where it remains at time of writing.[83]

Senator Boyer acknowledged legislation is only a tool, as are class actions; a "huge," "several-pronged," and "national approach" is needed to eradicate the practice.[84] Indeed, a broad approach is required to address coerced sterilization and the historical material relations giving rise to it and other forms of violence experienced by Indigenous people. For Boyer, it was evident sterilization practices were implemented to "ensure specific groups of people do not have the ability to reproduce," and "imposing measures intended to prevent births within the group" through coerced sterilization is genocide.[85] In passing this legislation, which received "overwhelming support" from the Survivors Circle for Reproductive Justice and community leaders across the country, Canada could set a good example for the international community by taking concrete action.[86] However, it is unclear why, if coerced sterilization is an act of genocide, new legislation is required considering there already exists legislation to address this crime.

Despite its limitations, one wonders if the passage of this legislation is a concrete step toward addressing the coerced sterilization of Indigenous women. It is certainly not enough to address the broader context that has led to the practice — a context that continues to be based on the disappearance of Indigenous Peoples (Tuck and Yang 2012). Perhaps here, one would do well to reflect on a piece of Black history in Upper Canada. Some considered passage of legislation in 1793, banning the importation of slaves, as a tangible step toward ending slavery, in support of Black liberation struggles — one that did not require a change to the consciousness of settlers or slave owners.[87] However, scholars note, this legislation was a compromise that "violated no existing public property" and "freed not one slave" (Winks 2021, 98, 97). Neither did it, or the gradual abolition of slavery, end anti-Black racism, which continues to impact all aspects of life and death for Black people and sometimes results in their coerced sterilization too (Maynard 2017; Roberts 2016).[88]

There is a fundamental tension in the words of Indigenous women who were coercively sterilized, who state clearly that they want individual accountability as they actively highlight the systemic or genocidal aspect of the practice. This fundamental tension reflects the space between remedies that seek to address personal-individual harms and their political-collective dimensions. The question for this author, who understands the need to push beyond binary thinking — it is rarely either or, this or that, good or bad — in liberation struggles, is at what point do we ensure systemic change grounded in an acknowledgement *and fundamental transformation* of historical material relations giving rise to violence against Indigenous bodies *and* lands if this is not a central part of the conversation? Indigenous women who have been coercively sterilized should not be asked to compromise in seeking justice for what was done to them.

Indigenous Rights, Responsibilities, and Resurgence

The fundamental tension in how to address personal-individual harms resulting from coerced sterilization and its political-collective dimensions reappears when considering the Indigenous rights–based approach to systemic racism in health care. Aboriginal rights exist to protect the collective and cultural distinctiveness of Indigenous Peoples (Kulchyski 2013) and are "recognized and affirmed" under section 35 (1) of the Constitution Act, 1982.[89] Many Indigenous Peoples hold Aboriginal rights to traditions, cultural practices, and subsistence activities stemming from historical land occupation and use. The right to self-determination "entails unconditional freedom to live one's relational, place-based existence, and practice healthy relationships" (Corntassel and Bryce 2012, 12). Boyer (2014b, 133) engages convincing evidence showing many Indigenous Peoples have pre- and post-contact practices of health and healing, and a "constitutionally protected Aboriginal right to health," including the right to reproduce and to traditional health practices and systems.

The land mass of Saskatchewan is covered by Treaties 2, 4, 5, 6, 7, 8, and 10, and Treaty Peoples may hold Treaty Rights to health and health care.[90] Those who signed treaties "did not relinquish their Aboriginal health regime/system to the British sovereign or to Canada. Rather, they protected these systems. Part of their intent ... was to supplement these systems with promises of medical care and medicines that were useful in treating European diseases."[91] In other words, many in Saskatchewan hold an Aboriginal right to practice their own ways of health and healing, and the right to access Western medicine through treaty. These "constitutionally entrenched rights" are unique to them (Boyer and Spence 2015, 95). Indigenous people also hold the right to health by virtue of being human, and to access health care in an equitable and non-discriminatory manner as guaranteed by international and domestic legal instruments.[92]

The *External Review* highlighted it was important for the SHR to acknowledge, as a starting point, that Indigenous health practices are "constitutionally-protected rights," and recommended it implement traditional medicine and knowledge approaches to health by relying on Indigenous laws and legal traditions.[93] In doing so, it needed to "consult and accommodate" holders of section 35 Aboriginal and Treaty Rights.[94] The SHR's commitment to adopt health principles set out in the UNDRIP was key to solidifying a "health rights based approach" for Indigenous Peoples, and here, "the usefulness of the UNDRIP cannot be understated."[95]

The UNDRIP recognizes the right of Indigenous Peoples to "self-determination," and by virtue of this, to "freely determine their political status" while maintaining "autonomy of self-government in matters relating to their internal and local affairs," and strengthening "their distinct political, legal, economic, social and cultural institutions."[96] Article 24 recognizes the right to "traditional medicines ... [and] health practices, including the conservation of their vital medicinal plants, animals and minerals," and to "access, without any discrimination," social and health services.[97] Boyer and Bartlett view the UNDRIP as a "forceful tool" for establishing the Indigenous right to health because it recognizes its interdependence with other rights, including those seeking to address economic and social conditions.[98]

The UNDRIP resulted from more than twenty-five years of efforts by the Working Group on Indigenous Populations, established in 1982. It is "the first human rights instrument to include the participation of those affected" and is considered the "gold standard" (Green 2014, 22-3) in international law for the protection of Indigenous human rights. It was adopted by the United Nations General Assembly in September 2007 (Charters and Stavenhagen 2009). In the lead up to its adoption, Canada engaged in "heavy lobbying" (Deer 2010, 25) against the UNDRIP, and together with Australia, New Zealand, and the United States, voted against it (Moreton-Robinson 2011). It expressed concerns with "overly broad" and "unduly restrictive" language that was "capable of a wide variety of interpretations" with respect to provisions addressing ownership of lands and resources, the need to obtain free, prior, and informed consent prior to development, utilization, or exploitation of these, and for being "overly pro-Indigenous peoples" in support of "self-determination," without giving adequate consideration to states and third parties.[99]

Canada changed course in November 2010 when it signed onto the UNDRIP with qualification. Prime Minister Stephen Harper stated it would be better for Canada to "endorse the UNDRIP while explaining its concerns, rather than simply rejecting the overall document" (cited in Boyer 2014b, 164). It viewed the document as "aspirational," "non-legally binding," and one that did not change Canadian laws, but endorsement would give government the opportunity to work in partnership with Indigenous Peoples in "creating a better Canada."[100] Canada reversed course again in May 2016 when Minister of Indigenous and Northern Affairs Carolyn Bennett announced it would support the UNDRIP "without qualification" and implement it in accordance with the Constitution. This "important step" toward reconciliation would provide a "full box of rights" to Indigenous Peoples.[101]

As a step toward implementation, Canada passed Bill C-15, the United Nations Declaration on the Rights of Indigenous Peoples Act (UNDA), on June 21, 2021.[102] Described by government as "a roadmap" for working with Indigenous Peoples to "advance lasting reconciliation" through "renewed, nation-to-nation, Inuit-Crown, government-to-government relationships with First Nations, Inuit, and Métis," it committed Canada to tabling an action plan to achieve the UNDA objectives within two years.[103] The Action Plan was released in 2023.[104] However, the Action Plan, the UNDA, and the UNDRIP are not without criticism.

Some contend the UNDRIP can be relied on to interpret section 35(1) of the Constitution to provide greater protection for Aboriginal rights (Boyer 2014a; Gunn 2014). Others argue the need to engage cautiously with the UNDRIP (Joffe 2014) in "defence of Indigenous struggles" (Kulchyski 2013, 1) as the rights contained within it are an extension of "universal human rights" or "equality rights" (57), reminiscent of the principle underlying "citizens plus," which can be deployed to undermine collective rights. Many agree the UNDRIP is a "worthy achievement" — Indigenous Peoples need to have their human rights respected (Kulchyski 2013, 58; Boyer 2014a; Green 2014). However, for Indigenous Peoples to retain their distinctive cultures — embedded in Indigenous forms of life, in relationship with the land — they require sovereignty, something missing from the UNDRIP (Churchill 2011; Kulchyski 2013).

Charmaine White Face (2013), Oglala Tituwan Oceti Sakowin and spokesperson for Sioux Nation Treaty Council, who participated in the drafting of the UNDRIP, shows how the final version approved by the United Nations General Assembly was not that approved by Indigenous Peoples. Indigenous sovereignty was undermined through wording changes and the deletion of text recognizing the right of Indigenous Peoples to freely determine their relationship with nation-states (White Face 2013). Indigenous Peoples were advised to "stop talking in terms of sovereignty and to argue instead for self-determination" (Pitty 2001, 59) to quell state fears of territorial secession. Self-determination, limited to "internal and local affairs" (White Face 2013, 41), is often interpreted as "self-government" (Alfred 2009). This has led at least one scholar to refer to the UNDRIP as "a travesty of a mockery of a sham" (Churchill 2011, 549).

Other criticisms revolve around how the UNDRIP, which presupposes the continued existence of Canada as a nation-state with right-granting capabilities (Kulchyski 2013), "valorizes the rule of the Rulers" (Green 2014, 22) that, whether in international or domestic law, is based on "colonial foundations" (Smith 2014, 84). Critics (Churchill 2011; Venne 1998; White Face 2013) point to Article 46(1), which reads, "Nothing in this Declaration may be ... construed as authorizing or encouraging any action which would dismember or impair, totally or in part, the territorial integrity or political unity of sovereign and independent States," as evidence the UNDRIP is vested in Indigenous dispossession.[105] In her reading of the UNDRIP, Irene Watson states, it "is a bit like states having their cake and eating it too ... on the one hand it recognizes the right of First Nations to self-determination, and, on the other hand, it limits self-determination to being exercised in accord with state power" (2018, 98).

Russ Diabo (2021) argues that, in adopting the UNDRIP, and through the UNDA and its proposed Action Plan, Canada is engaging in a "White Paper 2.0," which, if successful, will result in Indian bands being converted into "fourth level ethnic governments" below all others, the dissolution of Indigenous Services Canada, and the undermining of Aboriginal and Treaty Rights. Elsewhere, Diabo (2017) explains:

> First, section 91(24) of the Constitution, which states that the Crown has jurisdiction over "Indians, and Lands reserved for the Indians," will be used to impose national standards on the lives of Aboriginal peoples living on reserve through federal legislation, as has already been done with the *First Nations Land Management Act*, for example. With these laws, the Crown continues to set the parameters for how First Nations peoples are to live on their land ... Second, modern section 35 land claims and self-government agreements will be manipulated to modify, convert and extinguish the inherent sovereignty of First Nations. More self-government agreements will be signed with bands formed under the *Indian Act*. The political effect will be to convert these bands into a kind of ethnic Indigenous municipality rather than self-determining nations. Outlining a contingent set of rights through these agreements, rather than acknowledging the inherent right to self-determination, will in effect empty section 35 of any real political or economic meaning.

In his analysis, the outcome will be further conflict between grassroots Indigenous people engaged in land defense as part of broader sovereignty struggles, Indian Act–elected band councils, and the Canadian state. These and other shortcomings led White Face to conclude:

> If Bill C-15 is based on the [UNDRIP], it is based on a lie ... Having a Bill based on a lie makes the Bill a partner in the lie and therefore, not good law. To say that Bill C-15 will affirm the rights of Indigenous Peoples is not true. The UNDRIP was

> changed to satisfy colonizing governments' continued pursuit for control over Indigenous Peoples and resources. (Cited in Diabo 2021)

Beyond its central role in promoting population control activities worldwide, one would do well to remember the influence the Rockefeller Foundation exerted over the establishment of the United Nations (Mass 1976; Tournès 2014). Human rights have always been a Rockefeller family tradition (Urwin 1995).

Andrew Marshall argues corporate support for human rights needs to be understood within the context of a broader self-interest, one focused on "social control, top-down reforms, social engineering, and the desire to create and institutionalize a leadership cadre with whom foundations — and the ruling class they represent — can work" (2015, 775), while "sidelining" more "radical" (776) calls to address the root causes of social problems. The mandate of the United Nations, to maintain "international peace and security," needs to be considered together with the longstanding desire of corporate interests to keep the world safe for capitalism. Rights-based mechanisms like those under the UNDRIP rely on "state constructions that do not necessarily reflect inherent [I]ndigenous *responsibilities* to their homelands" (Corntassel and Bryce 2012, 152), and by investing in the "politics of recognition" (Coulthard 2014), or the "illusion of inclusion" (Corntassel 2007, 161), Indigenous struggles risk *reinforcing* colonialism and dispossession.

This fundamental tension has led some to reject this approach altogether by promoting a "radical reorientation towards land" (Smith 2014, 84) grounded in Indigenous sovereignty and resurgence (Simpson 2017). For Leanne Betasamosake Simpson, this means re-centring Indigenous responsibilities to work with "ancestors and those yet unborn" to ensure a "radical and complete overturning of the nation-state's political formations" (2017, 10). Similarly, for Jeff Corntassel, Indigenous resurgence "means having the courage and imagination to envision life beyond the state" (2012, 88–9). In this, there is a need to understand colonialism as a series of processes that are *always* designed to dispossess and contain Indigenous Peoples:

> The structure [of settler colonialism] is one of perpetual disappearance of Indigenous bodies for perpetual territorial acquisition ... the state sets up different controlled points

> of interaction through its practices — consultations, negotiations, high-level meetings, inquiries, royal commissions, policy, and law ... that slightly shift, at least temporarily and on microscales, our experience of settler colonialism as a structure. The state uses its asymmetric power to ensure it always controls the processes as a mechanism for managing Indigenous sorrow, anger, and resistance, and this ensures the outcome remains consistent with its goal of maintaining dispossession. It can appear or feel as though the state is operating differently because it is offering a slightly different process to Indigenous peoples. Goodness knows, we'd all like to be hopeful ... [However] it is shifting to further consolidate power, to neutralize our resistance, to ultimately fuel extractivism. Our history and our intelligence systems tell us we need to see this in the present. (Simpson 2017, 45–6)

The UNDRIP may be an "important tool" (Boyer 2014a, 14) that places Indigenous concerns in the international arena (Kulchyski 2013). It may provide a mechanism for Indigenous Peoples to organize, document human rights abuses, and form transnational coalitions (Smith 2014). It may also hold the possibility of improving the lives of some in the immediate or long term, including by accommodating or reinvigorating certain aspects of Indigenous cultures. However, to speak of reinvigorating culture apart from Indigenous forms of life is to speak of the potential for assimilation. Simpson writes, "Indigenous peoples require a land base and therefore require a central and hard critique of the forces that propel dispossession" (2017, 50). This critique is absent in responses to the coerced sterilization of Indigenous women, and this absence prevents us from considering how the avenues being pursued may reinforce dispossession. While there is no "pure strategy" (Smith 2014, 96) in the pursuit of justice, if we are not talking about dispossession, then we will "certainly not be talking about land restitution" (Simpson 2017, 42), a necessary component to addressing violence against lands and bodies.

Conclusion

The coerced sterilization of Indigenous women never stopped; it continued in different form — long after eugenics fell into disrepute. This work provides a context in which to understand this practice as part of a history of attempts on the part of the Canadian state to curb Indigenous reproduction to ensure continued access to Indigenous lands to the benefit of the political economy and those who depend on them for profit. Through a focus on Saskatchewan, it demonstrates that population control activities, funded and supported by corporate elites, were the ideological and material catalyst guiding the expansion of public health in Canada in ways that have resulted in the coerced sterilization of Indigenous women. It challenges the reader to reconsider the view that health and welfare interventions were ever value neutral. Rather, they have emanated from institutions, experts, and ideologies directly influenced by corporate interests who have everything to gain by ensuring the smooth functioning of a capitalist political economy; one that depends on violence against Indigenous lands and bodies. The expansion of family planning policy and practice is one manifestation of these interests, and through relations of global imperialism, this history links the experiences of Indigenous women here to that of others elsewhere, in the United States (López 2008; Torpy 2000), Central and South America (Kendall and Albert 2015; Menandro 2022; Mass 1976; Stavig 2017), Australia (Rademaker, Troy, and Hurst 2024), Indonesia, India, Africa, and Europe (Greve-Møller 2024; Open Society Foundations 2011; Zampas and Lamačková 2011).

The coerced sterilization of Indigenous women cannot be blamed on any one entity. The federal government has a unique relationship with Indigenous Peoples, a nation-to-nation relationship that in Saskatchewan is further cemented through treaties and other obligations owed to Cree, Dakota, Dene, Nakota, Saulteaux, Métis, and an increasing number of Inuit. While it has failed to meet its obligations, it is not solely responsible. Through federal devolution of responsibility to the province, it too is responsible for implementing systemically racist policies and practices that have resulted in the policing of Indigenous people. Health and welfare professionals — physicians, nurses, and social workers — sometimes imbued with their own racism and paternalism, have carried out policies and practices which have culminated in the coerced sterilization of Indigenous women. To this we must add the Canadian populace — of which government officials and health and welfare professionals are a part — which has supported narratives that deny the humanity of Indigenous people, blaming them for the conditions of life they often experience as we remain committed to a way of life — to jobs, consumption patterns, property rights, and more — that depends on violence. Then, there are the corporations, in their search for profits no matter the cost to land or life, who remain the largest beneficiaries of all.

The difficulty in assigning blame does not mean *no one* is to blame, it means *all are to blame.* In facing blame, there exists a possibility to do differently. We can join Indigenous Peoples in struggle against social relations of oppression. We are the "often forgotten" part of the colonial relationship after all, and a struggle this big requires all our efforts. However, to be of any use, we need to move past denial and toward facing the truth (Monture-Angus 1999a). Are we able to tell the truth about ourselves by recognizing our complicity in genocide? Many have yet to acknowledge the coerced sterilization of Indigenous women has happened. Perhaps this is a necessary first step. But then what? The fundamental tension in how to respond remains. It needs to be faced if our goal is to end the violence against Indigenous bodies and lands, and possibly, create a better world for all of us.

I have heard some say we need to do something to stop the coerced sterilization of Indigenous women, and doing something is better than doing nothing. We do, and it is. Others say change is incremental, it does not happen overnight. Indeed, the change required to bring about a transformation of historical material relations fueling colonialism, extractivism, and violence is massive, and there is an urgent need to act in the immediate, to do what we can, now. Perhaps proposed interventions will improve the lives of some at least. Perhaps. Then, there is the matter of principle. If the state is not willing to offer limited concessions to ensure the basic health and safety of Indigenous women, it will not be willing to do what is required to ensure justice for Indigenous Peoples, so maybe what we are doing is a start. Maybe all of this is true.

However, there is something risked when we only follow this logic. The many long-term struggles waged against colonialism, capitalism, heteropatriarchy, and white supremacy led by Indigenous, Black, Queer, and Trans people, women, and other oppressed groups offer lessons on what happens when our movements for justice are compromised and we settle for what is offered by those who continue to benefit from active and ongoing oppression — long-term goals are often lost, people are divided, gains are constantly under threat of being taken away (Alexander 2020; Kinsman 2023; Stote 2017; Tuck and Yang 2018), and our struggles continue. These lessons should serve as a warning of the ever-potential risk for co-optation by the state of any effort to address the coerced sterilization of Indigenous women.

In her writing on the mass incarceration of Black people in the United States, Michelle Alexander offers many lessons on the importance of repositioning reform work as movement building toward the dismantling of all systems of oppression. If this goal is not made explicit, she argues, reform work can and will be "easily absorbed or deflected" and accommodations offered by the state will serve to legitimate the system, not undermine it (2020, 293). For her, the central question becomes, are we serious about ending systems of control and oppression or not? If we are, there is a tremendous amount of work to do that must involve a fundamental change in public consciousness (290). She writes, "it is the failure to care, really care … that lies at the core of the system of control … here and elsewhere" (Alexander 2020, 290–1). If we are serious about ending violence and building a better world, we must move toward relationships of responsibility and care for each other and the lands on which we depend. We need to see each other in our humanity. And we need to re-learn how to dream, and to let those dreams guide us as we walk.

I often return to a question posed by Eve Tuck and K. Wayne Yang when they ask us to consider "towards what justice" we are headed in our struggles, what are the "lodestars" guiding our course, and how do we ensure they are reached by walking the paths we are on (2018, 10–1)? The actions we take in the immediate need to be connected to long-term goals and these goals must be made explicit, so we remain on course, determined, undivided, uncompromising, and strong. So that no one is left behind. Whatever risks making us lose focus by committing us to a path we did not intend to take, in directions we would rather not go, needs to fall away.

George Manuel wrote that for Canadians to deviate from the all too familiar road on which we walk and toward another that recognizes the humanity of Indigenous people, this will require a "genuine leap of imagination" (Manuel and Posluns 2019, 224). Métis legal scholar Marilyn Poitras, who resigned as commissioner after expressing concern with the "status quo" colonial structure of the MMIWG Inquiry, stated that our expectations of a particular course of action will determine whether something is successful or not (*CBC News* 2017). Similarly, Roland Chrisjohn wrote, "If we are less than honest in what we think it will take to undo what has been done, what right of complaint do we have if they [we] fail to undertake effective measures" (1997, 112). Is what is being offered enough to ensure justice for Indigenous women and their peoples? Is it the best any of us can imagine or hope for? Life is precious and beautiful. The ability to give life is magical, even if the capitalist system is incapable of recognizing it as such. Do we not all deserve to live a beautiful and magical life?

In her reflection on the importance of Indigenous resurgence as an alternative to continued engagement with the state, Leanne Betasamoke Simpson writes:

> I know that the current man-made global structures of the world are killing the planet and exploiting everything and everyone that is meaningful to me within my own nation. Resurgence is hope for me because of its own simultaneous dismantling of settler colonial meta-manifestations and its reinvigoration of Indigenous systemic alternatives — alternatives that have already produced sustainable, beautiful, principled societies. Yet we need more visioning, thinking, acting, and mobilization around these Indigenous systemic alternatives because creating the alternative is the mechanism through which freedom can be achieved. Engagement with Indigenous systems changes Indigenous peoples. It is a highly emergent and generative process. This requires ... more presence within Indigenous realities. This requires struggle and commitment. (2017, 49)

We are all being called on to locate ourselves in this struggle by demonstrating a similar commitment to dismantling colonialism as it intersects with the social relations that impact our health and well-being, too. To thinking, learning, and (re)envisioning alternatives that can co-exist in relationship with Indigenous Peoples and the land. Perhaps in this process we will change too. Audre Lorde (1988) once asked how we might use our differences in a common battle for a livable future. We must all ask ourselves this question. The state and its appendages cannot be relied on to build this future. The creation of this world is up to us.

Endnotes

Preface

1   On this history, see Daschuk (2013); Cardinal and Hilderbrant (2000); and Ray, Miller, and Tough (2000).
2   On settler colonialism and the need to "eliminate" Indigenous Peoples, see Tuck and Yang (2012); Wolfe (2006).

Introduction

1   *Base v. Hadley et al.* (2006) NWTSC 04.
2   *M.S.Z. v. M.* (2008) YKSC 73.
3   A judgment in August 2023 allowed the class action in Quebec to proceed. *Unetell et Madame X v. Centre Integre de Santé et de Services Sociaux de Lanaudiere et Richard Monday et Yvonne Brindusa Vasilie* (2023) P.Q. District de Joliette, 705-06-000011-214; *M.R.L.P. and S.A.T. v. The Attorney General of Canada, the Government of Saskatchewan, Saskatchewan Health Authority, Dr. Kristine Mytopher, Dr. Ahmed Ezzat, Dr. Ian Lund, John Doe and Jane Doe* (2007) Q.B.SASK. 1485; *P.D.I. and S.D.P. v. the Attorney General of Canada, The Government of Manitoba, Winnipeg Regional Health Authority, Southern Health-Santé Sud, Prairie Mountain Health, Northern Regional Health Authority, Interlake-Eastern Regional Health Authority, The College of Physicians & Surgeons of Manitoba, The College of Registered Nurses of Manitoba, St. Boniface Hospital, Jane Doe and John Doe* (2019) Q.B.MAN. CI19-01; *Jessica Horne v. Her Majesty the Queen in Right of the Province of British Columbia* (2019) S.C.B.C. 194010; *Cardinal v. HMQ* (2018) Q.B. AB. 1801-18051; *Lorraine Davis and Stephanie Roy v. His Majesty the King in Right of the Province of British Columbia* (2023) S.C.B.C. 231251.
4   Yvonne Boyer and Judith Bartlett, *External Review - Tubal Ligation in the Saskatoon Health Region: The Lived Experience of Aboriginal Women* (Saskatchewan: Saskatoon Health Region, 2017); Canada, Standing Senate Committee on Human Rights (SSCHR), *Forced and Coerced Sterilization of Persons in Canada* (Ottawa: SSCHR, 2021); SSCHR, *The Scars We Carry: Forced and Coerced Sterilization of Persons in Canada – Part II* (Ottawa: SSCHR, 2022).
5   A review of abortion services at the hospital was conducted in 1992; see Department of Health, *Report of the Abortion Services Review Committee* (NWT: Government of the Northwest Territories, 1992); on recommendations resulting from this review; see Department of Health, *Status Report: Implementation Plan for Recommendations of the Abortion Services Review Committee* (NWT: Government of the Northwest Territories, 1993).
6   British Columbia Task Force on Access to Contraception and Abortion Services, *Realizing Choices: The Report of the British Columbia Task Force on Access to Contraception and Abortion Services* (Victoria, BC: Province of British Columbia, 1994).
7   Suzy Basile and Patricia Bouchard, *Free and Informed Consent and Imposed Sterilizations Among First Nations and Inuit Women in Quebec* (Quebec: First Nations of Quebec and Labrador Health and Social Services Commission, 2022).
8   Boyer and Bartlett, *External Review,* 8.

9   Rockefeller funding was delivered through various agencies throughout the early to mid-twentieth century, including the Rockefeller Institute for Medical Research (1901); General Education Board (1903); Rockefeller Sanitary Commission for the Eradication of Hookworm (1909–15); Bureau of Social Hygiene (1919–34); Rockefeller Foundation (1913); Laura Spelman Rockefeller Memorial Fund (1918); and International Education Board (1923). For simplicity, the Rockefeller Foundation refers to any of these.
10 On Sanger, see Kennedy (1970); Takeuchi-Demirci (2018).
11 The League of Nations is considered the precursor to the United Nations; many of its activities were incorporated into the work of the United Nations after its formation in 1945 (Garcia, Rodogno, and Kozma 2016).
12 Thank you to an anonymous reviewer for highlighting this point, in this way.
13 Rockefeller Foundation, *Annual Report* (New York: The Rockefeller Foundation, 1933), 275–6.
14 In 1930, the Foundation gave the CNCMH $25,243.38; in 1931, $31,620; and in 1936, over $19,000. Rockefeller Foundation, *Annual Report* (New York: The Rockefeller Foundation, 1930), 18; Rockefeller Foundation, *Annual Report* (New York: The Rockefeller Foundation, 1931), 320; Rockefeller Foundation, *Annual Report* (New York: The Rockefeller Foundation, 1936), 372.
15 In Canada, rates per 1,000 were 27.2 (1946); 27.2 (1951); 28.0 (1958); 26.1 (1961); 19.4 (1966) (Schlesinger 1974, 114).
16 Canada, DNHW Task Force, *Recommendations of the First National Conference on Family Planning*, February 28 to March 2, 1972. (Ottawa: Health and Welfare Canada, 1974), comment 6. This definition initially included abortion, which was later deemed an "unacceptable" means of birth control. Abortion has a different history, was considered separately during legislative debates, and was addressed under separate legislative reform. The World Health Organization considers abortion a reproductive right if family planning does not go as expected. Abortion is not included in this discussion.
17 United Nations, *Final Act of the International Conference on Human Rights, Tehran*, April 22 to May 13, 1968 (New York: United Nations, 1968), para. 16, 4.
18 Provincial Archives of Saskatchewan (PAS), R-1453, File 1.156, Ken Svenson, Report: "Indian and Métis Issues in Saskatchewan to 2001," December 1978, 1.
19 Boyer and Bartlett, *External Review*, 18–19.
20 Ibid, 19.
21 Ibid, 6–8, 23–33.
22 National Inquiry into Missing and Murdered Indigenous Women and Girls (MMIWG), *Reclaiming Power and Place: The Final Report of the National Inquiry into Missing and Murdered Indigenous Women and Girls*, Volume 1A (Ottawa: MMIWG, 2019).

Chapter 1

1   Rockefeller Foundation, *Annual Report* (New York: The Rockefeller Foundation, 1928), 60, 209–10.
2   *The Welfare of Children Act*, R.S.S. 1927, c. 60, s. 4, ss. 2.
3   *The Welfare of Children Act*, s. 157–58.
4   PAS, R-33.5, File III 105 (13-4-3-3), Clarence Hincks, Samuel Laycock, and Oswald Rothwell, *Report of the Mental Hygiene Commission* (Regina: Government of Saskatchewan, 1930), 103.
5   Hincks, Laycock, and Rothwell, *Report of the Mental Hygiene Commission*, 105.
6   Ibid, 7–8.

7   Ibid, 8–10.
8   Ibid, 102.
9   Ibid, 103, 131.
10 *The Mental Defectives Act*, 1930, c.71, s.1; R.S.S. 1930, c.196, s.1; *The Mental Diseases Act*, 1921–22, c.75, s.1; R.S.S. 1930, c. 195, s.1. Hincks, Laycock and Rothwell, *Report of the Mental Hygiene Commission*, 105.
11 *An Act Respecting Mentally Defective and Mentally Ill Persons*, R.S.S. 1936, c. 91.
12 *An Act Respecting Mentally Defective and Mentally Ill Persons*, s. 59.
13 *An Act Respecting Mentally Defective, Mentally Ill and Other Persons*, R.S.S. 1950, c. 74, s. 60 (1).
14 *An Act Respecting Mentally Defective… Persons*, s. 41–46.
15 *An Act to Amend the Indian Act*, R.S.C. 1951, s. 2 (k).
16 Library and Archives of Canada (LAC), RG 29, Vol. 2971, File 851-4-300, pt. 1A, "Correspondence, C.A. Roberts, M. D., Principal Medical Officer, Mental Health, to Director, Indian Health Services," September 28, 1956.
17 *An Act Respecting the Solemnization of Marriage*, R.S.S. 1933, c. 59.
18 Rockefeller Foundation, *Annual Report* (New York: Rockefeller Foundation, 1935), 83.
19 PAS, R-1346, File 2.54e, A.V. Follett, *The Marriage Act: Summary of Meeting Held to Discuss Revisions of the Marriage Act and the Medical Health Certificate for Marriage*. PKU is a rare genetic disorder that, if left untreated, can cause "mental retardation." Medical genetics was informed by eugenics, and RF funding was instrumental to its development (Paul 1998).
20 LAC, RG29, Vol. 2730, File 812-2-2, pt. 1, "Correspondence, Dr. Thos. Robertson, Inspector of Indian Agencies, Saskatchewan, to R.A. Hoey, Indian Affairs Branch, re: Doctor and Dentist Services, Accounts, Schedule of Fees, 1936/01-1978/07," March 17, 1938.
21 LAC, RG29, Vol. 2730, File 812-2-2, pt. 1, "Correspondence, E.L. Stone, Secretary, Indian Affairs, to Dr. Thos. Robertson, Inspector of Indian Agencies," Saskatchewan, March 22, 1938.
22 As early as 1914, an amendment to the Indian Act allowed government to apprehend patients by force if they did not seek medical treatment. *An Act to Amend the Indian Act*, R.S.C. 1914, c. 35; *The Indian Act*, 1951, c. 29, s. 72.
23 *An Act to Amend the Indian Act*, R.S.C. 1951, c. I-5, s. 87 (now s. 88).
24 LAC, RG 29, Vol. 2936, File 851-1-X400, pt. 2A, "Circular Letter to All Superintendents," Indian Health Regulations (sec. 72 Indian Act, Order in Council, P.C. 193-1129), July 17, 1953. These regulations made special reference of tuberculosis and venereal disease (Lux 2016).
25 PAS, R-1342, File 2.54a, "Correspondence, Honourable Ed. Tchorzewski, Minister of Health, to Premier A.E. Blakeney, and all Cabinet Colleagues," December 29, 1977. In 1961, the Mental Hygiene Act was replaced with the Mental Health Act and the term "mentally defective" was changed to "mentally retarded."
26 Ibid. The Saskatchewan Mental Health Association formed through Hincks' advocacy, then general director of the Canadian Mental Health Association (CMHA), which obtained funding for provincial branches from federal Minister of Health and Welfare, Paul Martin Sr. The CMHA arose out of the CNCMH, with Hincks and Laycock as senior members. The CMHA in Saskatchewan had close links with government — Douglas and all his cabinet were members — and with the Psychiatric Services Branch — all senior psychiatrists were members (Mills 2007, 182–3). By the 1960s, to ensure legitimacy as governments updated policies and practices with human rights in mind, explicit eugenic rhetoric was avoided and the organization was renamed.
27 Ibid.

28 *Ibid.*
29 *The Marriage Act*, 1978, c. M-4 (effective February 26, 1979).
30 PAS, R-335, File 134, "Correspondence, G.F. Amyot, Provincial Health Officer, Government of British Columbia, to T.C. Douglas, Saskatchewan," September 1, 1944; "Correspondence, A. Sommerville, Director, Division of Communicable Diseases," Government of Alberta, August 30, 1944. R.O. Davison, Deputy Minister of Health, and M. Sheps, Secretary of the Health Services Survey Commission, also reached out to these provinces, and forwarded correspondence to Douglas on September 11, 1944, and November 7, 1944.
31 Henry Sigerist, *Saskatchewan Health Services Survey Commission* (Regina: Committee for Mental Hygiene, 1944), 7.
32 Sigerist, *Saskatchewan Health Services Commission*, 9.
33 For information on Hincks's eugenic activities, see McLaren (1990, 89, 93, 158–9).
34 Mental illness was considered a psychiatric diagnosis, while mental defectiveness referred to an individual of "below average intelligence," often identified through psychological testing.
35 Clarence Hincks, *Province of Saskatchewan Mental Hygiene Survey* (Regina: Committee for Mental Hygiene, 1945).
36 Hincks, *Mental Hygiene Survey*, 12. California was considered the epicentre of American eugenics.
37 There were over ten letters of protest in the files reviewed.
38 PAS, R-335, File 134, "Correspondence, Mrs. R.A. Pfeiffer, Diocesan President, Catholic Women's League, Prince Albert, to T.C. Douglas," December 22, 1945.
39 PAS, R-335, File 134, "Correspondence, Sodality of the Christian Mothers, Parish of St. Bruno, to T.C. Douglas," January 7, 1946.
40 PAS, R-335, File 134, "Correspondence, T.C. Douglas, to Loretta Ferlinski, Sodality of the Christian Mothers," January 18, 1946.
41 PAS, R-335, File 134, "Correspondence, A.R. Kaufman, to T.C. Douglas," March 1, 1946.
42 "Correspondence, Kaufman to Douglas."
43 PAS, R-335, File 134, "Correspondence, C.G Sheps, to T.C. Douglas," June 11, 1946. Sheps took leave the following year to study social medicine and public health at Yale University School of Medicine as part of a RF fellowship.
44 PAS, R-335, File 134, "Correspondence, T.C. Douglas, to A.R. Kaufman," June 13, 1946.
45 The involvement of the Rockefeller and Carnegie Foundations with eugenics and broader population control activities is well documented. The Julius Rosenwald Fund's involvement was less explicit, though no less problematic. Its funding of public health research included an initial syphilis control study that led to the development of the race-based Tuskegee Experiment, through which African American men were infected with syphilis; it also funded Margaret Sanger's American Birth Control League–initiated Harlem Clinic, a precursor to the "Negro Project," which brought birth control to African American communities in the American South in a way that some argue was racist and amounted to population control (Washington 2006, 160–2, 195–204). For all correspondence with corporate philanthropies, see PAS, R-33.5, File III 140 (14–35).
46 Will Keith Kellogg, brother to John Harvey Kellogg, the well-known medical doctor, was an active promoter of eugenics, and founder of the Race Betterment Foundation. Together, the brothers founded the Kellogg breakfast cereal company. Profits from the Kellogg company initially flowed into the Race Betterment Foundation, and later, into the W.K. Kellogg Foundation (Fee and Brown 2002). The Menninger Foundation was named after Charles Menninger and his sons, Karl and William, the founders of American psychiatry. Through the Menninger Clinic, foundation-trained psychiatrists

treated those considered mentally ill and drug addicted and established a school for "mentally retarded children" (Friedman 1992). Karl Menninger was considered by many to be a "liberal" and "progressive," but he ranked prostitution and homosexuality "high in the kingdom of evils," and evidence of mental illness. He also believed every woman who claimed rape should be required to have a psychiatric examination in order to separate false "fantasies" from true allegations; and that child sexual abuse may stimulate a child erotically; it was only traumatic if the child held "deep hostilities" (Menninger 1942, 284; Szasz 1997, 171–2; Wigmore 1970, 744). The Russell Sage Foundation funded research on feeblemindedness and eugenically segregated institutions, and according to its website, has continued to support research on the relationship between "genetic endowment" and socioeconomic status [i.e., Russell Sage Foundation (2014)]. The Millbank Memorial Fund was "induced" by Frederick Osborne, founding member of the American Eugenics Society, to help create the Office of Population Research at Princeton University, an institution that trained demographers in the study of population trends and generated many ideas central to the population control movement under the guise of "crypto eugenics" (Hanse and King 2013, 194–5). Together with Indian Affairs, the Hudson Bay Company, and the Royal Canadian Air Force, it carried out nutritional experiments on Indigenous children in residential schools across Canada (Mosby 2013). Despite being accused of engaging in population control activities — it insisted each of its public health projects include birth control services — in 2006, former President Daniel Fox denied it, or any senior staff ever considered birth control a means of reducing "undesirable characteristics" within populations. Rather, *economic factors* guided population policy (Fox 2006). Interestingly, in 2012, Fox received the Saskatchewan Distinguished Service Award for "outstanding contributions to the development of the provincial economy, culture and society" and was an appointed member of the Saskatchewan Health Quality Council, until 2019. Saskatchewan Health, "News Release: New York Doctor Recognized for Distinguished Service to Saskatchewan," March 27, 2012. saskatchewan.ca/government/news-and-media/2012/march/27/new-york-doctor-recognized-for-distinguished-service-to-saskatchewan.

47 PAS, R-326, File 167, "Correspondence, C.F.W. Hames, Deputy Minister Public Health, to TC Douglas, Premier," May 23, 1946. In the first year, cost would be shared between the RF and the province 50/50; in the second year, 40/60; and the third year, 30/70.

48 *An Act Respecting Mentally Defective... Persons,* R.S.S., 1950, c. 74. This may have influenced whether Indigenous people were always noted in institutional admissions (Dyck and Deighton 2017).

49 Rockefeller Foundation, *Annual Report* (New York: The Rockefeller Foundation, 1954), 110; also Mills (2007) and Dyck and Deighton (2017).

50 Douglas also corresponded with "international statesman of public health" (Bu and Fee 2008, 628), John B. Grant, from the RF. See PAS, R-326, File 167, "Correspondence, T.C. Douglas, to J.B. Grant," August 30, 1946. Grant assisted in the expansion of public health in China and India, which included birth control clinics, and supported a plan led by Margaret Sanger to secure American support for these (Katz, Harjo, and Engleman 2016). Together with Alan Gregg and Henry Sigerist, Grant was instrumental in the early relationship between the RF and the World Health Organization (Birn 2014).

51 PAS, R-326, File 167, "Correspondence, W.A. McIntosh, to C.F.W. Hames, re: Itinerary; For the Information of Dr. C.F.W. Hames." August 28, 1947.

52 PAS, R-326, File 167, "Correspondence, Leonard Rosenfeld, to Hugh Smith," September 9, 1946.

53 PAS, R-1346, File 1.26, C.F.W. Hames, Deputy Minister of Public Health, to T.C. Douglas, Memorandum: "Orders in Council Regulations Under the Mental Hygiene Act 1929-1949," December 6, 1946.
54 PAS, R-326, File 167, "Correspondence, Leonard Rosenfeld, to Hugh Smith," September 9, 1946.
55 There are similarities between this study and one begun in 1933 by R.G. Ferguson, director of Fort Qu'Appelle Sanatorium, Saskatchewan, who later worked at Fort Qu'Appelle Indian Hospital, funded by the Canadian Tuberculosis Association and National Research Council — which the RF helped establish — with support from Indian Affairs, which was based on the premise that "primitive" people were more vulnerable to tuberculosis. It sought to prove the bacillus-Calmette-Guerin vaccine could provide resistance in "less evolved races" (Lux 2016, 30).
56 PAS, R-33.5, File 127e, University of Saskatchewan, Document, "Mental Institutions (5 of 8)"; also Brison (2005).
57 PAS, R-33.5, File 127d, "Correspondence, T.C. Douglas, to unknown recipient," January 26, 1955; also Mills (2007).
58 PAS, R-33.5, File 554a, University of Saskatchewan, "Correspondence, T.C. Douglas, to Dr. D.G. McKerracher," April 5, 1960.
59 Eldorado Nuclear was established in the 1920s by Charles and Gilbert Labine, the latter a close friend to Liberal Minister of Supply and Munitions, C.D. Howe (Bothwell 1984). In 1943, the federal government secretly bought company shares and Eldorado became a Crown Corporation, after which it exerted great control over the uranium industry in Saskatchewan. Douglas supported uranium mining until 1963 when, as Member of Parliament, he became "outraged" at the federal plan to house nuclear missiles in the province (Harding 2007, 24). Despite this "about-turn," Harding (2007, 246) shows federal-provincial involvement in uranium production and the complicity of each in nuclear weapons proliferation. It was not until 1974 that the province formed the Saskatchewan Mining and Development Corporation, a Crown Corporation involved in uranium exploration and mining. Under an order-in-council, the entity could own up to 50 percent of uranium joint ventures. It partnered with the federal government in many mining pursuits, which continued after its merger, together with Eldorado, as Cameco (Bothwell 1984). Other than C.D. Howe, Douglas had the "greatest capacity" (Bothwell 1984, 281) to influence uranium mining in Saskatchewan, and Cadbury influenced his support for it.
60 LAC, RG29, Vol. 2915, File 851-1-A671, pt. 1A, "Correspondence, Medical Officer, Indian Office, Battleford, [name illegible], to Assistant Deputy and Secretary, Indian Affairs, S.L. MacDonald," July 10, 1933.
61 "Correspondence, Medical Officer, Battleford, to MacDonald." In another case, an audit of surgeries performed at the Notre Dame Hospital, North Battleford, Saskatchewan, from January 1953 to June 1955, revealed that of all appendectomies performed during this period, not more than 20 percent were cases of acute appendicitis. The other 80 percent involved removal of normal tissue. This led the auditors to conclude these were unnecessary procedures. However, hysterectomies were lower than at other hospitals. The report referenced Dr. G.J. Breton, who enjoyed preferred status in the hospital, and had been allowed to do hysterectomies without consultation or any evidence in the records to justify the operation. Consequently, this doctor's position was rescinded. See PAS, R-33.5, File 554b, Justice H.F. Thomson, Dr. M.G. Israels, and A.K. McTaggert, "Report to the Board of Inquiry," August 31, 1959, 32–42.
62 LAC, RG29, Vol. 2869, File 851-1-5, pt. 1, "Correspondence, J.P. Harvey, Regional Superintendent, Saskatchewan, to the Director of Indian Health Services," September 10, 1954.

63 LAC, RG29, Vol. 2919, File 851-1-A675, pt. 3, "Correspondence, Harvey to Director of Indian Health Services; attached Application for Special Treatment, [name withheld]," September 4, 1954.
64 LAC, RG29, Vol. 2869, File 851-1-5, pt. 1A, "Correspondence, Director of Indian and Northern Health Services, P.E. Moore to Regional Superintendent, Saskatchewan," August 20, 1957.
65 LAC, RG29, Vol. 2817, File 851-1-A673, pt. 1, "Correspondence, T.J. Orford, Regional Superintendent, Saskatchewan, to Dr. A.C. Taylor & Associates, Regina, Saskatchewan," March 25, 1960.
66 PAS, R-33.5, File III, 127 (14-8), "Correspondence, T.C. Douglas, to [name withheld]," November 16, 1950.
67 PAS, R-33.5, File III, 127 (14-8), "Correspondence, A.R. Coulter, to Dr. McKerracher, Director of Psychiatric Services," November 29, 1950.
68 PAS, R-33.5, File III, 127 (14-8), "Correspondence, T.C. Douglas, to [name withheld]," December 29, 1950.
69 "Proposed Grant to Provinces in Aid of Full Time Health Units," in Canada, House of Commons, *Debates*, 16th Parl., 4th Sess., Vol. 1 (March 3, 1930), 219.
70 "Proposed Grant to Provinces," 217.
71 *Ibid*, 217.
72 Grauer left the University of Toronto in 1939 to work at the BC Electric Company, where he became president. He sat on the board of the Royal Bank of Canada, the Ford Motor Company of Canada, and the Canadian Welfare Council.
73 A.E. Grauer, *Public Health: A Study Prepared for the Royal Commission on Dominion-Provincial Relations* (Ottawa: King's Printer, 1939), 60–1.
74 Grauer, *Public Health*, 69–70.
75 *Ibid*, 70, 71.
76 *Ibid*, 63, 23a.
77 *Ibid*, 23a.
78 *Ibid*, 23a.
79 *Ibid*, 63a, 69–70.
80 PAS, R-1675, File 9.144, Department of National Health and Welfare, "Minutes of the First Federal-Provincial Conference on Mental Health Directors," Ottawa, October 10–11, 1946, 2.
81 "Minutes, Federal-Provincial Mental Health Directors," 1–2.
82 *Ibid*, 2.
83 *Ibid*, 2.
84 *Ibid*, 3.
85 *Ibid*, 3. Stogdill was educated in psychology, and later, as a medical doctor at the University of Toronto. At the DNHW, he enabled the provinces to develop psychiatric services and universities to develop professional training and research programs. He helped establish a role for psychologists, psychiatrists, and social workers within the educational system (Griffin 1974).
86 "Minutes, Federal-Provincial Mental Health Directors," 3.
87 Canada, House of Commons, *Debates*, 20th Parl., 4th Sess., Vol. 4 (May 14, 1948), 3932.
88 Statistics Canada, excerpt "National Health Grant Program," 223. www66.statcan.gc.ca/eng/1962/196202410223_p.%20223.pdf.
89 PAS, R-33.4, File IX1d, J.H. Horowiczs, Senior Research Assistant, Health Insurance Studies, DNHW, "Health Grants: A Historical Review," 1948, 1.
90 The Rockefeller Foundation, *Annual Report* (New York: Rockefeller Foundation, 1948), 85.

91   Rockefeller, *Annual Report*, 85.
92   *Ibid*, 86.
93   The Rockefeller Foundation, *Annual Report* (New York: Rockefeller Foundation, 1951), 211.
94   PAS, R-326, File 167, "Correspondence, F.D. Mott, Chairman, Health Services Planning Commission, to Graham L. Davis, Hospital Director, W.K. Kellogg Foundation," October 26, 1946.
95   LAC, RG29, Vol. 2971, File 851-4-300, pt. 1A, "Correspondence, C.A. Roberts, M.D., Chief, Mental Health Division, to Director, Health Insurance Studies," November 10, 1953; "Correspondence, Gordon E. Wride, M.D., Assistant Director, Health Insurance Studies, to G.D.W. Cameron, M.D., Deputy Minister of National Health," November 14, 1953.
96   PAS, R-326, File 167, "Correspondence, F.D. Mott, to Dr. W.A. McIntosh," October 25, 1948.
97   For more detail on this history and how it informed Medicare, see Jones (2019); Marchildon (2012); Taylor (2009).
98   *Hospital Insurance and Diagnostic Services Act*, R.S.C., May 1, 1957.
99   In this instance, St. Laurent was speaking specifically to RF funding for the arts. Canada, House of Commons, *Debates*, 22nd Parl., 5th Sess., Vol. 1 (January 18, 1957), 393–4; also Brison (2005, 98–9).
100 LAC, RG29, Vol. 2995, File 851-8-8, pt.1, "Correspondence, Senior Administrative Officer, to Assistant Director, RE: Meeting with Officials of Saskatchewan Hospital Services Plan," June 12, 1959.
101 LAC, RG29, Vol. 2995, File 851-8-8, pt. 1, "Correspondence, O.J. Rath, Regional Superintendent, Indian and Northern Health Services, to Director," June 12, 1958.
102 It also informed medical care utilization research at the international level, including at the World Health Organization. PAS, R-999, File II 150, "Correspondence, J.C. Clarkson, Deputy Minister of Health, to Mr. M.B. Derrick, Attn: Mr. J. Sangster Re: WHO International Collaborative Study on Medical Care Utilization," April 29, 1968.
103 LAC, RG29, Vol. 2934, File 851-1-X300, pt. 1, "Correspondence, O.J. Rath, Regional Superintendent, Regina, to Director, Indian and Northern Health Services, RE: Policy Regarding Provision of Medical Care to Indian People," December 5, 1958.
104 PAS, R-328, File 3.97, "Correspondence, J.W. Monteith, Minister of National Health and Welfare, to J. Walter Erb, Minister of Public Health, re: Coverage of Indians," February 10, 1961.
105 PAS, R-328, File 2.18, "Correspondence, Ray Wollam, Director of Provincial Committee on Minority, to Dr. F.B. Roth, Deputy Minister of Public Health," June 21, 1960.
106 PAS, R-328, File 2.18, "Correspondence, M.S. Acker, Regional Health Services Branch, to Dr. F.B. Roth, Deputy Minister Public Health," May 16, 1961. This included the work of the public health nurse in "the early detection of retardates and follow-up aftercare in the home." See PAS, R-327, File 3.175, "Correspondence, M.S. Acker, Director, Regional Health Services Branch to Dr. J.G. Clarkson, Deputy Minister, Public Health, Saskatchewan," July 8, 1964.
107 *The Saskatchewan Medical Care Insurance Act*, R.S.S., 1961.
108 PAS, R-328, File 2.18, "Correspondence, Ray Wollam to V.L. Matthews," July 3, 1962.
109 PAS, R-328, File 2.18, "Correspondence, P.E. Moore to D.D. Tansley, of the Saskatchewan Medical Care Insurance Commission," August 2, 1962.
110 LAC, RG29, Vol. 3000, File 851-9.8, pt. 1, "Memorandum, T.J. Orford, Regional Superintendent, Saskatchewan Region, Medical Services, to the Director, Medical Services," September 24, 1962, 1.

111 "Memorandum, Orford to Director," 2.
112 LAC, RG29, Vol. 3000, File 851-9-8, pt. 1, "Correspondence, Judy Lamarsh, Minister of Health and Welfare, to Alan Blakeney," December 18, 1963.
113 House of Commons, *Debates*, 26th Parl., 3rd Sess., Vol. 1 (April 5, 1965), 2–3; cited in Taylor (2009, 332).
114 Federal-Provincial Conference, *Proceedings*, July 19–22, 1965 (Ottawa: Privy Council Office, 1968), 15.
115 Medicare became shorthand for insured services protected under federal law but administered by the provinces and territories following the principles of universality, comprehensiveness, public administration, portability, and accessibility. Medicare does not include all public-sector healthcare services, it is a subset of "public health care," and a "shrinking one at that" (Marchildon 2012, 5). In 1977, the Federal-Provincial Fiscal Arrangements and Established Programs Financing Act terminated the open-ended cost-sharing program by providing lump sum per capita payments, calculated based on income tax points and unconditional payments adjusted in accordance with the GNP. See Taylor (2009). The Canada Health Act generally ensures universal access to insured hospital care and primary care by doctors and other healthcare professionals.
116 LAC, RG29, Vol. 3000, File 851-9-8, pt. 1, "Correspondence, Minister of Health, Allan MacEachen, to Chief Walter Deiter, Federation of Saskatchewan Indians," February 23, 1968.
117 LAC, RG29, Vol. 2776, File 822-1-X300, pt. 2, "Correspondence, E.H. Baergen, Executive Secretary, Saskatchewan Medical Association, to Jean Chrétien, Minister of Indian Affairs," October 28, 1968. When prepayment plans worked as the collection agency for bills, it was reasonable to accept a reduction in the rendered fee listed in the fee schedule. In Saskatchewan, this reduction was 15 percent (Taylor 2009, 293).
118 LAC, RG29, Vol. 2776, File 822-1-X300, pt. 2, "Correspondence, John Munro, Minister of Health and Welfare, to E.H. Baergen, Executive Secretary, Saskatchewan Medical Association," November 14, 1968.
119 LAC, RG29, Vol. 2776, File 822-1-X300, pt. 2, "Correspondence, E.H. Baergen, Executive Secretary, Saskatchewan Medical Association, to Gordon B. Grant, Minister of Public Health, Regina," May 22, 1969.
120 LAC, RG29, Vol. 2934, File 851-1-X300, pt. 2, "Correspondence, Assistant Deputy Minister, Medical Services, to Dr. M.L. Webb, Regional Director, Saskatchewan Region," February 4, 1972. The supplementary health card was a paper card that allowed those who qualified access to non-insured medical services. Medical and hospital insurance cards, regardless of any welfare prefix to the registration number, did not mean that the holder was entitled to assistance for things like dental care. Registered Indians living on-reserve had an "R" on their card. Those living off-reserve, but who were on "needs tested" public assistance had a "Y" prefix on their Supplementary Health Card; if "means tested" public assistance, an "E"; if "child welfare," a "W." The province decided to issue an "R" for all Registered Indians, regardless of where they lived, or if on public assistance. Personal communication, Medical Services Branch, Ministry of Health, Government of Saskatchewan, June 15, 2018.
121 *The Saskatchewan Hospitalization Act*, R.S.S. s. 24 (1) and (2), and *the Saskatchewan Medical Care Insurance Act*, R.S.S. s. 39 (1) and (2), filed on November 15, 1972. In 1966, the federal government introduced the Canada Assistance Plan. The main purpose of this federal-provincial program was to cost-share welfare services. It covered the costs of certain health services required by welfare recipients not funded through Medicare or supplementary provincial insurance plans, including prescription

drugs, and dental and vision care. John Osborne, Special Adviser on Policy Development, DNHW, describes it in the following way: "Mothers' allowance cases and child welfare cases were no longer excluded from eligibility, and welfare services that would prevent people from becoming needy and non-insured health services became shareable items of a family's expenditure budget. The costs of extending provincial welfare administration beyond the level available in the base year became shareable. The provisions in the Unemployment Assistance Act for meeting a family's budgetary requirements (needs-testing), for supporting needy persons in homes for special care, and for prohibiting a provincial residence requirement were repeated in this Act. Other innovations were the extension of welfare services to people 'likely to become' poor and the offer to share in provincial administration costs." When costs were covered by the province through a welfare department, the federal government was still contributing. Indian Affairs continued to fund welfare services for Indians living on reserves. Appendix to the Neilson Task Force Report, John E. Osborne, *The Evolution of the Canada Assistance Plan*, 1985. https://web.archive.org/web/20180316192106/https://canadiansocialresearch.net/capjack.htm. Most health-related services were transferred from the Canada Assistance Plan to different federal-provincial arrangements known as Established Programs Financing, then the Canada Health and Social Transfer, and after 2004, the Canada Health Transfer. For a brief overview, see Canada, Department of Finance, "The History of Health and Social Transfers," June 15, 2023. https://www.canada.ca/en/department-finance/programs/federal-transfers/history-health-social-transfers.html. The history of federal-provincial financial transfers for health and welfare services is more complex than is discussed here.
122 *Canada Health Act*, 1984, R.S.C. c. 6.
123 Michael Kirby, Chair, *The Health of Canadians – The Federal Role Volume One – The Story So Far* (Ottawa: The Standing Committee on Social Affairs, Science and Technology, March 2001), 64; Government of Canada, Health Canada, First Nations and Inuit Health, "About the Non-Insured Health Benefits Program," May 16, 2024. https://www.sac-isc.gc.ca/eng/1576790320164/1576790364553.

Chapter 2

1 PAS, R.33.1, Box 1, File 864d, Government of Saskatchewan, Interdepartmental Committee on Minorities, "Submission by the Government of Saskatchewan to Joint Committee of the Senate and the House of Commons on Indian Affairs" (Ottawa: Joint Committee of the Senate and the House of Commons on Indian Affairs, 1960), IV 22, IV 24, VI 1, VII, 1–2.
2 National Aboriginal Health Organization (NAHO), *First Nations, Métis, and Inuit Women's Health*, No. 4 (Ottawa: NAHO, 2006), 16–17.
3 NAHO, *FNMI Women's Health*, No. 4, 15.
4 Truth and Reconciliation Commission of Canada (TRC), *Honouring the Truth, Reconciling for the Future: Summary of the Final Report of the Truth and Reconciliation Commission of Canada* (Ottawa, Truth and Reconciliation Commission of Canada, 2015).
5 TRC, *Summary of the Final Report*.
6 William Beveridge, *Social Insurance and Allied Services* (London: His Majesty's Stationary Office, 1942).
7 Marsh later served as welfare advisor to the United Nations Relief and Rehabilitation Administration and director of research in the School of Social Work, University of British Columbia (Moscovitch 2017).
8 Harry M. Cassidy, *Social Security and Reconstruction in Canada* (Toronto: Ryerson Press, 1943), 18, 89, 190.

9   Harry M. Cassidy, *Public Health and Welfare Reorganization: The Postwar Problem in the Canadian Provinces* (Toronto: Ryerson Press, 1945).
10 Laura Thompson, *Personality and Government: Findings and Recommendations* (Mexico: Ediciones del Instituto Indigenista Inter-Americano, 1951), 189–93.
11 Canada, Special Joint Committee of the Senate and the House of Commons Appointed to Examine and Consider the Indian Act, *Minutes of Proceedings and Evidence*, Fourth Report, June 22, 1948 (Ottawa: King's Printer 1948), 189–90, cited in Shewell (2002, 59).
12 The name of the Council has evolved from the Canadian Council on Child Welfare (1920–30), the Canadian Council on Child and Family Welfare (1930–35), the Canadian Welfare Council (1935–68), and the Canadian Council on Social Development (1968–2025).
13 LAC, MG 28 I 10, Vol. 118, "Joint Submission by the Canadian Welfare Council and the Canadian Association of Social Workers to the Special Joint Committee of the Senate and the House of Commons appointed to Examine and Consider the Indian Act," (Ottawa: King's Printer 1947), 2. For discussion, see Stevenson (2020, 113) and Shewell (2004, 190–2).
14 "Joint Submission by the Canadian Welfare Council and the Canadian Association of Social Workers," 6, cited in Stevenson (2015, 105).
15 Special Joint Committee, *Minutes*, June 22, 1948, 159, cited in Shewell (2002, 191).
16 *Ibid*, 160, cited in Shewell (2002, 192).
17 PAS, R-33.1, File 859a, "Conference of the Métis of Saskatchewan, Minutes of Proceedings, Regina," July 30, 1946.
18 M.W. Knudsen, "Conference of the Métis of Saskatchewan," 27–30.
19 *Ibid*, 29–30.
20 O.W. Valleau, "Conference of the Métis of Saskatchewan," 52.
21 *Ibid*, 53.
22 Green Lake was in the Île-à-la-Crosse district, in what was described as the "extreme north." The shelter housed twenty-five Métis children up to sixteen years old. Non-Aboriginal child welfare experts from the South of the province staffed the shelter, training Métis children in "Euro-Canadian hygienic standards prior to being fit for adoption into white, middle class family homes" (Dales 1954, 39); also Stevenson (2020, 96–104).
23 Métis were living on Crown land allocated for future roadbuilding, otherwise known as roadside allowances.
24 This entire situation has similarities to the forced relocation of Inuit to the Far North of Canada between 1939–63, which resulted in some Inuit starving to death. Symington and Valentine were both involved in this plan. See Tester and Kulchyski (1994).
25 PAS, A-85-308 933, File III 41, "Correspondence, John Sturdy to Paul Martin," April 5, 1952; see Barron (1997, 115).
26 Legislative Assembly of Saskatchewan, *Debates*, March 2, 1954; cited in Pitsula (1994, 29).
27 Legislative Assembly of Saskatchewan, *Debates*, February 23, 1956, 17; also debated on March 2, 1956.
28 Legislative Assembly of Saskatchewan, *Debates*, February 23, 1956, 26, (Douglas).
29 PAS, R-33.1, Box 1, File 864c, John Sturdy in Provincial Assembly, "Equal Rights for Treaty Indians," March 22, 1957, 8.
30 Sturdy, "Equal Rights for Treaty Indians," 8.
31 Canada, *Minutes of Proceedings and Evidence of the Joint Committee of the Senate and House of Commons on Indian Affairs*, 24th Parl., 3rd Sess., No. 12 (June 16, 1960), 1033–4. For a summary, see Leslie (1999, 368–77).

32 Canada, *Minutes of Joint Committee, No. 12,* 1038, 1071.
33 Ibid. Also PAS, R-33.1, Box 1, File 864d, "Submission by the Government of Saskatchewan," February 1960, IV 22, IV 24, VI 1, VII, 1–2.
34 Harry B. Hawthorn, ed., *A Survey of the Contemporary Indians of Canada: A Report on Economic, Political, Educational Needs and Policies, Vol. 1 and 2* (Ottawa: Department of Indian Affairs and Northern Development 1966), 1, 17, 22.
35 Hawthorn, *A Survey of the Contemporary Indians of Canada,* 1966, 28.
36 Ibid, 29.
37 Ibid, 29.
38 Ibid, 29, 30.
39 Ibid, 30.
40 United Nations, "Trusteeship Council," n.d. https://www.un.org/en/ccoi/trusteeship-council; also see United Nations Charter, Chapter XIII, "The Trusteeship Council," Art. 86–91, n.d. https://www.un.org/en/about-us/un-charter/chapter-13.
41 Hawthorn, *A Survey of the Contemporary Indians of Canada,* 1966, 31, 197.
42 Hawthorn, *A Survey of the Contemporary Indians of Canada,* 1967, 130.
43 Ibid, 108.
44 Hawthorn, *A Survey of the Contemporary Indians of Canada,* 1966, 102.
45 Ibid, 107.
46 Ibid, 17.
47 PAS, R-327, File 3-171, "Correspondence, O.E. Laxdal, to Dr. J. Clarkson, Deputy Minister of Public Health," April 16, 1964; "Correspondence, A.F. Huston, Medical Director, Regina Physical Restoration Centre, to V.L. Matthews," April 24, 1964.
48 Lawrence Joseph and Cindy Blackstock, "Human Rights Commission Complaint Form Against Indian and Northern Affairs Canada" 2007. https://fncaringsociety.com/sites/default/files/caring_society_afn_hr_complaint_2007.pdf; Rose-Alma McDonald and Peter Ladd, et. al., *Joint National Policy Review on First Nations Child and Family Services: Final Report* (Ottawa: Assembly of First Nations and Indian and Northern Affairs Development, 2000).
49 PAS, R-626, File 3, "Correspondence, Aldred H. Neufeldt, Director of Operations Research, to Dr. C. M. Smith, Director, Psychiatric Services," Regina, February 15, 1973.
50 "Correspondence, Neufeldt to Smith."
51 PAS, R-33.1, File 864c, John Sturdy in Provincial Assembly, "Equal Rights for Treaty Indians," March 22, 1957.
52 PAS, R-1453, File 2.176, John H. Hylton, *Report – Admissions to Saskatchewan Provincial Correctional Centres: Projections to 1993* (Regina: Prairie Justice Consortium, 1979), 1.
53 Hylton, *Report – Admissions to Saskatchewan Provincial Correctional Centres,* 1.
54 Ibid, 2.
55 Paul Robinson and Taylor Small, et. al., "Over-representation of Indigenous Persons in Adult Provincial Custody, 2019/2020 and 2020/2021," *The Daily,* July 12, 2023. https://www150.statcan.gc.ca/n1/pub/85-002-x/2023001/article/00004-eng.htm.
56 Office of the Correctional Investigator, "Correctional Investigator Releases Updated Findings on the State of Indigenous Corrections in Canada: National Indigenous Organizations Issue Statements of Support." Press Release, November 2, 2023. https://oci-bec.gc.ca/en/content/correctional-investigator-releases-updated-findings-state-indigenous-corrections-canada.
57 Government of Canada, Senate, Standing Committee on the Status of Women, *Minutes of Evidence,* 42nd Parl., 1st Sess. (December 7, 2017). https://www.ourcommons.ca/DocumentViewer/en/42-1/fewo/meeting-83/evidence (Vicki Chartrand). For more

on the expansion of the penal system in the post–World War II period, see Chartrand (2019).
58 Jean Chrétien, *Statement of the Government of Canada on Indian Policy* (Ottawa: Indian Affairs and Northern Development, 1969). https://publications.gc.ca/site/eng/9.700112/publication.html.
59 Omnibus Bill C-150, *The Criminal Law Amendment Act*, R.S.C. 1968–69, c. 38 amended several sections of the *Criminal Code*, including section 237, affecting abortion. It was passed on the same day as Bill S-15, which decriminalized contraception. *An Act to amend the Food and Drugs Act and the Narcotic Control Act* and to make a consequential amendment to the *Criminal Code*, R.S.C. 1968–69, c. 41, ss. 1–3, 13.

Chapter 3

1 LAC, RG29, Vol. 2869, File 851-1-5, pt. 1, "Correspondence, A.R. Kaufman to P.E. Moore, Director of Indian Health Services," November 28, 1963.
2 LAC, RG29, Volume 2869, File 851-1-5, pt. 1A, "Correspondence, S. Mallick to H.A. Proctor, Director General, Medical Services," December 15, 1964.
3 Mallick quoted an article entitled "Threepenny Answer to Starvation," published in the *Manchester Guardian* on December 10, 1964.
4 LAC, RG29, Vol. 2869, File 8851-1-5, pt. 1A, "Correspondence, R.A. Sprenger, Zone Superintendent, Northern Ontario, to Regional Superintendent, Medical Services, Eastern Region," June 1, 1965.
5 LAC, RG 29, Vol. 2869, File 851-1-5, pt. 1A, "Correspondence, Kahn Tineta Horn, to R.F. Battle, Director, Indian Affairs Branch, Indian and Northern Affairs," January 28, 1966.
6 Daniel Patrick Moynihan, *The Negro Family: The Case for National Action* (United States: Department of Labour, Office of Planning and Research, 1965).
7 Moynihan, *The Negro Family*, 19, 15–29.
8 *Ibid*, 29.
9 *Ibid*, 27.
10 *Ibid*, 47.
11 LAC, RG29, ACC 1996-97-698, Vol. 103, File 6780-1-0, "Correspondence, Director of Family Planning, to Dr. J.D. Bergevin, Senior Assistant Deputy Minister, Program Operations (Welfare), re: CIDA and IDRC – Family Planning Policies," October 24, 1972; also see Canadian Women's Committee on Reproduction, Population and Development (1995).
12 Lester Pearson, Chairman. *Partners in Development: Report of the Commission on International Development* (New York: Prager Publishers, 1969).
13 LAC, RG 29, Vol. 2869, File 8851-1-5, pt. 1A, "Correspondence, H.A. Proctor, Director of Medical Services, to Zone Superintendents," August 27, 1965.
14 LAC, RG29, Vol. 2869, File 851-1-5, pt. 1A, "Correspondence, M.L. Webb to Director General, Medical Services," September 13, 1965.
15 LAC, RG29, Vol. 2869, File 851-1-5, pt. 1A, "Correspondence, J.H. Wiebe, Regional Superintendent, Eastern Region, to Director General, Medical Services," September 14, 1965.
16 Canada, Senate Standing Senate Committee on Aboriginal Peoples, *Interim Report: Housing on First Nation Reserves: Challenges and Successes*, 41st Parl., 2nd Sess. (February 2015). https://sencanada.ca/content/SEN/Committee/412/appa/rep/rep08feb15b-e.pdf.
17 LAC, RG 29, Vol. 2869, File 851-1-5, pt. 1A, "Correspondence, H.A. Proctor, to Commander J. Coulter, Special Planning Secretariat," October 1, 1965.

18 "Correspondence, Proctor to Coulter," October 1, 1965.
19 LAC, RG29, Vol. 2869, File 851-1-5, pt. 1A, "Correspondence, T.J. Orford to H.A. Proctor, Director General, Medical Services," March 18, 1966.
20 *Criminal Code*, 1953-54, R.S.C., c.51.
21 For more details on this and numerous other bills introduced between 1963-69 proposing to amend the *Criminal Code*, see Appleby (1999, 19-28).
22 Canada, *House of Commons, Debates, 26th Parl., 2nd Sess., Vol. 7* (September 11, 1964), 7932-40.
23 Canada, *Debates*, 7933 (Robert Prittie).
24 *Ibid*, 7935.
25 *Ibid*, 7935 (Charles Willoughby).
26 Canada, *Minutes of Proceedings and Evidence of the Joint Committee of the Senate and House of Commons on Indian Affairs*, 24th Parl., 3rd Sess., No. 12 (June 16, 1960), 1033-4.
27 Canada, *Minutes of Joint Committee No. 12,* 1033, 1071.
28 Canada, *Minutes of Proceedings and Evidence of the Standing Committee on Health and Welfare*, 27th Parl., 1st Sess., No. 1 (March 1, 1966), 15-16.
29 Canada, *Minutes of Standing Committee, No. 1*, 17-8.
30 The Canadian Federation of Societies for Population Planning became a member of the International Planned Parenthood Federation in 1965, later changed its name to the Family Planning Federation of Canada, and then to the Planned Parenthood Federation of Canada. In 2005 it became the Canadian Federation for Sexual Health. In 2014, it amalgamated with Canadians for Choice (CARAL) and Action Canada for Population and Development (ACPD) as Action Canada for Sexual Health & Rights.
31 Planned Parenthood invited Kaufman and his Parents' Information Bureau to join in its activities. Kaufman preferred his service remain a separate organization but pledged continuing cooperation.
32 Canada, *Minutes of Proceedings and Evidence of the Standing Committee on Health and Welfare*, 27th Parl., 1st Sess., No. 5 (March 24, 1966), Appendix A, 121.
33 Canada, *Minutes Standing Committee, No. 5,* Appendix A, 123-4.
34 *Ibid*, 94 (Frank Fidler).
35 *Ibid*, 95 (Phillip Rynard).
36 *Ibid*, 96 (George Cadbury).
37 Erick Schmidt, *One Attack on Poverty – Family Planning* (Ottawa: Privy Council Office, 1966).
38 Schmidt, *One Attack*, 1.
39 *Ibid*, 3-4.
40 For an accessible discussion of the consequences of this reality, see Talaga (2017).
41 Schmidt, *One Attack*, 4-5.
42 Canada, *Minutes of Proceedings and Evidence of the Standing Committee on Health and Welfare*, 27th Parl., 1st Sess., No. 13 (June 9, 1966), 350-1.
43 Canada, *Minutes Standing Committee, No. 13*, 353.
44 PAS, R-327, File 1.226, *Leader Post*, (September 1964), "Poorest in the World Promised Action – Indian Situation Deplorable"; *Globe and Mail*, (May, 1966), "Indians Breed Like Rabbits, Thatcher says."
45 Canada, *Minutes of Proceedings and Evidence of the Standing Committee on Health and Welfare*, 27th Parl., 1st Sess., No. 10 (April 21, 1966), 251.
46 Canada, *Minutes Standing Committee No. 10*, 251-2 (Canadian Welfare Council).
47 *Ibid*, 271.
48 *Ibid*, 278 (John McNab).

49 *An Act to amend the Food and Drugs Act and the Narcotic Control Act* and to make a consequential amendment to the *Criminal Code*, R.S.C. 1968-69, c. 41, ss. 1-3, 13.
50 The argument can be made that this family planning "program" was in effect a "policy." Karen Lawford argues, "invisible policies" can exist and are made visible through a lens that seeks to highlight the allocation of resources, the material impacts resulting from these allocations, and the reactions of those impacted (2016, 149).
51 LAC, RG29, Vol. 2869, File 851-1-5, pt.1B, News Release, "Federal Government Initiates Family Planning Program," September 18, 1970.
52 The opposition Munro is referring to is not made clear, but Cabinet acknowledged Indigenous fears of population control earlier that year.
53 PAS, R-891, File 46e, Maurice Leclair and Joseph Willard, "Current Status of Family Planning in Canada" (Ottawa: DNHW, 1971), 25.
54 LAC, RG29, Vol. 2869, File 851-1-5, pt. 1B, "Correspondence, J.H. Wiebe to Dr. Maurice Leclair, Deputy Minister of Health," October 27, 1970.
55 "Correspondence, Wiebe to Leclair."
56 LAC, RG29, Vol. 2869, File 851-1-5, pt. 2, "Memorandum, J.H. Wiebe, to Dr. Maurice Leclair," October 19, 1971.
57 LAC, RG29, Vol. 2870, File 851-1-5, pt. 3B, "Correspondence, L.M. Black, Director General, Program Management, to F.J. Covill, Assistant Regional Director, Northwest Territories," October 30, 1974.
58 Canada, *House of Commons, Debates*, 28th Parl., 3rd Sess., Vol. 6 (May 6, 1971), 5549 (John Munro).
59 Dr. R.A.H. Kinch, "Service Aspects of Family Planning Clinics," in Department of National Health and Welfare, *Minutes of the Ad Hoc Meeting on Family Planning* (February 8-9, 1971), 14–15.
60 LAC, RG29, Vol. 2869, File 851-1-5, pt. 1, "Brief on Birth Control, G.C. Butler, Chief Medical Officer to S.M. Hodgson, Commissioner," June 11, 1968; Art Sorenson, "NWT Will Offer Birth Control Facts," *Edmonton Journal*. n.d.
61 LAC, RG29, Vol. 2869, File 851-1-5, pt. 2, "Correspondence, [Jeffrey Bishop], Food and Drug Directorate, to Dr. O. Schaefer, Northern Medical Research Unit," Edmonton, March 1, 1971.
62 LAC, RG29, Vol. 2869, File 851-1-5, pt. 2, "Correspondence, G.C. Butler, Regional Director, Medical Services, Northern Regional Headquarters, to Dr. S.S. Parlee, Chief, Department of Obstetrics/Gynaecology," Charles Camsell Hospital, April 2, 1972.
63 LAC, RG29, Vol. 2869, File 851-1-5, pt. 2, "Correspondence, Dr. S.S. Parlee, Chief, Department Obstetrics/Gynaecology, Charles Camsell Hospital, to Dr. G.C. Butler, Regional Director, Medical Services," Northern Regional Headquarters, April 2, 1971.
64 LAC, RG29, Vol. 2869, File 851-1-5, pt. 2, "Correspondence, Dr. Jeffrey Bishop, Director, Drug Advisory Bureau, Food and Drug Directorate, to Dr. O. Schaefer," Northern Medical Research Unit, April 15, 1971, 3.
65 "Correspondence, Bishop to Schaefer," 3.
66 LAC, RG29, Vol. 2869, File 851-1-5, pt. 2, "Memorandum, J.H. Wiebe, Assistant Deputy Minister of Health, Medical Services, Regional Director," Northern Region, April 22, 1971.
67 Canada, *House of Commons, Debates*, 28th Parl., 3rd Sess., Vol. 6 (May 6, 1971), 5549 (John Munro).
68 DNHW Task Force, *Recommendations of the First National Conference on Family Planning*, comment 6.
69 Cited in D.H. Berg and E.L. Jackson, *Delivering Family Planning Information and Services: A Review of the Literature Related to the Implementation and Maintenance of Family Planning Services, Vol. 1* (Winnipeg: University of Winnipeg, 1975), 128, 130,

132–3. The Canadian Institute on International Affairs is a "think tank" that provides a forum for the study and discussion of Canadian policies.
70 Berg and Jackson, *Delivering Family Planning*, 128.
71 *Ibid*, 128–9.
72 United Nations, *Final Act of the International Conference on Human Rights, Tehran*, April 22 to May 13, 1968, (New York: United Nations, 1968), para. 16, 4
73 United Nations, *Declaration on Social Progress and Development*, General Assembly Resolution 2542 (XXIV), December 11, 1969, U.N. Doc. A/7630. https://www.ohchr.org/sites/default/files/progress.pdf.
74 PAS, R-1274, File II.38, Frank Fidler, "Appendix F – Planned Parenthood Federation of Canada, re: Rapporteur's Report on Population Workshop," June 18, 1976.
75 PAS, R-891, File 99a, Family Planning Federation of Canada and Conservation Council, "A Population Policy for Canada?" Two-day seminars held at OISE," Toronto, November 20–21, 1972.
76 LAC, RG29, ACC 1996-97-698, Vol. 103, File 6780-1-0, "Briefing Notes for the Minister on Memorandum to Cabinet on Family Planning Policy," August 25, 1969.
77 Royal Commission on the Status of Women (RCSW), *The Report of the Royal Commission on the Status of Women* (Ottawa: Information Canada, 1970), vii.
78 In a memoriam following his death, Henripin is referred to as an "eminent colleague" of the Canadian Population Society (Lapierre-Adamcyk 2013), a "scientific association that seeks to improve knowledge and understanding about the quantitative and qualitative characteristics of human population" https://www.canpopsoc.ca.
79 RCSW, *The Report*, 395–420.
80 *Ibid*, vii.
81 *Ibid*, 275, 276.
82 *Ibid*, 279.
83 *Ibid*, 278.
84 *Ibid*, 280.
85 *Ibid*, 280.
86 *Ibid*, 281.
87 Omnibus Bill C-150, *The Criminal Law Amendment Act*, R.S.C., 1968–69, c. 38 amended a number of sections of the *Criminal Code*, including section 237, affecting abortion.
88 RCSW, *Report*, 285–7.
89 See, for example: Canada, *Report of the Committee on the Operation of the Abortion Law* (Ottawa: Minister of Supply and Services Canada, 1977).
90 Suzy Basile and Patricia Bouchard, *Free and Informed Consent and Imposed Sterilizations Among First Nations and Inuit Women in Quebec* (Quebec: First Nations of Quebec and Labrador Health and Social Services Commission, 2022).
91 PAS, R-891, File 46e, Dr. R.W. Tooley, Director, Family Planning Division, National Health and Welfare, "Family Planning in Canada: A Paper Presented to Alberta Conference on Family Planning," Edmonton, May 16, 1973, 11.
92 Tooley, "Family Planning in Canada," 11.
93 *Ibid*, 11.
94 LAC, RG 29, Box 77, File 3102-14-1, Phillip S. Corbet, Adrian Jones, Lorna Marsden, and Dixon Thompson. *Population: A Working Paper*, prepared by the Canadian Task Force on Population, for the Man and Resources Conference Programme, April 10, 1973, 19.
95 Canada, *House of Commons, Debates*, 29th Parl., 2nd Sess., Vol. 2 (April 2, 1973), 2817.
96 Tooley, "Family Planning in Canada," 5–6.

Chapter 4

1. PAS, R-1453, File 1.156, Ken Svenson, Report: "Indian and Métis Issues in Saskatchewan to 2001," December 1978, 1.
2. PAS, R-706, File I.198, "Minutes, Indian Health Services – Treatment Services, Canadian Public Health Association," Saskatchewan Division Meeting, April 5, 1967, 7.
3. "Minutes, Indian Health Services," 5.
4. Ibid, 6.
5. Ibid, 8.
6. PAS, R-706, File I.198, Indian Health Services (IHS), "Report of In-Service Training Regional Nursing Conference Saskatchewan Region, I.N.H.S.," October 17–27, 1960, 4.
7. IHS, "Report of In-Service Training," 4.
8. Ibid, 5.
9. Ibid, 9.
10. The Canadian Public Health Association offers technical and financial support, in association with other agencies and organizations, to promote public health in Canada (Canadian Public Health Association n.d.).
11. PAS, R-891, File 46e, Maurice Leclair and Joseph Willard, "Current Status of Family Planning in Canada," (Ottawa: DNHW, 1971), 25.
12. PAS, R-706, File 15.53, John Richards, Peter Beaglehole, Hugh Grocott, Vera Spencer, and Gisele Toupin, "Probe Committee," *A Report on Family Planning* (Regina: Department of Public Health, 1972), 3.
13. "Role of Public Health Nurse," in Probe Committee, *A Report on Family Planning*, 44.
14. PAS, R-706, File, 15.53, Family Planning Advisory Committee, *Report of the Family Planning Advisory Committee to the Committee of Ministers on Family Planning* (Regina: Saskatchewan Health, 1975), 6 and Appendix II.
15. Department of Public Health, Regional Health Services Branch, Policy Manual, cited in Probe Committee, *A Report on Family Planning*, 3.
16. A.W. Sihvon, "Department of Welfare Policy on Family Planning," in Advisory Committee, *Report*, 43.
17. Ibid, 18.
18. PAS, R-1412, File 11.1, "Correspondence, M.B. Derrick, Chairman, Thrust Group, to John Richards, Legislative Secretary to Minister of Public Health, re: Probe – Family Planning and Abortion," November 8, 1971.
19. PAS, R-1412, File 11.1, Saskatchewan Department of Public Health, Thrust Group, "Terms of Reference, Probe I. Abortion, Probe II., Family Planning," approved December 10, 1971.
20. Thrust Group, "Terms of Reference."
21. PAS, R-1412, File 11.1, Probe Committee, "Report on Abortion," January 14, 1972, 1.
22. Ibid, 1.
23. Ibid, 8.
24. Ibid, 8.
25. Ibid, 8.
26. PAS, R-517, File 1.202, "Correspondence, Ty Chiao, Medical Health Office, Health Department, City of Regina, to Walter Smishek," July 27, 1971. An earlier departmental memo discussing the "pros" of expanding the provision of therapeutic abortions noted a "positive outcome" of doing so was for "eugenic reasons," to allow society to protect itself against needing to maintain "hereditarily ill-endowed children." PAS, R-1346, File 1.57a, "Memorandum, Regional Health Services Branch, to Dr. S.L. Skoll, Deputy Minister, re: Information Paper on Therapeutic Abortion," October 21, 1971, 5.
27. PAS, R-1412, File 11.1, "Correspondence, John Richards to Walter Smishek, cc' 'all thrust members'," February 23, 1972.

28   Probe Committee, *A Report on Family Planning*, 2.
29   PAS, R-706, File 15.52, "Correspondence, E.L. Milner, Director, Division of Public Health Nursing, to Dr. D. Penman, Associate Deputy Minister," Public Health, October 26, 1972.
30   "Correspondence, Milner to Penman."
31   Probe Committee, *A Report on Family Planning*, 5.
32   *Ibid*, 5.
33   *Ibid*, 10, 5.
34   *Ibid*, 10. A motivating factor in the creation of the Department of the North was to enable resource extraction (Collier 1995; Quiring 2004).
35   *Ibid*, 1.
36   PAS, R-1412, File 11.1, Department of Public Health, *Proposals for a Family Planning Program for Saskatchewan*, Submitted for Consideration to The Minister of Public Health, April 1973.
37   PAS, R-1412, File 11.1, Walter Smishek, Minister of Public Health, "Press Release," June 20, 1973, 1.
38   Smishek, "Press Release," 2.
39   PAS, R-1412, File 11.1, "Correspondence, S.L. Skoll, Deputy Minister of Public Health, to Dr. D. Penman, Associate Deputy Minister, Public Health (Program Development), re: Comments on your proposal for a family planning program," June 20, 1973.
40   PAS, R-706, File 15.52, "Correspondence, M.B. Derrick, Associate Deputy Minister (Administration), to Dr. D. Penman, re: Family Planning," July 13, 1973.
41   PAS, R-706, File 15.52, "Department Memo, Walter Smishek, Minister of Public Health, to Allan Blakeney and All Cabinet Ministers, re: Family Planning Program," September 7, 1973; Family Planning Advisory Committee, *Report*, Appendix II.
42   PAS, R-706, File 15.53, "Ministerial Family Planning Meeting Minutes, re: Proposed Advisory Committee," October 22, 1973; Family Planning Advisory Committee, *Report*, 6.
43   This included Linda Berg, nursing student, University of Saskatchewan (resigned May 1, 1974); Bruce Cowie, General Manager, CKCK TV; Barbara Ellemers, Director of Nursing, Regina Department of Health; Rev. Williams Hordern, president, Luthern Theological Seminary; Glen Joice, Chief, Special Services to Youth and Families, Department of Social Services; Marcel l'Heureux, Director, Social Services, Department of Northern Saskatchewan; Joseph Megaw, Curriculum Consultant, Department of Education; Betsy Naylor, Chairman, Family Planning Association of Saskatchewan; Dr. Michael Spooner, Associate Professor, Head of Department of Family Medicine, Plains Health Centre (resigned May 15, 1974); Rev. Jim Weisgerber, Director, Roman Catholic Archdiocese of Regina; Rev. Peter Williams, Pastor, United Church, Lucky Lake; Meredith Moore, Family Planning Co-ordinator, Department of Health; Isobel McNab, President, SIWA; Vicki Wilson, Coordinator, SNWA (formerly Saskatchewan Native Women's Movement).
44   Public Health received comment from Leona Blondeau, fieldworker with the SNWA, on the "Proposals for a Family Planning Program for Saskatchewan." Blondeau indicated proposals for a family planning program would be "of benefit" to Indigenous Peoples, especially those relating to education and health. PAS, R-706, File 15.52, "Correspondence, Leona Blondeau, to Edward Tennant, Executive Director, Department of Public Health," August 27, 1973.
45   PAS, R-706, File 15.52, "Correspondence, Walter Smishek, Minister of Public Health, to Isobel McNab, President, Saskatchewan Indian Women's Association," November 14, 1973.

46   PAS, R-706, File 15.52, "Correspondence, Walter Smishek, Minister of Public Health, to Isobel McNab, President, Saskatchewan Indian Women's Association," January 2, 1974.
47   PAS, R-706, File 15.54, "Correspondence, Isobel McNab to Walter Smishek," n.d.; "Correspondence, Meredith Moore, Secretary to Family Planning Advisory Committee, to W.A. Robbins, Minister of Health," February 27, 1976.
48   PAS, R-706, File 15.53, "Correspondence, Vicki Wilson, SNWA, to Meredith Moore, Saskatchewan Family Planning Advisory Committee," July 14, 1975.
49   Family Planning Advisory Committee, *Report*, 7.
50   PAS, R-1346, File 1.61, "Correspondence, John D. Bury, Director, Regional Health Services Branch, to R.G. Ellis, Solicitor, re: Legal responsibility for unsolicited advice re: family planning to minors," December 20, 1973.
51   Family Planning Advisory Committee, *Report*, 18.
52   PAS, R-326, File 68, "Correspondence, C.F.W.Hames, Deputy Minister of Public Health, to Dr. G.G. Fergusson, Registrar, College of Physicians and Surgeons, Saskatchewan," January 27, 1948.
53   "Correspondence, Hames to Fergusson."
54   PAS, R-326, File 68, "Correspondence, Alex Blackwood, Deputy Attorney General, to C.F.W. Hames, Deputy Minister of Public Health," October 7, 1946.
55   PAS, R-1675, File 9.111, "Correspondence, F.S. Lawson, Director, Psychiatric Services Branch, to Dr. A.J. Beddie, Superintendent, Saskatchewan Training School, Moose Jaw," March 20, 1958.
56   PAS, R-1700, File 1.179, "Summary of Proceedings: Staff Conference for all Northern Retardation Workers, Chair, A. Hansen," Saskatoon, April 21, 1971, 2.
57   "Summary of Proceedings: Staff Conference," 3.
58   PAS, R-1346, File 1.61, "Correspondence, E.H. Baergen, Executive Secretary, Saskatchewan Medical Association, to Roy Romanow, Attorney General, Saskatchewan," November 1, 1971; n.a. "Uniformity Wanted for Age of Consent," *Leader Post*, January 6, 1972.
59   *Coming of Age Act*, 1970, R.S.S. 1970, c. 8.
60   PAS, R-1346, File 1.61, "Draft Memorandum, for signature of Dr. S.L. Skoll," June 18, 1971; "Correspondence, S.L. Skoll, Deputy Minister of Public Health, to Dr. H.D. Dalgleish, College of Physicians and Surgeons of Saskatchewan, re: problems of providing treatment services to minors without parental consent," June 21, 1971, 1.
61   "Draft Memorandum, Skoll," 2.
62   *Ibid*, 3.
63   PAS, R-1346, File 1.61, "Correspondence, T.L. Fisher, to Dr. E.H. Baergen, Executive Secretary, Saskatchewan Medical Association," September 20, 1971, 1–2.
64   PAS, R-1346, File 1.61, "Correspondence, S.L. Skoll, to Dr. K.W. Hodgins, re: Age of consent," January 6, 1972.
65   PAS, R-1346, File 1.61, "Correspondence, C. Beek, Executive Director, Southeast Regional Hospital Council, to R.G. Ellis, Solicitor," November 30, 1972.
66   PAS, R-1346, File 1.60, "Correspondence, R.G. Ellis, Solicitor, to Dr. W.R. Hatsell, Medical Consultant, Community Grants and Standards Division, Department of Social Services, Regina," May 11, 1973.
67   PAS, R-1346, File 1.60, "Correspondence, R.G. Ellis, Solicitor, to Dr. S.N. Banerjee, Assistant Regional Director, Psychiatric Centre, Weyburn," April 18, 1973.
68   PAS, R-1346, File 1.62, "Correspondence, R.G. Ellis to M.B. Derrick, Associate Deputy Minister of Public Health, 7 May 1970, re: Memorandum to deputy provincial treasurer, Mr. D.S. Dombowsky," May 1, 1970.

69   PAS, R-1346, File 1.59, "Correspondence, S.L. Skoll, to W.E. Smishek, re: Government Policy Relating to Legal Counsel for Professional Personnel Employed by Government," October 2, 1973.
70   PAS, R-1346, File 1.61, "Correspondence, R.G. Ellis, Solicitor, Public Health, to J.C. Reid, Saskatchewan Hospital Service Plan," December 3, 1970.
71   PAS, R-1721, File 4.59, "Correspondence, J.D. Fraser, Regional Director, Qu'Appelle Region, to D.A. Higgs, Director of Regional Operations, Central Office, re: Abortion – wards," January 1, 1980.
72   Family Planning Advisory Committee, *Report*, iii.
73   *Ibid*, 8.
74   *Ibid*, 8.
75   *Ibid*, 2, 8.
76   *Ibid*, 23.
77   *Ibid*, 22, 23, 19, 21 [recommendations 38, 39, 45, 26 and 34 respectively].
78   *Ibid*, 27 [recommendation 59, 60].
79   PAS, R-706, File 15.53, Family Planning Advisory Committee, "News Release," April 18, 1975.
80   PAS, R-706, File 15.53, "Memorandum, Minister of Health to Premier and all Cabinet Ministers, re: Recommendations of family planning advisory committee," February 24, 1975, Appendix III, response to recommendation 2.
81   "Memorandum, re: Recommendations," Appendix III, response to recommendations 39–40.
82   PAS, R-706, File 15.53, "Correspondence, Alice Caplin, Family Planning Advisory Committee, to W.A. Robbins," February 2, 1976, 1.
83   PAS, R-706, File 15.53, "Minutes of Meeting Between Committee of Ministers on Family Planning and Family Planning Advisory Committee, Legislative Building, Regina," May 27, 1976.
84   "Minutes, Committee of Ministers and Family Planning Advisory Committee," 1. Mr. Rolfes was opposed to abortion, and concerned with it being connected to family planning in any way.
85   *Ibid*, 2.
86   PAS, R-706, File 15.53, "Correspondence, Ed Tchorzewski, Minister of Education, to W.A. Robbins, re: disbanding of advisory committee," October 13, 1976.
87   PAS, R-891, File 44i, Report, *History of Family Planning Association of Saskatchewan*, n.d.; Family Planning Advisory Committee, "Background – Family Planning Association of Saskatchewan," n.d., 2.
88   Family Planning Advisory Committee, "Background," 1.
89   PAS, R-706, File 15.51, "Correspondence, John D. Bury, Director, Regional Health Services Branch, to Mr. K. Fyke, Associate Deputy Minister," November 7, 1975.
90   Probe Committee, *A Report on Family Planning*, 10. The province intended to offer a grant to the Association in 1974-75, but "red tape" delayed its transmission. In 1975-76, it offered $23,952. The Association also received support from Planned Parenthood and Health and Welfare Canada. In 1976–77, despite a year of budget cuts, the province gave the full budgeted amount of $25,000 to the Association. PAS, R-706, File 15.51, "Correspondence, N. Duane Adams, Assistant Deputy Minister, to W.A. Robbins, Minister of Health, Saskatchewan," February 6, 1976.
91   PAS, R-706, File 15.53, "Memorandum, Minister of Health to Premier and all Cabinet Ministers, re: Recommendations of family planning advisory committee," February 24, 1975, Appendix III, response to recommendation 36; PAS, R-706, File 15.53, "Correspondence, Walter Smishek, to Sally-Anne Williams, Executive Officer, Family Planning Association of Saskatchewan," March 17, 1975.

92   PAS, R-517, File I.202, "Correspondence, Dr. G.W. Piper, Director and Medical Health Officer, Public Health, to Ron Myhr, Family Planning Centre, Regina, Re: Proposal Regina Indigenous Worker Project," May 24, 1973.
93   "Correspondence, Piper to Myhr."
94   PAS, R-517, File I.202, "Correspondence, Ron Myhr, Coordinator of Services, 'Brief Outline of Current and Proposed Activities of Family Planning Association, Regina Branch,' to Division of Child Health," January 22, 1973, 1.
95   "Correspondence: Myhr, to Division of Child Health," 1.
96   PAS, R-706, File 15.65, Family Planning Advisory Committee, "Minutes of Meeting with Saskatchewan Family Planning Association," October 2, 1973, 4.
97   "Minutes, Saskatchewan Family Planning Association," 22.
98   PAS, R-891, File 44f, "Correspondence, Mrs. Sally Anne Williams, Executive Officer, Family Planning Association of Saskatchewan, to Honourable Ted Bowerman, Department of Northern Saskatchewan, 'Brief on Saskatchewan Family Planning,'" n.d. [1973], 1.
99   "Correspondence, Williams to Bowerman," 2.
100 Ibid, 3–4.
101 Ibid, 3–4.
102 Ibid, 4.
103 PAS, R-891, File 44i, Planned Parenthood, "Report of Activities, 1974-1975," November 18, 1975, 4; PAS, R-1274, File I.44P, "Correspondence, Nadia Grechuk, Executive Officer, to Myrna, Sonja, Marianne and Sheila," Re: President of Planned Parenthood of Saskatchewan Invited to Attend Annual Meeting of Native Women's Association of Canada," June 5, 1981.
104 Family Planning Advisory Committee, "Background," 1.
105 "Correspondence, Grechuk, to Myrna, Sonja, Marianne and Sheila," June 5, 1981.
106 Planned Parenthood, "Report of Activities, 1974–1975," 4–5.
107 PAS, R-1453, File 2.156, "A Brief History of Saskatchewan Native Women's Association," n.d., 1.
108 "History of Saskatchewan Native Women's Association," 1-2.
109 Ibid, 1.
110 PAS, R-891, File 72, "Correspondence, Nadia Greschuk, to Suzanne Brazeau, Director, Family Planning Division, Health and Welfare," September 15, 1976.
111 PAS, R-891, File 72, "Correspondence, Nadia Greschuk, to Lizette Ahenakew," Prince Albert, August 30, 1976.
112 PAS, R-891, File 72, "Correspondence, Nadia Greschuk, to Sir/Madam, Job Creation Branch, Dept. of Manpower and Immigration," Regina, September 14, 1976.
113 PAS, R-1274, File I.146, "Correspondence, Nadia Greschuk, to Bernard Daly, Interchurch Project on Population," June 16, 1976. In writing to Bernard Daly, a devout Catholic and part of the Christian Family Movement, who believed in natural family planning and opposed population control ideologies, Greschuk requested reading materials to assist in preparing a talk on the International Planned Parenthood Federation, to stimulate local discussion on population policy.
114 PAS, R-1274, File II.38, "Federal Minister of Manpower and Immigration, Robert Andras," on February 20, 1976; Frank Fidler, "Appendix F – Planned Parenthood Federation of Canada, Re: Rapporteur's Report on Population Workshop," June 18, 1976.
115 Fiddler, "Appendix F – Re: Rapporteur's Report."
116 PAS, R-1274, File II.38, John Dickinson, Chairman, Population Committee, Planned Parenthood Federation of Canada, "Appendix E – A Population Policy for Canada as

an Urgent Recommendation to the Federal Government from Planned Parenthood Federation of Canada," June 18, 1976, 2.
117 Dickinson, "Appendix E – A Population Policy for Canada," 2.
118 PAS, R-891, File30d, "Correspondence, Government of Saskatchewan Premier's Office, Statement by Marc Lalonde, Minister of National Health and Welfare," March 4, 1977, 2–3.
119 LAC, RG29, Vol. 103, File 6780-1-0, "Family Planning Insert Draft for Family Allowance Cheques" and "Memorandum, Suzanne Brazeau, Director of Family Planning, to Brian Iverson, Assistant Deputy Minister, Social Service Program Branch," July 7, 1977.
120 LAC, RG29, Vol. 103, File 6780-1-0, "Federal-Provincial Joint Promotion of Birth Planning" in Briefing Notes For Minister, Family Planning and Abortion, 1977, 3.
121 "Briefing Notes – Minister," 3.
122 PAS, R-935, File III 79b, Saskatchewan, Department of Health, "Statement on Family Planning," June 10, 1977, 1. The Department of Health provided limited funding to Serena Saskatchewan, a "natural" family planning organization founded in 1974 that taught the "symptom-thermal method." The national organization SERENA was founded in Quebec in 1955.
123 Department of Health, "Statement on Family Planning," 2. By the 1970s, "illegitimacy" and "out of wedlock birth" were being replaced by "teenage pregnancy" and "single parenthood," although marriage was still the preferred venue for "responsible motherhood" (Boyd and Flood 2015).
124 Government of Saskatchewan, Advisory Committee on Family Planning, *Toward Sexual and Reproductive Health in Saskatchewan* (Regina: Saskatchewan Health, 1993), 13.
125 Margaret Norum, "Preface," in *Proceedings of the Prevention of Adolescent Pregnancy Symposium*, November 25–26, 1982, edited by Catherine Fergusson (Saskatoon: Saskatchewan Institute for the Prevention of Handicaps, 1983), xxx.
126 Norum, "Preface," xxxvi.
127 *Ibid*, xxxvii–viii.
128 Dr. Melvyn Lavallée, "The Special Needs of the Native Adolescent," in *Proceedings of the Prevention of Adolescent Pregnancy Symposium*, November 25–26, 1982, edited by Catherine Fergusson (Saskatoon: Saskatchewan Institute for the Prevention of Handicaps, 1983), 16. Dr. Lavallée is "the first known Indigenous person to graduate from a medical doctor program in Western Canada" (Needham 2015), which raises the point that regardless of one's social location, one can adopt ideologies that blame the victim of oppressive social relations rather than highlighting their source.
129 PAS, R-935, File III 79b, "Correspondence, F.J. Bogdasavich, Deputy Minister, Department of Social Services, to K.J. Fyke, Associate Deputy Minister, Department of Health re: Draft Proposal on Family Planning," October 7, 1977.
130 PAS, R-935, File III 79b, Saskatchewan, Department of Health, "Draft Proposal: Roles of Department of Social Services and Education on Family Planning," June 10, 1977.
131 *The Children of Unmarried Parent Act*, 1973, R.S.S., 1973, c. 12, s. 25 (1) and (2).
132 *Ibid*, s. 26 (1); For "Report of Birth Form SSS 2090," see PAS, R-1655, File 3.7.10, "Services to Single Parents," November 12, 1981.
133 *Ibid*, s. 26 (2).
134 *The Family Services Act*, 1973, R.S.S., c. 38, s. 16 (1).
135 *Ibid*, s.15.
136 *Ibid*, s.16 (4).
137 *Ibid*, s.2 (A) (1).

138 PAS, R-935, File III. 74, "Correspondence, D. Cameron, Chairman, Social Services Policy Co-ordinating Committee, to F. Bogdasavich, Re: Children of Unmarried Parents Act," June 20, 1977.
139 "Correspondence, Cameron to F. Bogdasavich," 1.
140 *Ibid*, 1, 2.
141 *The Children of Unmarried Parents Act*, R.S.S., 1978, c.8 (effective February 26, 1979).
142 PAS, R-1655, File 3.7.10, "Services to Single Parents," November 12, 1981, 25.
143 PAS, R-1721, File 5.91, "Services to Unmarried Parents Meeting," September 20, 1978, appendix.
144 "Services to Single Parents," 26.
145 *Ibid*, 26.
146 *Ibid*, 27.
147 *Ibid*, 36.
148 "Services to Unmarried Parents Meeting," 1.
149 PAS, R-1721, File 3.107, "Correspondence, W.G. Bayne, Supervisor, Melfort, to G. Joice, Chief, Special Services to Youth and Families, Central Office, Re: Reporting legislation and services to Registered Indians, Family Services on Reserve 80/81," October 6, 1977.
150 "Correspondence, Bayne to Joice," 1.
151 PAS, R-1721, File 3.107, "Correspondence, R. Fontaine, Community & Personal Services, to R. Hikel, Associate Deputy Minister, Re: Policy statement – Treaty Indians," July 9, 1980; and enclosed Policy Statement: Department of Social Services, Re: Family/Child Care Services to Registered Indians, "Services to Registered Indians," 5.2.8.B.2.A.
152 PAS, R-1721, File 3.107, "Correspondence, W.G. Bayne, Program Coordinator, Family and Community Services, to G. Jacobs, Family Services, Re: Family/Child Care Services to Registered Indians," August 12, 1980, 1.
153 "Correspondence, Bayne to Jacobs," 1, 3.
154 PAS, R-1655, File 10.10.1, "Recommendation from the Working Together Conference," April 16, 1982. Notes forwarded from Deputy Minister, Social Services, to Ken Johns, Executive Director, Social Planning Secretariat.
155 PAS, R-1453, File 1.156, Ken Svenson, Report: "Indian and Métis Issues in Saskatchewan to 2001," December 1978, 1.
156 PAS, R-1453, File 1.53, The Social Planning Secretariat, "The Dimensions of Urban Poverty in Saskatchewan," First Draft, January 24, 1979, 16, 19.
157 Social Planning Secretariat, "The Dimensions of Urban Poverty," 20.
158 PAS, R-1671, File 6.127, Income Support Program Policy Division, "Background Paper: Registered Indians Receiving Saskatchewan Assistance Plan Benefits," April 1980.
159 The Social Assistance Plan was the province's "basic income support plan" to meet the cost of food, shelter, utilities, and other necessities of individuals and families. It was cost-shared under the Canada Assistance Plan, administered through regional Social Services, and was meant for those who had limited or no earning capacity. The Family Income Plan, administered by central offices, provided monthly supplements to low-income families with children under the age of eighteen. It too was cost-shared under the Canada Assistance Plan. Social Planning Secretariat, "The Dimensions of Urban Poverty," Table V, 24.
160 PAS, R-1655, File 3.7.11, "Correspondence, Sharon Kelly, to Richard Hazel et al., Teen Parent Project – Early Intervention for Young Single Mothers and Their Infants," November 19, 1982, 1.
161 PAS, R-1453, File 1.303, "Correspondence, T. Lynch, to N.D. Adams, Re: Summary of 1978 Vital Statistics for the Registered Indian Population of Saskatchewan," October 5, 1979, 1.

162 PAS, R-1453, File 1.266.2, "Correspondence, David Hawkes, Assistant Director, Social Planning Secretariat, to Dough McArthur, Director, Socioeconomic Policy, Planning and Research, Executive Council," July 12, 1978; PAS, R-1453, File 1.158, "People of Indian Ancestry in Regina, Major Conclusions from Statistics, June 1978," 1.
163 "Correspondence, Lynch to Adams," 2.
164 PAS, R-1665, File 5.18.7, "Confidential Report, Planning and Evaluation Branch, Saskatchewan Social Services, The Female Single Parent on Welfare: Overcoming Economic Dependency," March 1981, ii.
165 PAS, R-1655, File 3.7.11, "Correspondence, Sharon Kelly, to Richard Hazel et al., re: Teen Parent Project – Early Intervention for Young Single Mothers and Their Infants," November 19, 1982, 3.
166 "Correspondence, Kelly to Hazel et al.," 7–8.
167 La Loche and Pinehouse, in the northwest, are populated largely by Clearwater River Dene and Métis. Soiseth (1970) previously wrote that Indigenous child rearing practices based on "wide Indigenous community involvement" had reduced the number of children suffering from neglect. PAS, R-1655, File 3.7.11, "Correspondence, L. Soiseth, Coordinator, Foster Care Services, to S. Kelly, Administrative Coordinator, Regional Services Division, Re: Teen Parent Project," November 29, 1982.
168 PAS, R-1655, File 3.7.11, "Correspondence, Tanya Owen, Executive Director, Regina Native Women's Association, to Sharon Kelly, Coordinator, Preventative Services, Social Services," May 21, 1982.
169 PAS, R-1453, File 2.156, "Brief from Regina Native Women's Association to Social Planning Secretariat, in response to the position papers 'Attacking Urban Native Poverty: Alternative Government Responses' and 'The Dimensions of Indian and Native Urban Poverty in Saskatchewan,'" January 1980, 1.
170 "Brief – Regina Native Women's Association," Appendix A.
171 Ibid, Appendix A.
172 Ibid, Appendix A.
173 Ibid, Appendix A.
174 PAS, R-1671, File 6.126, "Correspondence, Chris Bailey, Research Officer, to Jim Balfour, Research Officer, Planning and Evaluation, Re: Status and non-Status Indians on Social Assistance," August 27, 1981.
175 "Correspondence, Bailey to Balfour."
176 PAS, R-1453, File 1.266.2, "Correspondence, David Hawkes, Assistant Director, Social Planning Secretariat, to Dough McArthur, Director, Socioeconomic Policy, Planning and Research, Executive Council," July 12, 1978.
177 Confidential Report, "The Female Single Parent on Welfare: Overcoming Economic Dependency," 18.
178 PAS, R-1453, File 1.360, "Health Assessment Seminars, Prince Albert and Yorkton, Saskatchewan Native Women's Association," n.d., in "Regina Native Women, 1981–1983."
179 "Health Assessment Seminars, Saskatchewan Native Women's Association," 1.
180 Ibid, 3, 7.
181 Ibid, appended Report of the Task Force on Women's Health, September 1980, 47.
182 Ibid, 50.
183 "Health Assessment Seminars, Saskatchewan Native Women's Association," 5–6.
184 "Brief – Regina Native Women's Association," 3.
185 PAS, R-1406, File 6.5, "Correspondence, L.M. Flynn, Northern Supervisor, Employment Support Services, to File," February 5, 1980. Subsequently forwarded from Toby Stewart to Ron Hikel (Associate Deputy Minister Social Services) and Jim Oxman, on February 8, 1980.
186 "Correspondence, Flynn forwarded to Stewart and Hikel," 1.

187　*Ibid*, 1.
188　*Ibid*, 1.
189　*Ibid*, 1.
190　PAS, RXG 43, CBKT (Regina) News Clip, "Métis Reaction to Love," March 3, 1980.
191　PAS, R-1406, File 6.5, "Correspondence, Rod Durocher, to Murray Koskie, Minister, Social Services, An Open Letter for Immediate Release," February 14, 1980.
192　PAS, R-1406, File 6.5, "Statement from Murray Koskie, Social Services Minister, on a Recommendation by Board of the Local Employment Services Project, Love, Saskatchewan," February 22, 1980.
193　"Statement from Koskie on Love."
194　Saskatchewan Health, *A Saskatchewan Vision for Health: Challenges and Opportunities* (Regina: Saskatchewan Health, 1992).
195　Minister's Advisory Committee on Family Planning, *Toward Sexual and Reproductive Health in Saskatchewan* (Regina: Saskatchewan Health, 1993), 15.
196　Advisory Committee, *Toward Sexual and Reproductive Health*, 8.
197　*Ibid*, executive summary.
198　*Ibid*, 13–14.
199　*Ibid*, 20, 12.
200　*Ibid*, 27. This change in focus was in keeping with that of the World Health Organization, which coined the term reproductive health in 1988 to reflect a change in the field of sexual health and reproductive rights as a result of the emergence of HIV/AIDS, and concerns regarding other sexually transmitted diseases.
201　*Ibid*, 28.
202　*Ibid*, 28.
203　*Ibid*, 39.
204　*Ibid*, 2–3.
205　PAS, F-193-3, File 12.114, Planned Parenthood Regina, "Briefing Note: Meeting with the Honourable Pat Atkinson and Planned Parenthood Regina," December 3, 1998.
206　PAS, BF 20-2, File 6.115, "Correspondence, Barb Schonhoffer, Executive Director, Planned Parenthood Birth Control Centre, to Eric Cline, Minister of Health," January 29, 1996.
207　PAS, BF 20-2, File 6.115, "Correspondence, Bonnie Johnson, Executive Director, Planned Parenthood Federation of Canada, to Eric Cline, Minister of Health," November 5, 1996.
208　"Correspondence, Johnson to Cline."
209　PAS, R-706, File 15.51, "Correspondence, John D. Bury, Director, Regional Health Services Branch, to K. Fyke, Associate Deputy Minister," November 7, 1975.
210　Advisory Committee on Family Planning, *Toward Sexual and Reproductive Health in Saskatchewan: Second Report* (Regina: Saskatchewan Health, 1995), 32.
211　Advisory Committee, *Toward Health: Second Report*, 31.
212　*Ibid*, viii.
213　*Ibid*, 14.
214　*Ibid*, 12.
215　*Ibid*, 12.
216　PAS, R-1700, File 1.177, "Correspondence, R. Baxter, Coordinator of Therapies, to Dr. A.J. Beddie, Medical Superintended, Dr. W. Zaleski, Clinical Director, Dr. K. Harrison, Director of Training and N. Steele, Supervisor of Social Services, Regional Mental Retardation Program," March 27, 1967.
217　Carole Legge, Gary Roberts, and Mollie Butler, *Situational Analysis: Fetal Alcohol Syndrome/Fetal Alcohol Effects and the Effects of Other Substance Use During Pregnancy* (Ottawa: Health Canada, 2000), 18.

218 Legge, Roberts, and Butler, *Situational Analysis*, 26.
219 *Ibid*, 26; Saskatchewan Prevention Institute, *Fetal Alcohol Spectrum Disorder Prevention Framework 2014* (Regina: Saskatchewan Health, 2014), 1.
220 The provincial government contributed $125,000 each year to the Institute's core operations. PAS, F-193-3, File 10.377, SIPH, "Fetal Alcohol Syndrome – New Saskatchewan Initiative on FAS." Prevention Post 9, no. 1 (Winter 1997), 1; "Fetal Alcohol Syndrome." Prevention Post 10, no. 1 (Winter 1998), 3.
221 PAS, F-193-1, File 8.28, "Correspondence, Eric Cline, to Lorne Calvert," September 20, 1996.
222 PAS, F-193-1, File 8.28, "Correspondence, Lorne Calvert, to Eric Cline," November 8, 1996.
223 Legge, Roberts, and Butler, *Situational Analysis*, 9; FAS/FAE Technical Working Group, *It Takes A Community: Framework for the First Nations and Inuit FAS/FAE Initiative and a Resource Manual for Community Based Prevention of Fetal Alcohol Syndrome and Fetal Alcohol Effects* (Ottawa: Health Canada, First Nations and Inuit Health Branch, 1997).
224 Legge, Roberts, and Butler, *Situational Analysis*, 9.
225 PAS, F-193-3, File 10.378, "Correspondence, Ann Schulman, Executive Director, SIPH, to Judy Junor, Associate Minister of Health," June 12, 1999; PAS, F-193-3, File 10.144, Minister's Advisory Committee on Family Planning, Special Programs for Aboriginal Youth, "Successful Mothers Program."
226 PAS, F-193-3, File 10.378, "Correspondence, Judy Junor, to Ann Schulman, SIPH," May 20, 1999.
227 Legge, Roberts and Butler, *Situational Analysis*, 61, 63, 28. Other programs like the "Healthiest Babies Possible" program, whereby prenatal counsellors visited pregnant Indigenous women in their homes, began in the early 1980s, delivered through the Regina Native Women's Association. PAS, R-1453, File 1.303, Native Alcohol Commission, "Healthiest Babies Possible Program," February 1981.
228 PAS, BF 20-2, File 6.155, Audrey Lunquist, "Cultural Issues in FAS Prevention," in *Conference Proceedings for FAS Prevention in Canada: Train the Trainer Working Conference* (Vancouver, B.C.: FAS Resource Society, 1994), 27.
229 Lunquist, "Cultural Issues in FAS Prevention," 27, 30.
230 PAS, F-193-3, File 10.146, Saskatchewan Health, "Briefing Note: FAS Prairie Province Initiative Meeting in Winnipeg," November 8, 1999.
231 PAS, F-193-3, File 10.147, Saskatchewan Health, "Briefing Note: Issue Alert – Saskatchewan FAS/Teratology Program Proposal," January 30, 2001; Pat Blakley and Richard Snyder, *Proposal for Establishment of Clinical Teratology Program* (Department of Pediatrics, University of Saskatchewan, 2001), 3.
232 Blakley and Snyder, *Proposal for Clinical Teratology Program*, 4.
233 PAS, F-193-3, File 10.147, "Correspondence, Neil Taylor, Saskatoon, to Pat Atkinson," December 6, 1999.
234 PAS, F-193-3, File 10.146, "Correspondence, R. Denson, to Pat Atkinson, Saskatchewan, Re: Fetal Alcohol Syndrome," March 16, 1999, 1-2.
235 PAS, F-193-3, File 10.146, "Correspondence, Judy Junor, to R. Denson," April 28, 1999, 1.
236 *Winnipeg Child and Family Services (Northwest Area) v. D.F.G.* (1997) 3 S.C.R. 925.

Chapter 5

1 *M.R.L.P. and S.A.T. v. The Attorney General of Canada, the Government of Saskatchewan, Saskatchewan Health Authority, Dr. Kristine Mytopher, Dr. Ahmed Ezzat, Dr. Ian Lund, John Doe and Jane Doe* (2007) Q.B.SASK. 1485; *P.D.I. and S.D.P. v. the*

Attorney General of Canada, The Government of Manitoba, Winnipeg Regional Health Authority, Southern Health-Santé Sud, Prairie Mountain Health, Northern Regional Health Authority, Interlake-Eastern Regional Health Authority, The College of Physicians & Surgeons of Manitoba, The College of Registered Nurses of Manitoba, St. Boniface Hospital, Jane Doe and John Doe (2019) Q.B.MAN. CI19-01; *Jessica Horne v. Her Majesty the Queen in Right of the Province of British Columbia* (2019) S.C.B.C. 194010; *Cardinal v. HMQ* (2018) Q.B.AB. 1801-18051; *Unetell et Madame X v. Centre Integre de Santé et de Services Sociaux de Lanaudiere et Richard Monday et Yvonne Brindusa Vasilie* (2023) P.Q. District de Joliette, 705-06-000011-214.

2   Canada, Senate Standing Committee on Human Rights (SSCHR), *Evidence*, 42nd Parl., 1st Sess. (April 3, 2019). https://sencanada.ca/en/Content/Sen/Committee/421/RIDR/54643-e (Lombard).

3   Post Partum Tubal Ligation Policy Number PP 7-3.6, in Yvonne Boyer and Judith Bartlett, *External Review - Tubal Ligation in the Saskatoon Health Region: The Lived Experience of Aboriginal Women* (Saskatchewan: Saskatoon Health Region, 2017), 32.

4   Royal University Hospital, "Post Partum Tubal Ligation Policy Number 1300," Maternal Services Policy and Procedure Manual, October 2016. https://web.archive.org/web/20190418173051/https://www.saskatoonhealthregion.ca/locations_services/Services/Maternal-Newborn-Care/Documents/1300%20PPTL%20Policy%20Oct%202016%20Leanne%20Signed%20off.pdf.

5   Access to Information and Privacy Request (ATIP) HE83-20G, Government of Saskatchewan, Ministry of Health, 11.8 Saskatoon Health Region – Investigation into Tubal Ligations, February 14, 2017, 14; Royal University Hospital, "Post Partum Tubal Ligation Policy." s. 4.0.

6   ATIP, HE83-20G, Ministry of Health, 11.8 Saskatoon Health Region – Investigation into Tubal Ligations, 14; Royal University Hospital, "Post Partum Tubal Ligation Policy." s. 4.2.

7   Ministry of Health, Royal University Hospital, "Post Partum Tubal Ligation Policy." s. 4.3.

8   Boyer and Bartlett, *External Review*, 9.

9   ATIP, HE83-20G, Government of Saskatchewan, Ministry of Health, "External Review Summary – Saskatoon Health Region –Investigations into Tubal Ligation," (taken directly from report, placed in Ministry format), July 25, 2017, Acute and Emergency Services Branch, 33.

10 Boyer and Bartlett, *External Review*, 32.

11 Alisa Lombard, Semaganis, Worme Lombard, "Submission to Special Rapporteur on Violence against Women Dubravka Šimonović, Re: Mistreatment & Violence Against Women During Reproductive Care, With Focus on Childbirth – RE: Forced Sterilization of Indigenous Women in Canada," May 17, 2019, 3–4. https://www.ohchr.org/Documents/Issues/Women/SR/ReproductiveHealthCare/SEMAGANIS%20WORME%20LOMBARD.pdf.

12 Lombard, "Submission to Special Rapporteur RE: Forced Sterilization of Indigenous Women in Canada," 3–4.

13 *Ibid*, 4.

14 ATIP HE83-20G, Government of Saskatchewan, Ministry of Health, "Saskatoon Health Region – Investigation into Tubal Ligations," December 21, 2015, 78.

15 Boyer and Bartlett, *External Review*, 33.

16 Ministry of Health, "Saskatoon Health Region – Investigation into Tubal Ligations," 78.

17 *Ibid*, 78.

18 *Ibid*, 77.

19 *Ibid*, 17.

20 ATIP HE83-20G, Government of Saskatchewan, Ministry of Health, "News Release: Saskatoon Health Region Launches External Review," January 20, 2017, 28.
21 Boyer and Bartlett, *External Review*, 15.
22 *Ibid*, 14–16.
23 *Ibid*, 9–10.
24 *Ibid*, 17–21.
25 *Ibid*, 17–8.
26 *Ibid*, 18.
27 *Ibid*, 18.
28 *Ibid*, 32.
29 *Ibid*, 28.
30 *Ibid*, 27.
31 *Ibid*, 32.
32 *The Child and Family Services Act*, R.S.S., 1989-90, c.-7.2 as amended by the *Statutes of Saskatchewan*, 1990-91, c.10 and c.C-8.1; 1992, c.21; 1994, c.27 and 35; 1996, c.11; 1999, c.14; 2000, c.6; 2001, c.33; 2004, c.5 and 65; 2006, c.19; 2014, c.E-13.1; 2016, c.13 and c.28; 2018, c.8 and c.42; and 2019, c.25; ATIP HE83-20G, Government of Saskatchewan, Ministry of Health, Acute and Emergency Services Branch, "Birth Alerts – SMA RA," October 17, 2019, 30–1.
33 ATIP HE83-20G, "Birth Alerts – SMA RA," 30–1.
34 MMIWG, *Reclaiming Power and Place*, 364–9.
35 *Ibid*, 367.
36 *Ibid*, 365.
37 *Ibid*, 365.
38 *Ibid*, 366–7.
39 Boyer and Bartlett, *External Review*, 19.
40 *Ibid*, 19.
41 *Ibid*, 19.
42 Canada, SSCHR, *Evidence*, 44th Parl., 1st Sess. (May 2, 2022), 8:2. (Witness A)
43 Boyer and Bartlett, *External Review*, 19.
44 *Ibid*, 25, 29.
45 *Ibid*, 25.
46 *Ibid*, 26.
47 *Ibid*, 26.
48 *Ibid*, 24.
49 *Ibid*, 24.
50 *Ibid*, 24.
51 *Ibid*, 24.
52 *Ibid*, 26.
53 *Ibid*, 27.
54 ATIP HE83-20G, "Birth Alerts – SMA RA," 30.
55 *Ibid*, 30–1. In British Columbia, more than half of birth alerts were issued against Indigenous mothers. The province agreed to end the practice in 2019 (Stuech 2019). In Manitoba, where doctors are required to issue a birth alert for any pregnant woman under the age of eighteen, government agreed to follow suit. Government of Manitoba, News Release, "Manitoba to End Use of Birth Alert," January 31, 2020. https://news.gov.mb.ca/news/index.html?item=46808&posted=2020-01-31.
56 *Ibid*, 30–1.
57 *Ibid*, 31.
58 *Ibid*, 31.

59 Canada, SSCHR, *Evidence*, 42nd Parl., 1st Sess. (April 3, 2019). https://sencanada.ca/en/Content/Sen/Committee/421/RIDR/54643-e (Lombard).
60 *Ibid.*
61 Alisa Lombard, "Fact Sheet on Indigenous Women - Forced Sterilization, Saskatchewan Canada," International Justice Resource Centre, February 2018. https://ijrcenter.org/wp-content/uploads/2018/02/Fact-Sheet-Forced-Sterilization-in-Canada.pdf.
62 Lombard, "Fact Sheet on Indigenous Women."
63 Bali Ram and Anatole Romaniuc (1985, 6) indicate both Manitoba and Saskatchewan had an identification code attached to the provincial health insurance number indicating Registered Indian Status.
64 PAS, R-1453, File 1.198, "Correspondence, E. Stepan, Director, Registration and Benefits, to G. Patchett, Executive Director, Medical Care Insurance Commission, Mr. S. [last name missing], Executive Director, Saskatchewan Prescription Drug Plan, Dr. M.H. Lewis, Director, Saskatchewan Prescription Drug Plan, Mr. H.L. Tobias, Director, Saskatchewan Aids to Independent Living, Mr. L.A. Hoffman, Director, Saskatchewan Hearing Aid Plan, Ms. Lucy Wynn, Director, Program Monitoring and Statistics, SHSP, Dr. H Walker, Executive Director, Community Health Services Branch, Re: Identification of Treaty Indians," September 14, 1979.
65 PAS, R-1453, File 1.198, "Correspondence, N.D. Adams, Assistant Deputy Minister, to E. Stepan, Registration and Benefits," September 28, 1979.
66 "Correspondence, Adams to Stepan."
67 This data was used in collaborative study with the World Health Organization in 1968. Dr. V.L. Matthews, Department of Social and Preventive Medicine, University Hospital, headed the Saskatchewan portion. PAS, R-999, File II. 150, "Correspondence, J.C. Clarkson, Deputy Minister of Health, to Mr. M.B. Derrick, 'Re; WHO International Collaboration Study on Medical Care Utilization,'" April 29, 1968. There have been calls from the MMIWG and other organizations for the state to collect "race-based" or "culturally specific" data to allow differentiation between the experiences of First Nations, Inuit, and Métis, white and Black, or LGBTQ2S, for instance, to track victims of crime, understand inequities in accessing services, or identify systemic discrimination. Without this being coupled with broader and transformative change, there is a risk this data can be used to the detriment of these groups.
68 PAS, R-1453, File 1.168, "Correspondence, Doug McArthur, to all Deputy Ministers, Re: Provision of Programs and Services to Treaty Indians," August 8, 1978, 3.
69 Alisa Lombard, "Statement to the Inter-American Commission on Human Rights – Forced Sterilization of Indigenous Women in Saskatchewan, Canada," February 27, 2018, 2. https://ijrcenter.org/wp-content/uploads/2018/02/Alisa-Lombard_IACHR-Statement-27.2.18.pdf; Alisa Lombard, "Submission to the United Nations Committee Against Torture, Re: Examination of Canada State Report, 65th Session," October 15, 2018, 9. https://ijrcenter.org/wp-content/uploads/2018/11/INT_CAT_CSS_CAN_32800_E.pdf.
70 Sterilization data is available from 1970 to 2018. This information is included in text.
71 The Indian Register provides a real-time count of the number of individuals registered under the Indian Act, and is said to be the "most appropriate source" (Amorevieta-Gentil, Daignault, Robitaille et al. 2014, 6) for examining demographic patterns among Registered Indians. It includes all persons with legal Indian Status, but is limited by under-declaration in cases where a child dies before their birth is recorded, and late declarations, when a Registered Indian birth is not registered due to administrative delays, a lack of legal incentive to declare, or changes to Indian Status eligibility rules (Morency, Caron-Malenfant, and Daignault 2018, 41–2).

72 Government of Canada, Aboriginal Affairs and Northern Development, *Aboriginal Demographics: From the 2011 National Household Survey* (Ottawa: Planning, Research and Statistics Branch, 2013), 12; also see Ram and Romaniuc (1985).
73 Statistics Canada, "Aboriginal Peoples in Canada: Key Results from the 2016 Census," *The Daily*, October 25, 2017. https://www150.statcan.gc.ca/n1/daily-quotidien/171025/dq171025a-eng.htm.
74 *Ibid*, 8, 18–19; Michael Tjepkema, Tracey Bushnik, and Evelyne Bougie, "Life Expectancy of First Nations, Métis and Inuit Household Populations in Canada," Statistics Canada, December 18, 2019. https://www150.statcan.gc.ca/n1/en/pub/82-003-x/2019012/article/00001-eng.pdf?st=2_mrjeez; Amanda Sheppard, Gabriel Shapiro, Tracey Bushnik et al., "Birth Outcomes Among First Nations, Inuit and Métis Populations," Statistics Canada, November 15, 2017. https://www150.statcan.gc.ca/n1/en/pub/82-003-x/2017011/article/54886-eng.pdf?st=ZZ0A2W1c.
75 This visual representation is for approximate conceptualization purposes only. Indigenous fertility rates are often difficult to calculate due to a lack of consistent and disaggregated data distinguishing Indigenous fertility levels from the rest of the Canadian or provincial population. Data often cannot be disaggregated for First Nations, Métis, and Inuit. To partially fill this gap, Morency, Caron-Malenfant, and Daignault (2018) relied on census data, the National Household Survey, Vital Statistics, and the Indian Register. However, considering this data cannot be broken down by province, it is supplemented with data drawn from Statistics Canada for 2006, 2010, and 2016, and a study conducted by Bakhtiar Moazzami (2015) on fertility trends in Saskatchewan. It also includes data from Bali Ram and Anatole Romaniuc (1985). See Claudine Provencher, Anne Milan, Stacey Hallman et al., "Fertility: Overview, 2012 to 2016" (Ottawa: Statistics Canada, 2018). www150.statcan.gc.ca/n1/en/pub/91-209-x/2018001/article/54956-eng.pdf?st=zGsvMLgb.
76 The Indian Registration System operates on the basis of affiliation to registry groups rather than geographic location. It covers all Registered Indians who meet the criteria established by the Indian Act regardless of their location, including those outside of Canada. The Census, on the other hand, is based on self-reporting to produce a domestic count of participating and self-identified Aboriginal persons in Canada at the time of enumeration. The Indian Registration System is all-inclusive in its count of individuals registered under the Indian Act. Census data does not include Indian reserves or settlements that chose not to participate, or where it is impossible to collect data because of natural events or when a portion of the total population of a reserve community experiences data quality issues (i.e., a certain level of non-response). Only the population in private dwellings (not in collectives or institutions) is surveyed by the Census. Registered Indian counts were extracted from INAC's Indian Registration System as at December 31, 2019 and have not been adjusted for late reporting of births or deaths. They reflect residency codes for individuals affiliated with these First Nations only. All later calculations relying on population estimates or the number of women of childbearing age, including delivery, abortion, and sterilization rates per 1,000 Registered Indian women, are based on data prepared by Denise Bisson, Statistics and Measurement Directorate, Planning, Research and Statistics Branch, Policy and Strategic Direction Sector, May 19, 2020.
77 The percent change in population growth rate was calculated with the following formula: PR= (V present - V past)/V past x 100 where PR = Percent Population Growth Rate; V present = yearly population value; V past = past/preceding yearly population value.
78 Statistics Canada, Table 13-10-0368-01, "Infant mortality, by birth weight," November 29, 2018. https://doi.org/10.25318/1310036801-eng. For Registered Indians, see Ram

and Romaniuc (1985). For a discussion of the lack of available data on infant mortality rates for Indigenous Peoples, see Elias (2014).

79 Amanda Sheppard, Gabriel Shapiro, Tracey Bushnik et al., "Birth Outcomes Among First Nations, Inuit and Métis Populations" (Ottawa: Statistics Canada 2017). https://www150.statcan.gc.ca/n1/pub/82-003-x/2017011/article/54886-eng.htm; Statistics Canada, Table 13-10-0713-01, "Infant deaths and mortality rates, by age group," November 27, 2023. https://doi.org/10.25318/1310071301-eng.

80 Government of Saskatchewan, Saskatchewan Health, *The Population of Saskatchewan* (Saskatchewan: Saskatchewan Health, n.d.), 3. https://pubsaskdev.blob.core.windows.net/pubsask-prod/108309/108309-The_Population_of_Saskatchewan.pdf.

81 ATIP HE67-20G, Saskatchewan Ministry of Health. Submitted August 20, 2019. Information received February 18, 2020. Delivery records were identified through a search for the following codes; ICD-9 Codes 64* complications mainly related to pregnancy; 65* normal delivery, and other indications for care in pregnancy, labour and delivery; 66* complications occurring mainly in the course of labour and delivery; 67* complications of the puerperium; 650 delivery in a completely normal case; V27* outcome of delivery (e.g., single live birth, single still birth, twins both born alive, etc.); with fifth digit 1, delivered, with or without mention of antepartum condition; or 2, delivered, with mention of post-partum complication. Records from 1970-71 to 1998-99 do not have a 5th ICD-9 digit so only those with a diagnosis code of 65*, 66*, or V27* are counted. This means deliveries may be over-counted slightly because the hospitalization may have been for a complication before or after the delivery hospitalization. A search was also conducted of records with ICD10-CA codes O1*, O2*, O3*, O40* to O48*, O60* to O75*, O85 to O92*, O95*, O98*, O99*, Z37*; with sixth digit 1, delivered, with or without mention of antepartum condition; or 2, delivered, with mention of post-partum complication. Deliveries with an induced abortion because of medical procedure or illness in the fetus or the pregnant woman were excluded. Counts for 1970-71 to 1998-99 are over counted by 0 percent to 4 percent because hospitalizations for complications before and after delivery cannot be excluded due to missing 5th digit on the diagnosis. The hospital files for 1998-99 have residence codes for Registered Indians assigned to the reserves corresponding to the band of origin rather than the community of residence. Some corrections were made for this issue in 1987-88 to 1998-99 data, based on postal code information. Starting in 1999-2000, residence codes for Registered Indians were assigned based on place of residence.

82 The General Fertility Rate = total number of live births to females 15-49 years of age/total number of females 15-49 years of age x 1,000. Due to data limitations, it is not possible to know the number of Registered Indian "live births" or the age at which they occurred. This work relies on the number of "deliveries" to Registered Indians and Other Saskatchewan Residents, which are assumed to involve females between 15-49 years, to calculate a "delivery rate per 1,000" for comparison purposes. No data on females of childbearing age was available for 1973, 1987, or 1989. In these years, an average was calculated using the number of females of childbearing age from the year previous and preceding, divided by 2. In all cases of data suppression, the number was assumed to be 10. This same practice was followed when calculating abortion and sterilization rates per 1,000.

83 There is a need for caution when considering infant deaths by health region; sometimes these rates reflect a small number of deaths. Saskatchewan Prevention Institute, *Infant Mortality in Saskatchewan: Evidence to Inform Public Health Practice* (Saskatchewan: Ministry of Health 2009), 95. https://skprevention.ca/resource-catalogue/child-development/infant-mortality-in-saskatchewan-evidence-to-inform-public-health-practice/; Saskatchewan Health, *The Population of Saskatchewan*, 3.

84 ATIP HE67-20G, "Abortions." A search was conducted for ICD-9 635* (Legally induced abortion), ICD-10-CA code O04* medical abortion (includes termination of pregnancy, therapeutic abortion). To be counted, the record also had to have one of the following procedure codes: CCP 1056 (other genitourinary instillation), 8193 (insertion of luminaria), 855 (medical induction of labour), 8641 (hysterectomy to terminate pregnancy), 870 (intra-amniotic injection for the termination of pregnancy), 871(vacuum aspiration for the termination of pregnancy), 872* (other termination of pregnancy); CCI codes 5CA88^^ (pharmacological termination of pregnancy), 5CVA89^^ (surgical termination of pregnancy. Records for 1970-71 to 1986-86 were selected based on the diagnosis code of 635* only because these records have only one intervention code. Counts are much lower than they should be as the data source is missing the day surgery records for these years. Abortions performed out of province as day surgeries or in non-hospital clinics are NOT counted in the table for any years of data. When the number of abortions in a health region was 5 or less, data was suppressed. In these cases, the number was assumed to be 3. The hospital files for 1998–99 have residence codes for Registered Indians assigned to the reserves corresponding to the band of origin rather than the community of residence. Some corrections were made for this issue in 1987–88 to 1998–99 data based on postal code information. Starting in 1999–2000, residence codes for Registered Indians were assigned based on place of residence.

85 ATIP HE67-20G, "Sterilizations." Sterilization records were identified by ICD-9 code V252 (Sterilization: admission for interruption of fallopian tubes or vas deferens); ICD-10-CA code Z302 (Sterilization: admission for interruption of fallopian tubes or vas deferens). Records for 1970–71 to 1986–87 were selected based on the diagnosis code of V252 and a sex of female because there is only one procedure code on the record and another procedure (e.g., a C-section) may have been recorded rather than tubal ligation. They may still be undercounted due to the small number of diagnosis codes available. For 1998–99 onward, selection was also based on the following procedure codes: CCP codes 782* (total bilateral salpingectomy; 783* (bilateral endoscopic destruction or occlusion of fallopian tubes); 784* (other endoscopic destruction or occlusion of fallopian tubes); 7853 (bilateral partial salpingectomy, unqualified, that for sterilization); CCI codes 1RF51^^ (occlusion, fallopian tube); 1RF59^^ (destruction, fallopian tube); 1RF89^^ (excision, fallopian tube). When the number of sterilizations in a health region was 5 or less, data was suppressed. In these cases, the number was assumed to be 3. The hospital files for 1998–99 have residence codes for Registered Indians assigned to the reserves corresponding to the band of origin rather than the community of residence. Some corrections were made for this issue in 1987–88 to 1998–99 data based on postal code information. Starting in 1999–2000, residence codes for Registered Indians were assigned based on place of residence.

86 Government of Saskatchewan, *Strong. Secure. Saskatchewan* (Saskatchewan: Government of Saskatchewan, n.d.), 2. https://pubsaskdev.blob.core.windows.net/pubsask-prod/93841/Economic%252BOverview-Digital-2020-FINAL.pdf.

87 Government of Saskatchewan, *Strong. Secure. Saskatchewan*, 7–8.

88 Government of Saskatchewan, "Crop Production," January 5, 2024. https://dashboard.saskatchewan.ca/business-economy/business-industry-trade/crop-production#saskatchewan-tab.

89 Government of Saskatchewan, *Strong. Secure. Saskatchewan*, 2.

90 Saskatchewan Mining Association, "Saskatchewan Uranium Fact Shee," 2025. https://saskmining.ca/wp-content/uploads/2025/06/SMA-Uranium-Infographic-2025-final-1.pdf. These include, among others, Rabbit Lake — the longest running uranium mine

in North America — from 1975 to 2016; in 2018, it suspended operations at McArthur River and Key Lake; it also has operations at Cigar Lake and McLean Lake. Areva Resources Canada (now Orano) previously operated the Cluff Lake Mine, which closed in 2002.

91 Two notable radioactive spills took place at Key Lake and Rabbit Lake. In January 1984, 87,330 cubic metres of radioactive liquid — the equivalent of more than thirty-four Olympic sized swimming pools — was released from the Key Lake mine into Gerald Lake. In 1989, 1,950 cubic metres of contaminated mine water — the size of three Olympic sized swimming pools — containing arsenic and radium-226, was released into the watershed that flows into Wollaston Lake, from the Rabbit Lake mine. Hundreds of spills involving three producing mines in Saskatchewan took place from 1981–91. For more recent examples, see Government of Canada, Canadian Nuclear Safety Commission, "Events Reporting: Uranium Mines and Mills." https://nuclearsafety.gc.ca/eng/acts-and-regulations/event-reports-for-major-nuclear-facilities/event-reporting/uranium-mines-mills.cfm.

92 *Smerek v. Areva Resources Canada Inc.* (2014) Q.B. SK. 282.

93 Fission Uranium Corp., "News Release: Fission Signs Engagement and Capacity Agreement with Clearwater River Dene Nation," March 25, 2021. https://www.newswire.ca/news-releases/fission-signs-engagement-and-capacity-agreement-with-clearwater-river-dene-nation-804412922.html.

94 Clearwater River Dene Nation, "News Release: Clearwater River Dene Nation Erects Security Checkpoint to Saskatchewan Uranium Fields," May 31, 2021. https://www.newswire.ca/news-releases/clearwater-river-dene-nation-erects-security-checkpoint-to-saskatchewan-uranium-fields-882773333.html.

95 Lisa Richardson, in Bill Casey, Chair, Standing Committee on Health, Letter to Ministers Petitpas Taylor, Goodale, and O'Regan, Re: Study on Forced Sterilization, August 2, 2019, 6. https://www.ourcommons.ca/content/Committee/421/HESA/WebDoc/WD10596408/421_HESA_reldoc_PDF/MinisterOfHealth-Final-e.pdf.

96 Alisa Lombard, "Statement to the Inter-American Commission on Human Rights: Forced Sterilization of Indigenous Women in Saskatchewan, Canada," February 27, 2018. https://ijrcenter.org/wp-content/uploads/2018/02/Alisa-Lombard_IACHR-Statement-27.2.18.pdf.

Chapter 6

1 Ironically (?), the NDP (formerly CCF) was in power during much of the history covered in this work, from 1943–60, 1971–82, and 1991–2007, times that were central to the expansion of a system of public health and family planning policies that approached Indigenous reproduction as problematic.

2 MMIWG, *Interim Report: Our Women and Girls Are Sacred* (Ottawa, MMIWG, 2017), 15–21. https://www.mmiwg-ffada.ca/wp-content/uploads/2018/03/ni-mmiwg-interim-report.pdf.

3 MMIWG, *Interim Report*, 17.

4 "Statement from Marilyn Poitras," July 11, 2017. https://assets.documentcloud.org/documents/3892277/Poitras-Words-of-Resignation-FINAL.pdf.

5 News Release, "National Inquiry Calls for Transformative Change to Eradicate Violence Against Indigenous Women, Girls and 2SLGBTQQIA," Gatineau, Quebec, June 3, 2019. https://www.mmiwg-ffada.ca/wp-content/uploads/2019/06/News-Release-Final-Report.pdf.

6 MMIWG, *Reclaiming Power and Place*, 53.

7 *Ibid*, 267.

8   *Ibid,* 584–94.
9   *Ibid,* 498–9.
10 Government of Saskatchewan, *Government of Saskatchewan Response to the National Inquiry into Missing and Murdered Indigenous Women and Girls* (Regina: Office of the King's Printer 2021). https://pubsaskdev.blob.core.windows.net/pubsask-prod/144082/MMIWGReport.pdf.
11 Government of Saskatchewan, *Response to the National Inquiry,* 4.
12 British Columbia, *Hansard,* April 25, 2006, 4000; *Apology Act,* S.B.C, 2006, c. 19.
13 *D.E. et al v. British Columbia* 2005. Others include *Richard v. HMTQ* and *A.W. and D.W. By Litigation Guardian, the Public Guardian and Trustee of B.C. v. HMTQ* (2003) BCSC 976; *Arishenkoff v British Columbia* (2002) BCSC 951; *L. R. v British Columbia* (1999) BCCA 698; *Rumley v British Columbia* (2002) BCSC 1300. These cases were brought up in discussions on the Apology Act. British Columbia, *Hansard,* March 29, April 6 and 25, 2006.
14 British Columbia, *Hansard,* March 29, 2006, 3456-67.
15 Government of Saskatchewan, *Hansard,* November 6, 2006, 196.
16 Government of Saskatchewan, *Hansard,* November 13, 2006, 358.
17 Boyer and Bartlett, *External Review,* 42.
18 Cited in Bill Casey, Chair, Standing Committee on Health, "Letter to Ministers Petitpas Taylor, Goodale, and O'Regan, Re: Study on Forced Sterilization," August 2, 2019, 5. https://www.ourcommons.ca/DocumentViewer/en/42-1/HESA/related-document/10596408.
19 Canada, Senate, *Debates of the Senate (Hansard),* 44th Parl., 1st Sess., Vol. 153, No. 132 (June 8, 2023), 3938. (Boyer)
20 *M.R.L.P. and S.A.T. v. The Attorney General of Canada, the Government of Saskatchewan, Saskatchewan Health Authority, Dr. Kristine Mytopher, Dr. Ahmed Ezzat, Dr. Ian Lund, John Doe and Jane Doe* (2017) Q.B.SASK. 1485.
21 *M.R.L.P. and S.A.T. v. The Attorney General of Canada et al.*
22 Tony Merchant of Merchant Law Group is a well-known lawyer who achieved a $1.9 billion settlement for survivors of residential schools, earning him $25 million (Gatehouse 2013). In 2020, Merchant was disciplined by the Law Society of Saskatchewan and had his licence suspended for eight months, beginning in February 2021, for alleged "inappropriate conduct" after he withheld $21,310 from a residential school survivor. *Law Society of Saskatchewan v. Merchant* (2020) SKLSS 6. https://www.lawsociety.sk.ca/wp-content/uploads/2020/09/2020-SKLSS-6-Merchant-00216970xB6EE0.pdf. He was previously investigated by the Canada Revenue Agency for allegedly storing $1.7 million in offshore tax havens, for which he named his wife, former Senator Pana Merchant and their three sons as beneficiaries (Shprintsen 2013).
23 See "Class Action Sixties Scoop Settlement – Official Documents," July 13, 2022. https://sixtiesscoopsettlement.info/official-documents/.
24 *Riddle v. Canada* (2018) FC 641.
25 An episode of *APTN InFocus* featured Coleen Rajotte and Marlene Orgeron, Sixties Scoop Survivors, and Garth Myers, lawyer at Koskie Minsky, LLP, who answered questions on many issues raised by the Settlement Agreement (APTN 2017).
26 Government of Canada, Indigenous and Northern Affairs, "Support for the Sixties Scoop Settlement Agreement to Move Forward," June 26, 2018. https://www.newswire.ca/news-releases/statement---minister-bennett-encourages-support-for-the-sixties-scoop-settlement-agreement-to-move-forward-686554941.html.

27 Koskie Minsky LLP, "Koskie Minksy Brings Métis and Non-Status Indian Sixties Scoop Class Action," December 20, 2018. https://www.newswire.ca/news-releases/koskie-minsky-brings-Métis-and-non-status-indian-sixties-scoop-class-action-703242491.html.
28 *Sharon Varley and Sandra Lukowich v. Canada (Attorney General of Canada)* (2024) FC T-2166-18.
29 Canada, SSCHR, *Evidence*, 44th Parl., 1st Sess. (April 25, 2022). https://sencanada.ca/en/Content/Sen/Committee/441/RIDR/55473-E. (Alisa Lombard)
30 Canada, SSCHR, *Evidence*, 44th Parl., 1st Sess. (May 2, 2022), 8:2.
31 Boyer and Bartlett, *External Review*, 40.
32 *Ibid*, 40.
33 *Ibid*, 39–40.
34 Truth and Reconciliation Commission of Canada, *Calls to Action* (Winnipeg: TRC, 2015), Calls 23 and 24.
35 Government of Saskatchewan, "Saskatoon Health Region Commits to Reconciliation," n.d. https://web.archive.org/web/20210602134622/https://www.saskatoonhealthregion.ca/locations_services/Services/fnmh/Documents/SHR%20Commitment%20to%20Reconciliation.pdf.
36 Boyer and Bartlett, *External Review*, 32, 34.
37 Indigenous Health Working Group (IHWG), *Indigenous Health in the New Saskatchewan Health Authority: Summary of Findings* (Saskatchewan: Saskatchewan Health, 2018). https://www.saskhealthauthority.ca/sites/default/files/2021-04/Report-2020-11-17-FNMR-IndigenousHealthSummary-vFINAL.pdf.
38 IHWG, *Indigenous Health*, 8–9.
39 Federation of Saskatchewan Indian Nations, "Cultural Responsiveness Framework," (Saskatchewan: FSIN, 2013), 5. https://www.saskhealthauthority.ca/sites/default/files/2021-06/FSIN-cultural-responsiveness-framework.pdf.
40 FSIN, "Cultural Responsiveness Framework," 5. An "Indigenous Cultural Responsiveness Theory" has been formalized as a "decolonized approach" that seeks to restore "community-based health and wellness systems," "establish a middle ground for engagement between mainstream and First Nations systems and worldviews" conducive to "mutually beneficial co-existence," and ensure Western service delivery is "culturally responsive." "Loss of land, resources," and the disturbance of "cultural ways and values" are acknowledged as factors affecting Indigenous health and well-being, and the authors call for recognition and respect of Indigenous health systems, including "healing approaches, medicines and practitioners" (Sasakamoose, Bellegarde, Sutherland et al. 2017, 4, 9, 11). However, they do not centre Indigenous lands and sovereignty as central conditions for these cultural practices to take place.
41 Frank Dobbin and Alexandra Kalev (2018) show some form of "anti bias," "racial bias" or "diversity training" goes back to the 1930s, but was stimulated by legal reforms brought about by the civil rights movement. Ambalavaner Sivanandan (1985) refers to "racial awareness training" as having its beginnings on a military base in Florida at the end of the 1960s, when "black rebellion" in American cities reverberated in the military and the institution found itself needing to uphold "individual dignity, worth and equal opportunity" within its ranks (18). For earlier examples and review, see Judy Katz (1975).
42 FSIN, "Cultural Responsiveness Framework," 10; also National Aboriginal Health Organization (NAHO), *Cultural Competency and Safety: A Guide for Health Care Administrators, Providers and Educators* (Ottawa: NAHO, 2008), 19–20.
43 NAHO, *Cultural Competency and Safety*, 6.

44 *Ibid*, 19.
45 *Ibid*, 14–15.
46 Mary Ellen Turpel-Lafond, *In Plain Sight: Addressing Indigenous-specific Racism and Discrimination in B.C. Health Care* (British Columbia: Ministry of Health, 2020), 213. https://engage.gov.bc.ca/app/uploads/sites/613/2020/11/In-Plain-Sight-Summary-Report.pdf.
47 Some examples: Royal Commission of Aboriginal Peoples, *Report of the Royal Commission on Aboriginal Peoples. Renewal: A Twenty-Year Commitment, Vol. 5* (Ottawa: Royal Commission on Aboriginal Peoples, 1996), esp. 202–258; NAHO, *Cultural Competency and Safety: A Guide for Health Care Administrators, Providers and Educators* (Ottawa: NAHO, 2008); MMIWG Inquiry, *Reclaiming Power and Place*; Mary Ellen Turpel-Lafond, *In Plain Sight*. The reader might find it useful to reflect on the warning issued by Sivanandan (1985) with respect to how the Black struggle against oppression was undermined when members of the Black community, which he describes as a "nascent black petit bourgeoisie" nourished by government aid, "leapt to embrace" this approach (14).
48 Indigenous Physicians Association of Canada and The Royal College of Physicians and Surgeons of Canada, *First Nations, Inuit, Métis Health Core Competencies. A Curriculum Framework for Undergraduate Medical Education* (Winnipeg and Ottawa: Indigenous Physicians Association of Canada and the Royal College of Physicians and Surgeons of Canada, 2009), 8.
49 Aboriginal Nurses Association of Canada, Canadian Association of Schools of Nursing and Canadian Nurses Association, *Cultural Competence and Cultural Safety in First Nations, Inuit and Métis Nursing Education: An Integrated Review of the Literature* (Ottawa: Aboriginal Nurses Association, 2009), 2.
50 In her important critique of cultural competency, Mary-Lyne Grenier (2020) argues "decolonization" is embedded within a cultural humility approach. However, this author is hard pressed to identify any substantial difference in approach other than "cultural humility" may have originated from the psychological literature.
51 Boyer and Bartlett, *External Review*, 40.
52 Saskatchewan Health Authority, "Streamlining Recruitment of First Nations and Métis Staff," August 13, 2019. https://web.archive.org/web/20210627161334/https://www.saskhealthauthority.ca/news/stories/Pages/2019/August/Streamlining-recruitment-First-Nations-M%C3%A9tis-staff.aspx.; "Program Provides Comfort, Support for Pregnant Women," October 29, 2019. https://web.archive.org/web/20210627155827/https://www.saskhealthauthority.ca/news/stories/Pages/2019/October/New-program-provides-support-pregnant-women.aspx.
53 ATIP, HE83-20G, Government of Saskatchewan, Ministry of Health, 1.11 Tubal Ligations – Royal University Hospital, 3; Saskatchewan Health Authority, "Nipawin Initiative Improving Cultural Competency," June 21, 2019. https://web.archive.org/web/20210627162230/https://www.saskhealthauthority.ca/news/stories/Pages/2019/June/Nipawin-initiative-improving-cultural-competency.aspx.
54 SHA, "Nipawin Initiative Improving Cultural Competency."
55 The report on forum proceedings is here: https://www.nccih.ca/495/Informed_Choice_and_Consent_in_First_Nations,_Inuit_and_M%C3%A9tis_Women%E2%80%99s_Health_Services.nccih?id=323.
56 Indigenous Services Canada, "Government of Canada actions to address anti-Indigenous racism in health systems," January 16, 2024. https://www.sac-isc.gc.ca/eng/1628264764888/1628264790978.

57 Assembly of First Nations (AFN), "Assembly of First Nations Calls for Criminalization of Forced Sterilization of First Nations Women," December 7, 2018. http://www.afn.ca/assembly-of-first-nations-calls-for-criminalization-of-forced-sterilization-of-first-nations-women/.
58 AFN, "Calls for Criminalization."
59 *Ibid.*
60 UN General Assembly, *Convention Against Torture and Other Cruel, Inhuman or Degrading Treatment or Punishment*, December 10, 1984, United Nations, Treaty Series, Vol. 1465, 85. Canada became signatory to this Convention on August 23, 1985, and ratified it on June 24, 1987. Government of Canada, "Reports on United Nations Human Rights Treaties." https://www.canada.ca/en/canadian-heritage/services/canada-united-nations-system/reports-united-nations-treaties.html.
61 *Canadian Charter of Rights and Freedoms*, R.S.C., s. 7, Part 1 of the *Constitution Act, 1982*, being Schedule B to the *Canada Act 1982* (UK), 1982, c. 11., Art. 12. https://laws-lois.justice.gc.ca/eng/const/page-15.html.
62 United Nations Committee Against Torture, *Concluding Observations on the Seventh Periodic Report of Canada*, December 21, 2018. https://www.ohchr.org/en/documents/concluding-observations/catccanco7-concluding-observations-seventh-periodic-report-canada.
63 Committee Against Torture, *Concluding Observations*, 51(a) and (b).
64 United Nations Committee Against Torture, *Information Received from Canada on Follow-Up to The Concluding Observations on Its Seventh Period Report*, February 21, 2020, 4. https://documents-dds-ny.un.org/doc/UNDOC/GEN/G20/094/90/PDF/G2009490.pdf?OpenElement. Accessed October 31, 2023.
65 UNCAT, *Information Received from Canada, Follow-Up*, 4.
66 *Ibid*, 5.
67 Canada, SSCHR, *Forced and Coerced Sterilization of Persons in Canada* (Ottawa: SSCHR, 2021), 27.
68 *Ibid*, 28–9.
69 SSCHR, *Evidence*, (May 2, 2022), 8:3.
70 *Ibid*, 8:4.
71 Canada, SSCHR, *Evidence*, 44th Parl., 1st Sess. (May 9, 2022), 9:25.
72 SSCHR, *Evidence* (May 2, 2022), 8:28.
73 Canada, SSCHR, *Evidence*, 42nd Parl., 1st Sess., No. 41 (April 10, 2019). https://sencanada.ca/en/Content/Sen/Committee/421/RIDR/41EV-54680-E.
74 SSCHR, *Evidence* (May 9, 2022), 9:10.
75 Senate of Canada, *Hansard*, 44th Parl., 1st Sess., No. 53, Vol. 153 (June 14, 2022), 1613. (Boyer)
76 Senate of Canada, *Hansard*, 44th Parl., 1st Sess., No. 97, Vol. 153 (February 2, 2023), 2875–76. (Boyer)
77 *Ibid*, 2876.
78 Senate of Canada, *Hansard*, 44th Parl., 1st Sess., No. 109, Vol. 153 (March 28, 2023), 3175. (Wells)
79 *Ibid*, 3175.
80 *Ibid*, 3176.
81 Senate of Canada, *Hansard*, 44th Parl., 1st Sess., No. 114, Vol. 153, (October 8, 2024). https://www.parl.ca/Content/Bills/441/Private/S-250/S-250_3/S-250_3.PDF.
82 Senate of Canada, *Hansard*, 45th Parl., 1st Sess., No. 7, Vol. 154, (June 5, 2025). https://www.parl.ca/Content/Bills/451/Private/S-228/S-228_1/S-228_1.PDF.

83 Senate of Canada, *Hansard*, 45th Parl., 1st Sess., No. 11, Vol. 154, (June 16, 2025). https://sencanada.ca/content/sen/chamber/451/debates/pdf/011db_2025-06-16-e.pdf.
84 Senate of Canada, *Hansard*, 44th Parl., 1st Sess., No. 97, Vol. 153 (February 2, 2023), 2877. (Boyer)
85 *Ibid*, 2876.
86 *Ibid*, 2876.
87 *An Act to Prevent the further Introduction of Slaves and to limit the Term of Contracts for Servitude Statutes of Upper Canada* c. 7, 33 George III, 1793.
88 The SSCHR heard testimony referencing the coerced sterilization of Black women. See Canada, SSCHR, *The Scars That We Carry: Forced and Coerced Sterilization of Persons in Canada – Part II* (Ottawa: SSCHR, 2022).
89 Boyer and Bartlett, *External Review*, 39. Canadian Charter of Rights and Freedoms, s.35(1).
90 Yvonne Boyer (2014b) engages evidence to demonstrate explicit references to medicine in the wording of treaties or records documenting oral negotiations in Treaties 6, 8 and 10. Elsewhere, Boyer and Sheyenne Spence (2015) demonstrate similar evidence in Treaties 2, 4 and 5, among others.
91 NAHO, *Aboriginal Health: A Constitutional Rights Analysis, No. 1* (Ottawa: NAHO 2003), 17.
92 The human right to health is recognized in many international and domestic human rights instruments including the Universal Declaration on Human Rights; the International Covenant on Economic and Social Rights; the Canadian Charter of Rights and Freedoms and other domestic laws that uphold the right to health. NAHO, *Aboriginal Health: A Constitutional Rights Analysis*; Gruskin, Ahmed, Bogecho et al. (2012).
93 Boyer and Bartlett, *External Review*, 33.
94 *Ibid*, 39.
95 *Ibid*, 34–5, 36.
96 *UNDRIP*, Articles 3, 4 and 5.
97 *UNDRIP*, Article 24.
98 Boyer and Bartlett, *External Review*, 35–6.
99 UN News, "United Nations Adopts Declaration on Rights of Indigenous Peoples," September 13, 2007, (Ambassador John McNee, Canada). https://news.un.org/en/story/2007/09/231062.
100 Government of Canada, "Canada's Statement of Support on the United Nations Declaration on the Rights of Indigenous Peoples," Indigenous and Northern Affairs Canada, November 12, 2010. https://web.archive.org/web/20240913172116/https://www.rcaanc-cirnac.gc.ca/eng/1309374239861/1621701138904.
101 Government of Canada, "Canada Becomes a Full Supporter of the United Nations Declaration on the Rights of Indigenous Peoples," Indigenous and Northern Affairs Canada, May 10, 2016. https://www.canada.ca/en/indigenous-northern-affairs/news/2016/05/canada-becomes-a-full-supporter-of-the-united-nations-declaration-on-the-rights-of-indigenous-peoples.html.
102 *United Nations Declaration on the Rights of Indigenous Peoples Act*, R.S.C., 2021, c. 14. https://laws-lois.justice.gc.ca/eng/acts/U-2.2/page-1.html.
103 Government of Canada, "The UN Declaration Explained," Justice Canada, July 20, 2023. https://www.justice.gc.ca/eng/declaration/what-quoi.html.
104 Government of Canada, *The United Nations Declaration on the Rights of Indigenous Peoples Act Action Plan* (Ottawa: Minister of Justice and Attorney General of Canada, 2023). https://www.justice.gc.ca/eng/declaration/ap-pa/ah/pdf/unda-action-plan-digital-eng.pdf.

105 UN General Assembly, *United Nations Declaration on the Rights of Indigenous Peoples: resolution / adopted by the General Assembly*, October 2, 2007, A/RES/61/295. https://www.refworld.org/docid/471355a82.html.

References

Abel, Ernest L. 1998. "Fetal Alcohol Syndrome: The 'American Paradox.'" *Alcohol and Alcoholism* 33, 3. https://doi.org/10.1093/oxfordjournals.alcalc.a008382.

Abel, Kerry, and John F. Leslie. 2000. *Native Policy Since 1945*. Canada: Indian and Northern Affairs.

Abner, Erika, and Mary Jane Mossman. 1990. "No More than Simple Justice: Assessing the Royal Commission Report on Women, Poverty and the Family." *Ottawa Law Review* 22, 3.

Ackerman, Katerina, and Shannon Stettner. 2019. "'The Public is Not Ready for This': 1969 and the Long Road to Abortion Access." *The Canadian Historical Review* 100, 2. https://doi.org/10.3138/chr.2018-0082-3.

Adam, Betty Ann. 2022. "Traditional Birthing a Step Toward Reclaiming Health Care Sovereignty." *National Post*, June 16, 2022. nationalpost.com/special-sections/national-indigenous-peoples-day/traditional-birthing-a-step-toward-reclaiming-health-care-sovereignty.

———. 2017. "Saskatoon Health Region Apologizes for Forced Tubal Ligations, Says Report 'Provides Clear Direction.'" *Saskatoon Star Phoenix*, July 28, 2017. thestarphoenix.com/news/local-news/saskatoon-health-region-apologizes-for-forced-tubal-ligations-says-report-provides-clear-direction.

———. 2015a. "Saskatchewan Women Pressured to Have Tubal Ligations." *Saskatoon Star Phoenix*, November 17, 2015. thestarphoenix.com/news/national/women-pressured-to-have-tubal-ligations.

———. 2015b. "NDP Decries 'Heinous' Sterilizations, Urges Action from Premier Wall." *Saskatoon Star Phoenix*, December 21, 2015. thestarphoenix.com/news/politics/ndp-decries-heinous-sterilizations-urges-action-from-premier-wall.

Ahmed, Sara. 2023. *The Feminist Killjoy Handbook: The Radical Potential of Getting in the Way*. New York: Seal Press.

Aivalis, Christo. 2020. "Pierre Trudeau, the Assault on Collective Bargaining, and Lowering Working-Class Expectations." *Journal of Canadian Labour Studies* 86. https://doi.org/10.1353/llt.2020.0041.

———. 2018. *The Constant Liberal: Pierre Trudeau, Organized Labour, and the Canadian Social Democratic Left*. Vancouver: UBC Press.

Alexander, Michelle. 2020. *The New Jim Crow: Mass Incarceration in the Age of Colorblindness*, 10th ed. New York: The New Press.

Allen, Holly, and Erin Fuller. 2016. "Beyond the Feeble Mind: Foregrounding the Personhood of Inmates with Significant Intellectual Disabilities in the Era of Institutionalization." *Disability Studies Quarterly* 36, 2. https://doi.org/10.18061/dsq.v36i2.5227.

Altink, Henrice. 2017. "The Black Scourge? Race and the Rockefeller Foundation's Tuberculosis Commission in Interwar Jamaica." *História, Ciências, Saúde – Manguinhos* 24, 4. http://doi.org/10.1590/S0104-59702017000500012.

Amorevieta-Gentil, Marilyn, David Daignault, Norbert Robitaille, et al. 2014. "Intergenerational Patterns of Fertility Among Registered Indian Teenage Girls in Canada." *The International Indigenous Policy Journal* 5, 3. https://doi.org/10.18584/iipj.2014.5.3.7.

Anderson, Kim. 2011. *Life Stages and Native Women: Memory, Teachings, and Story Medicine*. Winnipeg: University of Manitoba Press.

———. 2003. "Vital Signs: Reading Colonialism in Contemporary Adolescent Family Planning." In *Strong Women Stories: Native Vision and Community Survival*, edited by Kim Anderson and Bonita Lawrence. Toronto: Sumach Press.

———. 2000. *A Recognition of Being: Reconstructing Native Womanhood*. Toronto: Second Story Press.

Appleby, Brenda. 2001. "Canada and Birth Control." In *Encyclopedia of Birth Control*, edited by Vern Bullough. California: ABC - CLIO, Inc.

———. 1999. *Responsible Parenthood: Decriminalizing Contraception in Canada*. Toronto: University of Toronto Press.

APTN News. 2017. "The Sixties Scoop Settlement and the Issues Behind It." *APTN InFocus*, October 18, 2017. https://www.youtube.com/watch?v=Px5pWYiFm8g.

Argue, Cheryl, and Benjamin Schlesinger. 1974. "Family Planning and Social Work Practice." In *Family Planning in Canada: A Source Book*, edited by Benjamin Schlesinger. Toronto: University of Toronto Press.

Arnove, Robert (ed.). 1982. *Philanthropy and Cultural Imperialism: The Foundations at Home and Abroad*. Bloomington: Indiana University Press.

Arvin, Maile, Eve Tuck, and Angie Morrill. 2013. "Decolonizing Feminism: Challenging Connections between Settler Colonialism and Heteropatriarchy." *Feminist Formations* 25, 1. http://doi.org/10.1353/ff.2013.0006.

Azzopardi, Corry, and Ted McNeill. 2016. "From Cultural Competence to Cultural Consciousness: Transitioning to a Critical Approach to Working Across Differences in Social Work." *Journal of Ethnic & Cultural Diversity in Social Work* 25, 4. https://doi.org/10.1080/15313204.2016.1206494.

Bain, Ian. 1964. "The Development of Family Planning in Canada." *Canadian Journal of Public Health* 55, 8. https://www.jstor.org/stable/41983579.

Barona, Josep L. 2021. "The Rockefeller Foundation and the League of Nations: Public Health in Europe (1920–1945)." *Historia Debates E Tendencias* 21, 3. https://doi.org/10.5335/hdtv.21n.3.12845.

Barron, F. Laurie. 1997. *Walking in Indian Moccasins: The Native Policies of Tommy Douglas and the CCF*. Vancouver: UBC Press.

Barton, Walter. 1977. *The History and Influence of the American Psychiatric Association*. Washington, DC: American Psychiatric Press, Inc.

Bashford, Alison. 2014. *Global Population: History, Geopolitics, and Life on Earth*. New York: Columbia University Press.

Beagan, Brenda. 2018. "A Critique of Cultural Competence: Assumptions, Limitations, and Alternatives." In *Cultural Competence in Applied Psychology: An Evaluation of Current Status and Future Directions*, edited by Craig Frisby and William O'Donohue. Cham: Springer.

Bear Nicholas, Andrea. 2001. "Canada's Colonial Mission: The Great White Bird." In *Aboriginal Education in Canada: A Study in Decolonization*, edited by K.P. Binda and Sharilyn Caillou. Mississauga, ON: Canadian Educators Press.

Benassi, David. 2010. "'Father of the Welfare State'? Beveridge and the Emergence of the Welfare State." *Sociologica* 3. researchgate.net/publication/236962950_Father_of_the_welfare_state_Beveridge_and_the_emergence_of_the_welfare_state.

Berman, Edward. 1983. *The Influence of the Carnegie, Ford, and Rockefeller Foundations on American Foreign Policy: The Ideology of Philanthropy*. Albany, NY: State University of New York Press.

Berridge, Virginia. 2016. *Public Health: A Very Short Introduction*. Great Clarendon Street: Oxford University Press.

Beveridge, William. 1943. "Eugenic Aspects of Children's Allowances." *The Eugenics Review* 34, 4.

Bird, Florence. 1997. "Reminiscences of the Commission Chair." In *Women and the Canadian State*, edited by Caroline Andrew and Sandra Rodgers. Montreal and Kingston: McGill-Queen's University Press.

Birn, Anne-Emmanuelle. 2014. "Backstage: The Relationship Between the Rockefeller Foundation and the World Health Organization, Part I: 1940s–1960s." *Public Health* 128, 2. https://doi.org/10.1016/j.puhe.2013.11.010.

Bishop, Mary. 1983. "'The Politics of Abortion: Trends in Canadian Fertility Policy' by Larry Collins - Revisited." *Atlantis: Critical Studies in Gender, Culture & Social Justice* 9, 1.

Black, Edwin. 2003. *War Against the Weak: Eugenics and America's Campaign to Create a Master Race*. New York: Four Walls Eight Windows.

Blacker, Carlos P. 1935. "Fitness for Marriage." *The Eugenics Review* 27, 1.

Blackstock, Cindy. 2007. "Residential Schools: Did They Really Close or Just Morph into Child Welfare?" *Indigenous Law Journal* 6, 1. https://jps.library.utoronto.ca/index.php/ilj/article/view/27665.

Blackstock, Cindy, Nico Trocmé, and Marlyn Bennett. 2004. "Child Maltreatment Investigations among Aboriginal and Non-Aboriginal Families in Canada." *Violence Against Women* 10, 8. https://doi.org/10.1177/1077801204266312.

Bothwell, Robert. 1984. *Eldorado: Canada's National Uranium Company*. Toronto: University of Toronto Press.

Bowd, Alan. 1977. "Ten Years after the Hawthorn Report: Changing Psychological Implications for the Education of Canadian Native Peoples." *Canadian Psychological Review* 18, 4. https://doi.org/10.1037/h0081449.

Boyd, Susan B., and Jennifer Flood. 2015. "Illegitimacy in British Columbia, Saskatchewan, Ontario, and Nova Scotia: A Legislative History." *Allard Research Commons* (April). http://dx.doi.org/10.2139/ssrn.2636513.

Boyer, Yvonne. 2020. *Uncovering the Forced and/or Coerced Sterilization of Indigenous Women*. Keynote Address (transcript). National Collaborating Centre for Indigenous Health's National Gathering on Culturally Informed Choice and Consent in Indigenous Health Services, Ottawa, Canada, January 28, 2020. nccih.ca/docs/general/PODCAST-VoicesFromField-Boyer-Bartlett-Transcript-EN.pdf.

———. 2014a. "Using the United Nations Framework to Advance and Protect the Inherent Rights of Indigenous Peoples in Canada." In *The Internationalization of Indigenous Rights: UNDRIP in the Canadian Context*, edited by Terry Mitchell. Waterloo: Canadian Centre for International Governance.

———. 2014b. *Moving Aboriginal Health Forward: Discarding Canada's Legal Barriers*. Saskatoon, SK: Purich Publishing.

Boyer, Yvonne, and Sheyenne Spence. 2015. "Identifying and Advancing the Treaty Rights to Health… Signed from 1871 and 1906 in Manitoba." *Revue francaise d'etudes americanes* 3, 144. https://doi.org/10.3917/rfea.144.0095.

Boyko, John. 2016. *Cold Fire: Kennedy's Northern Front*. Toronto: Knopf Canada.

Bramadat-Willcock, Michael. 2021. "Clearwater River Dene Nation Blocks 'Business as Usual' Access to Uranium Fields." *Prince Albert Daily Herald*, June 7, 2021. paherald.sk.ca/clearwater-river-dene-nation-blocks-business-as-usual-access-to-uranium-fields/.

Bray, Debrah, and Perry Anderson. 1989. "Appraisal of the Epidemiology of Fetal Alcohol Syndrome Among Canadian Native Peoples." *Canadian Journal of Public Health* 80, 1. https://pubmed.ncbi.nlm.nih.gov/2702544/.

Breman, Jan, Kevan Harris, Ching Kwan Lee, et al. (eds.). 2019. *The Social Question in the Twenty-First Century: A Global View*. California: University of California Press.

Brison, Jeffrey. 2005. *Rockefeller, Carnegie, and Canada: American Philanthropy and the Arts and Letters in Canada*. Montreal: McGill-Queen's University Press.

Brodie, Janine, Shelley Gavigan, and Jane Jensen (eds.). 1992. *The Politics of Abortion.* Toronto: Oxford University Press.

Browne, Anette J., Colleen Varcoe, Victoria Smye, et al. 2009. "Cultural Safety and the Challenges of Translating Critically Oriented Knowledge in Practice." *Nurs Philos* 10, 3. https://doi:10.1111/j.1466-769X.2009.00406.x.

Brown, Theodore, and Elizabeth Fee. 2003. "Henry E. Sigerist: Medical Historian and Social Visionary." *American Journal of Public Health* 93, 1. http://doi.org/10.2105/ajph.93.1.60.

Brown, Richard. 1982. "Rockefeller Medicine in China: Professionalism and Imperialism." In *Philanthropy and Cultural Imperialism*, edited by Robert Arnove. Bloomington: Indiana University Press.

———. 1979. *Rockefeller Medicine Men: Medicine and Capitalism in America.* Berkeley, CA: University of California Press.

———. 1976. "Public Health in Imperialism: Early Rockefeller Programs at Home and Abroad." *American Journal of Public Health* 66, 9.

Brushett, Kevin. 2015. "Partners in Development? Robert McNamara, Lester Pearson, and the Commission on International Development, 1967–1973." *Diplomacy & Statecraft* 26, 1. https://doi.org/10.1080/09592296.2015.999626.

Bu, Liping, and Elizabeth Fee. 2008. "John B. Grant: International Statesman of Public Health." *American Journal of Public Health* 98, 4. https://doi.org/10.2105/AJPH.2007.129304.

Bunjun, Benita. 2018. "The Making of a Colonial Archive: The Royal Commission on the Status of Women." *Education as Change* 22, 2. https://doi.org/10.25159/1947-9417/3609.

Burton, Randy. 1999. "Social Cost of FAS Enormous." *The StarPhoenix*, June 3, 1999.

Caccia, Ivana. 2010. *Managing the Canadian Mosaic in Wartime, Shaping Citizenship Policy, 1939–1945.* Montreal; Kingston: McGill-Queen's University Press.

Cadbury, George. 1973. "A Population Policy? The Present Situation." In *A Population Policy for Canada?* Toronto: The Conservation Council of Ontario and The Family Planning Federation of Canada.

Cameron, G. Donald. 1959. "The Department of National Health and Welfare." *Canadian Journal of Public Health* 50, 8.

Campbell, Erika. 2020. "Combating Physician-Assisted Genocide and White Supremacy in Healthcare through Anti-Oppression Pedagogies in Canadian Medical Schools to Prevent the Coercive and Forced Sterilization of Aboriginal Women." Major Research Project. Queen's University.

Campbell, P.S. 1945. "Full-Time Health Services in Nova Scotia." *Canadian Journal of Public Health* 36, 10. https://www.jstor.org/stable/41978924.

Canadian Public Health Association. n.d. "Vision and Mission." https://www.cpha.ca/vision-and-mission.

Canadian Women's Committee on Reproduction, Population, and Development. 1995. "Canadian Policies and Practices in the Areas of Reproduction, Population and Development." *Canadian Woman Studies* 15, 2. https://cws.journals.yorku.ca/index.php/cws/article/view/9494.

Cardinal, Colleen. n.d. "The Sixties Scoop Payoff: Canada's Strategy for Settling Colonialism." *Sixties Scoop Network.* https://sixtiesscoopnetwork.org/60s-scoop-news-media?itemId=xglsbjysgu2r07iy4mrf9w58ua5ujt.

Cardinal, Harold and Walter Hilderbrant. 2000. *Treaty Elders of Saskatchewan.* Calgary: University of Calgary Press.

Cardinal, Harold. 1969. *The Unjust Society.* Toronto: D&M Publishers.

Carey, Michelle. 2015. "The Limits of Cultural Competence: An Indigenous Studies Perspective." *Higher Education Research & Development* 34, 5. https://doi.org/10.1080/07294360.2015.1011097.

Carter, Sarah. 2017. "Develop a Great Imperial Race": Emmeline Pankhurst, Emily Murphy, and Their Promotion of "Race Betterment" in Western Canada in the 1920s." In *Finding Directions West: Readings That Locate and Dislocate Western Canada's Past*, edited by Heather Devine and Goerge Colpitts. Calgary: University of Calgary Press.

———. 1993. "Categories and Terrains of Exclusion: Constructing the 'Indian Woman' in the Early Settlement Era in Western Canada." *Great Plains Quarterly* 13, 3. https://www.jstor.org/stable/23531720.

Cattapan, Alana, Samantha Moore, and Karen Lawford. 2021. *Reproductive Justice and Indigenous Women in Saskatchewan: Overview and Recommendations*. Johnson Shoyama. March 1, 2021. schoolofpublicpolicy.sk.ca/documents/research/policy-briefs/jsgs-policybriefs-reproductive-justice-and-indigenous-women-in-sk.pdf.

CBC Arts. 2004. "Tommy Douglas Crowned 'Greatest Canadian.'" *CBC News Online*, November 29, 2004. cbc.ca/news/entertainment/tommy-douglas-crowned-greatest-canadian-1.510403.

CBC News. 2021a. "'I won't comment on what's going on over in the U.K.' — Trudeau." *CBC News Online*, Mar 9, 2021. cbc.ca/player/play/video/1.5942642.

———. 2021b. "Northern Sask. First Nation Erects Security Checkpoint in Response to Uranium Exploration and COVID-19." *CBC News Online*, May 31, 2021. cbc.ca/news/canada/saskatchewan/uranium-first-nation-clearwater-river-dene-nation-1.6047439.

———. 2017. "Marilyn Poitras on Why She Resigned as MMIWG Commissioner and Her Hopes for Change." *CBC News Online*, July 16, 2017. cbc.ca/news/indigenous/marilyn-poitras-mmiwg-commissioner-resign-q-a-1.4207199.

———. 2015a. "Another Saskatoon Woman Says She Was Sterilized Against Her Will." *CBC News Online*, December 16, 2015. cbc.ca/news/canada/saskatoon/saskatoon-woman-says-she-was-sterilized-against-her-will-1.3366464.

———. 2015b. "'I Didn't Want it Done': Saskatoon Woman Was Sterilized Against Her Will." *CBCNews Online*, November 18, 2015. cbc.ca/news/canada/saskatoon/saskatoon-woman-sterilized-against-will-1.3324980.

———. 2015c. "'I Really Couldn't Do Anything': Saskatoon Woman Recalls Tubal Ligation." *CBC News Online*, December 21, 2015. cbc.ca/news/canada/saskatoon/i-really-couldn-t-do-anything-saskatoon-woman-recalls-tubal-ligation-1.3373945.

CBC Radio. 2018. "Indigenous Women Kept from Seeing their Newborn Babies until Agreeing to Sterilization, says Lawyer." *The Current*, November 13, 2018. cbc.ca/radio/thecurrent/the-current-for-november-13-2018-1.4902679/indigenous-women-kept-from-seeing-their-newborn-babies-until-agreeing-to-sterilization-says-lawyer-1.4902693.

Charlton, Jonathan. 2016. "Health Region Might Restart External Review: Woman Who Received Tubal Ligation Was Upset That She Was Not Contacted." *The Star Phoenix*, June 24, 2016.

Charters, Claire, and Rodolfo Stavenhagen (eds.). 2009. *Making the Declaration Work: The United Nations Declaration on the Rights of Indigenous Peoples*. Copenhagen: International Work Group for Indigenous Affairs. iwgia.org/images/publications/making_the_declaration_work.pdf.

Chartrand, Vicki. 2023. "The Quotidian Violence of Incarcerating Indigenous People in the Canadian State: Why Reform is Not an Option for Decolonization." In *The Routledge International Handbook on Decolonizing Justice*, edited by Chris Cunneen, Antje Deckert, Amanda Porter, Juan Tauri, and Robert Webb. London: Routledge Press.

———. 2019. "Unsettled Times: Indigenous Incarceration and the Links between Colonialism and the Penitentiary in Canada." *Canadian Journal of Criminology and Criminal Justice* 61, 3. https://doi.org/10.3138/cjccj.2018-0029.

Chase, Allan. 1977. *The Legacy of Malthus: The Social Costs of the New Scientific Racism.* New York: Alfred A. Knopf, Inc.

Cheng, Maria. 2023. "Canadian Police Won't Investigate Doctor for Sterilizing Indigenous Woman." *AP News*, September 27, 2023. apnews.com/article/canada-indigenous-women-sterilization-5a0ecfc3897ce4fc663281c40dc31f37#.

Chrisjohn, Roland. 1999. "You Have to be Carefully Taught: Special Needs and First Nations Education — A Report to the National Indian Education Council, The Assembly of First Nations, and the Chiefs Council on Education." *Native Psychologist Newsletter* 4, 4. https://web.archive.org/web/20061021000744/http://natpsycdn.brandonu.ca/News%209911.htm.

_____. 1997. *The Circle Game: Shadows and Substance in the Indian Residential School Experience in Canada.* Penticton, BC: Theytus Books.

Christie, Nancy. 2000. *Endangering the State: Family, Work and Welfare in Canada.* Toronto: University of Toronto Press.

Chunn, Dorothy. 1992. *From Punishment to Doing Good: Family Courts and Socialized Justice in Ontario, 1880–1940.* Toronto: University of Toronto Press.

Churchill, Ward. 2011. "A Travesty of a Mockery of a Sham: Colonialism as 'Self-Determination' in the UN Declaration on the Rights of Indigenous Peoples." *Griffith Law Review* 20, 3. https://doi.org/10.1080/10383441.2011.10854709.

Clarke, Adele. 2022. *Disciplining Reproduction: Modernity, American Life Sciences, and the Problem of Sex.* California: University of California Press.

Clarke, Tyler. 2013. "Cameco Shares Positives of Uranium Industry." *Prince Albert Daily Herald*, March 27, 2013.

Coale, Ansley J., and Hoover Edgar M. 1958. *Population Growth and Economic Development in Low Income Countries: A Case Study of India's Prospects.* Princeton, N.J.: Princeton University Press.

Cohen, Jamie, and T.F. Baskett. 1978. "Sterilization Patterns in a Northern Canadian Population." *Canadian Journal of Public Health* 69.

Collier, James. 1945. "United States Indian Administration as a Laboratory of Ethnic Relations." *Social Research* 12, 3. https://www.jstor.org/stable/40982119.

Collier, Ken. 1995. "Social Democracy and Underdevelopment: The Case of Northern Saskatchewan." In *Social Policy and Social Justice: The NDP Government in Saskatchewan During the Blakeney Years*, edited by Jim Harding. Waterloo: Wilfrid Laurier University Press.

Collins, Larry. 1982. "The Politics of Abortion: Trends in Canadian Fertility Policy." *Atlantis: Critical Studies in Gender, Culture & Social Justice* 7, 2.

Connelly, Matthew. 2008. *Fatal Misconception: The Struggle to Control World Population.* Massachusetts: Harvard University Press.

Cooper Owens, Dierdre. 2018. *Medical Bondage: Race, Gender, and the Origins of American Gynecology.* Athens, Georgia: The University of Georgia Press.

Corntassel, Jeff, and Cheryl Bryce. 2012. "Practicing Sustainable Self-Determination: Indigenous Approaches to Cultural Restoration and Revitalization." *The Brown Journal of World Affairs* 18, 2. https://www.jstor.org/stable/24590870.

Corntassel, Jeff. 2012. "Re-envisioning Resurgence: Indigenous Pathways to Decolonization and Sustainable Self-Determination." *Decolonization: Indigeneity, Education, and Society* 1, 1.

_____. 2007. "Partnership in Action? Indigenous Political Mobilization and Co-optation during the First UN Indigenous Decade (1995–2004)." *Human Rights Quarterly* 29, 2. http://doi.org/10.1353/hrq.2007.0005.

Coulthard, Glen. 2014. *Red Skins White Masks: Rejecting the Politics of Recognition.* Minneapolis: University of Minnesota Press.

Coutts, Jane. 1994. "Alberta Drug Plan to Provide Norplant." *Globe and Mail*, September 21, 1994.

Creighton, Jennifer. 2011. "Depression and the Depression: An Analysis of the Patient Ledgers of the Saskatchewan Hospital North Battleford from 1929 to 1935." MA thesis, University of Saskatchewan.

Critchlow, Donald T. 1999. *Intended Consequences: Birth Control, Abortion, and the Federal Government in Modern America*. New York: Oxford University Press.

Crow, James F. 2002. "C.C. Little, Cancer and Inbred Mice." *Genetics* 161, 4. https://doi.org/10.1093/genetics/161.4.1357.

Crozier, Cullen. 2017. "Against their Will." *APTN Investigates*, January 27, 2017. aptnnews.ca/against-their-will-cullen-crozier-aptn-investigates/.

Cull, Randi. 2006. "Aboriginal Mothering Under the State's Gaze." In *"Until our Hearts Are on the Ground," Aboriginal Mothering, Oppression, Resistance and Rebirth*, edited by D. Memee Lavell-Harvard and Jeannette Corbiere Lavell. Toronto: Demeter Press.

Cuthand, Doug. 2015. "Remembering William Wuttunee: Cree Lawyer Was a Trailblazer." *CBC News*, November 2, 2015. https://www.cbc.ca/news/indigenous/remembering-bill-wuttunee-1.3300662.

Dales, Alice. 1954. "Closing a Children's Institution in Saskatchewan." *Canadian Welfare* 30, 6.

Daschuk, James. 2013. *Clearing the Plains: Disease, Politics of Starvation, and Loss of Indigenous Life*. Regina: University of Regina Press.

Davies, Gareth. 1997. "Understanding the War on Poverty: The Advantages of a Canadian Perspective." *Journal of Policy History* 9, 4. https://doi.org/10.1017/S0898030600006163.

Davis, Angela, Gina Dent, Erica Meiners, et al. 2022. *Abolition. Feminism. Now.* Chicago: Haymarket Books.

Dawson, T. Brettel. 1998. "First Person Familiar: Judicial Intervention in Pregnancy, Again: G. (D.F.)." *Canadian Journal of Women and the Law* 10, 1.

Deighton, Alex. 2018. "The Nature of Eugenic Thought and Limits of Eugenic Practice in Interwar Saskatchewan." In *Eugenics at the Edges of Empire: New Zealand, Australia, Canada and South America*, edited by Diane Paul, Hamish Spencer, and John Stenhouse. New York: Palgrave Macmillan.

Diabo, Russ. 2021. "Commentary: With Bill C-15 (CANDRIP) and an Indigenous GG, Canada Spreads the Lie that It's Implementing UNDRIP." *The Georgia Straight*. August 7, 2021. straight.com/news/russ-diabo-with-bill-c-15-candrip-and-an-indigenous-gg-canada-spreads-lie-that-its-implementing.

———. 2017. "When Moving Past the Indian Act Means Something Worse." *Policy Options*, September 22, 2017. https://policyoptions.irpp.org/magazines/september-2017/when-moving-past-the-indian-act-means-something-worse/.

Dickason, Olive Patricia. 1992. *Canada's First Nations: A History of Founding Peoples from Earliest Times*. Toronto: McClelland & Stewart.

Douglas, Thomas C. 1933. "The Problems of the Subnormal Family." MA thesis, McMaster University.

Dobbin, Frank. 2009. *Inventing Equal Opportunity*. Princeton: Princeton University Press.

Dobbin, Frank, and Alexandra Kalev. 2018. "Why Doesn't Diversity Training Work? The Challenge for Industry and Academia." *Anthropology Now* 10, 2. https://doi.org/10.1080/19428200.2018.1493182.

Dowbiggin, Ian. 2014. "'Prescription for Survival': Brock Chisholm, Sterilization and Mental Health in the Cold War Era." In *Mental Health and Canadian Society: Historical Perspectives*, edited by James Moran and David Wright. Montreal and Kingston: McGill-Queen's University Press.

———. 2008. *The Sterilization Movement and Global Fertility in the Twentieth Century*. England: Oxford University Press.

———. 2006. "Prescription for Survival: Brock Chisholm, Sterilization and Mental Health in the Cold War Era." In *Mental Health and Canadian Society: Historical Perspectives*. Montreal; Kingston: McGill-Queen's University Press.

———. 1997. *Keeping America Sane: Psychiatry and Eugenics in the United States and Canada, 1880-1940*. New York: Cornell University Press.

Duffin, Jacalyn, and Leslie Falk. 1996. "Sigerist in Saskatchewan: The Quest for Balance in Social and Technical Medicine." *Bulletin of the History of Medicine* 70, 4. https://www.jstor.org/stable/44444726.

Dyck, Erika. 2013. *Facing Eugenics: Reproduction, Sterilization, and the Politics of Choice*. Toronto: University of Toronto Press.

Dyck, Erika, and Maureen Lux. 2020. *Challenging Choices: Canada's Population Control in the 1970s*. Montreal and Kingston: McGill-Queen's University Press.

———. 2016. "Population Control in the 'Global North'?: Canada's Response to Indigenous Reproductive Rights and Neo-Eugenics." *Canadian Historical Review* 97, 4. http://doi.org/10.3138/chr.Dyck.

Dyck, Erika, and Alex Deighton. 2017. *Managing Madness: Weyburn Mental Hospital and the Transformation of Psychiatric Care in Canada*. Winnipeg: University of Manitoba Press.

Ehrenreich, Barbara, and Deirdre English. 2010. *Witches, Midwives, & Nurses: A History of Women Healers*. New York: The Feminist Press.

———. 2005. *For Her Own Good: Two Centuries of Experts' Advice to Women*, 2nd ed. New York: Random House Inc.

Emery, John C. Herbert, and Ronald Kneebone. 2008. "Socialists, Populists, Resources, and the Divergent Development of Alberta and Saskatchewan." *Canadian Public Policy* 34, 4. https://doi.org/10.3138/cpp.34.4.419.

Eneas, Bryan. 2022. "Sturgeon Lake First Nation Marks Birth of Baby Boy, Celebrated as First Traditional Birth in Decades." *CBC News*, February 27, 2022. cbc.ca/news/canada/saskatchewan/sturgeon-lake-first-nation-traditional-birthing-1.6365339.

Eng, Ah-Yin. 1999. "Reflections of Life on the Reserve: From 1965 to 1971, A Husband-and-Wife Physician Team Helped Bring Better Health Care to Native Canadians." *Medical Post* 35, 40.

Engler, Yves. 2015. *Canada in Africa: 300 Years of Aid and Exploitation*. Halifax: Fernwood Publishing.

———. 2012. *Lester Pearson's Peacekeeping: The Truth May Hurt*. Halifax: Fernwood Publishing.

Elias, Brenda. 2014. "Moving Beyond the Historical Quagmire of Measuring Infant Mortality for the First Nations Population in Canada." *Social Science & Medicine* 123. http://doi.org/10.1016/j.socscimed.2014.10.056.

Farley, John. 2008. *Brock Chisholm, The World Health Organization, and the Cold War*. Vancouver: UBC Press.

Federation of Saskatchewan Indian Nations. 1973. "Health Plan for Indians." *Saskatchewan Indian* 3, 5. https://epe.lac-bac.gc.ca/100/205/301/ic/cdc/saskindian/a73may18ia.htm.

Federici, Silvia. 2004. *Caliban and the Witch: Women, the Body and Primitive Accumulation*. New York: Autonomedia.

Fedunkiw, Marianne. 2005. *Rockefeller Foundation Funding and Medical Education in Toronto, Montreal and Halifax*. Montreal and Kingston: McGill-Queen's University Press.

Fee, Elizabeth. 1996. "The Pleasures and Perils of Prophetic Advocacy: Henry E. Sigerist and the Politics of Medical Reform." *American Journal of Public Health* 86, 11. http://doi.org/10.2105/ajph.86.11.1637.

Fee, Elizabeth, and Theodore Brown. 2002. "John Harvey Kellogg, MD: Health Reformer and Anti-Smoking Crusader." *American Journal of Public Health* 92, 6. http://doi.org/10.2105/ajph.92.6.935.

Ferguson, R.G., and A.B. Simes. 1949. "BCG Vaccination of Indian Infants in Saskatchewan." *Tubercle* 30, 1. http://doi.org/10.1016/s0041-3879(49)80055-9.

Finkel, Alvin. 2006. *Social Policy and Practice in Canada: A History*. Waterloo: Wilfrid Laurier University Press.

———. 1995. "Origins of the Welfare State in Canada." In *Social Welfare Policy in Canada: Historical Readings*, edited by Raymond Blake and Jeff Keshen. Toronto: Copp Clark Ltd.

Finkle, Jason, and Barbara Crane. 1975. "The Politics of Bucharest: Population, Development, and the New International Economic Order." *Population and Development Review* 1, 1. https://doi.org/10.2307/1972272.

Fisher, Donald. 1999. "Rockefeller Philanthropy and the Creation of the Social Sciences Research Councils in the United States and Canada." In *The Development of the Social Sciences in the United States and Canada: The Role of Philanthropy*, edited by Theresa Richardson and Donald Fisher. Stamford, Connecticut: Ablex.

———. 1991. *The Social Sciences in Canada: 50 Years of National Activity by the Social Science Federation of Canada*. Waterloo: Wilfrid Laurier University Press.

———. 1983. "The Role of Philanthropic Foundations in the Reproduction and Production of Hegemony: Rockefeller Foundation and the Social Sciences." *Sociology* 17, 2. https://www.jstor.org/stable/42852563.

Fitzpatrick, Kathy. 2018. "Bear in Ottawa to Discuss Coerced Sterilization." *Saskatoon Star Phoenix*, December 12, 2018. thestarphoenix.com/news/local-news/bear-in-ottawa-to-discuss-coerced-sterilization.

Flett, Jaydon. 2016. "Saskatoon Women Recalls the Day She Was Sterilized Against Her Will." *APTN News*, February 2, 2016. aptnnews.ca/national-news/saskatoon-woman-recalls-the-day-she-was-sterilized-against-her-will/.

Folsom, Burton. 2010. *The Myth of the Robber Barons: A New Look at the Rise of Big Business in America*. 6th ed. Herndon, Virginia: Young America's Foundation.

Fortier, Craig, and Edward Hon-Sing Wong. 2019. "The Settler Colonialism of Social Work and the Social Work of Settler Colonialism." *Settler Colonial Studies* 9, 4. http://doi.org/10.1080/2201473X.2018.1519962.

Fox, Daniel. 2006. "The Significance of the Milbank Memorial Fund for Policy: An Assessment at its Centennial." *The Milbank Quarterly* 84, 1. http://doi.org/10.1111/j.1468-0009.2006.00411.x.

Freeman, Barbara. 2001. *The Satellite Sex: The Media and Women's Issues in English-Language, 1966–1971*. Waterloo: Wilfrid Laurier University Press.

———. 1998. "Same/Difference: The Media, Equal Rights and Aboriginal Women in Canada, 1968." *The Canadian Journal of Native Studies* 18, 1. https://cjns.brandonu.ca/wp-content/uploads/18-1-cjnsv18no1_pg87-116.pdf.

Friedman, Lawrence J. 1992. *Menninger: The Family and the Clinic*. Kansas: University Press of Kansas.

Fritz, W.B. 1978. "Indian People and Community Psychiatry in Saskatchewan." *Canadian Psychiatric Association Journal* 23, 1. http://doi.org/10.1177/070674377802300101.

———. 1976. "Psychiatric Disorders Among Natives and Non-Natives in Saskatchewan." *Canadian Psychiatric Association Journal* 21, 6.

Fritz, W.B., and Carl D'Arcy. 1982. "Comparisons: Indian and Non-Indian Use of Psychiatric Services." *Canadian Journal of Psychiatry* 27, 3. http://doi.org/10.1177/070674378202700303.

Frost, Stanley Brice. 1984. *McGill University for the Advancement of Learning, Volume II, 1895–1971*. Montreal & Kingston: McGill-Queen's University Press.

Gallegos, Joseph, Cherie Tindall, and Sheila Gallegos. 2008. "The Need for Advancement in the Conceptualization of Cultural Competence." *Advances in Social Work* 9, 1. https://doi.org/10.18060/214.

Garcia, Magaly Rodriguez, Davide Rodogno, and Liat Kozma. 2016. *The League of Nations Work on Social Issues*. Geneva: United Nations.

Gatehouse, Jonathan. 2013. "The Residential Schools Settlement's Biggest Winner: A Profile of Tony Merchant." *McLean's Magazine*, April 4, 2013. https://macleans.ca/news/canada/white-mans-windfall-a-profile-of-tony-merchant/.

Gaudry, Adam, and Danielle Lorenz. 2018. "Indigenization as Inclusion, Reconciliation, and Decolonization: Navigating the Different Visions for Indigenizing the Canadian Academy." *AlterNative: An International Journal of Indigenous Peoples* 14, 3. https://doi.org/10.1177/1177180118785382.

Giesbrecht, Lynn. 2019. "Rally Backs Lawsuit Alleging Forced Sterilization of Indigenous Women." *Regina Leader-Post*, November 26, 2019. https://leaderpost.com/news/saskatchewan/leaders-march-to-end-forced-sterilization-of-indigenous-women.

Gimenez, Martha. 2005. "Capitalism and the Oppression of Women: Marx Revisited." *Science and Society* 69, 1. http://doi.org/10.1521/siso.69.1.11.56797.

Ginzberg, Janet F. 1992. "Compulsory Contraception as a Condition of Probation: The Use and Abuse of Norplant." *Brooklyn Law Review* 58, 979.

Gleason, Mona. 1999. *Normalizing the Ideal: Psychology, Schooling, and the Family in Postwar Canada*. Toronto: University of Toronto Press.

Godel, John C., Henry F. Pabst, P.E. Hodges, et al. 1992. "Smoking and Caffeine and Alcohol Intake During Pregnancy in a Northern Population: Effect on Fetal Growth." *Canadian Medical Association Journal* 147, 2. https://www.ncbi.nlm.nih.gov/pmc/articles/PMC1336160/?page=1.

Goldstick, Miles. 1987. *Wollaston; People Resisting Genocide*. Montreal: Black Rose Books.

Gordon, Linda. 2002. *The Moral Property of Women: A History of Birth Control Politics in America*. Chicago: University of Illinois Press.

Gordon, Todd, and Jeffery Webber. 2016. *Blood of Extraction: Canadian Imperialism in Latin America*. Halifax: Fernwood Publishing.

Graham, Ron (ed.). 1999. *The Essential Trudeau*. Toronto: McClelland and Stewart Limited.

Green, James. 1999. *Cultural Awareness in the Human Services: A Multi-Ethnic Approach*, 3rd ed. Toronto: Allyn and Bacon.

Green, Joyce. 2014. "Denying Indigenous Human Rights: Colonialism and Rights Discourse in Canada." In *Indivisible: Indigenous Human Rights*, edited by Joyce Green. Halifax: Fernwood Publishing.

Grekul, Jana, Harvey Krahn, and Dave Odynak. 2004. "Sterilizing the 'Feeble-Minded': Eugenics in Alberta, Canada, 1929–1972." *Journal of Historical Sociology* 17, 4. https://doi.org/10.1111/j.1467-6443.2004.00237.x.

Grenier, Marie-Lyne. 2020. "Cultural Competency and the Reproduction of White Supremacy in Occupational Therapy Education." *Health Education Journal* 79, 6. http://doi.org/10.1177/0017896920902515.

Greve-Møller, Ann-Sophie. 2024. "A Vicious Campaign of Birth Control in Greenland." In *Sacred Bundles Unborn, Second Edition*, edited by Morningstar Mercredi and Firekeepers. Manitoba: Friesen Press.

Griffin, John. 1974. "Charles G. Stogdill." *Canadian Journal of Psychiatry* 19, 1. https://doi.org/10.1177/070674377401900109.

Gruskin, Sofia, Shahira Ahmed, Dina Bogecho, et al. 2012. "Human Rights in Health Systems Frameworks: What is There, What is Missing and Why Does It Matter?" *Global Public Health* 7, 4. http://doi.org/10.1080/17441692.2011.651733.

Guerra-Reyes, Lucia. 2019. *Changing Birth in the Andes: Culture, Policy, and Safe Motherhood in Peru*. Nashville: Vanderbilt University Press.

Gunn, Brenda. 2014. "Getting it Right: The Canadian Constitution and International Indigenous Rights." In *Indivisible: Indigenous Human Rights*, edited by Joyce Green. Halifax: Fernwood Publishing.

Gunn, Jennifer. 1999. "A Few Good Men: The Rockefeller Approach to Population, 1911-1936." In *The Development of the Social Sciences in the United States and Canada: The Role of Philanthropy*, edited by Theresa Richardson and Donald Fisher. Stamford, Connecticut: Ablex.

Guimond, Éric, and Norbert Robitaille. 2009. "Mère à L'Adolescence: Analyse de la Fécondité des Indiennes Inscrites âgées de 15 à 19 Ans, 1986 à 2004." *Cahiers Québécois de Démographie*, 38, 2. http://doi.org/10.7202/044817ar.

———. 2008. "When Teenage Girls Have Children: Trends and Consequences." *Horizons* 10, 1. Ottawa, Government of Canada.

Guimond, Éric, Norbert Robitaille, and Sacha Senecal. 2015. "Fuzzy Definitions and Demographic Explosion of Aboriginal Populations in Canada from 1986 to 2006." *Social Statistics and Ethnic Diversity*, edited by P. Simon, V. Piché and A. Gagnon. IMISCOE Research Series. Springer, Cham. http://doi.org/10.1007/978-3-319-20095-8_12.

Gurr, Barbara. 2015. *Reproductive Justice: The Politics of Health Care for Native American Women*. New Jersey: Rutgers University Press.

Habbick, Brian F., Josephine Nanson, Richard E. Snyder, et al. 1996. "Foetal Alcohol Syndrome in Saskatchewan: Unchanged Incidence in a 20-year Period." *Canadian Journal of Public Health* 87, 3. PMID: 8771927.

Hachey, Isabelle. 2021. "Après Joyce, Une Parole Libérée." *La Presse*, May 15, 2021. https://www.lapresse.ca/actualites/2021-05-15/apres-joyce-une-parole-liberee.php.

Hamilton, Charles. 2017. "MMIWG Inquiry Needs 'Reset' and 'Restructuring' after Resignation of Sask. Commissioner: FSIN Vice-Chief." *CBC News*, July 11, 2017. cbc.ca/news/canada/saskatoon/sask-mmiwg-commissioner-resigns-1.4199815.

Hande, D'Arcy. 2013. "Courting Collaboration." *Briarpatch Magazine*, November 13, 2013. https://briarpatchmagazine.com/articles/view/courting-collaboration.

Hanse, Randall and Desmond King. 2013. *Eugenics, Race, and the Population Scare in Twentieth Century North America*. New York: Cambridge University Press.

Haraway, Donna. 2003. "For the Love of a Good Dog: Webs of Action in the World of Dog Genetics." In *Race, Nature, and the Politics of Difference*, edited by Donald Moore, Jake Kosek and Anand Pandian. Durham and London: Duke University Press.

Harding, Jim. 2007. *Canada's Deadly Secret: Saskatchewan Uranium and the Global Nuclear System*. Halifax: Fernwood Publishing.

Hardon, Anita Petra. 1992. "The Needs of Women Versus the Interests of Family Planning Personnel, Policy-Makers and Researchers: Conflicting Views on Safety and Acceptability of Contraceptives." *Social Science and Medicine* 35, 6. https://doi.org/10.1016/0277-9536(92)90075-2.

Hartmann, Betsy. 1997. "Population Control I: Birth of an Ideology." *International Journal of Health Services* 27, 3. https://doi.org/10.2190/BL3N-XAJX-0YQB-VQBX.

———. 1995. *Reproductive Rights and Wrongs: The Global Politics of Population Control*. Boston: South End Press.

Haussman, Melissa. 2000. "What Does Gender Have to Do with Abortion Law?: Canadian Women's Movement-Parliamentary Interactions on Reform Attempts, 1969-91." *International Journal of Canadian Studies* 21, 1.

Hawaleshka, Danylo. 2005. "A Shot in the Dark?" *Maclean's Magazine*, November 28, 2005.

Heeswijk, Gail van. 1994. "'An Act Respecting Sexual Sterilization': Reasons for Enacting and Repealing the Act." MA thesis, University of British Columbia. https://dx.doi.org/10.14288/1.0087539.

Hepworth, H. Philip. 1980. *Foster Care and Adoption in Canada*. Ottawa: Canadian Council on Social Development.

———. 1977. *The Exercise of Responsibilities Towards Children by Parents and the State*. Ottawa: Canadian Council on Social Development.

Hodgson, Dennis. 1983. "Demography as Social Science and Policy Science." *Population and Development Review* 9, 1. https://www.jstor.org/stable/1972893

Hodson, Diana. 1990. "Child Welfare and Social Development: A History of the Canadian Council on Social Development, 1920–1941." Doctoral dissertation, University of Calgary. https://dx.doi.org/10.11575/PRISM/40110.

Hook, Joshua N. 2014. "Engaging Clients with Cultural Humility." *Journal of Psychology and Christianity* 33, 3.

Hook, Joshua N., Donald Davis, Jesse Owen, et al. 2017. *Cultural Humility: Engaging Diverse Identities in Therapy*. Washington, DC: American Psychological Association.

Horn, Michael. 1976. "Leonard Marsh and the Coming of a Welfare State in Canada." *Social History* 9, 17. https://hssh.journals.yorku.ca/index.php/hssh/article/view/40862.

Horowitz, Gad. 1966. "Conservatism, Liberalism, and Socialism in Canada: An Interpretation." *The Canadian Journal of Economics and Political Science* 32, 2. https://www.jstor.org/stable/139794.

Hyslop, Katie. 2021. "'It's Really Cruel': Thousands in Limbo Awaiting Sixties Scoop Settlement Money." *The Tyee*, January 25, 2021. https://thetyee.ca/News/2021/01/25/Thousands-Limbo-Awaiting-Sixties-Scoop-Settlement/.

Iacobelli, Teresa. 2022. "The Start of Something Big." Rockefeller Archive Center. https://resource.rockarch.org/story/the-rockefeller-foundations-20th-century-global-fight-against-disease/.

Irving, Allan. 1992. "The Scientific Imperative in Canadian Social Work: Social Work and Social Welfare Research in Canada, 1897–1945." *Canadian Social Work Review* 9, 1. https://www.jstor.org/stable/41669462.

———. 1988. "The Doctor Versus the Expert: Harry Morris Cassidy and the British Columbia Health Insurance Dispute of the 1930s." *BC Studies* 78. https://doi.org/10.14288/bcs.v0i78.1290.

———. 1981. "Canadian Fabians: The Work and Thought of Harry Cassidy and Leonard Marsh, 1930-45." *Canadian Journal of Social Work* 7, 1. https://www.jstor.org/stable/23458244.

Ittmann, Karl. 2003. "Demography as Policy Science in the British Empire, 1918–1969." *Journal of Policy History* 15, 4. http://doi.org/10.1353/jph.2003.0024.

Jacobs, Margaret. 2014. *A Generation Removed: The Fostering and Adoption of Indigenous Children in the Postwar World*. Lincoln: University of Nebraska Press.

Jahanbani, Sheyda. 2023. *The Poverty of the World: Rediscovering the Poor at Home and Abroad, 1941-1968*. Oxford: Oxford University Press.

James, Thia. 2023. "'So Much Work To Do': Indigenous Women Vastly Overrepresented in Federal Penitentiaries and Provincial Jails in Sask." *Sasktoon StarPhoenix*, November 14, 2023.

Jamieson, Kathleen. 1978. *Indian Women and the Law in Canada: Citizens Minus*. Ottawa: Supply and Services.

Jensen, Jane. 1992. "Getting to Morgentaler: From One Representation to Another." In *The Politics of Abortion*, edited by Janine Brodie, Shelley Gavigan and Jane Jensen. Toronto: Oxford University Press.

Joffe, Paul. 2014. "Undermining Indigenous Peoples' Security and Human Rights: Strategies of the Canadian Government." In *Indivisible: Indigenous Human Rights*, edited by Joyce Green. Halifax: Fernwood Publishing.

Johnston, Patrick. 1983. *Native Children and the Child Welfare System*. Toronto: James Lorimer Limited, Publishers.

Jones, Esyllt. 2019. *Radical Medicine: The International Origins of Socialized Health Care in Canada*. Winnipeg: ARP Books.

Jones, Kenneth L., and David W. Smith. 1973. "Recognition of the Fetal Alcohol Syndrome in Early Infancy." *The Lancet* 302, 7836. http://doi.org/10.1016/s0140-6736(73)91092-1.

Jones, Frank. 1968. "Trudeau on Welfare: Enough Free Stuff." *Toronto Star*, April 3, 1968.

Katz, Esther, Cathy Moran Harjo, and Peter Englement (eds). 2006. *The Selected Papers of Margaret Sanger: Round the World for Birth Control, 1920–1966, Volume 4*. Champaign: University of Illinois Press.

Katz, Judy. 1975. "A Systematic Handbook of Exercises for the Re-Education of White People with Respect to Racist Attitudes and Behaviours." Doctoral dissertation, University of Massachusetts. https://doi.org/10.7275/zeqp-ab15.

Kaufman, Bruce. 2004. *The Global Evolution of Industrial Relations*. Geneva: International Labour Office.

Kendall, Tamil, and Claire Albert. 2015. "Experiences of Coercion to Sterilize and Forced Sterilization Among Women Living with HIV in Latin America." *Journal of the International AIDS Society* 18, 1. https://doi.org/10.7448/IAS.18.1.19462.

Kennedy, David M. 1970. *Birth Control in America: The Career of Margaret Sanger*. London: Yale University Press.

Kent, Tom. 1988. *A Public Purpose: An Experience of Liberal Opposition and Canadian Government*. Kingston & Montreal: McGill-Queen's University Press.

Kinsman, Gary. 2023. *The Regulation of Desire, Third Edition: Queer Histories, Queer Struggles*. Montreal: Concordia University Press.

Kirkup, Kristy. 2018a. "Feds Won't Change Criminal Code to Outlaw Forced Sterilization, Despite First Nations Outcry." *Global News*, December 07, 2018. https://globalnews.ca/news/4739302/forced-sterilization-criminal-code-first-nations/.

———. 2018b. "Indigenous Women Coerced into Sterilizations Across Canada: Senator." *Saskatoon StarPhoenix*, November 12, 2018. https://thestarphoenix.com/news/local-news/indigenous-women-coerced-into-sterilizations-across-canada-senator.

Kirmayer, Lawrence. 2013. "Embracing Uncertainty as a Path to Competence: Cultural Safety, Empathy, and Alterity in Clinical Training." *Culture, Medicine and Psychiatry* 37, 2. 10.1007/s11013-013-9314-2.

Kotaska. Andrew. 2023. "NWT Obstetrician Apologizes for Unprofessional Conduct." August 30, 2023. https://cabinradio.ca/wp-content/uploads/2023/09/Media-Statement-2023.08.30.pdf.

Kowalewski, Karolina, and Yasmin Mayne. 2012. "The Translation of Eugenic Ideology into Public Health Policy: The Case of Alberta and Saskatchewan." In *The Proceedings of the 18th Annual History of Medicine Days Conference 2009*, edited by Lisa Peterman, Kerry Sun, and Frank W. Stahnisch. Newcastle upon Tyne: Cambridge Scholars Publishing.

Kozyrskyj, Anita L. 1996. "History of Public Health in Canada." *Canadian Journal of Public Health / Revue Canadienne de Santé Publique* 87, 1. https://www.jstor.org/stable/41991588.

Kühl, Stefan. 2013. *For the Betterment of the Race: The Rise and Fall of the International Movement for Eugenics and Racial Hygiene*. New York: Palgrave Macmillan.

———. 1994. *The Nazi Connection: Eugenics, American Racism, and German National Socialism*. London: Oxford University Press.

Kulchyski, Peter. 2013. *Aboriginal Rights Are Not Human Rights: Essays on Law, Politics and Culture*. Winnipeg: ARP Books.

Kumaş-Tan, Zofia, Brenda Beagan, Charlotte Loppie, et al. 2007. "Measuring Cultural Competence: Examining Hidden Assumptions in Instruments." *Academic Medicine* 82, 6. http://doi.org/10.1097/ACM.0b013e3180555a2d.

Kurbegovic, Erna. 2020. "Full-Time Health Services in Nova Scotia." In *Psychiatry and the Legacies of Eugenics Historical Studies of Alberta and Beyond*, edited by Frank W. Stahnisch. Edmonton: Athabasca University Press.

Kyba, Patrick. 1964, "The Saskatchewan General Election of 1929." MA Thesis, University of Saskatchewan.

Ladd-Taylor, Molly. 2017. *Fixing the Poor: Eugenic Sterilization and Child Welfare in the Twentieth Century*. Baltimore: John Hopkins University Press.

Lagace, Naithan, and Niigaanwewidam Sinclair. 2015. "The White Paper, 1969." *Canadian Encyclopedia*, September 24, 2015. https://www.thecanadianencyclopedia.ca/en/article/the-white-paper-1969.

Lam, Vincent. 2011. *Extraordinary Canadians: Tommy Douglas*. Toronto: Penguin Canada.

Lampard, Robert. 2012. "The Hoadley Commission (1932-34) and Health Insurance in Alberta." In *Making Medicare: New Perspectives on the History of Medicare in Canada*, edited by Gregory P. Marchildon. Toronto: University of Toronto Press.

Langford, William. 2017. "Helping People Help Themselves: Democracy, Development, and the Global Politics of Poverty in Canada, 1964-1979." Doctoral dissertation, Queen's University.

Lapierre-Adamcyk, Évelyne. 2013. "HENRIPIN, Jacques – 1926-2013." *Canadian Population Society Newsletter* 38, 3.https://www.canpopsoc.ca/sites/cps/assets/File/publications/newsletter/news_38_3.pdf.

Larson, Scott. 2014. "Lawsuit against Cameco, Areva Dismissed." *The Leader-Post*, September 10, 2014.

Lauren, Baba. 2013. *Cultural Safety in First Nations, Inuit and Métis Public Health: Environmental Scan of Cultural Competency and Safety in Education, Training and Health Services*. Prince George, BC: National Collaborating Centre for Aboriginal Health.

Lawford, Karen. 2016. "Locating Invisible Policies: Health Canada's Evacuation Policy as a Case Study." *Atlantis: Critical Studies in Gender, Culture & Social Justice* 37, 2. https://atlantisjournal.ca/index.php/atlantis/article/view/147-160%20PDF/147-160.

Lawford, Karen, and Audrey Giles. 2012. "Marginalization and Coercion: Canada's Evacuation Policy for Pregnant First Nations Women Who Live on Reserves in Rural and Remote Regions." *Pimatisiwin: A Journal of Aboriginal and Indigenous Community Health* 10, 3. https://journalindigenouswellbeing.co.nz/wp-content/uploads/2013/02/06LawfordGiles.pdf.

Lavoie, Josée. 2018. "Medicare and the Care of First Nations, Métis and Inuit." *Health Economics, Policy and Law* 13. https://doi.org/10.1017/S1744133117000391.

_____. 2013. "Policy Silences: Why Canada Needs a National First Nations, Inuit and Métis Health Policy." *International Journal of Circumpolar Health*, 72. https://doi.org/10.3402/ijch.v72i0.22690.

Leader Post. 1980. "Sterilization Resolution Awaited." *The LeaderPost*, February 13, 1980.

Leslie, John. 1999. "Assimilation, Integration or Termination? The Development of Canadian Indian Policy, 1943–1963." Doctoral dissertation, Carleton University. https://doi.org/10.22215/etd/1999-04189.

Levitan, Tyler and Emilie Cameron. 2015. "Impact and Benefit Agreements and the Neoliberalization of Mineral Development in the Canadian North." In *Mining and Communities in Northern Canada: History, Politics, and Memory*, edited by Arn Keeling and John Sandlos. Calgary: University of Calgary Press.

Lewis, Deborah J. 1995. "Coercive Sterilization: Its Eugenical Underpinnings and Current Manifestations." MA thesis, Carleton University. https://doi.org/10.22215/etd/1995-03029.

Lewis, Oscar. 1966a. "The Culture of Poverty." *Scientific American* 215, 4. https://www.jstor.org/stable/24931078.

_____. 1966b. *La Vida: A Puerto Rican Family in the Culture of Poverty-San Juan and New York*. New York, NY: Random House.

_____. 1960. "The Culture of Poverty in Mexico City-Two Case Studies." *Economic and Political Weekly* 12, 23/24/25.

_____. 1951. *Life in a Mexican Village: Tepoztlan Restudied*. Champaign: University of Illinois Press.

Linton, Ralph. 1947. "The Vanishing American Negro." *The American Mercury* 64, 278.

Little, Margaret. 1998. *"No Car, No Radio, No Liquor Permit": The Moral Regulation of Single Mothers in Ontario, 1920-1997*. Toronto: Oxford University Press.

Loh, Shirley, and M.V. George. 2003. "Estimating the Fertility Level of Registered Indians in Canada: A Challenging Endeavour." *Canadian Studies in Population* 30, 1. https://doi.org/10.25336/P66G6Z.

López, Iris Ofelia. 2008. *Matters of Choice: Puerto Rican Women's Struggle for Reproductive Freedom*. New Brunswick, NJ: Rutgers University Press.

Loo, Tina. 2019. *Moved By the State: Forced Relocation and Making a Good Life in Postwar Canada*. Vancouver: UBC Press.

Lorde, Audre. 1988. *A Burst of Light: And Other Essays*. New York: Ixia Press.

Lotz, Jim. 1968. "Social Science Research and Northern Development." *Arctic* 21, 4. https://www.jstor.org/stable/40507577.

Lowell, JoAnn. 1995. "NWT Abortion Review Puts Spotlight on the Politics of Medicine." *Herizons* 9, 1.

Lux, Maureen. 2016. *Separate Beds: A History of Indian Hospitals in Canada*. Toronto: University of Toronto Press.

_____. 2010. "Care for the 'Racially Careless': Indian Hospitals in the Canadian West, 1920-1950s." *Canadian Historical Review* 91, 3. https://doi.org/10.3138/chr.91.3.407.

_____. 1998. "Perfect Subjects: Race, Tuberculosis, and the Qu'Appelle BCG Vaccine Trial." *Canadian Bulletin of Medical History* 15, 2. https://doi.org/10.3138/cbmh.15.2.277.

MacDonald, Nancy. 2016. "Canada's prisons are the 'new residential schools.'" *MacLean's*, February 18, 2016. https://macleans.ca/news/canada/canadas-prisons-are-the-new-residential-schools/.

MacDougall, Heather. 2009. "Into Thin Air: Making National Health Policy, 1939–45." *Canadian Bulletin of Mental Health* 26, 2. https://doi.org/10.3138/cbmh.26.2.283.

Mackenzie King, William Lyon. 1973. *Industry and Humanity*. University of Toronto Press.

Maioni, Antonia. 2004. "New Century, New Risks: The Marsh Report and the Post-War Welfare State in Canada." *Policy Options*, August 2004. https://irpp.org/wp-content/uploads/assets/po/social-policy-in-the-21st-century/maioni.pdf.

Maki, Krys. 2021. *Ineligible: Single Mothers Under Welfare Surveillance*. Halifax: Fernwood Publishing.

Malone, Kelly Geraldine. 2022. "Ending Birth Alerts a 'Red Herring' that Doesn't Address Root Causes of Child Apprehensions, Experts Say." *CBC News*, September 19, 2022. https://www.cbc.ca/news/canada/manitoba/birth-alerts-child-welfare-agencies-indigenous-children-1.6587623.

Mann, Emily, and Patrick Grzanka. 2018. "Agency-Without-Choice: The Visual Rhetorics of Long-Acting Reversible Contraception Promotion." *Symbolic Interaction* 41, 3. https://doi.org/10.1002/symb.349.

Manuel, Art, and Grand Chief Ronald Derrickson. 2017. *The Reconciliation Manifesto: Recovering the Land, Rebuilding the Economy*. Toronto: James Lorimer Limited, Publishers.

Manuel, George, and Michael Posluns. 2019. *The Fourth World: An Indian Reality*. Minneapolis: University of Minnesota Press.

Marchildon, Gregory. 2016. "Douglas versus Manning: The Ideological Battle over Medicare in Postwar Canada." *Journal of Canadian Studies* 50, 1. https://doi.org/10.3138/jcs.2016.50.1.129.

———. 2012. *Making Medicare: New Perspectives on the History of Medicare in Canada*. Toronto: University of Toronto Press.

———. 2011. "A House Divided: Deinstitutionalization, Medicare and the Canadian Mental Health Association in Saskatchewan, 1944–1964." *Social History* 44, 88. http://doi.org/10.1353/his.2011.0014.

Marcus, George. 1983. "Elite Communities and Institutional Orders." In *Elites, Ethnographic Issues*, edited by George Marcus. Albuquerque: University of New Mexico Press.

Marsh, James (ed.). 1999. *The Canadian Encyclopedia*. Toronto: McLelland & Stewart.

Marsh, Leonard. 2017. *Report on Social Security for Canada New Edition*. Montreal & Kingston: McGill-Queen's University Press.

———. 1938. *Health and Unemployment: Some Studies of Their Relationships*. London: Oxford University Press.

Marshall, Andrew. 2015. "Black Liberation and the Foundations of Social Control." *The American Journal of Economics and Sociology* 74, 4. https://doi.org/10.1111/ajes.12109.

Marshall, Dominique. 2006. *The Social Origins of the Welfare State*. Waterloo: Wilfrid Laurier University Press.

Martens, Kathleen. 2022. "60s Scoop Survivor Compensation Payments Capped at $25K." *APTN News*, April 7, 2022. https://www.aptnnews.ca/national-news/60s-scoop-survivor-compensation-payments-capped-at-25k/.

Mass, Bonnie. 1976. *Population Target – The Political Economy of Population Control in Latin America*. Toronto: Latin American Working Group.

———. 1974. "An Historical Sketch of the American Population Control Movement." *International Journal of Health Services* 4, 4. https://doi.org/10.2190/KNDY-DL4J-YTP3-479M.

Maynard, Donna, and Don Kerr. 2007. "From Pre-Contact to the Present: The Demography of the Aboriginal Peoples of Canada." In *The Changing Face of Canada: Essential Readings in Population*, edited by Roderic Beaujot and Don Kerr. Toronto: Canadian Scholar's Press Inc.

Maynard, Robyn. 2017. *Policing Black Lives: State Violence in Canada from Slavery to the Present*. Halifax: Fernwood Publishing.

Menandro, Leila. 2022. ""Close the Baby Factory, Woman!" The Family Planning Agendas of the Brazilian National Congress and the Media." Doctoral dissertation, Federal University of Espírito Santo.

Merchant, Emily Klancher. 2022. "Environmental Malthusianism and Demography." *Social Studies of Science* 52, 4. https://doi.org/10.1177/03063127221104929.

Mercredi, Ovide, and Clem Chartier. 1981. *The Status of Child Welfare Services for the Indigenous Peoples of Canada: The Problem, the Law and the Solution*. Paper presented at the Indian Child Welfare Rights Conference, Regina Saskatchewan, March 19, 1981.

McCallum, Mary Jane Logan. 2014. *Indigenous Women, Work and History 1940-1980*. Winnipeg: University of Manitoba Press.

McCormack, Thelma. 1999. "Fetal Syndromes and the Charter: The Winnipeg Glue-Sniffing Case." *Canadian Journal of Law and Society* 14, 2. https://doi.org/10.1017/S0829320100006074.

McDougall, William. 1934. *Religion and the Sciences of Life, With Other Essays on Allied Topics*. London: Methuen & Company, Limited.

McEwen, Ernest R. 1968. *Community Development Services for Canadian Indian and Métis Communities*. Toronto: Indian-Eskimo Association of Canada.

McKenzie, Holly, Colleen Varcoe, Dory Nason et al. 2022. "Indigenous Women's Resistance of Colonial Policies, Practices, and Reproductive Coercion." *Qualitative Health Research* 32, 7. https://doi.org/10.1177/10497323221087526.

McLaren, Angus. 1990. *Our Own Master Race: Eugenics in Canada, 1885-1945*. Toronto: University of Toronto Press.

McLaren, Angus, and Arlene Tigar McLaren. 1986. *The Bedroom and the State: The Changing Practices and Politics of Contraception and Abortion in Canada, 1880- 1980*. Toronto: McClelland & Stewart.

McLaren, Robert. 1995. "George Woodall Cadbury: The Fabian Catalyst in Saskatchewan's 'Good Public Administration.'" *Canadian Public Administration* 38, 3. https://doi.org/10.1111/j.1754-7121.1995.tb01059.x.

McNaughton, Dunn Ardys. 2002. "Cultural Competence and the Primary Care Provider." *Journal of Pediatric Health Care* 16, 3. https://doi.org/10.1067/mph.2002.118245.

Menninger, Karl. 1942. *Love Against Hate*. New York: Harcourt, Brace and Company.

Meren, David. 2017. "'Commend Me the Yak': The Columbo Plan, The Inuit of Ungava, and 'Developing' Canada's North." *Social History* 50, 102. https://doi.org/10.1353/his.2017.0039.

Midzain-Gobin, Liam, and Heather Smith. 2021. "Debunking the Myth of Canada as a Non-Colonial Power." *American Review of Canadian Studies* 50, 4. https://doi.org/10.1080/02722011.2020.1849329.

Mills, John. 2007. "Lessons From the Periphery: Psychiatry in Saskatchewan, Canada, 1944-68." *History of Psychiatry* 18, 2. https://doi.org/10.1177/0957154X06073011.

Moazzami, Bakhtiar, 2015. *Strengthening Rural Canada: Fewer & Older: Population and Demographic Crossroads in Rural Saskatchewan*. Ottawa: Adult Learning, Literacy and Essential Skills Program.

Monture-Angus, Patricia. 1999a. "Considering Colonialism and Oppression: Aboriginal Women, Justice and the "Theory" of Decolonization." *Native Studies Review* 12, 1.

———. 1999b. *Journeying Forward: Dreaming First Nations' Independence*. Black Point: Fernwood Publishing.

———. 1995. *Thunder in My Soul: A Mohawk Woman Speaks*. Black Point: Fernwood Publishing.

Moore, Samantha, and Alana Cattapan. 2020. *A Safe Place to Have my Baby: A Narrative Evaluation of Sanctum 1.5 in its First Year*. May 2020. https://issuu.com/alana.cattapan/docs/sanctum_1.5_final_report__may_2020_.

Moore, Holly. 2018. "Saskatchewan Health Policy Raises New Questions About Gerald Stanley Jury Selection." *APTN Investigates*, April 6, 2018. https://www.aptnnews.ca/national-news/saskatchewan-health-card-policy-raises-new-questions-about-gerald-stanley-jury-selection/.

Morency, Jean-Dominique, Éric Caron-Malenfant, and David Daignault. 2018. "Fertility of Aboriginal People in Canada: An Overview of Trends at the Turn of the 21st Century." *Aboriginal Policy Studies* 7, 1. https://doi.org/10.5663/aps.v7i1.29326.

Morency, Jean-Dominique, Éric Caron-Malenfant, Simon Coulombe, et al. 2015. *Projections of the Aboriginal Population and Households in Canada, 2011 to 2036*. Ottawa: Statistics Canada.

Moreton-Robinson, Aileen. 2011. "Virtuous Racial States: The Possessive Logic of Patriarchal White Sovereignty and the United Nations Declaration on the Rights of Indigenous Peoples." *Griffith Law Review* 20, 3. https://doi.org/10.1080/10383441.2011.10854714.

Mosby, Ian. 2013. "Administering Colonial Science: Nutrition Research and Human Biomedical Experimentation in Aboriginal Communities and Residential Schools, 1942–1952." *Social History* 46, 91. http://doi.org/10.1353/his.2013.0015.

Moscovitch, Allan (ed.). 2017. "Introduction to the New Edition." In *Report on Social Security for Canada New Edition* by Leonard Marsh. Montreal & Kingston: McGill-Queen's University Press.

Mullally, Sasha. 2009. "Between Community and State: Practicing Public Health in Cape Breton, 1938–1948." *Acadiensis* 38, 2. https://journals.lib.unb.ca/index.php/Acadiensis/article/view/12737.

Nanson, Josephine, Roxana Bolaria, Richard E. Snyder, et al. 1995. "Physician Awareness of Fetal Alcohol Syndrome: A Survey of Pediatricians and General Practitioners." *Canadian Medical Association Journal* 152, 7. https://pubmed.ncbi.nlm.nih.gov/7712419/.

Nanson, Josephine. 1997. "Binge Drinking During Pregnancy: Who are the Women at Risk?" *Canadian Medical Association Journal* 156, 6. https://www.ncbi.nlm.nih.gov/pmc/articles/PMC1227044/pdf/cmaj_156_6_807.pdf.

Navarro, Vincente. 1981. *Imperialism, Health and Medicine*. New York: Baywood.

Naylor, C. David. 1986. *Private Practice, Public Payment: Canadian Medicine and the Politics of Health Insurance, 1911–1966*. Kingston; Montreal: McGill-Queen's University Press.

Needham, Fraser. 2015. "U of S Medical Program Graduates Highest Percentage of Aboriginal Doctors in Canada." *Eagle Feather News*, July 10, 2015. https://web.archive.org/web/20230923234351/https://www.eaglefeathernews.com/news/index.php?detail=1415.

Nerestant, Antoni. 2021. "Racism, Prejudice Contributes to Joyce Echaquan's Death in Hospital, Quebec Coroner Inquiry Concludes." *CBC News*, October 1, 2021. https://www.cbc.ca/news/canada/montreal/joyce-echaquan-systemic-racism-quebec-government-1.6196038.

Niessen, Shuana. 2017. *Shattering the Silence: The Hidden History of Indian Residential Schools in Saskatchewan*. Regina: Faculty of Education.

Open Society Foundations. 2011. "Against Her Will: Forced and Coerced Sterilization of Women Worldwide." October 4, 2011. https://www.opensocietyfoundations.org/publications/against-her-will-forced-and-coerced-sterilization-women-worldwide.

Ordover, Nancy. 2003. *American Eugenics: Race, Queer Anatomy, and the Science of Nationalism*. Minneapolis: University of Minnesota Press.

Ostry, Aleck. 2009. "The Foundations of a National Public Hospital Insurance." *Canadian Bulletin Medical History* 26, 2. https://doi.org/10.3138/cbmh.26.2.261.

Palko, M., R. Lennox, and C. Mcquarrie. 1971. "Current Status of Family Planning in Canada." *Canadian Journal of Public Health* 62, 6. https://pubmed.ncbi.nlm.nih.gov/5133827/.

Palmater, Pamela D. 2011. *Beyond Blood: Rethinking Aboriginal Identity and Belonging*. Saskatoon: Purich Publishing.

Palmer, Bryan. 2009. *Canada's 1960s: The Ironies of Identity in a Rebellious Era*. Toronto: University of Toronto Press.

Papps, Elaine, and Irihapeti Ramsden. 1996. "Cultural Safety in Nursing: The New Zealand Experience." *International Journal for Quality Health Care* 8, 5. https://doi.org/10.1093/intqhc/8.5.491.

Patrias, Carmela. 2006. "Socialists, Jews, and the 1947 Saskatchewan Bill of Rights." *Canadian Historical Review* 87, 2. https://doi.org/10.3138/CHR/87.2.265.

Patterson, Thomas. 2020. *A Social History of Anthropology in the United States*. London: Routledge.

———. 2018. *Social Change Theories in Motion*. New York: Routledge.

Paul, David, Shauna Hill, and Shaun Ewen. 2012. "Revealing the (in)Competency of "Cultural Competency" in Medical Education." *AlterNative: An International Journal of Indigenous Peoples* 8, 3. https://doi.org/10.1177/117718011200800307.

Paul, Diane. 1998. *The Politics of Heredity: Essays on Eugenics, Biomedicine, and the Nature-Nurture Debate*. New York: SUNY Press.

Pearson, Lester. 1970. "A New Strategy for Global Development." *The UNESCO Courier: a Window to the Open World*, February. https://unesdoc.unesco.org/ark:/48223/pf0000056743.

Perelman, Michael. 2000. *The Invention of Capitalism: Classical Political Economy and the Secret History of Primitive Accumulation*. North Carolina: Duke University Press.

Perraux, Leslie. 1999. "Life Sentence for Nicotine." *The Star Phoenix*, May 29, 1999.

Pickles, Katie. 2002. *Female Imperialism and National Identify: Imperial Order Daughters of the Empire*. Manchester: Manchester University Press.

Pitsula, James. 1994. "The Saskatchewan CCF Government and Treaty Indians, 1944–64." *Canadian Historical Review* 71, 1. https://doi.org/10.3138/CHR-075-01-02.

Pitty, Roderic. 2001. "Indigenous Peoples, Self Determination and International Law." *The International Journal of Human Rights* 5, 4. https://doi.org/10.1080/714003733.

Polaschek, Nick. 1998. "Cultural Safety: A New Concept in Nursing People of Different Ethnicities." *Journal of Advanced Nursing* 27, 3. https://doi.org/10.1046/j.1365-2648.1998.00547.x.

Pols, Hans. 1999. "The World as Laboratory: Strategies of Field Research Developed by Mental Hygiene Psychologists in Toronto, 1920-1940." In *The Development of the Social Sciences in the United States and Canada: The Role of Philanthropy*, edited by Theresa Richardson and Donald Fisher. Stamford, Connecticut: Ablex Publishing Corporation.

Pon, Gordon. 2009. "Cultural Competency as New Racism: An Ontology of Forgetting." *Journal of Progressive Human Services* 20, 1. https://doi.org/10.1080/10428230902871173.

Powell, Clare. 1980. "Gov't Waffles on Love Proposal." *Briarpatch Magazine* (March).

Prince Albert Daily Herald. 1980. "Sterilization 'Not Government Policy.'" February 14, 1980.

Quiring, David M. 2004. *CCF Colonialism in Northern Saskatchewan*. Vancouver: UBC Press.

Rademaker, Laura, Jakelin Troy, and Julia Hurst. 2024. "Friday Essay: 'Too Many Aboriginal Babies' – Australia's Secret History of Aboriginal Population Control in the 1960s." *The Conversation*. April 11, 2024. https://theconversation.com/friday-essay-too-many-aboriginal-babies-australias-secret-history-of-aboriginal-population-control-in-the-1960s-189249.

Ralstin-Lewis, D. Marie. 2005. "The Continuing Struggle against Genocide: Indigenous Women's Reproductive Rights." *Wicazo Sa Review* 20, 1. https://www.jstor.org/stable/4140251.

Ram, Bali. 2004. "New Estimates of Aboriginal Fertility, 1966-1971 to 1996-2001." *Canadian Studies in Population* 31, 2. https://doi.org/10.25336/P6C31T.

Ram, Bali, and A. Romaniuc. 1985. *Fertility Projections of Registered Indians, 1982 to 1996*. Ottawa: Indian Affairs and Northern Development.

Ramsden, Irihapeti. 1990. "Cultural Safety." *New Zealand Nursing Journal* 83, 11.

Ray, Arthur, Jim Miller, and Frank Tough. 2000. *Bounty and Benevolence: A History of Saskatchewan Treaties*. Montreal & Kingston: McGill-Queen's University Press.

Reed, James. 1978. *From Private Vice to Public Virtue: The Birth Control Movement and American Society since 1830*. New York: Basic Books.

Revie, Linda. 2006. "More Than Just Boots! The Eugenic and Commercial Concerns behind A. R. Kaufman's Birth Controlling Activities." *Canadian Bulletin of Medical History* 23, 1. https://doi.org/10.3138/cbmh.23.1.119.

Richardson, Theresa. 1999. "The Rockefeller Boards: The Organization of Philanthropy and the Origins of Social Sciences." In *The Development of the Social Sciences in the United States and Canada: The Role of Philanthropy*, edited by Theresa Richardson and Donald Fisher. Stamford, Connecticut: Ablex.

———. 1989. *The Century of the Child: The Mental Hygiene Movement and Social Policy in the United States and Canada*. New York: State University of New York Press.

Richardson, Theresa, and Donald Fisher (eds.). 1999. *The Development of the Social Sciences in the United States and Canada: The Role of Philanthropy*. Stamford: Ablex Publishing Corporation.

Roberts, Dorothy. 2016. *Killing the Black Body: Race, Reproduction, and the Meaning of Liberty*. New York: Vintage Books.

———. 1995. "The Only Good Poor Woman: Unconstitutional Conditions and Welfare." *Denver University Law Review* 72, 4. https://digitalcommons.du.edu/dlr/vol72/iss4/8.

Roberts, Gary, and Josephine Nanson. 2000. *Best Practices: Fetal Alcohol Syndrome/Fetal Alcohol Effects and the Effects of Other Substances Use During Pregnancy*. Ottawa: Canada's Drug Strategy Division, Health Canada.

Romaniuc, Anatole. 2000. "Aboriginal Population of Canada: Growth Dynamics Under Conditions of Encounter of Civilisations." *The Canadian Journal of Native Studies* 20, 1. https://doi.org/10.25336/P6B605.

Ross, Loretta. 2017. "Trust Black Women: Reproductive Justice and Eugenics." In *Radical Reproductive Justice: Foundation, Theory, Practice, Critique*, edited by Loretta Ross, Lynn Roberts, Erika Derkas, Whitney Peoples, and Pamela Bridgewater. New York: The Feminist Press.

Ross, Loretta, Erika Derkas, Whitney Peoples, et al. (eds.). 2017. *Radical Reproductive Justice: Foundation, Theory, Practice, Critique*. New York: The Feminist Press.

Roth, F. Burns, and R.D. Defries. 1958. "Canadian Journal of Public Health / Revue Canadienne de Santé Publique." *The Saskatchewan Department of Public Health* 49, 7. https://www.ncbi.nlm.nih.gov/pmc/journals/3761/.

Rousseau, Nicole. 2009. *Black Women's Burden: Commodifying Black Reproduction*. New York: Palgrave MacMillan, 2009.

Roy, Chunilal, Adjit Choudhuri, and Donald Irvine. 1970. "The Prevalence of Mental Disorders among Saskatchewan Indians." *Journal of Cross-Cultural Psychology* 1, 4. https://doi.org/10.1177/135910457000100410.

Rusco, Elmer. 1991. "John Collier: Architect of Sovereignty or Assimilation?" *American Indian Quarterly* 15, 1. https://doi.org/10.2307/1185213.

Russell, Peter. 1970. "The Co-Operative Government in Saskatchewan, 1929-1934: Response to the Depression." MA thesis, University of Saskatchewan. http://hdl.handle.net/10388/6175.

Russell Sage Foundation. 2014. "How Genetics Can Enrich the Way We Study Social Inequality." May 22, 2014. https://www.russellsage.org/news/how-genetics-can-enrich-way-we-study-social-inequality.

Ryan, William. 1971. *Blaming the Victim*. New York: Pantheon Press.

Sachse, Carola. 2009. "What Research, to What End? The Rockefeller Foundation and the Max Planck Gesellschaft in the Early Cold War." *Central European History* 42, 1. https://doi.org/10.1017/S0008938909000041.

Salmon, Amy. 2004. "'It Takes a Community': Constructing Aboriginal Mothers and Children with FAS/FAE as Objects of Moral Panic in/through a FAS/FAE Prevention." *Journal of the Motherhood Initiative for Research and Community Involvement* 6, 1. https://jarm.journals.yorku.ca/index.php/jarm/article/view/4889.

Sandor, George, David Smith, Patrick MacLeod, et al. 1981. "Intrinsic Defects in the Fetal Alcohol Syndrome: Studies on 76 cases from B.C. and the Yukon." *Neurobehavioral Toxicology* and *Teratology* 3, 2.

Sanger, Margaret. 1922. *The Pivot of Civilization*. New York: Bretano's Publishers.

Sangster, Joan. 1999. "Criminalizing the Colonized: Ontario Native Women Confront the Criminal Justice System, 1920-60." *The Canadian Historical Review* 80, 1. https://doi.org/10.3138/CHR.80.1.32.

Sarra, Janis. 1982. "The Case Against Depo Provera." *Healthsharing* 3, 1.

Sarkadi, Laurie. 1995. "Paying the Price for Birth Control." *Horizons* 9, 1.

Sasakamoose, JoLee, Terrina Bellegarde, Wilson Sutherland, et al. 2017. "Miyo-Pimātisiwin Developing Indigenous Cultural Responsiveness Theory (ICRT): Improving Indigenous Health and Well-Being." *The International Indigenous Policy Journal* 8, 4. https://doi.org/10.18584/iipj.2017.8.4.1.

Schlesinger, Benjamin. 1974. "Poverty and Family Planning." In *Family Planning in Canada: A Source Book*, edited by Benjamin Schlesinger. Toronto: University of Toronto Press.

Schlesinger, Joel. 2022. "Potash Sales Anticipated to Reach Unprecedented High in 2022." *Saskatoon StarPhoenix*, November 16, 2022. https://thestarphoenix.com/special-features/potash-in-our-province/potash-sales-anticipated-to-reach-unprecedented-high-in-2022.

Scott, Frank R. 1937. "The Privy Council and Mr. Bennett's "New Deal" Legislation." *Canadian Journal of Economics and Political Science* 3, 2.

Schouler-Ocak, Meryam, Iris T. Graef-Calliess, Ilaria Tarricone, et al. 2015. "EPA Guidance on Cultural Competence Training." *European Psychiatry* 30, 3. https://doi.org/10.1016/j.eurpsy.2015.01.012.

Scoffield, Heather. 1993. "Health and Welfare Dumps Depo Bid." *Horizons* 7, 2.

Scully, Judith M. 2000. "Cracking Open CRACK: Unethical Sterilization Movement Gains Momentum." *A Publication of the Population and Development Program at Hampshire College*, 2 (Spring). https://ssrn.com/abstract=1646144.

Sear, Rebecca. 2021. "Demography and the Rise, Apparent Fall, and Resurgence of Eugenics." *Population Studies* 75, 1. https://doi.org/10.1080/00324728.2021.2009013.

Sewell, Dennis. 2009. *The Political Gene: How Darwin's Ideas Changed Politics*. London, UK: Pan Macmillan.

Shaheen-Hussain, Samir. 2020. *Fighting for a Hand to Hold: Confronting Medical Colonialism against Indigenous Children in Canada*. Montreal; Kingston: McGill-Queens University Press.

Shapiro, Thomas M. 1985. *Population Control Politics: Women, Sterilization, and Reproductive Choice*. Philadelphia: Temple University Press.

Shea, Laura. 2007. *Reflections on Depo Provera: Contributions to Improving Drug Regulation in Canada*. Ottawa: Women and Health Protection.

Shevell, Michael. 2012. "A Canadian Paradox: Tommy Douglas and Eugenics." *The Canadian Journal of Neurological Science* 39, 1. http://doi.org/10.1017/s0317167100012658.

Shewell, Hugh. 2016. "Why Jurisdiction Matters: Social Policy, Social Services and First Nations." *Canadian Journal of Native Studies* 36, 1.

——. 2004. *'Enough to Keep Them Alive': Indian Welfare in Canada, 1873-1965*. Toronto: University of Toronto Press.

——. 2002. "'Bitterness Behind Every Smiling Face': Community Development and Canada's First Nations, 1954-1968." *Canadian Historical Review* 83, 1. http://doi.org/10.3138/CHR.83.1.58.

——. 2001. "What Makes the Indian Tick?" The Influence of Social Sciences on Canada's Indian Policy, 1947-1964." *Social History* 37, 67.

Shewell, Hugh, and Annabel Spagnut. 1995. "The First Nations of Canada: Social Welfare and the Quest for Self-Government." In *Social Welfare with Indigenous Peoples*, edited by John Dixon and Robert Scheurell. London: Routledge.

Short, Jim. 1999. "Refusal to Fully Examine FAS Scandalous." *Saskatoon Star Phoenix*. December 3, 1999.

Shprintsen, Alex. 2013. "Senator's Husband put $1.7 Million in Offshore Tax Havens." *CBC News*, April 3, 2013. https://www.cbc.ca/news/canada/senator-s-husband-put-1-7m-in-offshore-tax-havens-1.1329197.

Shrubsole, Nick, and P. Whitney Lackenbauer. 2014. "The Gustafsen Lake Standoff." In *Blockades or Breakthroughs? Aboriginal Peoples Confront the Canadian State,* edited by Yale Deron Belanger and P. Whitney Lackenbauer. Kingston & Montreal: McGill-Queen's University Press.

Sigerist, Henry E. 1951. *A History of Medicine. Vol. 1: Primitive and Archaic Medicine.* New York: Oxford University Press.

———. 1943. *Civilization and Disease.* Ithaca: Cornell University Press.

Silliman, Jael. 2004. "Women of Color and Their Struggle for Reproductive Justice." In *Undivided Rights: Women of Color Organize for Reproductive Justice,* edited by Jael Silliman. Cambridge, Mass: South End Press.

Simpson, Audra. 2014. *Mohawk Interruptus: Political Life Across the Borders of Settler States.* Durham: Duke University Press.

Simpson, Leanne Betasamoke. 2017. *As We Have Always Done: Indigenous Freedom through Radical Resistance.* Minneapolis: University of Minnesota Press.

Sirrs, Christopher. 2020. "Promoting Health Protection Worldwide: The International Labour Organisation and Health Systems Financing, 1952–2012." *The International History Review* 42, 2. https://doi.org/10.1080/07075332.2019.1582550.

Sivanandan, Ambalavaner. 1985. "RAT and the Degradation of Black Struggle." *Race & Class* 26, 4. https://doi.org/10.1177/030639688502600401.

Soiseth, Len. 1970. "A Community that Cares for Children." *Canadian Welfare* 46, 3.

Smiley, Donald. 1963. *The Rowell-Sirois Report: An Abridgement of Book 1 of the Royal Commission on Dominion-Provincial Relations.* Toronto: McClelland and Stewart Limited.

Smith, Andrea. 2014. "Human Rights and Decolonization." In *Indivisible: Indigenous Human Rights,* edited by Joyce Green. Halifax: Fernwood Publishing.

———. 2013. "Unsettling the Privilege of Self-Reflexivity." In *Geographies of Privilege,* edited by France Winddance Twine and Bradley Gardner. London and New York: Routledge.

———. 2012. "Indigeneity, Settler Colonialism, White Supremacy." In *Racial Formation in the Twenty-First Century,* edited by Daniel Martinez HoSang, Oneka LaBennett, and Laura Pulido. Berkely: University of California Press.

———. 2005. *Conquest: Sexual Violence and American Indian Genocide.* Cambridge, Mass: South End Press.

Smith, Keith D. 2009. *Liberalism, Surveillance, and Resistance: Indigenous Communities in Western Canada, 1877–1927.* Edmonton: Athabasca University Press.

Smith, Jason. 2014. *A Concise History of the New Deal.* New York: Cambridge University Press.

Smith, Joanna. 2016. "'The Pass System' Explores Dark Chapter in Canadian History." *Toronto Star,* January 10, 2016. thestar.com/news/canada/the-pass-system-explores-dark-chapter-in-canadian-history/article_7afb4f5f-a6fb-5a77-9e5a-a08407856cde.html.

Smylie, Janet, Deshayne Fell, and Arne Ohlsson. 2010. "A Review of Aboriginal Infant Mortality Rates in Canada: Striking and Persistent Aboriginal/Non-Aboriginal Inequities." *Canadian Journal of Public Health* 101, 2. http://doi.org/10.1007/BF03404361.

Smylie, Janet, Sue Crengle, Jane Freemantle, et al. 2010. "Indigenous Birth Outcomes in Australia, Canada, New Zealand and the United States – an Overview." *Open Womens Health Journal* 4. https://www.ncbi.nlm.nih.gov/pmc/articles/PMC3563669/.

Splane, Richard. 2003. *George Davidson: Social Policy and Public Policy Exemplar.* Ottawa: Canadian Council on Social Development.

Spaulding, William. 1993. "Why Rockefeller Supported Medical Education in Canada: The William Lyon MacKenzie King Connection." *Canadian Bulletin of Medical History* 10. https://www.utpjournals.press/doi/pdf/10.3138/cbmh.10.1.67.

Star Phoenix. 2016. "Complaints Badly Handled." *Star Phoenix*, June 25, 2016. https://thestarphoenix.com/opinion/editorials/0625-edit-editorial.

Stavig, Lucia. 2017. "Feminist Assemblages: Peruvian Feminisms, Forced Sterilization, and Paradox of Rights in Fujimori's Peru." MA Thesis, University of Lethbridge. https://hdl.handle.net/10133/4850.

Steffler, Jeanette. 2008. "Aboriginal Peoples: A Young Population for Years to Come." *Horizons* 10, 1.

Stern, Alexandra Minna. 2006. *Eugenic Nation: Faults and Frontiers of Better Breeding in Modern America*. Berkeley: University of California Press.

_____. 2005. "Sterilized in the Name of Public Health: Race, Immigration, and Reproductive Control in Modern California." *American Journal of Public Health* 95, 7. https://doi.org/10.2105/AJPH.2004.041608.

Stevenson, Allyson. 2020. *Intimate Integration: A History of the Sixties Scoop and the Colonization of Indigenous Kinship*. Toronto: University of Toronto Press.

_____. 2015. "Intimate Integration: A Study of Transracial Adoption in Saskatchewan, 1944–1984." PhD thesis, University of Saskatchewan.

Stote, Karen. 2022. "From Eugenics to Family Planning: The Coerced Sterilization of Indigenous Women in Post 1970 Saskatchewan." *Native American and Indigenous Studies Journal*, 9, 1.

_____. 2017. "Decolonizing Feminism: From Reproductive Abuse to Reproductive Justice." *Atlantis* 38, 1.

_____. 2015. *An Act of Genocide: Colonialism and the Sterilization of Aboriginal Women*. Halifax: Fernwood Publishing.

_____. 2012. "An Act of Genocide: Eugenics, Indian Policy, and the Coercive Sterilization of Aboriginal Women in Canada." Doctoral dissertation, University of New Brunswick.

Stout, Madeline Dion, and Bernice Downey. 2006. "Nursing, Indigenous Peoples and Cultural Safety: So What? Now What?" *Contemporary Nurse* 22, 2. https://pubmed.ncbi.nlm.nih.gov/17026439/.

Struthers, James. 1983. *No Fault of Their Own: Unemployment and the Canadian Welfare State, 1914-1941*. Toronto: University of Toronto Press, 1983.

Stueck, Wendy. 2019. "B.C. Ends Controversial Birth Alert System That Affected Indigenous Mothers Disproportionately." *The Globe and Mail*, September 16, 2019. https://www.theglobeandmail.com/canada/british-columbia/article-bc-ends-controversial-birth-alert-system-that-affected-indigenous/.

Summergrad, Paul, and Thomas P. Hackett. 1987. "Alan Gregg and the Rise of General Hospital Psychiatry." *General Hospital Psychiatry* 9, 6. https://doi.org/10.1016/0163-8343(87)90054-5.

Swartz, Donald. 1993. "The Politics of Reform: Public Health Insurance in Canada." *International Journal of Health Services* 23, 2. https://doi.org/10.2190/JJGJ-NGHE-R2CL-H75A.

Symington, D.F. 1953. "Métis Rehabilitation." *Canadian Geographical Journal* 46, 4.

Szasz, Thomas. 1997. *Manufacture of Madness: A Comparative Study of the Inquisition and the Mental Health Movement*. New York: Syracuse State University.

Alfred, Taiaiake. 2009. *Peace, Power, Righteousness: An Indigenous Manifesto, 2nd ed.* Canada: Oxford University Press.

Tait, Caroline. 2013. "Resituating the Ethical Gaze: Government Morality and the Local Worlds of Impoverished Indigenous Women." *International Journal of Circumpolar Health* 72, 1. https://doi.org/10.3402/ijch.v72i0.21207.

_____. 2008. "Simpering Outrage During an "Epidemic" of Fetal Alcohol Syndrome." *Canadian Woman Studies* 26, 3. https://cws.journals.yorku.ca/index.php/cws/article/view/22115.

———. 2003. "The Tip of the Iceberg: The 'Making' of Fetal Alcohol Syndrome in Canada." Doctoral dissertation, McGill University. https://escholarship.mcgill.ca/concern/theses/w0892d25n.

Takeuchi-Demirci, Aiko. 2018. *Contraceptive Diplomacy: Reproductive Politics and Imperial Ambitions in the United States and Japan*. California: Stanford University Press.

Talaga, Tanya. 2017. *Seven Fallen Feathers: Racism, Death, and Hard Truths in a Northern City*. Toronto: House of Anansi Press.

Tasker, John Paul. 2019a. "Premier Scott Moe Disagrees with MMIWG Inquiry's Genocide Finding." *CBC News*, June 10, 2019. https://www.cbc.ca/news/canada/saskatchewan/premier-scott-moe-disagrees-with-indigenous-inquiry-s-genocide-finding-1.5169622.

———. 2019b. "Inquiry into Missing and Murdered Indigenous Women Issues Final Report with Sweeping Calls for Change." *CBC News*, June 3, 2019. https://www.cbc.ca/news/politics/mmiwg-inquiry-deliver-final-report-justice-reforms-1.5158223.

———. 2017. "Missing and Murdered Inquiry Needs Extension and New Approach, Families and Activists Say." *CBC News*, May 15, 2017. https://www.cbc.ca/news/politics/mmiwg-inquiry-letter-extension-1.4115681.

Taylor, Graham. 2019. *Imperial Standard: Imperial Oil, Exxon, and the Canadian Oil Industry from 1880*. Calgary: University of Calgary Press.

Taylor, Malcolm G. 2009. *Health Insurance and Canadian Public Policy: The Seven Decisions that Created the Canadian Health Insurance System and their Outcomes*. Montreal: McGill-Queen's University Press.

Taylor, Stephanie. 2019a. "Saskatchewan to Continue Using 'Birth Alert' Despite Calls by Inquiry to Stop." *The Star Phoenix*, June 20, 2019. https://thestarphoenix.com/news/local-news/saskatchewan-to-continue-using-birth-alerts-despite-calls-by-inquiry-to-stop.

———. 2019b. "Indigenous Group Renews Calls for Saskatchewan to End 'Birth Alerts.'" *CBC News*, September 18, 2019. https://www.cbc.ca/news/canada/saskatoon/sask-birth-alerts-1.5289154.

Tester, Frank, and Peter Kulchyski. 1994. *Tammarniit (Mistakes): Inuit Relocation in the Eastern Arctic, 1939–63*. Vancouver: UBC Press.

The Canadian Press. 2017. "Saskatoon Health Region Apologizes for Tubal Ligations on Indigenous Women." *CTV News Saskatoon*, July 27, 2017. https://www.ctvnews.ca/health/saskatoon-health-region-apologizes-for-tubal-ligations-on-indigenous-women-1.3522436.

———. 2018. "Judges, Lawyers at Odds Over Deal to Pay $75M in '60s Scoop Legal Fees." *CBC News*, August 17, 2018. https://www.cbc.ca/news/canada/toronto/60s-scoop-legal-battle-1.4789650.

Theobald, Brianna. 2019. *Reproduction on the Reservation: Pregnancy, Childbirth, and Colonialism in the Long Twentieth Century*. Chapel Hill: University of North Carolina Press.

Thomas, Susan L. 1998. "Race, Gender, and Welfare Reform: The Antinatalist Response." *Journal of Black Studies* 28, 4. https://doi.org/10.1177/002193479802800401.

Thorne, F.C. 1952. "Samuel W. Hamilton, M.D., 1878–1951." *Journal of Clinical Psychology* 8, 1.

Thoronton, Russell. 1987. *American Indian Holocaust and Survival. A Population History Since 1492*. Norman: University of Oklahoma Press.

Toledano, Michael. 2015. "Indigenous Canadians are Fighting for the Uranium Industry." *Vice News*, February 11, 2015. https://www.vice.com/en/article/jmbwx8/a-dene-alliance-formed-to-resist-uranium-and-tar-sands-mining-in-saskatchewan-892.

Torpy, Sally J. 2000. "Native American Women and Coerced Sterilization: On the Trail of Tears in the 1970s." *American Indian Culture and Research Journal* 24, 2.

Tournès, Ludovic. 2014. "The Rockefeller Foundation and the Transition from the League of Nations to the UN (1939–1946)." *Journal of Modern European History* 12, 3. http://doi.org/10.17104/1611-8944_2014_3_323.

Tough, David. 2014. "'At Last! The Government's War on Poverty Explained': The Special Planning Secretariat, the Welfare State, and the Rhetoric of the Poverty in the 1960s." *Journal of the Canadian Historical* 25, 1. http://doi.org/10.7202/1032802ar.

Trocmé, Nico, Bruce MacLaurin, Barbara Fallon et al. 2006. *Understanding the Overrepresentation of First Nations Children in Canada's Child Welfare System: An Analysis of the Canadian Incidence Study of Reported Child Abuse and Neglect (CIS-2003)*. Toronto: Centre of Excellence for Child Welfare.

Trocmé, Nico, Della Knoke and Cindy Blackstock. 2004. "Pathways to the Overrepresentation of Aboriginal Children in Canada's Child Welfare System." *Social Service Review* 78, 4. http://doi.org/10.1086/424545.

Trovato, Frank 1987. "A Macrosociological Analysis of Native Indian Fertility in Canada: 1961, 1971, and 1981." *Social Forces* 66, 2.

Tuck, Eve, and K. Wayne Yang (eds.). 2018. *Toward What Justice? Describing Diverse Dreams of Justice in Education*. New York, NY: Routledge.

———. 2012. "Decolonization Is Not a Metaphor." *Decolonization: Indigeneity, Education & Society* 1, 1. https://jps.library.utoronto.ca/index.php/des/article/view/18630/15554.

Tunney, Catharine. 2017. "Jody Wilson-Raybould's Father Calls Missing and Murdered Inquiry a 'Bloody Farce.'" *CBC News*, May 24, 2017. https://www.cbc.ca/news/politics/bill-wilson-mmiwg-inquiry-1.4129627.

Turner, Stephen P. 1999. "Does Funding Produce Its Effects? The Rockefeller Case." In *The Development of the Social Sciences in the United States and Canada: The Role of Philanthropy*, edited by Theresa Richardson and Donald Fisher. Stamford, Connecticut: Ablex Publishing Corporation.

Turpel-Lafond, Mary Ellen. 1996. "Patriarchy and Paternalism: The Legacy of the Canadian State for First Nations Women." In *Women and the Canadian State*, edited by Caroline Andrew and Sandra Rodgers. Montreal and Kingston: McGill-Queen's University Press.

Tuhiwai Smith, Linda. 1999. *Decolonizing Methodologies: Research and Indigenous Peoples*. New York: Zed Books.

Twohig, Peter. 2002. "The Rockefellers, the Cape Breton Island Health Unit and Public Health in Nova Scotia." *Journal of the Royal Nova Scotia Historical Society* 5.

Urwin, Cathy Kunzinger. 1995. "'Nobless Oblige' and Practical Politics: Winthrop Rockefeller and the Civil Rights Movement." *The Arkansas Historical Quarterly* 54, 1. https://doi.org/10.2307/40030926.

Valentine, Victor F. 1954. "Some Problems of the Métis of Northern Saskatchewan." *The Canadian Journal of Economic and Political Science* 20, 1. https://doi.org/10.2307/138417.

Valverde, Mariana. 1991. *The Age of Light, Soap, and Water: Moral Reform in English Canada, 1885-1925*. Toronto: McClelland & Stewart Inc.

Vecchio, Jaryn. 2023. "Sturgeon Lake Holds Sod-Turning Ceremony for New Birthing Centre." *Battlefords Now*, October 10, 2023. https://battlefordsnow.com/2023/10/10/sturgeon-lake-holds-sod-turning-ceremony-for-new-birthing-centre/.

Venne, Sharon H. 1998. *Our Elders Understand Our Rights: Evolving International Law Regarding Indigenous Peoples*. Penticton: Theytus Books.

Verburg, Peter. 1994. "Super-Pill for the Poor." *Alberta Report* 21, 43.

Vescera, Zac. 2021. "Saskatchewan to Discontinue Practice of Birth Alerts." *Saskatoon StarPhoenix*, January 26, 2021. https://thestarphoenix.com/news/saskatchewan/saskatchewan-to-discontinue-practice-of-birth-alerts.

Vincent, George. 1918. *The Rockefeller Foundation — A Review of Its War Work, Public Health Activities, and Medical Education Projects in 1917*. New York: Rockefeller Foundation.

Ward, Norman. 1973. "Mike: The Memoirs of the Right Honourable Lester B. Pearson, I: 1897–1948 by Lester B. Pearson (review)." *The Canadian Historical Review* 54, 2.

Warick, Jason. 2018. "'Justice Was Not Served': Sixties Scoop Survivors Unhappy After Approval of $875 Settlement." *CBC News*, May 11, 2018. https://www.cbc.ca/news/canada/saskatoon/sixties-scoop-hearing-saskatoon-1.4658197.

Wasacase, Tanya. 2003. "The Empty Mirror: Western Theories of Identity and the Attack on Indigenous Peoples." BA Honours Thesis, St. Thomas University. https://web.archive.org/web/20070816155112/http://www.darknightpress.org/index.php?i=print&article=2.

Washington, Harriet A. 2006. *Medical Apartheid: The Dark History of Medical Experimentation on Black Americans from Colonial Times to the Present*. New York, NY: Doubleday.

Watson, Irene. 2018. "First Nations, Indigenous Peoples: Our Laws Have Always Been Here." In *Indigenous Peoples as Subjects of International Law*, edited by Irene Watson. New York: Routledge. https://hdl.handle.net/11541.2/128338.

Weaver, Sally M. 1981. *Making Canadian Indian Policy: The Hidden Agenda 1968–1970*. Toronto: University of Toronto Press.

Webster, David. 2011. "Development Advisors in a Time of Cold War and Decolonization: The United Nations Technical Assistance Administration, 1950–59." *Journal of Global History* 6, 2. https://doi.org/10.1017/S1740022811000258.

Weinberg, Paul. 2019. *When Poverty Mattered: Then and Now*. Halifax: Fernwood Publishing.

Weindling, Paul. 2012. "Julian Huxley and the Continuity of Eugenics in Twentieth-century Britain." *J Mod Eur Hist* 10, 4. https://pubmed.ncbi.nlm.nih.gov/25798079/.

_____. 2003. "Modernizing Eugenics: The Role of Foundations in International Population Studies." In *American Foundations in Europe: Grant-Giving Policies, Cultural Diplomacy and Trans-Atlantic Relations, 1920s–1980*, edited by Giuliana Gemelli and Roy MacLeod. New York: P.I.E.-Peter Lang.

_____. 1988. "The Rockefeller Foundation and German Biomedical Sciences, 1920-40: From Educations Philanthropy to International Science Policy." In *Science, Politics and the Public Good: Essays in Honour of Margaret Gowing*, edited by N.A. Rupke. London: Palgrave MacMillan.

Western Oil. 1949. "Thirty-six Million Saskatchewan Acres Now Under Lease for Oil Exploration." *Western Oil* (July), 98.

White Face, Charmaine. 2013. *Indigenous Nations' Rights in the Balance: An Analysis of the Declaration on the Rights of Indigenous Peoples*. St. Paul, Minnesota: Living Justice Press.

Wiebe, Sarah Marie, and Erin Marie Konsmo. 2014. "Indigenous Body as Contaminated Site? Examining Reproductive Justice in Aamjiwnaang." In *Fertile Ground: Exploring Reproduction in Canada*, edited by F. Scala & S. Paterson. Montreal and London: McGill-Queen's University Press.

Wigmore, John. 1970. *Evidence in Trials at Common Law, Volume 3A*. Toronto: Little Brown & Company.

Winks, Robin. 2021. *Blacks in Canada: A History*, 5th ed. Montreal & Kingston: McGill-Queen's University Press.

Wolfe, Patrick. 2006. "Settler Colonialism and the Elimination of the Native." *Journal of Genocide Research* 8, 4. https://doi.org/10.1080/14623520601056240.

Zakreski, Dan. 1999. "Blood and Betrayal: The Deadly Effects of Fetal Alcohol Syndrome on Our Society." *The Star Phoenix*, November 27, 1999.

Zampas, Christina, and Adriana Lamačková. 2011. "Forced and Coerced Sterilization of Women in Europe." *International Journal of Gynecology & Obstetrics* 114, 2. https://doi.org/10.1016/j.ijgo.2011.05.002.

Zingel, Avery. 2022. "Tuktoyaktuk Woman Files $6M Lawsuit Claiming N.W.T. Doctor Sterilized Her Without Consent." *CBC News*, March 10, 2022. https://www.cbc.ca/news/canada/north/nwt-sterilization-claim-1.6360857.

Zinn, Howard. 1990. *The Politics of History,* 2nd ed. Champaign Illinois: University of Illinois Press.

Zunz, Olivier. 2012. *Philanthropy in America: A History.* Princeton, N.J.: Princeton University Press.

Index

2SLGBTQQIA people, violence facing, 178–9, 243n67; *see also* Two-Spirit people

abortions, 19, 148, 216n16
   consenting to, 117–19
   increasing access to, 75, 105, 109–10, 114
   Indigenous women's forced, 2, 16, 101
   policy making on, 94, 99, 109–10, 114–18, 125–6, 227n59
   rates of, 115–16, 168–70
   see also Therapeutic Abortion Committees
Adams, N.D., 157
adoption, Indigenous child, 12, 22, 64, 113, 152
   Sixties Scoop, 74–5, 123, 184–6
Advisory Committee on Family Planning (Saskatchewan),
   from 1973: 116, 119–21
   from 1993: 134–7, 139
Africa, 62, 89, 91, 96, 210
Alberta, 97, 131
   class action lawsuits in, 2, 185
   forced sterilization/birth control in, 143
   public health system in, 40
   sterilization policies in, 1, 28–31, 42, 107–8
Alexander, Michelle, 212
Alvin Buckwold Child Development Program (ABCDP), 137, 140, 142
American Birth Control League (ABCL), 6–7, 33, 218n45
Anderson, Kim, 19
Anishinaabe people, 200
Appleby, Brenda, 12
Archibald, RoseAnne, 198
Asia, 62, 89, 97, 104
Assembly of First Nations, 76, 198
assimilation, 163, 191–2, 209
   colonial justifications for, 88, 154
   federal/provincial efforts to hasten, 30, 47–8, 61, 67–8
   Indigenous choice between segregation and, 11, 54–6, 76, 79, 176
   "integration" and, 62–4, 67–8, 73–4, 87, 159

Baergen, E.H., 50
Bartlett, Judith, 21, 204
   SHR External Review, 149–50, 153–4, 188
Basford, Ron, 96
Bashford, Alison, 8, 13, 18, 31, 108, 160
Bates, Gordon, 42
Bayne, W.G., 128–9
Bear, Heather, 198
Bear Nicholas, Andrea, 73
behavioural genetics, 33
Bennett, Carolyn, 184, 205
Bennett, Richard, 40
Berezowsky, William, 67
Beveridge Report, 58–60
Bighead, Shirley, 197
Bird, Florence, 105–6
birth alerts, 127–8, 151–5, 183
birth control,
   abortion as, 99, 216n16
   advocates of, 31, 33, 44, 82
   aggressive colonial dissemination of, 15–16, 101–3, 115–17, 131–2
   anti-Indigenous/genocidal use of, 71, 83–4, 93–4, 122–3
   clinics, 6, 219n50
   decriminalization of, 11–12, 16, 80, 96–9, 109
   as eugenics/population control, 6–8, 15–16, 44, 81, 170–1, 218nn45–6
   government economic concerns and, 98
   organizations, 6–7, 96
   pills, 84, 98, 102–3, 122
   poverty/justice beyond, 9, 19, 21, 93–4
   public support for, 6, 71, 99–100, 105, 123
   as reproductive right, 18, 97
   RF support for, 6, 13
   variable access to, 12, 97–9, 105–7
   War on Poverty and, 11, 85, 93, 98–9
   women historically seeking out, 12, 122
   world overpopulation and, 7, 89–90, 96
Bishop, Jeffrey, 102–3
Blacker, C.P., 12, 58
Black people, 189, 250n47
   coerced birth control of, 88, 210, 218n45, 252n88

persistent racist perceptions of, 34, 62, 202–3
state pathologizing/criminalizing of, 87–8, 143, 212
Blackstock, Cindy, 76, 156
Blake, Jennifer, 183
Blakeney, Allan, 133
Blondeau, Leona, 55, 233n44
Boyer, Yvonne, 21, 204, 252n90
  on CFS birth alerts, 153–4
  efforts to criminalize coerced sterilization, 199, 201–4
  SHR External Review, 149–50, 183, 188, 204
British Columbia, 70
  Apology Act, 181
  class action lawsuits in, 2, 181
  Gustafson Lake standoff, 142
  Indigenous women's forced abortion/sterilization, 2, 181
  public health system in, 40, 60
  racism in health care, 191, 243n55
  sterilization policies in, 1, 28, 42, 107, 181
British Eugenics Society, 58–9, 96
Brown, Richard, 5
Bunjun, Benita, 106–7
Burton, Randy, 142
Butler, G.C., 101

Cadbury, George, 100
  Canadian Planned Parenthood founding, 96, 99, 104
  sterilization promotion, 43, 96–7, 104
  uranium mining support, 36–7, 104, 220n59
Cameco, 172–3, 220n59
Cameron, Don, 128
Cameron, G.D.W., 44–6
Canada Health Act, 51, 223n115
Canada Assistance Plan (CAP), 74, 86, 223n121, 238n159
Canadian Medical Association, 41, 117
Canadian Medical Protective Association (CMPA), 118
Canadian National Committee for Mental Hygiene (CNCMH), 217n26
  funding for, 10, 45, 216n14
  policy influence of, 23, 35, 41–2, 44
Canadian National Council for the Control of Venereal Disease (CNCCVD), 42

Canadian Public Health Association, 112–13
Canadian Welfare Council (CWC), 63–4, 75, 88, 98, 221n72, 225n12
capitalism,
  colonialism intersecting with, 11, 15, 18–19, 201
  eugenics/population control serving, 8, 89, 159–60
  growth of industrial, 4–5, 159
  Indigenous genocide/dispossession and, 18–19, 63, 159, 176–7, 193–4
  individualism under, 19, 72, 87
  philanthropy amid, 4–5, 32, 36, 52
  politician/institutional support for, 37–40, 44, 52, 60–1, 208–10
  public health system/provision in, 32, 39–40, 52–3, 56
  scientific medicine as integral to, 5, 9, 63, 193
  struggles against, 212–13
  welfare state provisions in, 10–11, 15, 59, 80
Caplin, Alice, 116, 120
Cardinal, Colleen, 185–6
Carnegie Foundation, 32, 89, 218n45
Carriere, Jeannine, 156
Carter, Sarah, 42
Cassidy, Harry, 33, 60–1, 64
Catholic Church, 30, 109, 115
charity organizations, 4, 9, 56
Charter of Rights and Freedoms, 183, 199, 252n92
Chartier, Danielle, 178
Chartrand, Vicky, 79
child care, 105, 130
Child and Family Services (CFS), 143, 151, 153
Child and Family Services Act, 151; *see also* Family Services Act
children,
  adoption of Indigenous, *see* adoption, Indigenous child
  apprehension of, 35–6, 55, 106, 150–6, 179, 184–6
  experimentation on, 34, 102–3
  family allowances for, 43–4, 56–7, 60, 66–7, 70, 76, 125
  FAS and, *see* fetal alcohol syndrome/effects
  "illegitimate"/"unwanted," 6, 23–6, 93–4, 110–16, 119, 125–9

Indigenous valuing of, 19, 88, 94, 101–3, 131–2, 148, 197
legislation pertaining to, 22–6, 100, 128–30
"mentally defective," 22–5, 28, 97, 109
needed support for existing, 9, 19, 21, 75, 93–4, 102
poverty impacts on, 112, 132–6, 167
pressure to space/limit, 12–14, 22, 56–8, 83–4, 122–3
revoked Indian Status for, 105, 163
segregation/assimilation of Indigenous, 64–7, 73–7
social assistance for, 75, 143, 172
training of, 35, 159
see also residential schools
Child Welfare Act (Saskatchewan), 22–3, 119
child welfare system, 41, 223n120
child apprehension via, 35–6, 74–6, 97, 151–2
funding for, 45, 63
Indigenous assimilation/segregation in, 11, 74–6, 79, 156, 171
policy making, 11, 63–4, 76, 79, 98
systemic anti-Indigenous violence in, 179–80
Chisholm, Brock, 43–4
Chrétien, Jean, 50
Chrisjohn, Roland, 144–5, 213
citizens plus, concept of, 70, 73, 206
civil rights, 61, 87–8
movement, 189, 250n41
Clark, Teddy, 174
class action litigation, 215n3
for coerced sterilization, 2, 17, 147, 181, 184
Indigenous experiences in, 147, 186–7
provincial responses to, 181–2
role of, 184, 186–7, 202
Sixties Scoop, 184–6
Claxton, Brooke, 43–4, 46
Cline, Eric, 135–6, 138–9
Coale, Ansley, 90–2, 96
Collier, John, 61–2, 70, 72, 86
colonialism,
aggressive birth control dissemination in, 15–16, 101–3, 115–17, 131–2
anti-Indigenous racism in, 78–9, 88, 178–9
assimilation, see assimilation

capitalism intersecting with, 11, 15, 18–19, 32, 53, 201
coerced sterilization as, 170, 186
family planning in, 18–19, 82
FAS/FAE and, 140–1, 144
Indian policy as tool of, 15, 54, 62, 160–1
institutional perpetuation of, 154, 179–80, 186, 193–5
land theft in, 20, 54–5, 95–6, 201–3, 207
poverty resulting from, 62, 84, 156, 176
public health expansion as, 1, 11, 29, 37, 190, 197
reproductive violence in, 20, 106, 172–3, 200–1
resource exploitation/expropriation, 20, 64–6, 80, 89, 174–6, 207–8
as shaping Indigenous women's experiences, 3, 17–19, 107, 158–9
struggles against, 21, 89, 178–9, 190–8, 211–13
systemic racism in, 3, 11, 21, 145–7, 158, 170
UNDRIP and, 206, 208–9
in United States, 20, 62, 87–9
welfare state expansion, 15, 53, 61, 153
Western medicine as, 9, 15, 26, 53, 72, 193–5
Committee to End Sterilization Abuse, 19–20
Community Health Representatives (CHR) program, 72
consent, 141
age of medical, 114–19
coerced, 110, 143, 146–7, 150
lack of, 1–2, 84–5, 147–8, 173
parental/spousal, 108, 117, 129
policies/laws on, 108, 114, 117–19, 148–9
requirement to obtain informed, 118–20, 148–9, 182–3, 195–6, 199–201, 205
contraceptives, 13
counselling/pressuring Indigenous use of, 2, 22, 28, 107, 121–2
breastfeeding and use of oral, 102–3
decriminalizing, 11–12, 15, 80, 92, 227n59
dependence on doctors for, 8
free distribution of, 75, 114, 122–3, 164
global population control and, 43, 89

long-acting, 2, 141, 143
oral, 84, 102-3, 114, 122
policy making on, 28, 99-100, 125, 201
sterilization versus, 3, 111, 141
Cook, Katsi, 19-20
Co-operative Commonwealth Federation (CCF), 27
actions regarding Indigenous communities, 67, 72, 248n1
(shifting) healthcare policies of, 36-7, 40, 49
Corntassel, Jeff, 208-9
corporations,
interests of, 3, 8, 11-12, 171-5, 208
federal-provincial shared interests with, 37, 46, 189, 211
philanthropy of, 4-5, 32, 36, 52-3, 89
public health/population control influence, 8-10, 89, 111, 210
see also Rockefeller Foundation; uranium mining
COVID-19 pandemic, 175
Cree Nation,
coerced sterilization of women from, 196, 200
state attempts to assimilate, 69, 106, 161, 185, 191-2
treaty lands and obligations, 21, 210
Criminal Code,
coerced sterilization in, 199, 201-2
decriminalizing contraceptives, 93-5, 227n59
dissemination of birth control knowledge, 80, 99
cultural competency training/framework, 17
concept origins, practising/use of, 181, 189, 194-6, 199
critiques of, 190-4, 198
cultural humility versus, 195
cultural safety versus, 181, 189-90
in Saskatchewan/Canada, 187-8, 195-6
culture of poverty discourse, 87-8, 139

Davidson, George, 43, 64
Davies, Gareth, 86
D.D.S. (coerced sterilization case), 148, 183
decolonization, 197-8, 250n40, 251n50
dehumanization, Indigenous, 158, 179-80, 194, 201
Deighton, Alex, 24
Dene Nation, 21, 161, 210, 238n167

mining resistance, 173-5
Denson, Raymond, 142-3
Department of National Health and Welfare (DNHW),
Community Health Representatives program, 72
Indigenous child apprehension support, 74-5
Indigenous population control, 98, 103
mental hygiene initiatives, 41, 44-6, 221n85
ministers/advisors of, 43-6, 48, 60, 50, 99
Depo-Provera, 2-3, 141
"developing countries," 72, 83, 91-2
Diabo, Russ, 207-8
Dickason, Olive Patricia, 160
Diefenbaker, John, 70, 91
Dornstauder, Frank, 74-5
Douglas, Tommy,
early eugenic tendencies of, 10, 27-8, 31, 95, 217n26
Indigenous community relations, 38-9, 47-8, 65-8
master's thesis on "subnormal" family, 10, 22, 27-8
policies/public health programs of, 10, 28, 30-5, 58, 68-9
premiership of, 10, 30-1, 36, 48, 72
RF support, 14, 32-3
shifts from socialism, 36-8
Dowbiggin, Ian, 33
Duncan, Dustin, 178
Durocher, Rod, 133
Dyck, Erika, 12, 17-18, 20, 24, 84-5
Dyson, W.A., 86

Echaquan, Joyce, 2
education, 134-5
birth control access and higher, 95, 107, 163
calls to address Indigenous, 20, 62-5, 106
contraception, 6-7, 94, 100, 121-6, 132
culturally safe/competent, 180-1, 189-90, 195
on FAS, 138-41
jurisdictional responsibilities for, 30, 67-8, 72
low Indigenous formal, 73, 77, 88, 98, 113

mental health, 40–1
RF investing in public health, 6, 9, 39, 53
see also residential schools
Elders, 144
cultural advisory roles of, 135, 187, 196
Ellis, R.G., 117–18
Emery, Herbert, 37
Eng, Ah-Yin, 83–5
English River First Nation, 172
eugenics,
birth control as, 6–8, 15–16, 44, 81, 170–1, 218nn45–6
capitalist interests in, 8, 89, 159–60
concept/ideology, 4, 12
fertility control, 3, 11–13, 43, 78, 83, 90, 119
institution involvement with, 3, 27, 58, 89, 171, 193
mental hygiene movement and, 6, 14, 23–5, 45
politician tendencies toward, 10, 27–8, 31, 95, 217n26
in population control movement, 3–4, 8, 31, 109
in post–World War II period, 7–8, 35, 38, 159, 162
in psychiatry, 4, 24, 117, 142
RF support for, 13–14, 25–8, 32, 43, 58–9, 86–7, 159
in Saskatchewan history, 3, 22, 27, 96, 132–3
welfare state expansion and, 9, 33, 35–6

family planning,
in colonialism, 18–19, 82
education, 6–7, 94, 100, 121–6, 132
Eurocentric notions of, 84, 113, 132
fertility and, 80, 99, 104, 110
foreign aid, ties to, 91–2, 97
as human right, 12–13, 103
infant mortality and, 4, 7, 12, 90
on-reserve initiatives, 122–4, 128, 135
poverty and pressure for, 11, 19, 21, 85, 93–4, 98–9
Rockefeller support for, 13, 83, 109
in Saskatchewan, 71, 93–4, 98, 112–17, 119–27, 134
social worker roles in, 114–15, 120, 137
United Nations support for, 13, 43, 60, 89–92, 103–4, 171

Family Services Act (Saskatchewan), 120, 127, 134, 151
Far North, 78, 225n24
federal-provincial relations,
assimilation of Indigenous people via, 47, 60–3, 67–8, 72–4, 80
birth control approaches, 21, 101–3, 113–14, 120, 125–32
child welfare in, see child welfare system
collaborative, 11, 73, 86, 107, 111, 139
conferences on, 44–6, 49, 100
corporate influence in, 9–10, 45–6, 111
expanding provincial jurisdiction in, 11, 47, 63–4, 67–8
funding for Indigenous health care, 29–30, 67–8
healthcare provision and, 3, 9, 40–1, 157–8
Indigenous healthcare provision, 11, 24–6, 47–51, 86, 100, 199
mental healthcare provision, 24–5, 44–6, 55, 77
social service provision, 60–1, 74, 139, 151
see also Royal Commission on Dominion-Provincial Relations
Federation of Saskatchewan Indian Nations (FSIN), 47–8, 157, 189, 198
"feeblemindedness,"
legislation on, 24–5
philanthropic/state work to eliminate, 6–7, 25, 34, 79, 218n46
as "social evil," xiv, 6–7, 25, 34, 42
feminism,
approaches to reproductive choice, 16, 19, 21, 105, 108–10
population control ideas and, 13, 42
fertility,
eugenic efforts to control, 3, 6–8, 12–13, 43, 90
family planning policy and, 80, 99, 104, 110
Indigenous women's agency over, 17–20, 131
rates of Indigenous, 112, 115, 141, 159–64, 167, 244n75
research on, 90, 99
total rates of, 107, 162–4, 166–7, 246n82
women's seeking to control, 13, 19–20
fetal alcohol syndrome/effects (FAS/FAE),
association of Indigenous women with, 127, 137–40, 141–2

colonialism and, 140–1, 144
diagnosis/cases of, 137–9, 144
initiatives to address, 138–40
Feusi, Arnold, 67
Finkel, Alvin, 56–7
First Nations Child and Family Caring Society, 76, 156
Fisher, Donald, 10
Fisher River (reserve and Indian Hospital), 83–4
Fisher, T.L., 118
Flynn, L.M., 132–3
foreign aid, Canadian,
economic objectives in, 71–2, 91–2
family planning, ties to, 91–2, 97
Fosdick, Raymond, 7
Fraser, J.D., 118
Fritz, Wayne, 77–8

Galton, Francis, 12, 33, 58
genocide, Indigenous,
coerced sterilization as, 3, 20, 100–1, 179, 187, 202–3
efforts to deny, 122–3, 149, 180, 192–3
Indian policy and, 76, 79, 122–3, 131, 154
land dispossession and, 61, 79, 174, 176–7
ongoing, 21, 76, 79, 145, 193
struggles against, 190, 200, 211
Grauer, Albert, 40–1, 221n72
Gregg, Alan, 28, 33, 219n50
Greshuck, Nadia, 124, 236n113
Guimond, Éric, 159, 163–4
Guttmacher, Alan, 82–3

Habbick, Brian, 137–8
Hainault, Walter, 175
Hames, C.F.W., 32, 117
Hamilton, Samuel W., 34
Harper, Stephen, 205
Hawthorn Report, 70–1, 73–4
Heagerty, J.J., 39, 41–2, 44, 52
Henripin, Jacques, 105–6
Hepworth, Philip, 75
heteronormativity, 6, 14, 25, 54, 105
heteropatriarchal notions of family, 22, 55–7, 87, 197, 201, 212
Hincks, Clarence,
CNCMH leadership, 23, 41, 44–5, 217n26

RF support for, 35, 45, 59
survey/report recommendations, 30–1, 41
HIV/AIDS, 147
Advisory Committee reports on, 135–6
rates of, 135, 239n200
support for those with, 155–6
Horner, S.A., 24
Horowitz, Gad, 37
housing, 177
inadequate supply of, 65, 84, 93, 123, 130, 167
as necessary for well-being, 20, 43, 75, 106
state investment in, 67, 96, 124
substandard/slumlike on-reserve, 62–4, 75, 84, 154
humanitarianism,
capitalist interests and, 60, 63
Indian policy and, 46, 69, 79
population control and, 15, 29, 109
human right(s), 134, 208
complaints filed against state practices, 76, 156–7, 199
efforts to ensure, 117, 142–3, 181, 188, 206, 217n26
family planning as, 12–13, 103
legislation/declarations to protect, 69, 105, 205–6, 209, 252n91
state violations of, 153, 178–80, 198–202
Huxley, Julian, 171
Hylton, John, 78

imperialism, 70
economic, 73, 89
public health/Western medicine as, 9, 14, 53, 89, 193, 210
Indian Act,
definition of "Indian" under, 25, 105, 127–8, 156, 163
Indigenous regulation via, 11, 25–6, 54, 63, 207, 217n22
service delivery and, 11, 47, 51, 156
Indian Affairs, 220n55
assimilation/integration via, 63, 68–9, 72–3, 129–30
criticism/recommendations toward, 65, 68–9, 84
funding for Indigenous health care, 24, 26, 41, 50, 56, 223n121
institutionalization/regulation via, 24–6, 65, 84, 161, 218n46

Joint Committees on, 69, 95
ministers/commissioners of, 38, 50, 61
reorganization of, 63, 68, 100
Indian Agents, 26, 55, 65
Indian Health Services, 25, 38, 47–50, 112, 123
Indian hospitals, 51
Indigenous segregation via, 11, 24–5, 56
coerced sterilization at, 1, 83–5
experimentation and abuse at, 56, 220n55
Indian New Deal, 61–3
Indian policy,
assimilation via, 61–4, 67–8, 73–6, 79, 87–8, 159–61
federal-provincial, 15, 25, 62, 69
foreign aid and, 62, 92
land theft via, 54, 61, 63, 161
"new," 61–5, 76
as responsible for Indigenous poverty and ill health, 62–3, 163
Saskatchewan's, 60, 69
"Indian problem," 75
coerced contraception/sterilization as solution to, 81, 141
extending the welfare state and, 10–11, 64–5
transnational, 87
Indian Register, 161, 165, 244n71
Indian Status, 204
assimilation/integration via, 48, 74, 80, 105–6
denial of women's/children's, 105–6, 163, 179, 184
disproportionate sterilization/abortion based on, 16, 158–9, 168–70, 187
health service funding and, 50–1, 53, 156
institutionalization and, 74, 78
pregnancy/birth/mortality rates based on, 126, 161–2, 167
tracking based on, 47, 156–8, 243n63
see also non-Status Indians; Registered Indians
Indigeneity, 25, 148; see also Indian status
Indigenous Health Working Group (IHWG), 188–9
Indigenous Peoples,
assimilation of, see assimilation
CCF actions toward, 38–9, 47–8, 65–8, 72, 248n1

children, see children
dispossession of, 18–19, 63, 159, 176–7, 193–4
education data of, 73, 77, 88, 98, 113
genocide of, see genocide, Indigenous
healthcare provision, 11, 24–6, 47–51, 86, 100, 199
institutionalization of, 11, 25, 76–7, 171
mining resistance, 173–5
policing of, 10, 78, 211
policy making on, see Indian policy
poverty, 126, 129, 131, 134–6, 157
public health care for, 11, 24–6, 46–51, 86, 100, 134, 199
racism facing, 2–3, 26, 70, 78–9, 112, 132–3, 190–6
struggles for sovereignty, 21, 142, 172–3, 177, 193–7, 250n40
systemic discrimination facing, 3, 11, 21, 145–7, 158, 170, 191, 243n55
theft of land, 20, 54–5, 95–6, 201–3, 207
violence to, 21, 75, 107, 145, 170–3, 193, 209–12
see also Anishinaabe people; Cree Nation; Dene Nation, Elders; Inuit; Métis, non-Status Indians; Registered Indians
Indigenous resurgence, 203, 208, 213
Indigenous rights, 17, 179–80, 203–4; see also Treaty Rights
Indigenous women,
coerced abortions for, 2, 16, 101
colonialism shaping experiences of, 3, 17–19, 106–7, 158–9, 200–1
FAS, associations with, 127, 137–40, 141–2
fertility, seeking to control, 12–13, 19–20, 122–3, 125
Indian Status, denial of, 105–6, 163, 179, 184
mental health of, 109, 126–7, 155–6
policing of, 23, 110, 145, 179
prostitution, associations with, 25, 27, 38, 55, 64
stereotypes of, 23, 27, 55, 66, 95, 113, 141
struggles for reproductive agency, 17–21, 105–6, 110, 131, 183
surveillance of, 2, 65, 107, 114, 127–30, 146, 150–4
systemic discrimination experiences, 1–3, 21, 146–51, 154–6

treatment of pregnant, 135, 143, 152, 243n55
violence against, 106, 136, 140–2, 144, 170–1, 177–80
Western medicine and, 19–21, 131–2, 197, 204, 250n40
see also MMIWG Inquiry; sterilization, coerced
infant mortality rates,
definition of, 163, 165
higher rural/Third World, 41, 64
Indigenous, 64, 102, 112, 115, 165–7, 170
mental hygiene/family planning movement on, 4, 7, 12, 90
Saskatchewan's, 165
institutionalization, 199
of Indigenous people, 11, 24–5, 38, 74, 76–8, 154, 179
"mental defectiveness" and, 23–5, 34
of public health care, 3, 8–9
institution building,
elite/RF influence via, 1–10, 39, 58–9, 89, 193, 208
eugenics in, 3, 27, 58, 89
Indigenous-led, 197, 204
philanthropy and, 3, 10, 34–6, 53
institutions,
assimilation/segregation via, 23–5, 66, 218n46
capitalist, 60, 210
colonialism/racism, perpetuation via, 154, 179–80, 186, 193–5
conditions in, 74, 83
eugenics in, 3, 27, 171, 193
federal, 55, 91
health/welfare, 3, 179–80, 210
Indigenous admissions to, 11, 24–5, 38, 55, 76–8, 171
mental, 34–5, 44
policing of individuals via, 23–4, 55–6, 131, 179–80, 210
provincial, 24, 55
psychiatric, 25, 76–8, 117, 171
shifts in/overhauling, 182, 197, 204
Inter-American Indian Institute, 62, 86
International Labour Organization (ILO), 8, 59–60
intrauterine devices (IUDs), 114, 122
coerced prescribing of, 2, 82, 93–4
global/colonial population control via, 82–3, 93–4

Inuit, 79
coerced sterilization/contraception, 2–3, 21, 101–3, 126, 158, 169–70
colonial violence against women, 106, 200–1
demographic data, 158, 161–2, 165, 169–70
forced relocation/dispossession, 18, 21, 225n24
government service obligations to, 51, 189, 205, 210–11
IQ scoring, 34, 130, 137–8

Jackson, Mary, 98
Jahanbani, Sheyda, 62
Jensen, Jane, 109–10
Johnston, Patrick, 75
Junor, Judy, 139, 142–3

Kahnawake, 84, 105
Kaufman, A.R., 31, 43–4, 82–3, 228n31
Kaufman, Bruce, 59
Kelly, Sharon, 130
Kent, Tom, 85–6
Kineepick Métis Local Inc., 173
Kkailther, Hector, 174
Knowledge Keepers, 179, 196
Koskie Minsky, 184
Koskie, Murray, 133–4
Kulchyski, Peter, 18

Lalonde, Marc, 125
land,
Canada as Indigenous, 3, 14, 37, 142, 160, 185, 191
capitalist wealth via expropriating, 4, 21, 36, 44, 53, 125, 176–7
corporate/state ensuring unimpeded access to, 6, 14–17, 18, 37, 89, 176, 210
genocidal colonial theft of, 20, 54–5, 96, 201–3, 207
Indigenous assimilation to exploit, 60–2, 65–6, 69, 80, 161, 186
responsibilities to, 79, 177, 208, 212
struggles for Indigenous sovereignty over, 21, 142, 172–3, 177, 193–7, 250n40
uranium mining on, *see* uranium mining
violence against Indigenous bodies and, 21, 107, 145, 171–7, 180–1, 210–11

Langford, William, 89
Latin America, 62, 86–7, 89–91, 96, 104, 164
Lavallée, Melvyn, 126–7
Laycock, Samuel, 23, 35, 217n26
League of Nations, 8, 59–60, 216n11
Leslie, John, 65, 76
Lewis, Oscar, 86–7
Little, C.C., 33
Lombard, Alisa, 147–8, 156, 158, 182–3, 187
London School of Economics (LSE), 58, 75
Loo, Tina, 92
Lorde, Audre, 214
Lotz, Jim, 101–2
Love, Saskatchewan, 132–4
Lozorko, D.M., 65
Lunquist, Audrey, 140
Lux, Maureen, 17–18, 20, 49–50, 84–5

Mackenzie King, William Lyon, 91
    public health plan promotion, 39–40, 43, 45
    Rockefellers, relationships with, 39, 52, 59
    social policy approach, 39, 43, 52, 58–60
Mallick, S., 82–3
Manitoba, 2, 40
    Indigenous demographic data, 135, 162, 243n63
    treatment of pregnant Indigenous women in, 135, 143, 152, 243n55
Mann, Jackie, 148, 181
Manuel, Art, 176
Manuel, George, 73, 78, 213
Marcus, George, 1
marriage,
    birth control and middle class notions of, 12, 14, 23, 115–16
    chastising lack of, 88, 94–5, 106–7, 134–5, 115–20
    Indigenous births outside of, 115–16, 119–20
    restrictive legislation on, 10, 23–8, 31, 127, 134–5, 151
    segregation/regulation of Indigenous, 4, 22–4, 42, 66, 106
    see also unmarried women
Marshall, Andrew, 208
Marshall, Dominique, 43
Marsh Report, 57, 59–60, 64
Martin Sr., Paul, 44, 67, 217n26
Mass, Bonnie, 82, 89, 109

maternal mortality rate, 7, 41
McKerracher, D.G., 32–3, 44
McIntosh, W.A., 33, 46
McNab, Isobel, 116, 122
McNab, John, 99
MCR KY AHA region (Mamawetan Churchill River, Keewatin Yatthé, and Athabasca), 166, 169, 171
Medical Care Act, 49, 100
Medicare, 49, 86, 223n115
Mental Defectives Act, 24
mental deficiency/defectives,
    mental hygiene views on, 4, 10, 27, 34, 77
    training/surveillance/sterilization of, 22–5, 31, 35
Mental Diseases Act, 24
mental health,
    conferences, 44
    funding/support for, 44–5
    Indigenous women's, 109, 126–7, 155–6
    policy making, 40–1, 117
    programs/services, 35, 41, 117, 155–6
    studies/surveys on, 10, 23, 28–9, 34
Mental Hygiene Act, 24–5, 32, 217n25
mental hygiene movement,
    eugenics, associations with, 6, 14, 25
    legislation, *see* Mental Hygiene Act
    research/initiatives, 6, 9, 30, 33–5
    views of, 4, 23–4, 45
    see also Canadian National Committee for Mental Hygiene
Meren, David, 92
Merriman, Paul, 155
Métis, 21
    Cameco/uranium development work, 172–5
    coerced sterilization/contraception for, 129–30, 139, 149, 158, 179–80
    compensation for violence faced by, 179–80, 184, 188, 205
    demographic data, 77–8, 97, 126, 129, 161–2, 165
    jurisdictional responsibility for, 51, 210–11
    living conditions of, 65–6, 97–8, 129
    organizations representing, 65–6, 106, 116, 133
    population control initiatives against, 66–8, 74, 121, 210
    scholars/researchers, 3, 153, 156, 178, 213

Sixties Scoop/child apprehension
  experiences, 74-5, 106, 129-30,
  152-3, 225n22
  targeted state segregation/assimilation
  of, 65-8, 77-8
Missing and Murdered Indigenous Women
  and Girls, 170-1; see also MMIWG
  Inquiry
MMIWG Inquiry, 152, 155, 178-180, 213
Moe, Scott, 180
Monteith, J.W., 48
Monture-Angus, Patricia, vii, 186
Moore, P.E., 38, 48
morality, 30
  healthcare professional responsibilities
  and, 183, 195
  "mental defectiveness" and, 10, 23, 27
  perceptions of Indigenous women
  lacking, 14, 23, 27, 66, 95, 113
  synthesis of public health and, 4, 27, 86
  White, Anglo-Saxon Protestant notions
  of, 4, 23, 86, 145
Morgan, Cora, 152-3
Moynihan Report, 87-8
M.P. (coerced sterilization case), 147, 149
Munro, John, 50, 99-101, 229n52

Nanson, Josephine, 137-8, 140, 142
National Aboriginal Health Organization,
  55, 190
National Health Grants Program, 45-6
natural resources, 36
  "collaborative agreements" for, 172-5
  colonial theft of, 20, 64-6, 80, 89, 174-6,
  207-8
  Indigenous people as gatekeepers of,
  3, 18-19, 37
  Indigenous sovereignty over, 21, 205
  industrial extraction of, 18-19, 172-5, 180
  political economy concerns over
  distribution of, 3, 8, 15, 29, 60,
  229n50
  population control and, 3, 11, 18, 31,
  52-3, 90-1
Navarro, Vincente, 176
Nazis, 5, 7, 12, 29-30
neo-Malthusians, 8, 90
Neufeldt, Aldred, 77
New Democratic Party (NDP), 36, 48, 94,
  178, 248n1; see also Co-operative
  Commonwealth Federation

non-Status Indians,
  compensation for violence faced by,
  173-4, 184
  demographic data, 78, 126, 158, 161-2,
  169-70
  government service provision to, 51
  organizations representing, 116, 133, 173
  Sixties Scoop/child apprehension, 74
North, the, 1, 102, 121-2, 162, 171
  Department of, 115, 232n34
  disseminating birth control in, 1, 102,
  115, 121-2
  Indigenous population rates in, 102,
  162, 171
North Battleford, 38, 93, 120, 137, 141
  Saskatchewan Hospital in, 24, 35, 56,
  76-7
North-West Mounted Police, 55
Northwest Territories, 1, 101-2, 135, 147
Notestein, Frank, 91, 159
Nunavut, 17, 200-1

O'Keefe, Joseph, 95
Ontario, 31, 184, 198
Orano Canada Inc. 172-3, 247n90
Orford, T.J., 38, 48-9, 94, 113
Orgeron, Marlene, 185
overpopulation,
  as cause of poverty, 83, 91, 95
  demography as tool to study, 58, 159
  fear of Indigenous/"Third World"
  growth and, 15, 68, 85, 102
  recommended contraceptive use for, 81,
  83, 90, 96

paternalism, state,
  control of Indigenous people via, 54, 84,
  110, 211
  Eurocentric family planning and, 84,
  113, 132
  Indigenous poverty from, 61, 211
  in public health/welfare provision, 1-2,
  106, 113, 145, 211
Pearson, Lester, 49, 70, 85-6, 91-2
philanthropy, 108
  capitalist goals in, 4-5, 32, 36, 52
  corporate, 4-5, 32, 36, 52-3, 89
  institution building and, 3, 10, 34-6, 53
  mental hygiene, 6-7, 25, 34, 79
  racist roots of, 32, 70, 87
  see also Rockefeller Foundation

Pinehouse First Nation, 130, 172–4, 238n167
Planned Parenthood, 228n30
    forced Indigenous sterilization/contraception and, 75, 82–3, 97–8, 104
    formation and population control support, 7, 12, 91, 97–100
    policy/program influence of, 12, 16, 75, 94–100, 104–7
Planned Parenthood Saskatchewan,
    (lack of) Indigenous consultation, 116, 123–5
    programming/services by, 125–6, 135–6
    vision and state support for, 115, 120–2, 126
Poitras, Marilyn, 178–9, 213
police, 55, 57
    child welfare system collaboration, 151, 154
    see also RCMP
Pon, Gordon, 193
population control (movement), 82, 236n113
    coerced Indigenous sterilization and, 79, 81, 146
    concept/eugenic ideology of, 3–4, 8, 31, 109
    corporate interest in, 6, 8, 13–15, 208, 210, 218n45
    feminist support for, 13, 42, 108, 110
    humanitarian/political economy arguments for, 8, 15, 29–31, 109, 218n46
    Indigenous reproductive agency versus, 17–19, 78–9, 81, 97, 100
    international/UN proponents of, 81–3, 89–91, 96, 208
    policies of, 1, 13–15, 28, 170, 210
    promotion of, 4, 43, 57, 91, 208
    see also overpopulation
Population Council (Rockefeller institute), 13, 43, 83, 89–91, 159
post–World War II period, 90
    eugenics/mental hygiene movement in, 7–8, 35, 38, 159, 162
    Indian policy in, 15, 53, 62, 76, 79, 97
    public health services in, 10, 53, 56
    welfare state policy making in, 15, 56, 58–9, 71
poverty,
    birth control and, 11, 19, 21, 85, 93–4, 98–9
    children, impacts on, 112, 132–6, 167
    colonialism and, 62, 84, 156, 176
    discourse on culture of, 86–8, 92, 131, 139
    global, 60, 71–2, 96
    Indian policy and, 62–3, 163
    Indigenous, 126, 129, 131, 134–6, 157
    overpopulation as cause of, 12–13, 83, 91, 95
    on reserves, 83–5, 93, 98, 112, 135
    state paternalism and, 61, 211
    systemic racism and, 14, 155–6, 174–7
    violence and, 75, 112, 135–6
    war on, *see* War on Poverty
    welfare state approaches to, 11, 15, 56–7, 79–80
Powell, Clare, 133
Prince Albert Parkland region (PA Parkland), 118, 166–7
Prittie, Robert, 94–5
Proctor, H.A., 92–4, 98
promiscuity,
    "feeblemindedness" and, 4, 6
    Indigenous women as associated with, 106–7, 113
    population control and, 12–13, 95, 120
psychiatry, 218n34
    eugenics/birth control and, 4, 24, 117, 142
    funding of care, 32, 35, 37
    Indigenous institutionalization in, 11, 25, 76–7, 171
    in public health system, 26–7, 217n26, 221n85
    Saskatchewan research in, 32–5, 37, 44
public health,
    capitalist provision of, 32, 39–40, 52–3, 56
    colonial expansion of, 1, 11, 29, 37, 190, 197
    corporate influence over, 8–10, 89, 111, 210
    federal-provincial provision of, 3, 9, 40–1, 157–8
    funding for Indigenous, 24–30, 41, 47–53, 56, 67–8, 156–8, 223n121
    as imperialism, 9, 14, 53, 89, 193, 210
    Indigenous care provision, 11, 24–6, 47–51, 86, 100, 199
    institutions, 3, 8–9, 179–80, 210
    moral narratives of, 4, 27, 86, 183, 195
    paternalism in, 1–2, 106, 113, 145, 211

philanthropic investment in, 6, 9, 39, 53
policies/programs, 10, 28, 30–7, 39–40,
  49, 58, 68–9
post–World War II period, 10, 53, 56
provincial systems, 40,43, 45, 60
psychiatry in, 26–7, 217n26, 221n85
racism in, 2, 113, 132–3, 190–7, 243n55
reforms, 134–6
Rockefeller involvement in, 8–10, 22,
  31–6, 39–40, 45–7, 193
Saskatchewan as pilot project, 10–11,
  22, 40, 43, 52
stereotypes in, 55, 106, 141, 187, 190
systemic discrimination in, 11, 21, 52,
  156, 181, 190–7, 210–11
tracking/profiling of Registered Indians,
  16, 47, 50–1, 156–8
welfare state expansion and, 10–11,
  39–40, 56

Quebec, 2, 40, 118, 179
queer people/queerness, 6, 14, 34, 107, 212
Quiring, David, 66–7

racialized women,
  coerced sterilization of, 18–20, 141, 143,
    199
  erasing experiences of, 107–9, 130–1
  reproductive justice for, 18, 109, 201
racial profiling, 112
  of Indigenous people, 54–5, 151, 153,
    156–8
  mental hygiene movement and, 4–7, 29,
    42
racism, 105, 110
  anti-Indigenous, 2, 70, 78–9, 132–3, 190–6
  anti-Black, 87–8, 143, 202–3, 212, 218n45
  coerced sterilization support and, 70,
    132, 142–3, 203
  corporate/philanthropic roots in, 32, 70,
    87
  fetal alcohol syndrome/effects and,
    141–2
  healthcare policies, 2, 113, 132–3, 190–7
  systemic, *see* systemic racism
Ram, Bali, 161, 164
Ramsden, Irihapeti, 189–90
RCMP, 55
  (lack of) investigation into state
    violence, 179, 185, 201
  removal of land defenders, 142, 173

Regina Native Women's Association
  (RNWA), 130, 132
Regina Qu'Appelle region, 26, 56, 65, 119,
  220n55
  demographic data, 166, 168–9, 171
Registered Indians, 26, 116
  assimilation of, 48, 80, 158
  demographic data/"fuzziness" for, 126,
    158–67
  disproportionate sterilization of, 16, 38,
    158, 168–71, 178
  funding of health care for, 47, 49–51, 98,
    156–8
  health service tracking/profiling of, 16,
    47, 50–1, 156–8
  institutionalization of, 76–8
  jurisdictional disputes/transfer over,
    46–51, 131, 156–8
  off-reserve, 50–1, 54, 69, 130–1, 161,
    223n120
  on-reserve, 51, 73, 105, 162
  poverty of, 129, 131
  pregnancy/birth/infant mortality rates,
    115, 126, 129, 136, 162–7
  Sixties Scoop/child welfare system
    involvement, 74, 76
Relling, Sandra, 185
relocation, forced, 18, 66, 179, 225n24
reproduction,
  eugenic efforts to control, 8, 11–12, 22,
    78, 83, 119
  government desire to curb Indigenous,
    78, 88, 141, 171, 210
  perceived economic threat of
    Indigenous, 125, 132, 145, 159–60,
    177
  politics of, 11, 14–17, 149, 158–9
  women's desire to control, 12, 20, 123,
    125
reproductive justice approach, 18, 109, 171
  on coerced sterilization, 20, 183, 201–2
reserves, 196
  child welfare involvement/removal
    from, 38–9, 64, 74–6, 128–9, 152
  exodus from, 16, 54–5, 73–4, 113
  family planning initiatives for, 122–4,
    128, 135
  FAS/FAE programs on, 139, 141
  health coverage differences for, 49, 83,
    144
  ill health on, 41, 51, 64

increasing surveillance on, 63–4, 74–6, 122–4, 128, 139, 207
individualizing of social problems on, 37, 53, 71–2, 87, 130, 187
limited funding/service provision to, 30, 41, 46, 51
policy to "empty," 15, 54, 60–1, 63–9, 76, 163
population rates on, 54, 65, 67–9, 83, 93–5, 162
poverty on, 83–5, 93, 98, 112, 135
segregation on, 11, 25, 54–5, 64–7, 73
sterilization of women from, 38, 158, 168–71, 178
see also Registered Indians
residential schools, 218n46
   assimilation through, 55–6, 73
   child welfare system as replacing, 64, 76, 78–9
   Indigenous segregation via, 11, 25, 55, 73
   phasing out of, 55, 64, 73
   survivors/legacy of, 38, 106, 154, 188, 249n22
Ringrose, C.A.D., 97
Robbins, W.A., 120
Roberts, Dorothy, 143
Robertson, Thos., 26
Robitaille, Norbert, 159, 163–4
Rockefeller III, John D., 91
   family planning and contraception support, 13, 83, 109
Rockefeller Jr., John D., 39, 59
   eugenic beliefs of, 6, 11
Rockefeller Sr., John D.,
   oil company ownership, 4, 36, 40, 70
   wealth and philanthropy of, 4–5, 9, 27, 36
Rockefeller Foundation (RF), 53
   eugenics and population control support, 13–14, 25–8, 32, 43, 58–9, 86–7, 159
   funding of public health programs/research, 8–10, 22, 31–6, 39–40, 45–7, 193
   ideologies and expansion of, 4–7, 13–15, 35–7, 90, 189, 208
   politicians' relationships with, 32, 34, 39–40, 52, 91
   United Nations involvement, 8, 13, 46, 60, 89–91, 208

Rockefeller, Nelson, 62
Romaniuc, Anatole, 161, 164
Roy, Chunilal, 76
Royal Canadian Mounted Police, *see* RCMP
Royal Commission on Dominion-Provincial Relations (RCDPR), 40–1
Royal Commission on the Status of Women (RCSW), 16, 105–9
Royal University Hospital (Saskatoon), 35, 137, 140, 146
Rynard, Phillip, 97

Sanger, Margaret, 6–7, 11, 79, 218n45, 219n50
Saskatchewan,
   anti-Indigenous racism in, 3, 26, 112, 132–3, 142–3, 149
   attempted assimilation of Indigenous people, 37, 54, 68–9, 72
   birth alerts/Sanctum program, 151–2, 154–5, 183
   class action lawsuits in, 2–3, 147, 183
   coerced sterilization/birth control in, 21, 38, 117–21, 132–6, 142–3, 170, 177–8, 183
   culturally responsive programming, 187–8, 195–6
   demographic trends in, 77–8, 112, 129, 161–70
   Department of Public Health, *see* Saskatchewan Department of Public Health
   eugenics in history of, 3, 22, 27, 96, 132–3
   Evidence Amendment Act, 182
   Family Services Act in, 120, 127, 134, 151
   FAS cases in, 137–42
   healthcare reform, 134–6
   family planning policy, 71, 93–5, 98, 112–17, 119–27, 134
   health care for Indigenous communities in, 46–51, 56, 71, 156–8
   Indian policy in, 54, 60, 67–72, 156–8
   Indigenous children in care in, 75–7
   Indigenous living conditions in, 65–6, 75–8, 95, 98, 129–36
   Indigenous organizations in, 65, 116, 133, 157, 189, 198
   as public health pilot project, 10–11, 22, 40, 43, 52

psychiatry research/work in, 32–7, 142
resource extraction in, 37, 171–5
segregation of Indigenous people in, 11, 24, 54–5, 65–6, 77
treaty obligations in, 204, 210
see also Advisory Committee on Family Planning
Saskatchewan Advisory Panel on Health System Structure, 188
Saskatchewan Assistance Plan, 129
Saskatchewan Department of Public Health, family planning/birth control policies, 31–2, 113–15
Probe Committee, 114–16, 121
Saskatchewan Health Authority (SHA), 166
birth alerts/Sanctum program, 151, 155, 183
culturally responsive programming, 140, 187–8, 195
Saskatchewan Health Services Planning Commission, 31, 34, 46
Saskatchewan Hospital, 24, 35, 38, 56, 76–7
Services Plan, 34, 46–9
Saskatchewan Indian Women's Association (SIWA), 116, 122, 124
Saskatchewan Institute for the Prevention of Handicaps (SIPH), 136, 138–40
Saskatchewan Medical Care Insurance Act, 48, 50
Saskatchewan Mental Health Association, 26, 217n26
Saskatchewan Native Women's Association (SNWA), 116, 122–4, 131–2
Saskatchewan Task Force on Women's Health (STFWH), 131
Saskatoon, 67, 120
coercion/surveillance of Indigenous women in, 2, 114, 128–30, 146, 155
FAS cases in, 137, 141
Health Region, *see* Saskatoon Health Region
psychiatric facilities in, 35, 55–6
Registered Indian deliveries/abortions in, 166, 168
Saskatoon Health Region (SHR), birth alerts involvement, 151
coerced sterilization involvement/review, 146, 148–50, 188
sterilization apology/reparative measures by, 17, 181–3, 188, 195, 204

SC FH C H region (Sun Country, Five Hills, Cypress, and Heartland), 166, 168, 171–2
Schmidt, Erick, 97–8
self-determination, 106, 203–7
settler colonialism, 192, 197–8, 208–9, 213; *see also* colonialism
Sheps, C.G., 31
Shewell, Hugh, 47, 63
Shumiatcher, Morris, 69–70
Sigerist, Henry, 33–4, 38
views/work on public health, 28–31, 219n50
Simpson, Audra, 192
Simpson, Leanne Betasamosake, 208–9, 213
single mothers/parents,
birth alerts for, *see* birth alerts
birth control pressure facing, 113–14, 136, 147
Indigenous, 129–30, 134–6, 157
measures to surveil, 23, 110, 136, 139, 151
poverty of, 126, 134–6, 157
programs for, 128–30
Sivanandan, Ambalavaner, 250nn41,47
Sixties Scoop,
apprehension experiences, 74–6, 106, 129–30, 152–3, 225n22
class action litigation for, 184–6
Skoll, S.L. 116–18
Smishek, Walter, 116
Smith, David, 137
Smith, George, 174
Smith, Hugh G., 34
Smith, Leanne, 149
Smylie, Janet, 153
social insurance, 52, 57–9
socialism, 28
politicians' support for capitalism versus, 36–7, 44, 52
social reform/ers, 4, 58, 61; *see also* morality
social workers,
in child welfare apprehensions, 35–6, 39, 42, 65, 73–5, 152
family planning/population control work, 114–15, 120, 137
policing "mental defectives," 4, 6, 24, 27, 35
policy involvement, 60, 63–4, 156, 211, 221n85

surveillance/coerced sterilization of Indigenous women, 65, 107, 127, 146, 150–4
Special Planning Secretariat, 85–6, 92–3, 96–7
Spencer, H.E., 40
Standing Committee on Health and Welfare, 95–9
Stanton Territorial (Yellowknife) Hospital, 1–2, 147
Status Indians, *see* Registered Indians
stereotypes,
   addressing negative healthcare, 187, 190
   of Indigenous women, 55, 106, 141
sterilization, coerced,
   apology/reparative measures for, 17, 181–3, 188, 195, 204
   cases, 2–3, 101–3, 126–30, 143, 147–9, 179–83, 196, 200
   class action litigation for, 2, 17, 147, 181, 184
   as colonial violence, 1, 83–5, 170, 186
   contraceptives versus, 3, 111, 141
   in Criminal Code, 199, 201–2
   criminalization of, 199, 201–4
   disproportionate Indigenous, 38, 81, 141, 158–9, 168–71, 178, 187
   as Indigenous genocide, 3, 20, 100–1, 179, 187, 202–3
   "mental deficiency" and, 22–5, 31, 35
   as personal-individual harm, 186–7, 203
   Planned Parenthood and, 75, 82–3, 97–8, 104
   as political-collective harm, 186–7, 203
   population control movement on, 79, 81, 146
   promotion of, 43, 96–7, 104
   provincial policies, 1, 28–31, 42, 107–8, 181
   of racialized women, 18–20, 141, 143, 199
   racism in, 70, 132, 142–3, 203
   reproductive justice approach on, 20, 183, 201–2
   in Saskatchewan, 21, 93–5, 117–21, 132–6, 142–3, 170, 183
   social worker support for, 65, 107, 127, 146, 150–4
   systemic discrimination in, 1, 16, 146–7, 177, 180–1, 193, 197

"underdeveloped" countries, promotion
   in, 43, 81, 90–1, 97, 102, 104
   in United States, 19–20, 87–8, 210
   violence of, 2, 17–18, 177–9, 187, 199–202
Stevenson, Allyson, 68. 75, 123, 151–2
St. Laurent, Louis, 47, 91
Stogdill, C.G., 44–5, 221n85
Stone, E.L., 26
Sturdy, John, 67–8
Sturgeon Lake First Nation, 196
Survivors Circle for Reproductive Justice, 183, 202
Swartz, Donald, 52
Symington, D.F., 66, 225n24
systemic racism,
   addressing, 87–8, 108, 140, 186–8, 191–6, 203, 250n41
   Canadian political economy reinforcement of, 14, 145, 176–7, 194
   coerced sterilization and, 1, 16, 146–7, 177, 180–1, 193, 197
   colonialism and, 3, 11, 21, 145–7, 158, 170
   Indigenous women's experiences of, 1–3, 21, 146–51, 154–6
   poverty and, 14, 155–6, 174–7
   public health, 11, 21, 52, 156, 181, 190–7, 210–11
   Saskatchewan-based, 3, 149
   see also racism

Tait, Caroline, 3, 139–41
"tangle of pathology," 88, 113, 139
Tchorzewski, Ed, 26
teen pregnancy, 126–7, 130, 135–6, 157, 163
Tepoztlán, Mexico, 87
Thatcher, Ross, 49, 98, 122
Theobald, Brianna, 18, 20
Therapeutic Abortion Committees, 109–10, 114
Thibodeau, Nora, 151–2
"Third World" countries, 89, 91, 102, 104
Tineta-Horn, Kahn, 83–4
Tooley, R.W., 110
Tootoosis, John, 69
trans people, 14, 212
Treaty Indians, 67, 69, 116, 161, 204
treaty responsibilities, 11, 46–7, 68, 72, 157–8, 204

Treaty Rights, 47, 51, 63, 70, 173, 204, 207
Trudeau, Justin, 194
Trudeau, Pierre Elliott, 79–80
Truth and Reconciliation Commission (TRC), 178, 187–8
tubal ligation, 114, 141
    doctors seeking consent for, 84–5, 118, 151
    reviewing policies on, 148, 150–1, 182–3, 187
tuberculosis,
    eugenic beliefs about, 4, 220n55
    public health measures against, 8, 29, 34, 45, 55–6
    rates on reserves, 41, 64
Tuck, Eve, 212
Tutt, Sherrie, 142
Two-Spirit people, 170, 180

"underdeveloped" countries,
    promotion of sterilization in, 43, 81, 90–1, 97, 102, 104
    Western political/economic interests in, 89–90, 125
"underdevelopment," government initiatives addressing, 72, 90, 97–8, 104
United Nations, 64
    birth control/family planning agenda of, 13, 43, 60, 89–92, 103–4, 171
    Canadian involvement in, 46, 60, 64, 91–2, 96–7, 225n7
    global poverty, work to counter, 60, 71–2, 96
    inception of, 8, 60, 89, 216n11
    Population Conferences, 90, 96–7, 104
    Rockefeller involvement with, 13, 46, 60, 89, 208
United Nations Committee Against Torture (UNCAT), 199
United Nations Declaration on the Rights of Indigenous Peoples (UNDRIP), 188, 204–9
United Nations Declaration on the Rights of Indigenous Peoples Act (UNDA), 205, 207
United States, 189, 205
    anti-Black racism in, 62, 87–8, 212
    coerced sterilization in, 19–20, 87–8, 210
    colonial dispossession/extraction in, 20, 62, 87–9

    mental hygiene movement in, 6, 34, 46, 91
University of Toronto, 40, 60, 91
    School of Hygiene, 9, 35, 46
unmarried women,
    birth alerts on, 127–8
    institutionalization of, 77
    policy making on, 23, 127, 134–5, 151
    surveillance/chastising of, 14, 88, 94–5, 107, 119–20
uranium mining,
    capitalist support for, 36–7
    in Saskatchewan, 171–5, 220n59, 247n90

Valentine, Victor, 66, 225n24
Valleau, O.W., 65–6
Valverde, Mariana, 4
venereal disease,
    organizations to control, 41–2
    perceptions of feeblemindedness and, 4, 6, 25, 42, 117
    as pressing issue, 25, 29, 45
    stereotypes of Indigenous women and, 55, 217n24
Vincent, George, 53
violence, 59, 80
    2SLGBTQQIA people facing, 178–9, 243n67
    alcohol consumption/FAS, and, 136, 138, 140–4
    anti-Indigenous, 3, 75, 145, 156, 170, 202
    coerced sterilization/obstetrical, 2, 17–18, 177–9, 187, 199–202
    domestic, 136, 138, 142, 156
    on Indigenous women, 106, 136, 140–2, 144, 170–1, 177–80
    to the land and Indigenous bodies, 21, 107, 145, 171–3, 193, 209–12
    poverty and, 75, 112, 135–6
    struggles to address, 145, 179–81, 185–7, 193, 201, 209–12
    systemic, 135–6, 140, 179, 193, 195–7, 211

Wall, Brad, 172, 178
War on Poverty, 86, 96
    Indigenous population control as part of, 11, 15, 80, 85–6, 92–3, 99
Wasacase, Tanya, 191–2

Watson, Irene, 206–7
Webb, M.L., 93, 112
Weinberg, Paul, 74, 88
welfare state expansion,
    assimilation/surveillance of Indigenous people in, 11, 35–6, 53, 64–5, 70, 74, 79
    capitalist/RF influence in, 10–11, 15, 39–40, 56–7
    ideological approaches, 11, 15, 56–7, 79–80
    mental hygiene/eugenics movement in, 9, 33, 35–6
    policy making, 11, 39–42, 57–60, 74, 79–80, 85–6
    proponents of, 9, 33, 39, 42, 57–8
    public health in, 10–11, 39–40, 56
    see also Marsh Report; War on Poverty
Western medicine,
    assumptions of, 159, 193
    colonial/imperial imposition of, 9, 15, 26, 53, 72, 195
    Indigenous women's/people's negotiation of, 19–21, 131–2, 197, 204, 250n40
    reinforcing segregation/assimilation, 55, 159
Western nations,
    cultural assumptions of, 64–5, 131–2, 159, 180
    geopolitical concerns, 11–12, 89, 160, 193
    population control concerns, 8, 11–12, 89, 102–4
    poverty discourse of, 86–7, 92, 131
White Face, Charmaine, 206–8
White Paper(s), 69, 80, 101–1, 207
Wiebe, J.H., 93, 100, 103
Williams, Anne, 121–3
Willoughby, Charles, 95
Wilson-Raybould, Jody, 198
World Bank, 89–92, 96
Wride, G.E., 46

Yang, K. Wayne, 212
Yukon, 135

Zinger, Ivan, 78